INTERNATIONAL NEGOTIATION

Evangelos Raftopoulos explores international negotiation as a structured process of relational governance that generates common interest between and among international participants and in relation to the international public order. He challenges prescriptive models of negotiation – developed in international relations and positivistic approaches to international law, which artificially separate treaties from negotiation in the name of "objectivity" – and opens a window through which to look at international negotiations from a novel, international law perspective. Using an interdisciplinary approach that incorporates law, philosophy, politics, and linguistics, he proposes a holistic, theoretical model of multilateral international negotiation that not only offers a "subjective" view of international law in practice but also demonstrates the importance of understanding the horizontal normativity of international ordering. This work should be read by academics and practitioners of international law and negotiations, officials of international organizations, and anyone else interested in international law and international relations.

Evangelos Raftopoulos is Professor of International Law and International Environmental Law at Panteion University in Athens, Greece. He is also Founding Director of MEPIELAN Centre/Panteion University, which is an officially accredited UNEP/MAP partner and a member of the Mediterranean Commission on Sustainable Development. Educated in Cambridge (PhD (Cantab), LLM (Cantab), and Athens (LLB), he has been recently a visiting scholar at Downing College, University of Cambridge and he is a Fellow at the Cambridge Centre for Environment, Energy and Natural Resource Governance (C-EENRG), University of Cambridge. For more than two decades, he has been consulted by the Mediterranean Action Plan/Barcelona Convention Secretariat as MAP/UNEP legal advisor. He has participated in more than seventy international environmental conferences and meetings and has authored eleven books and numerous articles and international reports. He holds a diploma in the piano.

CAMBRIDGE STUDIES ON ENVIRONMENT, ENERGY AND NATURAL RESOURCES GOVERNANCE

Cambridge Studies on Environment, Energy and Natural Resources Governance publishes foundational monographs of general interest to scholars and practitioners within the broadly defined fields of sustainable development policy, including studies on law, economics, politics, history, and policy. These fields currently attract unprecedented interest due to both the urgency of developing policies to address climate change, the energy transition, food security and water availability and, more generally, to the progressive realization of the impact of humans as a geological driver of the state of the Earth, now called the "Anthropocene."

The general editor of the series is Professor Jorge E. Viñuales, the Harold Samuel Chair of Law and Environmental Policy at the University of Cambridge and the Founder and First Director of the Cambridge Centre for Environment, Energy and Natural Resource Governance (C-EENRG).

International Negotiation

A PROCESS OF RELATIONAL GOVERNANCE FOR INTERNATIONAL COMMON INTEREST

EVANGELOS RAFTOPOULOS

Professor of International Law, Panteion University, Athens

CAMBRIDGE
UNIVERSITY PRESS

CAMBRIDGE
UNIVERSITY PRESS

University Printing House, Cambridge CB2 8BS, United Kingdom

One Liberty Plaza, 20th Floor, New York, NY 10006, USA

477 Williamstown Road, Port Melbourne, VIC 3207, Australia

314–321, 3rd Floor, Plot 3, Splendor Forum, Jasola District Centre, New Delhi – 110025, India

79 Anson Road, #06–04/06, Singapore 079906

Cambridge University Press is part of the University of Cambridge.

It furthers the University's mission by disseminating knowledge in the pursuit of education, learning, and research at the highest international levels of excellence.

www.cambridge.org
Information on this title: www.cambridge.org/9781107196643
DOI: 10.1017/9781108164870

First published 2019

Printed and bound in Great Britain by Clays Ltd, Elcograf S.p.A.

A catalogue record for this publication is available from the British Library.

Library of Congress Cataloging-in-Publication Data
NAMES: Raftopoulos, Evangelos, author.
TITLE: International negotiation : a process of relational governance for international common interest / Evangelos Raftopoulos.
DESCRIPTION: Cambridge [England] ; New York, NY : Cambridge University Press, [2019] | Series: Cambridge studies on environment, energy and natural resource governance | Includes bibliographical references and index.
IDENTIFIERS: LCCN 2018017142 | ISBN 9781107196643
SUBJECTS: LCSH: Diplomatic negotiations in international disputes. | Diplomatic negotiations in international disputes – Methodology. | Mediation, International.
CLASSIFICATION: LCC JZ6045 .R335 2019 | DDC 327.2–dc23
LC record available at https://lccn.loc.gov/2018017142

ISBN 978-1-107-19664-3 Hardback

Contents

Preface and Acknowledgments — *page* xi
List of Abbreviations — xv

Introduction — 1
The Theoretical Quest — 1
The Narration of Negotiation in International Relations Theory — 2
Treaties, Negotiations, and International Common Interest Relations: A Theoretical Refocusing of International Law — 4
Unveiling the Theoretical Voice of This Book — 6

PART I THEORETICAL APPROACHES TO INTERNATIONAL NEGOTIATIONS AND INTERNATIONAL COMMON INTEREST — 11

1 **The Theorization of International Negotiation: Autonomous Prescriptive Theoretical Models and Their Deficiencies** — 13
1 A Panoramic Critical View — 13
2 Zero-Sum Situations and Distributive or Positional Negotiation — 15
3 Non-Zero-Sum Situations and Integrative Negotiation — 18
3.1 The Methodological Model of the Harvard Principled Negotiation — 22
3.2 The Prescriptive Transformative Model: A Theoretical Message from Game Theory — 26
3.2.1 Structural Characteristics and Contextuality — 28
3.2.2 Situational Characteristics and Contextuality — 32
3.2.3 Strategy Choice and Contextuality — 38

2 **International Creative Negotiation: A Relational Theoretical Framework** 41
1 International Negotiation as a Holistic Theoretical Approach: International Creative Negotiation as Governance of International Common Interest 41
2 "Dancing in a Relationship," or, on the Relational Nature of International Creative Negotiations 43
3 On the Textuality of International Creative Negotiation 48
4 On the Phased Structure of International Creative Negotiation 54
5 On the Contextuality of International Creative Negotiation 59
6 On the Subjectivity of International Creative Negotiation 69
6.1 The Setting Up of a Negotiation Team 69
6.2 The Organization and Decisional Configuration of the Negotiation Team 74
6.3 The Accountability of the Negotiation Team 79
6.4 The Process Advisory Role of the Negotiation Team 81

PART II THE NEGOTIATION PHASES IN THE CONVENTIONAL CONSTRUCTION OF INTERNATIONAL COMMON INTEREST 83

3 **The Prenegotiation Phase as a Process of Transformative Governance** 85
1 Introductory Critical Remarks 85
2 The Diagnostic Level 87
2.1 Generating the Level of Negotiation Focus 87
2.2 The Leading Role of the Initiator of Prenegotiation 88
2.3 The Determination of Negotiable Issues 90
2.3.1 Thematic Diagnostic Approach: The Management of Knowledge 90
2.3.2 The Subjective Diagnostic Approach: The Management of Subjective Framings 97
2.3.3 The Management of Contextuality of the Prenegotiation Transformation 100
2.3.4 The Management of Alternative Solutions to Prenegotiation 103
3 The Multilateral Governance Level 105
3.1 Institutional Organization and Management of the Prenegotiation Process 105
3.1.1 Structure and Function of Ad Hoc Multilateral Conference 106
3.1.2 The Techniques of Managing Ad Hoc Multilateral Conference 108

3.2 The Patternment of the Content of Declarative Instruments 113
4 The Outcome of Prenegotiation 118

4 The Constitutive Negotiation Phase as a Process of Constructing Treaties of International Common Interest 120
1 Overview 120
2 Initiation and Institutional Organization of Constitutive Negotiation 121
2.1 The Political Initiative 121
2.2 The Negotiation-Generating Decision 122
2.3 The Ad Hoc Body of Conferential Negotiation 122
2.4 The Role of the Secretariat as a Guardian of the Constitutive Negotiation Process 123
3 The Consensus Procedure as a Negotiating Practice of Constructing Common Interest 127
3.1 The Two Aspects of the Consensus Procedure 127
3.2 The Consensus Relational Level 128
3.3 The Strategic Management Level 131
3.4 The Organizational Management Level 132
3.4.1 The Procedural Techniques of Lateral Expansion and Fragmentation of Issues 133
3.4.2 The Conference-Scaling Practices: Sub-fora and Miniaturization of Conferences 134
4 Rules of Procedure and Practices 136
4.1 Purpose and Definitions 137
4.2 Place and Time of Meetings 138
4.3 Invitation of Observers 138
4.4 Public and Private Sessions of the Meetings 138
4.5 Agenda Setting 139
4.6 Representation 140
4.7 The Bureau of the Negotiating Meeting or Conference 140
4.8 The Organization of the Negotiating Meeting or Conference 142
4.9 Conduct of Business 143
4.10 Decision-Making 144
4.11 The Languages of the Negotiating Meeting or Conference 145
4.12 Amendments: Relationship to the Conventional Regime 148
5 Negotiation of the Textual Pattern of International Agreements 149
5.1 Patternment at the Level of Context of Reference (Referential Patternment) 150
5.1.1 Identifiability of the Context of Reference (Context Identification) 150
5.1.2 Consistency with the Context of Reference (Contextual Consistency) 152

5.1.3 An Added-Value or Constructive-Heuristic Field 154
5.2 Morphological Patternment 155
5.2.1 The Framework Agreement-Performative Protocols *in Processu* Approach 156
5.2.2 The Integrative Agreement-Performative Annexes *in Processu* Approach 158
5.3 Normative Patternment or Patternment of Content 159
5.3.1 The Preamble 160
5.3.2 Legislative Use of Terms: Legislative Definitions 161
5.3.3 Purpose and Scope of Application 164
5.3.4 General Duties-Obligations 170
5.3.5 The System of Multilateral ICI Governance 172
5.3.5.1 Thematization 172
5.3.5.2 Institutionality 182
5.3.5.3 Controllability 187
5.3.5.4 Transformability 197
5.3.5.5 Subjectivity 202
6 Special Techniques and Practices of Constitutive Textual Negotiation 210
6.1 Organizational Techniques and Practices 210
6.1.1 Opening Statements 210
6.1.2 Brainstorming Sessions 211
6.1.3 Inter-Sessional Workshops 213
6.1.4 Side-Events 215
6.2 Textual Techniques and Practices 216
6.2.1 The System of Brackets 216
6.2.2 Recording the Names of Negotiating Participants in the Reports of the Meetings and Conferences 217
6.2.3 Non-Negotiation Text: "Non-Paper" 218
7 The Outcome of Constitutive Negotiation 219

5 The Renegotiation Phase as a Process of Revisionary Governance of Conventional Regimes 222

1 Negotiable Transformation Mutatis Mutandis 222
2 Initiation and Institutional Organization of Renegotiation 223
2.1 The Initiation of Renegotiation 223
2.2 The Institutional Guardianship of the Secretariat in the Renegotiation Process 224
3 Renegotiation of the Textual Pattern of an International Agreement 227
3.1 The Contextuality of Renegotiation 227
3.2 The Morphological Patternment of Amendment 229

3.3 Amendment or Replacement? The Dynamic of the Renegotiation Process 231
3.4 Alternative Options to Renegotiation? 234
3.5 Renegotiating the Treaty Regime Declarative Components 235
4 The Outcome of Renegotiation 239
5 In the Twilight Zone between Renegotiation and Constitutive Negotiation: Renegotiating the Under-Determinate Edges of a Treaty Regime 239
5.1 Renegotiating the Undetermined Crime of Aggression of the Rome Statute of the ICC and the Way to the Kampala Revisionary Compromise 240
5.1.1 Referential Context, the Rome Compromise, and Institutional Layers of Renegotiation 240
5.1.2 The Twinning Renegotiating Process 243
5.2 The Kampala Revisionary Compromise 246

Bibliography 250

Index 257

Preface and Acknowledgments

This book offers an attempt to reconstruct the theoretical link between international negotiation and treaty in an international law perspective and within the realm of interstate negotiations. It analyses their complementary relationship as a structured process of relational governance referring to the construction and reconstruction of the international common interest that is the soul of the polycentric public international order. Its purpose is to unveil the relational character of international negotiation as a process generating international common interest that goes beyond the numerous publications on negotiation produced in the framework of the international relations theory or by experts describing the intricacies of a particular negotiation process on a specific topic.

This book is not the result of a funded project or a special event. It is the product of a life journey and of uncountable series of events, involving research, international negotiating practice, teaching, and conferential exposure shedding light on the need for an integrated theoretical approach to negotiation and treaties in the quest for an order of international common interest. My long exploration and teaching of the theory and practice of international law and the continuum of treaty–international negotiations – coupled with a privileged, long involvement in international environmental negotiations as a UNEP/MAP external legal advisor in Mediterranean marine environment affairs – laid the field for developing and testing my relational approach to international negotiation. The advancement of this theoretical approach inevitably brings with it the way we think about international law and international relations and the way we understand and use their limiting methodological exclusivities. And in this connection, the embedded element of life in my theoretical quest inevitably invites fundamental philosophical underpinnings that permeate and consolidate not only the articulation of the theoretical language but also, more importantly, the broader, more pragmatic understanding of knowledge of international law as relational public law between public entities forming the horizontally structured, polycentric international society.

This book is a book "about international creative negotiation," not a book "of negotiation." I have written this book in a theoretical attempt to show that international negotiation should be understood and explained on the basis of a holistic, interdisciplinary approach that conceptualizes it as a relational, context-dependent, textual, phased-structured, and authoritatively intersubjective process governing conventionally constituted relations of international common interest in patterns. International negotiations need to be understood as an integral dimension of treaties, as a structured relational process of preparation, formation, operation, and development of international conventional regimes serving common interest with coexisting conditions of certainty and uncertainty, efficiency and inefficiency, and within a horizontally developing international order. In consequence, its understanding requires an interdisciplinary approach to law and policy supported by philosophical, linguistic, and psychological considerations, and a concomitant "openness" to a basic quantum understanding of reality. Such an approach is not only closer to the unceasing interaction between stability and fluidity in the relational construction of international common interest through conventional instruments, but it also explains why and how international negotiation matters to international ordering.

Such an approach makes immediately conceivable how international negotiations may take their due in the construction of international common interest and, as a result, be effectively and efficiently conducted as a collective process. At the same time, one can easily infer from the book how inadequate it can be when a negotiating party (from the point of view of his specific role rather than from that of the popularized abstract "personality") dissociates its conduct of international negotiation from the construction of international common interest, or when a national delegate exclusively negotiates through the lenses of its national interest (thus ignoring the importance of understanding its promotion dialectically, through its creative interaction with international common interest and the knowledge for it). It is also insufficient when a delegate of a non-state entity is exclusively oriented towards the progress of the sectorial purposes pursued by that entity (thus having no perception of the need for its interconnection with international common interest and knowledge of the techniques leading to it), or when an international law expert negotiates, holding firm to the indoctrinated "lawyer's view" of international law, defending the methodological borderline between law and non-law and, as a result, taking more of an external advisory role to the negotiating process. Limiting his contribution to the clarification, explanation, or defence of the relevant rules, principles, and sources of international law regarding the issues involved, he chooses to refrain from being properly involved in the negotiation of the subject matter and adopting a "legislator's view" in this process. Finally, it is also not enough when technical/scientific delegates overstep their authority and claim a predominant negotiating role because of their special knowledge of the subject matter, sometimes armed with their long experience in negotiations. Paying an entirely superficial – if any – attention to the legal elements of the negotiating process, ranging from the proper drafting of treaty text to its interrelationship with its context and the construction of international common interest (ICI), they clearly overstep the limits of their role, risking future inconsistencies and implementation problems.

This book was first written and published in Greek and in a more general version at the beginning of 2014. It integrated my long experience in international negotiations as a UNEP/MAP external legal advisor and was built on my multilevel teaching of this subject as a special undergraduate and graduate course at the Panteion University in Athens (which I still do) or in the form of international seminars and international training schools in the framework of the MEPIELAN Centre, which I founded in 2008. Seeds of this book, from the special perspective of the environment, came from a chapter I wrote for the book *Contributions to International Environmental Negotiation in the Mediterranean Context*, which I co-edited with Moira McConnell in 2004. Returning to Cambridge after many years as a visiting scholar in my College (2016 and 2017), I embarked on the translation of the book and the incorporation of new ideas, making substantial improvements to the text. In fact, and as expected, the demanding task of translation was inevitably creative and guided me not only to the substantial reconstruction of a large part of the book but also to the development of more elaborate ideas in my effort to offer better explanation of its central tenets.

In a peculiar manner, this book has a special relationship with Downing College. Downing has been the intellectual and learning place where I originally developed my basic approach to the knowledge of the international and the relational nature of treaties when writing my PhD thesis under the inspiring and insightful supervision of Clive Parry, a superb intellectual thinker of international law. And after many years, it happened that the completion of a more developed and reconstructive English version of my book on international negotiations, initially written in Greek, was made possible in Downing College, where my theoretical voice was born and to which I returned as a visiting scholar. The incomparable accommodation gracefully offered to me by the College, coupled with its unique collegiate atmosphere and discussions with old and new friends and colleagues, linked the past with the present in a wonderful circle creating this book. Words may be poor to describe how grateful I am to Downing College for this unique life experience. And how deeply indebted I remain to Clive Parry and to the unfailing long friendship of John Hopkins, the soul of Downing College for highly reputable studies in law.

In the course of this project, I most gratefully acknowledge the invaluable, openhanded support and advice of my distinguished colleague Jorge Viñuales, who embraced and directed my efforts to reach the prestigious Cambridge University Press and honoured me with his proposal to include this book in his new series, Cambridge Studies on Environment, Energy and Natural Resource Governance.

I am grateful to the three anonymous reviewers contacted by Cambridge University Press for their excellent comments. Special thanks go to Matt Gallaway at Cambridge University Press, together with his first-rate team (Rebecca Jackaman, content editor, Jayavel Radhakrishnan, project manager, Ami Naramor, copyeditor, as well to James Diggins and Jackie Grant), who have taken care of this manuscript through its editing and production process, for their impeccable professionalism and enthusiasm in materializing this project. Last but not least, I wish to express my deep gratitude to Anna, my wife of thirty years, and George, my son, who embarked on his own challenging international law and policy journey towards a world order of common interest, for their unfailing love and constant encouragement throughout the writing of this book.

Abbreviations

AJIL	*American Journal of International Law*
APEC	Asia Pacific Economic Council
BATNA	Best Available Solution to a Negotiated Agreement
BATNDE	Best Available Solution to a Negotiated Declaration
BITS	Bilateral Investment Treaties
BWM Convention	International Convention for the Control and Management of Ships' Ballast Water and Sediments (2004)
BYBIL	*British Yearbook of International Law*
CHGM	Commonwealth Heads of Government Meeting Communiqué (2013)
CITES	Convention on International Trade in Endangered Species of Wild Fauna and Flora (1973)
COLREG	Convention on the International Regulations for Preventing Collisions at Sea (1972)
COPs	Conferences of the Contracting Parties
CRP	Conference Room Paper
EJIL	*European Journal of International Law*
EU	European Union
FAO	Food and Agricultural Organization
FCCC	Framework Convention on Climate Change
GEF	Global Environmental Facility
GESAMP	Group of Experts on Scientific Aspects of Marine Pollution
GYIL	*German Yearbook of International Law*
HNS Convention	International Convention on Liability and Compensation for Damage in Connection with the Carriage of Hazardous and Noxious Substances by Sea (1996)
IAEA	International Atomic Energy Agency
ICAO	International Civil Aviation Organization
ICI	International Common Interest

ICJ	International Court of Justice
ICLQ	*International & Comparative Law Quarterly*
ICSID	International Centre for Settlement of Investment Disputes
ICZM Protocol	Barcelona Convention Protocol on Integrated Coastal Zone Management in the Mediterranean (2008)
IEA	International Energy Agency
IGBP	International Geosphere-Biosphere Programme
IHDP	International Human Dimension Programme on Global Environmental Change
ILM	International Legal Materials
IMO	International Maritime Organization
INC	Intergovernmental Negotiating Committee
IPBES	Intergovernmental Platform on Biodiversity & Ecosystem Services
IPCC	Intergovernmental Panel on Climate Change
ITO	International Trade Organization
IUCN	International Union for Conservation of Nature
JVI	Joint Vienna Institute
LIFE	International Convention for the Safety of Life at Sea (1974)
LJIL	*Leiden Journal of International Law*
MAP	Mediterranean Action Plan
MARPOL	International Convention for the Prevention of Pollution from Ships, 1973, as modified by the Protocols 1978 and 1997
MEPIELAN	Mediterranean Programme for International Environmental Law and Negotiation/Panteion University
MLR	*Modern Law Review*
MOP	Meetings of the Contracting Parties
MOU	Memorandum of Understanding
NEA	Nuclear Energy Agency
NGO	Nongovernmental Organization
OECD	Organisation for Economic Co-operation and Development
OPCW	Organisation for the Prohibition of Chemical Weapons
OPRC Convention	International Convention on Oil Pollution Preparedness, Response and Cooperation (1990)
OSPAR	Convention for the Protection of the Marine Environment of the North-East Atlantic (1992)
PIC	Prior Informed Consent
POPs	Persistent Organic Pollutants
SAB	Scientific Advisory Board
SBSTTA	Subsidiary Body on Scientific, Technical and Technological Advice

STCW	International Convention on Standards of Training, Certification and Watchkeeping for Seafarers (1978)
SWGCA	Special Working Group on the Crime of Aggression
TRIPS Agreement	Agreement on Trade-Related Aspects of Intellectual Property Rights (1994)
UNCLOS	United Nations Convention on the Law of the Sea
UNCTAD	United Nations Conference on Trade and Development
UNDP	United Nations Development Programme
UNECE	United Nations Economic Commission for Europe
UNEP	United Nations Environment Programme
UNESCO	United Nations Educational, Scientific and Cultural Organization
UNFCC	United Nations Framework Convention on Climate Change (1992)
UNGA	United Nations General Assembly
UNITAR	United Nations Institute for Training and Research
WHO	World Health Organization
WMO	World Meteorological Organization
WTO	World Trade Organization

Introduction

THE THEORETICAL QUEST

This book explores international negotiation as a structured process of relational governance generating international common interest (ICI) between and among international participants and in relation to the international public order. In its theoretical quest, this book systematically unveils the missing theoretical link between international negotiation and treaty. Both concepts, in their creative complementarity, are conducive to the construction and continuous operation of relations of ICI and, further, to a pragmatic, contextually relevant, and fundamentally relational approach to international public ordering. Providing an interdisciplinary analysis of the nature and working of this complementarity, this book places it under the perspective of public international law: as a structured process constructing ICI upon which the polycentric public international ordering is founded and evolves.

Such a perception of international negotiation challenges the one-dimensional way international relations theorizes negotiations and positivist international law understands it. The former, exclusively concentrating on the political feature of international negotiation, elaborates its explanations in terms of prescriptive, and unceasingly enriched, models pursuing prevalence or accommodation of interests in international power relations. The latter perceives international negotiation as a distinctive political process – and for this reason as theoretically untouchable – which is simply a flexible and effective means that can be used for achieving "objective" international law solutions with no further inquiry into international negotiation's nature and its relation to treaty. In fact, treaty, being approached as an objective concept of international law, analogous to contract and governed by rules and principles establishing a contract view of treaties, is the legal superstar in the positivist theory of international law, and its concept cannot be "theoretically contaminated" through linkages with political processes. Thus, both theories, chained with their methodological assumptions and serving their methodological barriers, provide a complacently authoritative version of a discrete and autonomous understanding of "negotiation" and "treaty." Understood as separate constructs, they only marginally meet, always within the strictly defined bounds of their respective methodologies.

However, treaty and negotiation in their complementary relationship fundamentally challenge these methodologically imposed barriers. Shedding light on this complementary relationship, this book attempts to advance a self-sustained theoretical approach to the negotiation process as a multilateral structured governance process, between and among international participants, for preparing, constructing, and developing relational treaty regimes of ICI. It is a central tenet of this book that states and non-state entities negotiate in order to establish relations serving ICI. They do not simply negotiate in order to produce solutions to a problem. They negotiate for continuity, not for finality. And this book demonstrates, going into theoretical and practical depth, that such an approach is associated with certain fundamental qualities of international negotiation that make possible its authoritative creative role in the construction of ICI. It is relational (a complementary relationship with a legal [treaty] or declarative instrument), textual (a multilateral legislative-like function between the negotiating participants), contextual (a creative relation to the referential, international, and political ordering), process-phased (a development in three phases marking the distinguishing process characteristics), and subjective (an authoritative intra-subjective and intersubjective decision-making process governing the construction of ICI). This conceptualization of creative international negotiation and its fundamental qualities are equally ignored by the international relations theories and the positivist theory of international law.

THE NARRATION OF NEGOTIATION IN INTERNATIONAL RELATIONS THEORY

Negotiation is undoubtedly one of the central concepts of international relations theory. But within the bounds of its methodology, its theoretical narration is distinctly one-dimensional. Focusing on negotiation as a general process of achieving distributive or integrative solutions in power relations, international relations theory has basically embarked on the development of two competitive prescriptive models of negotiation.

The older distributive or positional negotiation model promotes a popular way of looking at negotiation as a subtle "bargaining," how to achieve the best distribution of benefits and losses at the expense of the other side. It is an autonomous prescriptive model that views negotiation in the most individualistic terms flattering the egotistic aspect of human nature: as a discrete process of intersubjective competitive manipulation with the aim to win, irrespective of consequences, relational context, interests of the other side or, of course, common interest. Inescapably, therefore, only incidentally and only if it is "winning," an agreement may be within the purview of this model. On the other hand, the more recent integrative model attempts to offer, as an alternative to the distributive or positional mode, a more human and social – and hence more relational – perspective of negotiation. It views negotiation as a discrete intersubjective process integrating all interests involved with a view to create benefit for all. And its influential version, the Harvard principled negotiation model, brings to the fore the importance of specifically achieving what it calls a "wise agreement," focusing on the merits to achieve the most feasible balance between "relationship" and "substance" of this agreement. Yet the achievement of the "wise agreement" is carried out through a policy approach: a detailed elaboration of par excellence methodological standards setting out the programme that axiomatically leads to a wise agreement "of any kind." In doing so, it sets out a widely appealing anthropocentric model of principled negotiation that, however, simplifies and rationalizes the negotiation process by manipulating context, relation, process, and agreement instrumentality with a sweeping and unswerving generalization.

Perhaps, when the narration of negotiation in international relations theory takes a more contextually "coloured" turn, it draws particular interest. This is illustrated in a marginally developed and neglected model, rooted in game theory, which I call the prescriptive transformative model and which developed as an empirical, practice-oriented – and for this reason "open-ended" – negotiation model in the framework of the United Nations Institute for Training and Research (UNITAR) with a view to transforming the East–West conflict situation into a cooperative relation. Unlike the other two general prescriptive models, the transformative model sets out the elements of negotiating the transition to a cooperative relation at the international level – and with it, the transformation of the relations between international actors. Thus, it avoids the pitfalls of a grand theory-like perception of negotiation applicable everywhere and swallowing structural and contextual characteristics that are specific to the international negotiation process, and their management is reflected in its agreed outcome (e.g., the Helsinki Final Act, 1975). And as a practice-oriented theory, it calls for continuous enrichment and development of the model.

Nevertheless, all prescriptive models of negotiation do not touch the theoretical link between international negotiation and treaty and distance themselves from their conspicuous dialectical interrelationship in the construction of ICI. In their generalized approach to negotiation as a political process, both treaty and ICI perception become methodologically crippled. In the first place, it is abundantly clear that international relation theorists have an inadequate understanding of law. In particular, they assume law in general, and international law in particular, as a private law conceptualization and logic (a system of clear-cut, objective rules in a hierarchically organized national legal order, authoritatively established and enforced upon individuals when freely entering into objective relations determined by law). And it is this approach to law as a "state" rather than as a "process" that determines the way they envisage the role of law in their political analyses. Process understanding is assumed to belong to the privileged sphere of the political analysis of international relations theory regarding power relations where international law and its concepts, in their static, objective, private law-like normativity, may be either entirely excluded or appropriately embedded into their theoretical models as mere factors. Overall, the static "private law" perception of international law by international relations theorists is, not only, hardly interesting, but, more importantly, hardly convincing for its anticipated force, accuracy, and effectiveness in their power relations modelling schemes.

On the other hand, it is clear that the knowledge of law as public law or as relational law governing continuous relations between social entities, private entities, or individuals generating distinct relational normativity for the attainment of public or social purposes in continuity (in a process) and in context, and the concomitant conceptualization of international law as a relational law construct of a public law nature, as a subjective law of relational governance performing ICI in context, remains – not surprisingly – a terra incognita for international relations theorists. Otherwise, they would have been more inquisitive about the linkage between treaty and negotiation, less mono-disciplinary in their vehemently defended approach, and more philosophically sensitive to interrelationships. Instead, they overall maintain an oversimplified and misguiding attitude about law, identified with an unquestionable and a rather opaque private law understanding, which leads them to misconceptions producing poor judgments about normativity and to the projection of a closed-shop approach to the negotiation process. In defence of the methodological borderline between international law and international relations, international relations theorists embrace international negotiation – and positivist international law theorists eagerly concur – as a political construct exclusively explained within the realm of international relations. So perpetuating this closed-shop approach to the negotiation process, theoretical books on negotiations in general, and recently on international negotiations or aspects of them, are predominantly written by political scientists, but also by managers, economists, or even by international lawyers practicing them on specific subjects and approaching them in an ad hoc-ish manner. Not by legal theorists.

TREATIES, NEGOTIATIONS, AND INTERNATIONAL COMMON INTEREST RELATIONS: A THEORETICAL REFOCUSING OF INTERNATIONAL LAW

The answer to the need for such theoretical refocusing given by this book is subsumed to the following thesis: treaties – and with them related declarative instruments operating either precursorily or systemically for the development of treaties – and negotiations should be viewed as the two inextricably interwoven aspects of one intersubjective process governing ICI. Under this integrating theoretical approach, treaties should be understood as patterned activities constituting relational regimes between states and relevant non-state entities serving ICI in continuity and not as "concluded" agreements, as completed projects entailing objective legal consequences like private law contracts. In fact, states and other relevant institutional entities "are in treaty relations" governing their common interest as an aspect of ICI.[1]

Such a theoretical perception of treaties automatically "subjectifies" them: it points to the direction of the subjects performing this activity and, with it, it reveals the importance of properly understanding the way they perform this activity; they negotiate. At the same time, its process aspect is indicated through the integrated structured negotiation. In practice, states and other non-state entities, operating as "legislators" of their own relations within and in consistency with their "legislated" contexts (international and national), negotiate the establishment or the development of their relational ICI treaty regime in a structured negotiating process and in view of the patterned elements of treaties as well as the patterned management of the related multilevel context. As a result, the missing theoretical link between treaty and negotiation is unfolded and their complementary relationship is restituted. This theoretical refocusing requires a consistent and thorough analysis of the performance of the treaty activity, a theory of international negotiation constructing ICI as a purposive complementary relationship with international normative instruments, conventional (treaties) or declarative (declarations, decisions, action plans, strategies, etc.).

Unsurprisingly, there is no room for such an approach in the realm of the positivist theory of international law. Accordingly, it is completely ignored by mainstream international lawyers who are methodologically directed to basically limit their conceptual understanding of treaties to private law contracts, as legally "concluded" agreements to which international law attaches legal consequences analogous to private law contracts. The negotiating aspect of treaties is entirely subdued to the logic and application of its methodological objectification. As a result, international negotiation only emerges under the mantle – and within the methodological limitations – of a general (private) law rule-approach. As a distinct political process, because of its mysterious qualities, it may constitute a means for peaceful settlement of international disputes or for the creation of new international norms of conduct. And the only anticipation is that its "general" application takes place within the frame of relevant principles of international law and would be conducted following a few general guidelines for the achievement of its objective. This is a kind of second-order negotiation. Projecting an exclusive "lawyer's view" of objective treaty law – as opposed to a "legislative view" of treaty relational normativity aimed at ICI – the positivist theory of international law methodologically denies the process element of treaty expressed as intersubjective relational governance of ICI.

1 As Parry insightfully put it, "to treat is but to negotiate and to be 'in treaty' is but to be in negotiation." International law "is essentially public law and the relations of public bodies inter se, whether within the State or without, are not governed by rules of law related to market or money economics." C. Parry, "Of Treaties," in A. Parry (ed.), *Collected Papers of Clive Parry*, vol. II, Wildy, Simmonds and Hill Publishing, 2012, 289, 305.

UNVEILING THE THEORETICAL VOICE OF THIS BOOK

The theoretical approach developed in this book and its attempt to point to a different theoretical perspective in the international negotiation process unfolds in two Parts. The general Part I contains two chapters that elaborate on the inadequacies of the theoretical narration on negotiation advanced by international relations theory and on the need for a holistic theoretical approach to international negotiation as a process creating and governing relations of ICI based on the complementarity between negotiation and treaty.

Chapter 1 sets the stage for exploring, with a critical look, the terrain of the efforts to theorize the international negotiation process through autonomous prescriptive models in the field of international relations theory. It argues for two distinct and competitive prescriptive models of negotiation, the "distributive" or "positional" negotiation model and the "integrative" or "principled" negotiation model. The former, prescribing the elements of negotiation as a discrete intersubjective process of competitive manipulation leading to the best possible distribution of benefits at the expense of the others, clearly ignores common interest. The latter, and its eminent Harvard version, prescribes the elements and method of negotiation as a process for integrating, in a unitary manner, all interest involved in achieving agreements of common interest, while its anthropocentric negotiation model eliminates relational contextuality. In a less celebrated manner, an interesting prescriptive transformative model of international negotiation, developed from game theory, sets up the elements of an agreed, practice-oriented, and open-ended model of historically transforming the East–West conflict situation into a cooperative one. The chapter explains why, although different in theoretical significance, all these models are inadequately equipped to go beyond a general managerial approach to international negotiation and describe how it constructs ICI as an ICI governance process. Providing autonomous, generalized, one-dimensional approaches to the negotiation process, they are set to prescribe their par excellence methodological standards that objectify negotiation as a political process that, in all cases, may lead to the attainment of their final theoretical aim.

Chapter 2 advances a holistic theoretical approach to the international negotiating process as a creative process instrumentation for preparing, constituting, and expanding relational treaty regimes performing ICI in correlation with their constantly unveiling contexts. Focusing on the theoretically neglected complementarity relationship between "treaty" and "negotiation" in the process of creating and governing relations of ICI, it sails through the methodologically limiting, generalizing, and mono-disciplinary approaches of international relations (negotiations as "autonomous prescriptive models") and positivist international law theory (a "contract view" of treaties) and brings to light the relational, process-related, and intersubjective ICI normativity of treaty. The chapter contends that international creative negotiation reinforces the relational link between "treaty and negotiation" and provides a holistic understanding of the reality of ICI governance enshrined in the continuity construction of ICI treaty regimes. The chapter specifically demonstrates that international creative negotiation has four distinguishing features: it is conceptually relational in the sense that it rests on the complementarity between "treaty" and "negotiation" in the process of creating and governing relations of ICI; it is focused on the language of a negotiating text and its intricacies (textuality); it is structured in three distinct phases, Prenegotiation, Constitutive Negotiation, and Renegotiation (phase-structured); it operates in relation to a generic context of an idiomorphic international "societas" and the evolving public international legal order (contextuality); and it is an authoritatively formed intra-subjective and inter-subjective decision-making process of collective governance through specially organized collectivities, the negotiating teams, vested with a multifaceted role subjectivity.

Part II of this book unfolds a specific in-depth analysis of the three phases of the international creative negotiation process – preparing, constituting, and renegotiating relational treaty regimes of ICI – thus providing a comprehensive and interdisciplinary view of complex issues that, so far, are fragmentally and inadequately treated. In this process, these phases develop a certain *relational governance structure*: each consecutive phase builds upon certain appropriate elements of the previous one.

Chapter 3 analyses the Prenegotiation phase of the international negotiation process as a collective attempt to transform a seemingly "zero-sum" or "distributive" situation into a negotiable relationship reflecting a "non-zero-sum" or "integrative" situation serving ICI. Such collective transformative governance has a declarative character and serves as a precursor for the constitutive phase of international negotiation. Prenegotiation, as an exercise of transformative governance of international relations, is a structured intersubjective process, generating the negotiation focus, and heavily dependent upon the perception of the role of its initiator-leader. It is constructed in two interrelated levels. First, the diagnostic level encompasses the identification of the negotiable issues through cognitive management carried out knowledgeably (diagnostic thematic management), intersubjectively (management of "subjective framings"), and contextually (management of the special context of reference). Second, the level of multilateral governance is featured by its tiered structure, its comprehensive negotiating approach and management of the subject matter, and the collective framing of its declarative product. It is properly initiated by standard techniques employed by the initiator-leader consisting of the drafting of a supporting report dealing with the issues under negotiation, the drafting of a single negotiating text setting out the negotiable elements of the intended Declaration/ Decision etc., and the drafting of the agenda. The content of the declarative outcome of Prenegotiation is patterned and is formally adopted by consensus.

Chapter 4 embarks on an extensive analysis of the Constitutive phase of the international negotiation process, which refers to the collective establishment of an ICI treaty regime or to its expansion through a performative Protocol. Here negotiation is rigorously examined as an intersubjective relational process whereby a new treaty or a new Protocol related to it are "constituted" as collective normative activities pursuing the protection and promotion of ICI on a consensual basis and by consistent reference to their context. The product generated by Prenegotiation is part of this context; however, the transition from the Prenegotiation phase to the Constitutive Negotiation phase is nonlinear, linked to the efficient management of a variety of contextual factors. Constitutive Negotiation applies, mutatis mutandis, certain methodical elements of the diagnostic level of Prenegotiation. This phase is generated from a multilateral, institutional, or conventional regime action and is carried out by an ad hoc body of conferential negotiation. In this process, the role of the Secretariat is central, operating as its guardian, vested with a catalytic administrative, creative, and diplomatic role, protecting it from possible breaks. The adoption of the consensus procedure is the basic procedural safeguard providing the necessary negotiation space for forming decisions constituting a relational treaty regime in pragmatic terms and legitimating it. Having an important "constructing-negotiating" aspect, it is structured in three distinctive and interrelated levels, the consensus-relational, the strategic management, and the organizational management levels. Correspondingly, the adoption of the patterned rules of procedure, supplemented by international practice, set up the organizational and functional framework of the negotiating forum. The chapter then proceeds from the more institutive to the more legislative-like constructive processes of constitutive ICI treaty negotiation. Here, the negotiation of the textual pattern of the treaty instrument takes centre stage in the Constitutive Negotiation process. It is specifically associated with three levels of treaty patternment that provide the necessary normative material for the construction of ICI: referential patternment (context identification, contextual compatibility, and "added value" or constructive heuristic); morphological patternment ("framework agreement – performative protocols" or "integrative agreement – executing annexes"); and normative patternment. The latter lies at the heart of Constitutive Negotiation because the knowledge and proper management of treaty-patterned elements constitute the pillars around which the Constitutive Negotiation process is unveiled. Correspondingly, the knowledge and appropriate use of organizational and textual techniques and practices, variably applied in all negotiation phases, creatively contribute to the progress of negotiation and the consensus-building of the ICI treaty relation.

Finally, Chapter 5 develops the Renegotiation phase of the international negotiation process as a structured intra-institutional process of revisionary governance of an operating treaty regime. It reinforces its relational resilience, indicating the ingrained "negotiability" of its normative force. Renegotiation builds on the structural and procedural characteristics and the treaty-patternment approach of Constitutive Negotiation, and employs the same techniques, while it properly integrates some methodical elements of the diagnostic level of Prenegotiation. It is initiated by an institutionally provided regime action prescribed in the amendment clause of the treaty. The Secretariat, operating as an institutional guardian of the regime, is endowed with institutional due diligence relating to the conferential renegotiation body, the report of the proposed amendments identifying the zone of renegotiation, institutional diplomacy, and the diplomatic conference for the adoption of treaty amendment or its replacement. The contextuality of the revisionary negotiation encompasses a particular internal context of reference, generated by the institutional life of the treaty regime (derivative context). The morphological patternment of Renegotiation refers to the textual negotiating technique applied to the amendment of the text pattern of the treaty. Alternatively, it may take the form of replacement as a result of a collective decision shaped by negotiation, of a multifactorial basis. "Withdrawal" or "denunciation" hardly constitute alternatives to Renegotiation because of relational and contextual considerations; they may, however, be used as an intermediate strategy to trigger Renegotiation. Renegotiation may also refer to the declarative components of a treaty regime, such as actions plans, leading to their "refinement" or "reassessment." In some cases, Renegotiation may develop in the twilight zone between Constitutive Negotiation and Renegotiation when related to the development of the underdetermined aspects of a particular treaty, undergoing subtle structural transformations and producing new negotiating techniques.

All in all, the theoretical voice of this book is tuned to provide an interdisciplinary, international law-based account for an international negotiator on how to be involved not only effectively but also perceptively and in perspective in the phased international negotiation process between and among states and relevant non-state actors constructing ICI. Through this process and offering a "legislative view" of international law, this book reveals why it matters to understand the horizontal normativity of international ordering, especially when positivist thinking does not seem to be an appealing option.

PART I

Theoretical Approaches to International Negotiations and International Common Interest

1

The Theorization of International Negotiation

Autonomous Prescriptive Theoretical Models and Their Deficiencies

1 A PANORAMIC CRITICAL VIEW

This chapter sets the stage for exploring the terrain of the efforts to theorize the international negotiation process through autonomous prescriptive models developed in the field of international relations theory. Thus, at the international level, the attempt to build a theory of the international negotiation process was generally connected with the development of a theoretical and, at the same time, empirical approach referring to the management of two distinct "situations," which, in turn, provided the cause and the starting point of two distinct and competitive prescriptive models of international negotiation:

- The "zero-sum" or "distributive" situation, which provided the basis for the model of "distributive negotiation" or "positional negotiation."
- The "non-zero-sum" or "positive-sum" situation, which is associated with the model of integrative negotiation – the latter is more specifically and, to an extent, convincingly articulated by the more recent methodological model of "principled negotiation" developed in the framework of the Harvard Negotiation Project, which was broadly spread.

Viewed as general prescriptive models, both the model of distributive negotiation and the model of integrative negotiation are theoretically deficient. Being in a competitive relation, each theoretical model requires the exclusive guidance of those who adopt one or the other in a binding manner, so that they will embark on a course of action by following a certain negotiating roadmap. In doing so, each theoretical model determines the purpose pursued by negotiation (prevalence or predominance over the other side – a "positive solution for all" or a "commonly accepted solution") and provides a description and analysis of all those elements that axiomatically make up the negotiation path and lead to the attainment of its final purpose. Remaining within the strict framework of their par excellence methodological standards, both prescriptive theoretical models seem unable to conceptualize the catalytic complementarity of the special referential context and to incorporate it to their distinctive theoretical construction. Instead, they compete at the level of the usefulness and adequacy of the theoretical generalization of their prescriptive force. At the same time, they are exhausted in the formulation of techniques and methods that the negotiating parties must adopt in order to be instrumental in achieving their different objectives. As a result, they ignore the complexity, distinctiveness, and intricacies of the reality of the international negotiation process that lie in the crucial importance of the phases of international negotiation (Prenegotiation, Constitutive Negotiation, and Renegotiation), its textual character (language and the "patterned" text – treaty or collective declaration or organizational decision – generated by international negotiation), its institutional characteristics (a multilevel constitution of negotiating conferences and negotiating teams) – notably, the key features that build up the proposed approach of this book. That is, to view international negotiation as *a structured process of multilateral construction of a conventional regime of ICI, in harmony with the horizontally evolving international order of justice as well as with the subjectivity and openness of its context of operation*.

Undoubtedly, the eventual theoretical synthesis of these two prescriptive models may cover, to a certain extent, their admitted theoretical and practical inconsistencies;[1] however, it will continue to feed the underlying generalized approach to the negotiation process. Orienting towards the generality of negotiation as method blurs the significance of "interconnections" and "particular differences" related to the very nature of international negotiation.[2] At the same time, it undermines the possibility for a better, more careful, but also deeper, observation and understanding of the imponderable factors, the experiences, and the refined differences and processes that have a determining impact on the international negotiating process.

Likewise, a theorization of international negotiation through a prescriptive construct also emerges from game theory. This is what is described here as a *transformative model* that, focusing on the transition from a conflict situation to a cooperative situation, develops those general concepts and elements associating this transition with a guided negotiating action. Starting from a clearly defined empirical framework, the paradigm of rapprochement of the relations between East and West and the Helsinki Final Act (August 1975), the transformative model

[1] B. M. Patton, "On Teaching Negotiation," in M. Wheeler (ed.), *Teaching Negotiation: Ideas and Innovations*, PON Books, 2000, 7, 12–16.

[2] The "craving for generality" and the pursuance of manipulating the complex and subtle inner aspects of reality through uniform methods and techniques, independently from contextual references, actually hinders the attempt towards more and better understanding of "imponderable evidence," declares Wittgenstein; see R. Monk, *Ludwig Wittgenstein: The Duty of Genius*, Vintage, 1991, 547–548; also L. Wittgenstein, *Philosophical Investigations* (transl. by G. E. M. Anscombe), Basil Blackwell, 1976, Part II, 223 ("if a lion could talk, we could not understand him!"). In fact, the "craving for generality" underlying both the distributive negotiation, aiming at "the dominance of position," and the principled negotiation, aiming at achieving "a wise agreement," may function, although from opposing directions, equally misleadingly.

pursues the theorizing of international negotiation within the gradual development of general and commonly accepted prescriptive elements and perceptions managing the transition to cooperative relations between parties with heterogeneous interests. Like the two previous prescriptive theoretical models, the transformative model feeds the generalized approach to the negotiation process, displaying analogous deficiencies and falling subject to the same criticism. On the other hand, it searches for the plausibility of its prescriptive elements in the fact that they are commonly accepted under the aegis of the insightful global research perspective and coordination of UNITAR, as well as in their propounded "openness" to further development – an aspect that is, perhaps, the reason for its much less celebrated discussion in international relations theory. Arriving at a commonly accepted practice-oriented theory, this theoretical model is rooted in conceptually agreed perceptions related to the dynamics – rather than to the causality – of the pursued "transformation" of the conflict situation into a cooperative one.

All in all, these three prescriptive theoretical models, developed in the field of international relations, remain faithful to the traditional methodological entrenchment of this field, producing a one-dimensional approach to the international negotiation process. They focus on negotiation as a distinct, generic process, rationalizing it either as a discrete process of intersubjective, competitive manipulation leading to the best possible distribution of benefits at the expense of the others, or as a discrete intersubjective process integrating all interests involved, achieving wise agreements for the benefit of all, or, even as a process of building solutions serving a common benefit through a calculated transition from a historically distributive situation to an integrative cooperative solution.

2 ZERO-SUM SITUATIONS AND DISTRIBUTIVE OR POSITIONAL NEGOTIATION

The *zero-sum* or *distributive situation* refers to situations where the expected benefit is considered or perceived as limited from the beginning, for it is part of a strictly defined totality. In consequence, it is considered or perceived only in terms of distribution to the effect that one side's benefit is the other side's loss. This process of limited distribution of benefits and losses, rooted in the historical perception or attitude of the negotiating sides, may be expressed as $(+) + (-) = 0$. A characteristic example of this situation is the conflict between two neighbouring states on the demarcation of their borders or on the delimitation of their maritime zones or of their continental shelf. The perception of the conflict as a zero-sum or distributive situation usually leads the states involved to avoid negotiations in order to evade the risk or the uncertainty of limited distribution. Such a perception also generally characterizes conflict situations before they become the subject of negotiation.[3] If,

[3] I. W. Zartman and M. R. Berman, *The Practical Negotiator*, Yale University Press, 1982, 13.

however, the states involved finally decide to proceed to negotiations guided by this perception, then the negotiation process becomes an instrument for the advancement of such a perception. The negotiation process is viewed as a process of intersubjective competitive manipulation to be performed in the light of strictly defined individualistic goals and rigidly static terms. This is the so-called *distributive negotiation* or *positional negotiation* whereby negotiation is approached as a process of competitive manipulation by the negotiating sides so that each of them attempts to achieve the best possible distribution of benefits at the expense of the rest. In fact, this model of negotiation seems to be commonly identified with the bargaining model or the model of the bazaar.

The *distributive* or *positional negotiation,* as a prescriptive theoretical model, displays the following characteristics:

1) **The power of parties plays a determinative role.** Negotiations, carried out on the basis of an individualistic approach adopted by the states involved, develop in a framework of an open competition of power, where "good faith" and "rationality" are displaced and, instead, "realism" and "intransigence of conduct" dominate. The "domination" (or the "win") of the strongest, securing the maximum satisfaction of its own objectives, is considered the ultimate purpose of this type of negotiation.
2) **The opening of the negotiating process anchors the final outcome of negotiations.** Negotiations neither have a preventive character nor seek the creation of regimes intended to govern relations of common interest between the parties involved. Instead, they are designed to achieve a durable solution of conflicts to the effect that their opening anchors the final outcome of negotiations. In other words, their opening has a strong "anchoring effect" exerting a strong pull throughout the rest of the negotiation.[4]
3) **The negotiators adopt a clearly distributive attitude.**Pursuing domination or a win over the other party/ies, the negotiating party projects views that give little or no consideration to the opposing objectives of the other party/ies, while it systematically contests their legitimacy, refusing to accept their consequences. At the level of multilateral negotiations, the adoption of a clearly distributive attitude in positional negotiations degenerates into the formation of inflexible coalitions between the parties, with an obscure, and rather symbolic, community of interests.
4) **The negotiators apprehend the limited frame of their positions in a linear manner and they organize it in a clearly individualistic and strict gradation.** Ignoring the significance of establishing or maintaining relationships and

[4] At a more general level, the "anchoring effect" of a negotiation related to the first offer or the first draft of a text may have a considerable impact on the rest of the negotiation process and on its final outcome, precisely because the negotiating situations are surrounded by great uncertainty and ambiguity. See, e.g., A. D. Galinksy, "When to Make the First Offer in Negotiations," available at: http://hbswk.hbs.edu/archive/4302.html.

generating a continuous accommodation of interests, as well as the potential impact of the negotiation process on creating and evaluating new options by the parties, the negotiators organize from the very beginning, and on the basis of individualistic – and usually inadequately grounded – evaluations and choices, the concrete scaling of positions that determines their negotiating conduct. This is a strictly perceived linear scaling of positions consisting of: the opening position, the secondary position, the subsequent position, the fallback position, and the bottom-line or red-line[5] position. On the basis of this perception, a *multitiered framework* is defined within which the "rival party/ies" will be confronted, whereby the negotiating steps are guided in a mandatory, inflexible, and polarizing manner. Being "framed" within this individually determined linear scaling of their positions, the negotiators are called to make decisions on what and how to offer, what to reject, and what concessions to make. Their creativity is burned out on how effectively to exercise advocacy in support of the multitiered framework of their positions, an advocacy that becomes an end in itself.

5) **The progress of the negotiations is realized through successive phases of individualistic practices of power competition and strategies of misrepresentation.** The intensification of competition and the exercise of pressures are sought to the maximum extent for the progress of negotiations through the systematic use of *coercive tactics* (e.g., threats, intimidation, blackmail, bluffing, fait accompli, harassment, ultimatum [do this or do not do this, otherwise . . .], deadline), and the designing and systematic application of *destabilizing tactics* and *strategic misrepresentations* by acts or omissions (e.g., reversing of positions, continual postponement, voluntary leaks of information generating destabilization, deceit, surprise by new facts and information, silence, engineering incidents and disturbing actions, no-show in negotiations, imposition of a "negotiation marathon," abrupt withdrawal from negotiations). As a result, the required synergy between the negotiating states is limited to the minimum possible, whereas the risk of exposure of the negotiating states as well as of a fiasco of a negotiation is visible. Small concessions are possible only to the extent that

5 It is no coincidence that the lowest acceptable position in negotiations is commonly described by the use of the term "red line," since the phrase "thin red line" was made up of the material of "heroism" and, hence, equipped with "communicative force": it was used to depict succinctly the "heroic resistance" of the 93rd British Highland Regiment at the Battle of Balaklava, on 25 October 1854, during the Crimean War. The phrase "thin red line" was used by London *Times* correspondent William Russel, who, observing the battle from a distance, wrote that he could only see "a thin red streak tipped with a line of steel" of the 93rd Highland Regiment, a phrase that, metaphorically used, became synonymous with heroic resistance. For the event, see the National Archives, *British Battles Exhibition*, Crimea 1854 – The Battle of Balaklava, available at: www.nationalarchives.gov.uk/battles/crimea/battle.htm. Also, *The Argyll and Sutherland Highlanders (Princess Louise's), Battle Honours 1806–1902*, "The Thin Red Line" – "Balaklava," Crimean War, 25th October 1854, available at: www.theargylls.co.uk/battlebalaklava.php.

they are considered mandatory, at that particular time, for the continuance of negotiations.

It is evident that the model of *distributive* or *positional negotiation* is organized and evolved around a basic methodological assumption that may even be regarded as largely a commonplace: that when one negotiates, one only seeks, on the basis of one's positions, to maximize material reward or competitive prevalence against the other side. This model, however, ignores arbitrarily all those essential elements inherent in the negotiation process that characterize the possibility of its consensual shaping, impact the field of options of the negotiating parties, and constitute the material of constructing regimes of common interest: that is, "process," "interest," "relations," and "legitimacy." Equally arbitrarily, this model ignores, as well, the need for transforming the perceived distributive situation into a positive-sum situation. Perhaps even more important is that it ignores or pays too little attention to the impact of the generated outcome and on whether and how it partakes of common interest in general.

3 NON-ZERO-SUM SITUATIONS AND INTEGRATIVE NEGOTIATION

The *"non-zero-sum"* or *"positive-sum" situation* is associated with situations where the anticipated benefit is considered to be common, and, in consequence, it is perceived *as a possibility to shape a relationship of common interest*, so that each state-party participates in the benefit generated by the relationship in general (even though not equally), having ensured that its basic interests would be protected and that none of the other state-parties involved would be unilaterally or exclusively benefited. As a situation geared to create a common-interest relationship between states, it is perceived either as an *initial situation* or as a *transformed or resulting situation*.

More specifically, as an initial situation, it refers to the understanding of international issues and problems of a generally functional character that constantly require, through negotiation, a coordinated and integrated management either at the global or at the regional level, but also at the bilateral level (problematic issues ranging from economic cooperation, protection of the environment, and sustainable development, to the prohibition of chemical weapons, the control of nuclear energy, the fight against terrorism or piracy, or the prohibition of all forms of inhuman and degrading treatment). As a transformed or resulting situation, it refers to the perception that the existing international dispute or conflict of interests associated with it may ultimately be dealt with effectively and efficiently only if creatively transformed, through negotiation, into a non-zero-sum situation. This resulting situation may be related to certain cases where a disputed territorial area comes to be approached by the parties to the dispute in the light of the valuable resources this area may contain (e.g., oil and gas in a disputed continental shelf area) and the mutual benefit that the parties may draw from the possibility of reaching an equitable agreed solution through negotiation. More commonly, it may be related to cases where a seemingly conflict situation arises, for the first time, in the international domain – a *primae impressionis* perception of new problematic issues of an outstanding and intrinsically unusual nature for which there is not, as yet, an international regulatory regime and a shaped international policy – and, as a result, an initiative is undertaken for its negotiated transformation into a relationship of ICI.

Resorting to negotiations in such situations, it becomes conspicuous that a distinct form of international negotiation is developed, differing substantially from the distributive or positional negotiation. Instead of pursuing manipulation and an individualistically favourable distribution of benefits, this form of negotiation seeks to consolidate a collective creation of relations managing ICI, thus completely opposing the individualistic approach of distributive negotiation, as explained earlier. This is the so-called *integral* or *creative* international negotiation, which has the character of a multilateral determination and management international public interest, and as such it includes the following essential elements:

1) **Collective identification and determination of the issues of negotiation for the creation of a relationship of ICI.** In contrast to the distributive negotiation, the parties to the integrative international negotiation are approaching the negotiating process with the prospect of the possible creation of a relationship to function for mutual or common benefit. They search for and jointly define, therefore, the issues that may be the subject matter of this negotiation and may potentially offer the possibility of establishing between them a relational regime of ICI. Since the negotiating parties evaluate the identified issues differently at the time of the initiation of the negotiation process, their common goal is to create a common management pattern capable of integrating the originally different or "negotiably crude" evaluations with a view that, in the end, all negotiating parties will benefit. The key to this process is the packaging of the jointly identified issues. In fact, the issues are incorporated or integrated into a "package" to the effect that the outcome of negotiations will represent an overall and balanced compromise with reference to *all* identified issues. Through the continuous management of diverging and converging interests and values, the negotiations outcome will reflect the creation of *a relational regime of common interest operating pluralistically*.
2) **Adoption of a dialectical approach for the creation of a relationship of ICI.** From the outset, the negotiating parties adopt a dialectical approach, cooperating to achieve a multilateral enlightenment, learning, and informed consensual solutions to problems associated with the subject matter of negotiation. Learning how to cooperate and consult each other, by asking more than demanding and by arguing convincingly, the negotiators learn to shape collectively and creatively, in a time-space context, the construction of an appropriate relational regime

serving ICI. Such a relational regime will be geared to enable the parties to understand, evaluate, and manage, more thoroughly and effectively, the specific problems they will face, while, at the same time, it will safeguard the continual coexistence of their individual and collective perspectives, without the latter absorbing the former and vice versa. The negotiating parties are guided to an exploratory examination of the assumptions interwoven with their claimed positions in order to bring out the substratum of their underlying interests and to trace the field of their common interest. It is clear that in this process, in contrast to distributive negotiation, the negotiators take into account, to a varying extent, the objectives of the other negotiating parties, recognizing, explicitly or implicitly, the legitimacy of these objectives. In addition, the negotiators may develop multilaterally, in the context of uncertainties surrounding the prospect of establishing a regime of ICI, important "lateral considerations" revealing new, originally silent, problems and generating joint innovative ideas for the creative management of thorny problems.[6] In this latter case, it seems that integrative negotiation embraces *the logic of complementarity* – beyond rationalism and a step-by-step approach – since, as explained later, the negotiating search for ICI is generated and progressing through a nonlinear development associated with: the intersubjectivity of the negotiating parties, the interconnection of the negotiated relationship with its dynamically evolving context, the "open" (imperfect and continuously developing) multilateral legislative will – and not the "perfect" contractual agreement – of the parties negotiating under conditions institutionalizing the negotiating process.

3) **Adoption and implementation of relational norms as elements of the negotiating process.** The negotiating parties adopt and implement a series of regulatory norms that support the strengthening of the constructive negotiation of a relationship of ICI (relational norms). These relational norms constantly guide the negotiators to the issues that they need to focus on in order to be able to arrive, more assuredly, at the shaping of a resilient relationship of ICI, properly adjusted to the management of the uncertainties that characterize the targeted non-zero-sum situations. These relational norms include:
   - A *quasi-fiduciary adoption of a long-term perspective of creating a regime relationship that will consistently secure ICI*. In this context, the potential benefits and costs associated with such a relational regime will be considered and evaluated not in absolute terms, but in terms of "complementarity."[7]

[6] On "lateral thinking" and its importance to the "non-conventional" generation of creative ideas see, generally, E. de Bono, *Lateral Thinking: Creativity Step by Step*, Harper & Row, 1970, *passim*; also his *Serious Creativity: Using the Power of Lateral Thinking to Create New Ideas*, HarperBusiness, 1992, *passim*.

[7] "Complementarity" constitutes a basic concept in the language of quantum physics and denotes that conceptual dichotomies are illusions. As such, complementarity is directly related to the prominent Stoic motto ΟΥΔΕΝ ΚΑΚΟΝ ΑΜΙΓΕΣ ΚΑΛΟΥ ("There's no evil without some good"), and, in fact,

Since the creation of the ICI regime and its continuous-time function does not actually allow accurate "measurements" of benefits and costs; since also, in reality, the emergence of common interest and the allocation of common benefits are multilaterally determined and dynamic in nature and, therefore, relative and intersubjective related to many different factors that determine the "individual-collective" perception and the action of the negotiating parties (relevant social, economic, cultural, technological, and spatial/regional factors, as well as subjective evaluations concerning the participation or nonparticipation of each negotiating party); and, finally, since the more the "benefits" and "costs" are measured in a time-space context under conditions of ICI, the more their relevant attitudes and behaviour are altered, it is the quasi-fiduciary adoption of a long-term perspective of creating a regime relationship to consistently secure ICI that constitutes a factor that supports the relational perspective of negotiation.

- *Ensuring the stability of the negotiation process through unravelling different levels of institutionalization and participation and the avoidance of disrupting the negotiation process.* This relational norm assures a steadily recurrent flow of interaction opportunities, the widening of the progress of negotiation through synergies, and the reinforcing of the significance of arguments related to society and science, while it facilitates the "joint learning" of the problems associated with the tracing and determination of ICI aspects of the issue under negotiation.[8] As is explained in what follows, the ad hoc institutionalization of the negotiating process between states, in conjunction with the appropriate engagement of competent institutional mechanisms and the participation of the relevant non-state entities, buttresses, in actuality, the continuation of the negotiating process and the collective perspective of reaching consensus,

it should provide the "space" for the overall evaluation of the outcome of the negotiation process for it denotes the relativity of a successful or an unsuccessful negotiation. For an intellectually refreshing approach to the deeper understanding and construction of law (a "look beyond law in order to understand law") by reference to the "epistemological space" of the insights of contemporary physics (general relativity and quantum theory), see L. H. Tribe, "The Curvature of Constitutional Space: What Lawyers Can Learn from Modern Physics," 103 *Harvard Law Review* (1989), 1–39. On the other hand, it is noteworthy that the positivistic approach to international law and its methodologically pursued epistemological "objectivity" rested on the perceived analogy of domestic law, and was inescapably founded on the logic and method of classical physics; see, e.g., E. Raftopoulos, *The Inadequacy of the Contractual Analogy in the Law of Treaties*, Publications of the Hellenic Institute of International and Foreign Law, Athens, 1990, *passim*; also his *Course, Theory and Language of International Law: "Objectivity" or International Common Interest?* (in Greek), Nomiki Bibliothiki SA, 2014 (Repr. first edn 1997), 3ff. and 20ff.

8 This "joint learning," however, may encompass the pursuit of the primacy of certain parties in cases where uncertainty surrounds the understanding of the essence of the issues or it penetrates into the scientific consideration of the problems involved; see J. K. Sebenius, "International Negotiation Analysis," in V. A. Kremenyuk (ed.), *International Negotiation: Analysis, Approaches, Issues*, 2nd edn, Jossey-Bass, a Wiley Company, 2002, 229, 254.

against any disrupting individual actions. In fact, any disruption of the negotiation process tends to inflate politically the problems associated with the issues under negotiation and seriously undermines the confidence of the negotiating parties, while the cooperative response and management of these problems is abandoned in the uncertainty of the flow of time. And this can only make infinitely more difficult any future return to the negotiating table.

3.1 *The Methodological Model of the Harvard Principled Negotiation*

The development of *principled negotiation* as an autonomous prescriptive theoretical model of negotiation, being at the opposite end of distributive or positional negotiation,[9] is relatively recent and was articulated in the framework of the Harvard Negotiation Project.[10]

Harvard principled negotiation propounds *a generalizing* model of negotiation as an alternative to the model of positional negotiation, through which the efficient and amicable production of the so-called wise outcomes is methodically designed.[11] The negotiating parties should recognize that their goal is to direct their negotiating focus on both "the relationship" and "the substance" of their respective merits.[12] This model identifies four methodological axes that refer to "the basic points of negotiation," around which the negotiating process should revolve and unfold, and that transcend all levels of negotiation (individual, local, national, regional, and international), applying "almost in all cases." These four methodological axes are formulated as "negotiation commandments":

- *Separate the people from the problem* (people problem): the negotiator should disentangle the people's problem from the substance of the issue under negotiation and deal with it separately; this will enable him to advance a direct engagement and effective communication with the other negotiator/s as "human beings," so as to be dissociated from the positions he puts forward and to be, in effect, converted into a problem solver, thus making possible the reaching of an efficient and amicable "wise outcome."

[9] R. Fisher and W. Ury, with B. Patton (ed.), *Getting to YES: Negotiating Agreement without Giving In*, Penguin Books, 1991, *passim*.

[10] Program on Negotiation, Harvard Law School, "About the Harvard Negotiation Project," 19 April 2009, available at: www.pon.harvard.edu/research_projects/harvard-negotiation-project/hnp/.

[11] Ibid., 10.

[12] Adversely, the positional negotiation sacrifices the relationship to the pursuance of achieving substantive individual benefits or vice versa; see Patton, "On Teaching Negotiation," *supra* 1, 7, 14–15.

- *Focus on interests, not positions* (interests problem): the negotiator should focus on the interests highlighting the importance of their exploration, recognition, and satisfaction, since, if caged in positions, either he may face the reduction of the possibility of reaching an agreement or he may be led to an insufficient and unworkable agreement.
- *Invent options for mutual gain* (options problem): the negotiators should support creativity in the negotiation process, pursuing a wide range of possible solutions that may creatively advance their shared interests and lead to reconciling their differing interests.
- *Insist on using objective criteria* (criteria problem): the negotiators should be directed towards the development and proper use of objective criteria and procedures during the negotiation process, so that they will reach results based on criteria and standards independent of their will, the reason takes hold in acts and decisions, and any yielding "turns colorless," being the outcome of principle rather than of pressure.

In the framework of this generalizing approach and the establishment of the four par excellence methodological axes, principled negotiation postulates, expanding on the same generalizing direction, three programmatic stages of negotiation for reaching agreement:

- *The analysis stage*, referring to the period when the party merely attempts to diagnose systematically the situation of the prospective negotiation (perception of the problems, identification of the related interests, the prima facie resulting options and the criteria for establishing an agreement).
- *The planning stage*, referring to the period when the party, on the basis of the diagnosis, proceeds to generate ideas and actions for the prospective negotiation (possible approaches to the management of problems, issues, and important interests, selection of realistic objectives, decision on alternative options, strategies or prescriptions to reach an agreement).
- *The discussion stage*, referring to the period when the parties communicate with each other by exchanging views on the foregoing considerations in order to reach an agreement built on mutually beneficial options and objective criteria, by adopting common approaches to their understanding and management while recognizing and addressing the diversity of their individual approaches and determinations.

At this point, note that the prescriptive theoretical model of principled negotiation provides an "anthropocentric" model of negotiation comprising par excellence methodological standards gearing to achieve any kind of agreement. This conspicuous generalization of the model permeates through all fields and levels of negotiation, centring around the "personal" character of negotiation. In effect, the anthropocentric generalization of the model expands to cover, in a linear manner, international negotiations as well, relinquishing completely superficially – and obviously artificially – the particularities and complexity of the specific referential field of its context. In a paradoxical way, the methodological assimilation of the anthropocentric negotiation method – attaining *any kind* of "bloodless" "wise agreement" – with the negotiation creating an international agreement establishing, in fact, a relational regime of ICI seems to meet, through a different path, the inadequate "unitary contractual view" of the law of treaties adopted by the postwar positivistic theory of international law.[13] Without underestimating the significance of the human factor in the negotiating process and its appropriate utilization, the dynamic construction of a relational regime of ICI through negotiation for the preparation, constitution, and development of treaties requires negotiators to focus on "the interconnections" featuring the international negotiation process and, at the same time, differentiating it from other forms of negotiation, notably:

- Its complementary relationship to its special context of reference, international and domestic.
- Its analysis as a heavily structured process of constructing ICI evolving through three distinct phases.
- Its institutional characteristics.
- Consideration of the features of its textuality and the nature of its language.
- The normative significance of the formal patterns (treaties, declarations, action plans, etc.) that it generates.

A vivid illustration of these remarks is given by the proposed standard of "Best Available Solution to a Negotiated Agreement" (BATNA) for which the principled negotiation model reserves a special position. It is "the standard against which any proposed agreement should be measured,"[14] ensuring a more pragmatically perceived clarity of the bottom line of the attempted negotiation and the value of determining the best options if negotiation fails and no agreement can be reached. It is "the only standard which can protect you both from accepting terms

[13] At the international level, this theoretical approach to the law of treaties was conspicuously reflected in the codifying Vienna Convention on the Law of Treaties, 1969; nevertheless, the Vienna Convention makes serious concessions to the public nature of the treaties and the subjectivity of their application, especially by the open-ended formulation of the rules concerning "invalidity, termination and suspension of the operation of the treaties" and their specified procedural implementation, as well as their *ex nunc* prescribed consequences where the importance of a "relational view" of treaty and "subjectivity" in serving solutions of ICI are plainly prescribed. See E. Raftopoulos, *The Inadequacy of the Contractual Analogy in the Law of Treaties*, 1990, *supra* note 7, 207–254; also his *Course, Theory and Language of International Law, supra* note 7, 270–289. For the importance of the "relational contract law" see esp. I. R. MacNeil, *The New Social Contract: An Inquiry into Modern Contractual Relations*, Yale University Press, 1980, *passim*.

[14] Fisher, Ury, and Patton, *Getting to YES, supra* note 9, 100.

that are too unfavorable and from rejecting terms it would be in your interest to accept."[15]

It is beyond any doubt that BATNA is conducive to a more pragmatic function regarding the determination of the scope of negotiation *individually* by each negotiating party, since it produces more clarity and dynamic evaluation of the bottom line of negotiation. As stated, "[y]our BATNA not only is a better measure but also has the advantage of being flexible enough to permit the exploration of imaginative solutions."[16] And it proceeds to describe the three distinctive operations generating BATNA: inventing a list of actions that could be taken if no agreement is reached, improving some of the more promising ideas and converting them into practical alternatives, and selecting, tentatively, the one alternative solution that seems to be the best.[17]

It is obvious that BATNA, by introducing the measure for evaluating the bottom line of negotiation with regard to the minimum acceptable degree of reaching an agreement at the individual level and irrespective of the field of negotiation, directs the negotiating party to expand its investigation into the identification of the pragmatic field into which it will creatively shape its possible alternative solutions and, eventually, its final decision. Developing and improving BATNA during the negotiation process, is, no doubt, an operation that may generally have a positive effect on reaching an agreement even beyond the minimum acceptable limit. At the same time, it may, in its generality, provide a powerful negotiating tool in the hands of the weaker party against the unwilling and seemingly stronger party. There is, of course, always the possibility in two-party negotiations, according to the principled negotiation model, that an abortive effort to reach an amicable agreement may also be effected, if both the negotiating parties realize that they have an equally powerful and attractive BATNA.

However, the "craving for generality" and the individualistic-anthropocentric sourcing of BATNA, as forged within the bounds of the methodology of the principled negotiation model, operate misleadingly to the extent that they are conceived to penetrate, in an identical manner, all fields of negotiation: from the field of individual-personal negotiations into the field of negotiation between collective entities and, particularly, into that of states, regardless of the nature of the relationships to be established and the context in which they will be developed (a methodological relegation). Thus, this model can play a very small role in international negotiations aiming at constructing ICI. As is explained later,[18] the BATNA at the Prenegotiation phase (which may be renamed as BATNDE – the "Best Alternative to a Negotiated Declaration" – because of its declarative outcome) appears to be particularly weak: the delicate transformative nature of the situation

15 Ibid.
16 Ibid.
17 Ibid., 103–105.
18 See Chapter 3, Section 4, 141–209.

that becomes the subject of Prenegotiation, coupled with the declarative nature of the textual product of Prenegotiation, form the two interrelated factors that may substantially affect the weight and the force of BATNDE. Relatedly, at the Constitutive Negotiation phase, the adoption of the consensus procedure as a technique of constructing common interest, coupled with the structured negotiation process for the establishment of a treaty relational regime – with its interrelationship with the Prenegotiation but also with its focus on the textual pattern of the treaty aiming at the effective and efficient encapsulation of common interest (*contextual or referential patternment, morphological patternment, normative patternment*) – renders obviously quixotic, even at the individual level, the very issue of the measure assessing the bottom line of negotiation (the best alternative to Constitutive Negotiation).

3.2 *The Prescriptive Transformative Model: A Theoretical Message from Game Theory*

The development of the *prescriptive transformative model* is associated, to a certain extent, with the operative conception of an aspect of the non-zero-sum situation as a *transformed or resulting situation*: thus, an already existing international dispute or conflict of interests (a zero-sum situation) is attempted to be tackled effectively and efficiently through its positive transformation into a cooperative situation of potentially mutual benefit and common interest. Starting from the game theory approach to the non-zero-sum situation and, particularly, the familiar paradigm of the "prisoner's dilemma," the prescriptive transformative model basically refers to the general management of problems that are largely characterized, on the one hand, by a lack of trust and conflicting or diverging interests and, on the other hand, by the need for cooperation. In this context, it generates a series of variables that may disentangle the parties from the "mini-max" rational strategy of the prisoner's dilemma to be considered as the best strategy, and may ascribe a certain substance to the gradual development of cooperation between the parties, despite their fears and their mutual lack of trust. In other words, how is it then possible that two powers, opposing each other – but assumed to be equal – escape from the logic of achieving the best, but unrealistic, solution (a "win-defeat logic") and endeavour, instead, to transform the existing enmeshed situation into a progressively developing situation of cooperation?

At the end of the 1970s, Frei, relying on empirical facts and research findings concerning the process of rapprochement between East and West in the all-European context and of developing cooperation between them, pursued the theorization of the relevant findings of this evolving relationship, which were collected from both sides, the Western and Eastern worlds, and he proposed a joint *practice-oriented theory*,[19] open to further development and under the auspices of UNITAR.[20] This is, in fact, a theoretical construction within a clearly defined empirical framework, where its prescriptive articulation was based on the paradigm of the advancing of cooperation between East and West marked by the Helsinki Final Act, 1975, and its aftermath. It refers, in other words, to the perception of the dynamic process of a clearly defined aspect of international reality: that is, the development of cooperative relations between heterogeneous parties representing different political systems. In this context, it identified, exclusively and inductively, three groups of factors or variables that could have a positive impact on the cooperative effort and being solely associated with the relevant empirical findings. The first grouping of factors or variables referred to the "structural characteristics affecting cooperation," which were more specifically ascertained as "size of payoffs" and "number of issues." The second grouping referred to the "situational characteristics affecting cooperation," which were specifically identified as "time pressure," "information," and "time horizon." Finally, the third grouping was overall characterized as "strategy choice."[21]

At this point, it should be emphasized that the theoretical interest of this theoretical version of the prescriptive transformative model is eventually tempered not so much by its imperfect articulation, a natural consequence of its interrelationship with a historically determined international reality and the time-dependent research findings. More significantly and directly, it is tempered by the high degree of selectivity and inductivity that underlie its "out-of-context" *generalized* theoretical approach: the three groupings of factors or variables mentioned earlier are displayed as theoretical standards that could be commonly accepted and applied in any case where a positive transformation of a conflict situation is being attempted, since they are deemed to have "generally" an effective explanatory power. However, the current reality of international relations and their application is significantly interrelated with other factors that seem to be arbitrarily considered as "stable" even though they are characterized by complexity, subjectivity, and complementarity and exert decisive influence in the negotiation process. And this is precisely the delicate and central point that also delineates the limits – and with them the weakness – of

[19] D. Frei, *Evolving a Conceptual Framework of Inter-Systems Relations: Elements for a Common Theoretical Approach to Cooperative Transactions in East–West Relationships*, UNITAR 1980, Research Report No. 25, 26ff.

[20] It is noteworthy that the formulation of the transformative mode Frei proposed was part of the cutting-edge research policy of UNITAR at that time concerning the building of a comprehensive common theoretical approach and concepts with respect to the growing interactions between East and West and the development of an all-European inter-systems cooperation based on common scientific consensus from East and West. In consequence, Frei's work corresponds to a similar theoretical approach and conceptualization developed by Evgeny Chossudovsky in a companion study, also under the auspices of UNITAR; see E. M. Chossudovsky, *The Helsinki Final Act Viewed in the United Nations Perspective: Towards Strengthening the Continuity and Coherence of the Follow-Up to the Conference on Security and Cooperation in Europe*, UNITAR 1980, Research Report No. 24.

[21] Ibid., 28–37.

game theorists in general to provide an adequate theory for international negotiations,[22] even within the framework of a generalized theoretical model and its inherent limitations. This can be better understood if the three groupings of factors or variables are to be summarily presented, but in the light of a broader critical approach related to the contextuality of their theoretical standing and function as it unfolds from the preceding general remarks.

3.2.1 Structural Characteristics and Contextuality

Regarding the structural characteristics, the "size of payoffs" and the "number of issues" are considered able to affect, in their interrelationship, the process of developing cooperation in situations of a prisoner's dilemma type.

As far as "the size of payoffs," it is contended that, in accordance with the empirical findings, the smaller the payoffs of the envisaged cooperation, during the transformation process of a zero-sum situation into a non-zero-sum situation, the more feasible seems cooperation between the opposing parties. And this is reasonable because, if cooperation is built on small payoffs, "the opposing parties will not have to worry about possible asymmetries in their payoffs at their expense."[23] In other words, negotiation for cooperation at this level ensures a high degree of foreseeability. In consequence, the process of transformation may start effectively if it refers to marginal or even insignificant agreements or arrangements in those fields where there is an obvious symmetry or complementarity between the opposing parties (e.g., educational exchanges, research cooperation, or tourism cooperation). On the other hand, vigorous claims for attempting direct cooperation in more substantial or vital issues (e.g., matters of international security, consolidation of peace, mutual reduction or limitation of weapons, or nonproliferation of nuclear weapons) would be inevitably dangerous because of the lack of trust between the opposing parties and the perception of high probability of unequal payoffs and imbalances that could be generated by their direct negotiation. It is precisely this lack of foreseeability that traps even more in the prisoner's dilemma and may easily lead to deadlocks, thus causing irreparable damage to the transformation process for a long period of time.

As is further explained, in order to keep the total size of payoffs at a low level, both during the crucial initial period and throughout the whole period of the process, all the individual steps of the transformation process must be kept small as well. For this reason it is suggested that the "piecemeal procedure" would seem to be the most appropriate approach. Major steps are to be understood only as the cumulative effect of small and patient steps. Respectively, any search for identifying the qualitative development of the relations between opposing parties should, in fact, look back to

[22] As prominent game theorist Howard Raiffa indirectly admits in the prologue of his book; see H. Raiffa, *The Art and Science of Negotiation*, Harvard University Press, 1982, Prologue, 2–5.

[23] Frei, *supra* note 19, 29.

the historical past rather than to the perspectives of the immediate future (notably, how their relations were two or five years ago and how they are today).

This "gradation" in the process of transforming a zero-sum situation into a non-zero-sum situation with a view to achieve cooperation seems to correspond, in very general terms, to the logic of the "phases" of international creative negotiation to be analysed in what follows (Prenegotiation, Constitutive Negotiation, Renegotiation). Nevertheless, it remains at a level of generality that, quite artificially, bypasses the most complicated problems directly linked to the understanding of gradation and, even more importantly, to its negotiation management that may construct ICI. In fact, it is on these aspects that the analysis of international creative negotiation is focused through its three phases. In addition, it does not investigate either the subjectivity of the gradation of payoffs and its interconnection with the specific context of the anticipated development of a cooperative relationship, or its instrumental function in the development of common interest. According to the transformative model, the issues should be "cut" and "scaled" in a manner that is inversely proportional to their importance intersubjectively, always reflecting an agreement between the parties. It is, however, more than obvious that the evaluation of the cutting and scaling of the issues has not an objective character, for it is related to the way in which the parties to the dispute seem to jointly perceive it in a specific context. In fact, the very issues that are of small payoffs and, therefore, high in the position of the hierarchy of the issues under negotiation, may be substantially differentiated. This may happen by reference to the time or the particularity of the relationship under negotiation, but also, more subtly, by the intersubjectivity in the evaluation of the "scaled" issues that is associated with the complementarity of their political and apolitical dimension, since, in any case, conceptual dichotomies are misleading – "there is no evil without some good."[24]

Nor should it escape attention that the "piecemeal procedure" has an instrumental character of teleological targeting. Its true value is to be found right at the transition from "fringe" or "minor" agreements to agreements of "major importance" with respect to the conflicting interest, thus allowing a relationship of ICI eventually to be built. In actuality, the "piecemeal procedure" further refers to the operative interconnection of the scaled or gradated issues as a whole, thus serving more effectively a way out of the prisoner's dilemma situation and the creation of a cooperative relationship or a relationship of common interest. It is, therefore, clear that the focal point in this process is the negotiating management of the transformation of the situation based on its teleological targeting and the systematic consideration and elaboration of the overall interconnection of the negotiation issues. The "cutting" and "scaling" of the issues on the basis of their size of payoffs aims at the transformation of the whole climax of the relationship – not merely at some

[24] For instance, it is characteristic of the differentiated hierarchies attributed to issues related to the protection and management of the environment in "gradated" multifarious issues in the course of time and in different contexts.

steps of progress (namely, the reaching of agreements of small payoffs) that can be devalued by the lapse of time if the opportunity of transformation, at the crucial time period, is lost in clouds of complacency or gets bogged down in non-tolerance for further change efforts. The theoretical deficit displayed by the prescriptive transformative model of game theory, with respect to the negotiating management of the teleologically targeted transformative process, demonstrates the simplistic way by which the manipulation of the constantly fluxing and participatory constructed international reality is handled.

As far as the "number of issues, it is argued in general that, in accordance with the empirical findings, multidimensional situations lead more effectively to the transformation of a zero-sum situation into a non-zero-sum situation in comparison with one-dimensional situations. The identification of a large number of issues that seem appropriate to negotiate constitutes a key management practice of the transformation pursued that ensures, to a significant extent, the continuity of the negotiating process and its balanced outcome. Of course, the pursuit of negotiating multiple issues (*thematic multiplicity*) inevitably increases the time span of the negotiation process, but ensures creative flexibility and the required resilience between the negotiating parties. As is stated, the criterion of multidimensionality has been successfully applied in the negotiations between East and West, before and after the Helsinki Final Act, 1975, when, for the first time in diplomatic history, a great variety and number of issues were identified, negotiated, and incorporated into the final framework of cooperation.[25]

Thematic multiplicity presupposes the functional interlinking of different issues in the broader field where negotiation takes place, so that negotiators can more easily and more productively move from one theme to another when faced with obstacles or deadlocks. In other words, what is required is thematic interrelation-in-multiplicity and not thematic individuality-in-multiplicity in the course of negotiation. The separate negotiation of each theme on the basis of the initial perception of "its own merits" may clearly prove counterproductive. However, it should be clarified that thematic interrelation-in-multiplicity should be undertaken with care. It should not be forgotten that both its logic and its productivity have a teleological purpose and instrumental character, namely the dynamic construction of ICI in context, and therefore their underpinning is primarily intersubjective. Hence, in certain cases and under certain circumstances, there is the looming risk that thematic interrelation-in-multiplicity or, otherwise, a package deal may be perceived as an effort to blackmail and, as a result, it becomes fragile and

25 Frei, *supra* note 11, 30. These issues depict an overall approach to the relationship between the parties and are listed in the following order: issues concerning security in Europe; cooperation in the fields of economy, science and technology, and the environment; the development of transport; the promotion of tourism; labour migration; personnel training; security and cooperation in the Mediterranean; cooperation in humanitarian fields and in the dissemination and exchange of information; cooperation and exchanges in the cultural field; and cooperation and exchanges in the field of education. Conference of Security and Cooperation in Europe, Final Act, Helsinki, 1975, *passim*.

dysfunctional, particularly if it happens to include extremely sensitive issues prematurely, without the required collective elaboration and pragmatism or willingness to compromise.

Finally, thematic multiplicity in negotiations, materialized through a package deal agreement where it is agreed that multiple – and scaled or gradated – issues will be negotiated as a whole with a view to simultaneously accept or reject them, is also associated with the application of two specific negotiating techniques to ensure the dynamic pliability and, therefore, the durability of the negotiating process. These negotiating techniques are: (a) *the procedure of lateral expansion of the issues under negotiation* or *the procedure of adding new and related issues* where an attempt is being made to add new and additional issues associated with the wider relational horizon of the negotiators, and (b) *the procedure of fragmenting or even subtracting existing issues* so that the remaining ones become smaller and more manageable.

The procedure of adding new and related issues attempts, through the agreed enlargement of the scope of the negotiation, to contain matters generally associated with the wider horizon of the relations between the parties and not directly linked, from the point of view of substance, to the thematic multiplicity of the package deal. The new and additional issues are emerging through general international problems that the negotiating parties may jointly face with converging perceptions, and linked with their common international role. Though located outside and beyond the particular thematic field of the specific negotiation (e.g., issues concerning global security, international economic development/developing states, or international trade), these issues, when introduced to negotiation, may operate in support of the effort to overcome the impasses resulting from the specified thematic field under negotiation, creating additional "tanks" for pumping common interest. The measure of this lateral expansion is determined intersubjectively and to the degree that it attains the removal of barriers to the progress of negotiation and the construction of the necessary field of relational transformation. At the same time, the negotiating parties become conscious of the significance of this broader horizon of developing cooperation, something that strengthens the overall negotiating prospects. Depending on the course of negotiations, these issues may either be part of the final negotiated outcome or be excluded from it, in accordance with the discretion of the negotiating parties, thus constituting the so-called negotiation chips.[26]

On the other hand, the procedure of fragmenting or even subtracting existing issues may be used for creating a multiplicity "from the inside" or a consistency: when new and additional issues cannot be found, the existing issues may be increased if subdivided into smaller, more manageable issues or, even, if some of

[26] In general, as has been rightly pointed out in regard to negotiations concerning the coupling of international disputes, "paradoxically, some gaps may be narrowed by widening the frame." A. E. David, *The Strategy of Treaty Termination: Lawful Breaches and Retaliations*, Yale University Press, 1975, 132.

them are subtracted in order to enhance the coherence of the remaining issues. And, here, it should be pointed out that, without any doubt, the possibility of reframing the issues through their appropriate fragmentation or subtraction constitutes an important negotiating technique in the process of transforming their relationship – as, indeed, and of any creative negotiation – since through such a reframing the limits of negotiation are restated and new opportunities are created for a successful outcome of this process. Equally important is the next step, which, in the case of fragmenting or subtracting of issues, remains largely unexplored: that is the assessment of the importance of the interaction of the new interconnections between the issues arising from the process of fragmentation. This interaction, if it is to be creative, should have *a positive sign in a paratactic perspective*, so that the negotiating parties will be pushed into a creative, flexible, and constructive-coherent transition from one issue to another, thus increasing, continually and step by step, the chances of achieving a successful outcome of the overall negotiation of multisided issues. However, if the interaction operates in such a manner that an issue cannot be resolved without causing chain effects in other interconnected issues (*hypotactic perspective*), then the deadlock is imminent. In fact, such a creation of a multiplicity of issues "from the inside" through fragmentation or subtraction may be dysfunctional from the start and, ultimately, unworkable, even raising strong suspicions that a coercive fragmentation or subtraction of the issues may be imposed.

Overall, this dynamic reframing of the negotiating issues, both through adding new related issues and through the fragmentation or subtraction of existing issues, does not only cluster a particularly high degree of difficulty. In pragmatic terms, it is also of key importance for the marginal or the creative directions that international negotiation will be geared to follow.

3.2.2 Situational Characteristics and Contextuality

Concerning the situational characteristics, three elements are considered able to affect, in their interrelationship, the process of developing cooperation in situations of a prisoner's dilemma type: "time pressure," "information," and "time horizon."

As to the time pressure, it is contended that, according to the empirical findings, the time pressure in negotiations, on the one hand, tends to considerably reduce negotiators' demands, but, on the other hand, it can hardly affect their willingness to grant concessions. Time pressure, in other words, may reduce the extent of the claims, but it does not, as a result, facilitate the emergence of a creative will. In fact, the higher the pressure, the more the parties adhere to their initial demands and appear less prepared to reconcile. In this case, the practice shows that the creation of an *adequate time frame*, through the management of the multiple dimensionality of the issues under negotiation, may contribute to the transformation of a zero-sum situation to a non-zero-sum situation. The disclosure of active thematic subfields resulting from the process of the fragmentation of issues, or even the addition of new issues operating as "a concomitant negotiation element," as explained earlier, may create an adequate negotiation frame (*negotiation margin*). Thus, through the corresponding thematic management operated in subdivided time, new initiatives and proposals may be put forward that may lead to cooperation, provided of course that the input of new demands is frozen or kept at the minimum possible level. At the discretion of the parties, some of the new proposals may be included in the final product of negotiation or may be excluded from it, considered "negotiation chips" and, as such, having played an important intermediate constructive role.

As regards this element, the determination of the specific management technique generating the artificially created time horizon and the adequate negotiation margin remains unexplored. In fact, both the process of thematic fragmentation and the process of adding new issues as "concomitant negotiation elements" can be organized from the multiple perspectives of different disciplines and practices: any negotiation problem can be deconstructed and discussed in the light of the perspectives of different experts (legal, social, economic, technical-technological) or constraints (budgetary discipline) and professional practice, with the view of creating multiple choices of common interest and, possibly, enlargement of the participants. This requires a diagnosis of the situation and a determination of the approaches generated from this diagnosis, but also of the practical measures emanating from these approaches.[27]

Equally constructive can be the effective management of both the level of force and the scope of application of the pursued regulatory framework of cooperation. Thus, an adequate negotiation margin may be offered by proposals for *an appropriate gradation of the regulatory force* of the agreement under negotiation through the formulation of weaker versions of this force. The effectiveness and the level of adoption of these weaker versions become operable if the negotiating parties find and agree that their initial perception of the level of the regulatory force of the proposed agreement is not attainable at this particular point in time. As a result, a sequential transition from the stronger to the weaker versions of the regulatory force of the proposed agreement may be effectuated that can take the form of a "procedural" rather than a "substantive," a "partial" rather than a "comprehensive," a "provisional" rather than a "permanent," a "nonbinding" rather than a "binding" agreement.[28] Similarly, an adequate negotiation margin may be offered by proposals for *an appropriate gradation of the scope of application of the proposed agreement* through the formulation of "weaker" versions regarding the "territorial" or "substantive" or "time" limitation of the scope of application, but also the "addition of a new, strong partner" in the negotiation process, the participation of which will make the proposed agreement more attractive and functional (e.g., involving a competent international economic organization). In all these cases of gradation

[27] This sequence of generating ideas is well reflected in the "Circle Chart" presented by Fisher, Ury, and Patton in their *Getting to YES*, *supra* note 9, 66–69.

[28] For this gradation, see ibid., 71–72.

of the regulatory force, it is necessary that the negotiating parties should identify, as clearly as possible, the zone of their disagreement so that the specific points of their disagreement become manifest.

As to *the information*, it is argued that, in the light of the existing evidence and international practice, the transformation of a zero-sum situation into a non-zero-sum situation and the resulting stabilization and encouragement of the pursued cooperation process of parties with diverse interests require an increase of the flow of information and their effective and efficient management. The increase in the flow of information about the issues as well as the positions, the related interests, the preferences, and the behaviour of the parties, and their appropriate channelling to the negotiation process, associated with frequent contacts for an exchange of information, may contribute positively to the building of relations between the parties. And here, the various forms of "institutionalization" of the negotiating process ensure the smooth flow of information. When negotiations become institutionalized to a greater or lesser extent, by the creation of a chain of periodic multilateral conferences and the parallel establishment of specific thematic committees, as well as the use of appropriate international organizations for regular and more flexible contacts and exchange of information, then the stability, the comprehensiveness, and the reliability of the collected information are secured, but also the effective and continuous access to the information, for the mutual benefit of the parties. And this is a great service in the effort to transform the situation.

At this point, it should be observed that the procedural safeguarding of the increasing flow of information, achieved through various forms of institutionalization and effective access to them, should be coupled, on the one hand, with the identification of reliable international sources of information and, on the other hand, with a more instrumental and a more sustainable management of information. The latter refers to both the integration of technical/technological data into the negotiation process and the systematic construction of an effective internal informational infrastructure.

More specifically, the prevalence of the well-known authoritative global or regional international organizations – particularly of those that are thematically competent ("the competent organizations") as regards their ability both to create invaluable informational infrastructure and to ensure direct and permanent access to the relevant information and its effective communication is well established. As is rightly stressed by José Alvarez, "International Organizations possess 'knowledge assets' which give them a competitive advantage to produce knowledge-based goods and services that enhance states' ability to cooperate,"[29] and, indeed, one would add, to negotiate. And in this context, the Secretariats of international organizations play a key catalytic role in ensuring effective management of information and communication in a variety of forms, characterized by free access and a high degree of

[29] J. E. Alvarez, *International Organizations as Law-Makers*, Oxford University Press, 2005, 341.

impartiality. As is explained in the relevant sections of this book, the important creative role of the Secretariats of international organizations or international institutional entities exerted in all stages of the negotiation process, together with the provided wide access to information and the more general institutional buttressing the continuum of recurring negotiations, lies at the core of the structured negotiating process related to the preparation, creation, and adaptation of all ICI conventional regimes.

On the other hand, and depending on the nature of the negotiations and the particularities of the case, independent scientific institutes or research centres of international prestige can also bear an important degree of reliance regarding information and knowledge.[30] Nongovernmental organizations, of global or regional character with a recognized contribution to the field of their special interests, may also provide reliable information and knowledge in the negotiating process – although, in their case, issues relating to transparency, democracy, and accountability as to the formation of their decisions may always be creeping.[31] Relatedly, reliable and good quality information can also be drawn from some states in reference to specific areas in which they are particularly distinguished for the progress achieved, the innovation attained, or the embedded experience, the value of which can exceed the contextuality of such information associated with their statehood (e.g., special legislation, particular legal concepts and approaches flourishing in certain legal systems, and cultures that may be "paradigmatically" used in developing, for instance, international environmental governance with significant implications[32]). Things become simpler if these states are generally perceived as

[30] As Haas rightly observes, the reliability of scientific consensus in these cases and their political acceptance is directly related, on the one hand, to the reputation of the expertise of the scientists involved – and the generation of knowledge does not raise any suspicion of policy bias from donors – and, on the other hand, to the fact that the information is disseminated to governments through scientific communities supported by relevant international organizations or associated with them. See P. M. Haas, "Science Policy for Multilateral Environmental Governance," in N. Kanie and P. M. Haas (eds.), *Emerging Forces in Environmental Governance*, United Nations University Press, 2004, 115–136.

[31] See, e.g., J. McGann and M. Johnstone, "The Power Shift and the NGO Credibility Crisis," 11 *Brown Journal of World Affairs* (2005), 159–171. With regard to the credibility of NGOs, the risk of their possible "tunnel vision," should also be considered, that is, the deliberate neglect on their part of the "big picture" and the broader social, economic, and political context. See J. T. Matthews, "Power Shift," 76(1) *Foreign Affairs* (1997), 56–66. Also available at: www.foreignaffairs.com/articles/52644/jessica-t-mathews/power-shift.

[32] The legal concept of "public trust" and the possibility of its application with a view to building a more effective public participation in environmental governance at the national as well as at the international level of implementation of conventional environmental regimes, is characteristic. See, e.g., P. Sand, "Sovereignty Bounded: Public Trusteeship for Common Pool Resources?" 4(1) *Global Environmental Politics* (2004), 47–71; E. Raftopoulos, "Theorizing about Conventional Environmental Sea-Regimes as International Trusts: The Case of the Barcelona Convention System," in R. Wolfrum, M. Seršić, and T. M. Šošić (eds.), *Contemporary Developments in International Law: Essays in Honour of Budislav Vukas*, Brill-Nijhoff, 2015, Part 2: Law of the Sea, pp. 263–290.

"neutral," but in areas of advanced specialization it may be perfectly possible that the information itself acquires an autonomous value being "neutralized" from the state from which it emanates.[33]

This identification of reliable international sources of information requires further consideration: it should be effectively linked to capacity building, ensuring the proper integration of the externally derived specific information and scientific reports – and particularly the technical/technological data – into the dynamic and the requirements of the negotiating process. For such capacity building, a structural approach is required to address both the individual and the collective/multilateral levels. Thus, the diplomatic delegations should include experts in the specific scientific area, so that the proper understanding and communication of such information will be facilitated and its integration into the negotiation process will be adequately assessed. Also, the negotiating forum should be organized on an additional technical basis, in order to ensure that the assessment and integration of scientific/technical information into the negotiating process is first channelled to subsidiary "technical working groups" and, then, introduced, for further discussion, into ad hoc negotiating conferences or meetings – commonly described in international practice as "Ad Hoc Working Groups of Legal and Technical Experts"[34] – which, in fact, have an overall view of the evolving logic of negotiation.

At the same time, it is worth stressing that a systematic construction of an effective domestic informational infrastructure should be pursued, that is, a reliable, dynamically evolving, and effectively communicated database, mainly featuring the following elements: *institutionalization* (it should be structured as a special mechanism properly adapted to the particular realities of state administration); *supportiveness to negotiation* (it should operate and be systematically used as a supportive platform for the stabilization of a negotiating process); *autonomy* (it should be centrally diffused and properly accessible to the negotiating teams but also to the widely involved relevant stakeholders; it should be sufficiently heterogeneous and systematically evolving and expanding regardless of the stage and the route of the particular negotiation process).

The special value of developing a domestic information infrastructure for supporting each phase of the negotiating process may be interesting in another more subtle and less conspicuous respect. Its function may also be geared to generate more loosely applicable information, incorporating a "factual" perspective, so that a controllable problem solving, a contextually satisfactory solution, is to be pursued.

33 Such neutralization of information is normally associated with special knowledge generated from certain states in areas where there is a "vacuum" or "uncertainty": a characteristic case is that of controlling the impact of seismic surveys noise (and particularly their chronic and cumulative effects) on the marine environment, which are carried out at the exploration phase of offshore hydrocarbons, on which there is special innovative legislation only in a few developed states (Australia, Canada, Norway, the United Kingdom, and the United States).

34 For a detailed reference of their function and role in the Constitutive Negotiation and Renegotiation processes, see Chapters 4 and 5.

It may, thus, also operate as *an observatory*, substantially contributing to the consolidation of a more heuristic approach to the shaping of the relevant decisions.[35] Thus, the individual pursuit of "reasoned judgments" by the negotiating parties becomes increasingly related to the understanding of their "open-ended" character and, eventually, of the importance of the *decision space* (options awareness, including the inherent uncertainty in the potential outcomes)[36] for shaping, more intuitively, collective decisions serving the common interest in the particular case and arriving at suitable, controllable, and contextually effective problem-solving.[37]

Finally, the openness of the time horizon is considered a major condition that plays a key role in the process of transforming a zero-sum situation into a non-zero-sum situation. There is no doubt that, in general, the possibility of a continuing flow of negotiations and the assurance of its periodicity considerably facilitates the approximation of the rival parties and reinforces their desire for a joint management of the conflict. When negotiation is ongoing, enabling repetitive interaction, the negotiating parties have the opportunity to learn each other, to understand more fully the range, the strength, and the depth of their respective interests underlying their projected positions, and, hence, to turn progressively to adopt common views regarding the framework of an appropriate cooperative relationship.

More specifically, the attempt to maximize the time horizon of negotiations in the process of transforming a zero-sum situation into a non-zero-sum situation should be mutually controlled both *procedurally* and *substantively*. In the first case, as the practice shows, the extension of the time horizon is to be ensured by the appropriate institutionalization of the negotiating process at various levels, either within the realm of existing "competent organizations" or through the creation of ad hoc international organs or organizations that guarantee the uninterrupted conduct of negotiation and the necessary periodicity of the contacts between the parties. The "quasi-institutionalization" of the negotiating process is noteworthy since it refers to the diligent creation of a de facto situation of an unbreakable and

35 For the nature and function of the "heuristic decision," see, e.g., G. Gigerenzer and W. Gaissmaier, "Heuristic Decision Making." 62 *Annual Review of Psychology* (2011), 451–482, available at: http://dx.doi.org/10.1146/annurev-psych-120709-145346.

36 On the "decision space" as generally applicable, contextually informed option awareness, see, e.g., D. L. Hall, B. Hellar, and M. McNeese, "Rethinking the Data Overload Problem: Closing the Gap between Situation Assessment and Decision Making," in *Proceedings of the 2007 National Symposium on Sensor and Data Fusion (NSSDF) Military Symposia (MSS)*, McLean, VA, 2007; J. L. Drury, G. L. Klein, J. Mathieu, Y. Liu, and M. S. Pfaff, "Sympathetic Decisions: Incorporating Impacts on Others into Emergency Response Decision Spaces," in T. Comes, F. Fiedrich, S. Fortier, J. Geldermann, and T. Müller (eds.), *Proceedings of the 10th International ISCRAM Conference*, Baden-Baden, Germany, May 2013, 199–209, also available at: www.iscramlive.org/ISCRAM2013/files/132.pdf.

37 Interestingly, Rolf Dobelli, in his list of systematic cognitive errors analysed in his bestselling book, includes "information bias" whereby accumulated knowledge reflected in countless papers, research reports, comments, and forecasts was rendered worthless by the financial crisis of 2008 (*The Art of Thinking Clearly* [transl. by N. Griffin], Harper, 2013, 176–178), and similarly – I would add – by the amazing collapse of the Soviet Union in 1991.

undisturbed relationship between the parties, avoiding any drastic rupture of this relationship. In the second case, the maximization of time horizon is to be carried out by giving priority to the negotiation of issues or measures involving long-term commitments by the parties (e.g., developing economic and commercial cooperation between the parties or, to put it in a more contemporary perspective, adopting common actions towards a sustainable management of natural resources). Giving priority to the negotiation of such matters, the parties have an opportunity to put to a time test their respective readiness to support long-term commitments. Thus, through a constantly developing positive feedback effect, they may gradually build confidence on a relationship of common interest, governed by their ongoing collective determination of its specific conditions.

3.2.3 Strategy Choice and Contextuality

Finally, the third grouping, characterized as "strategy choice" and emphatically focused on the gradual building of confidence as a fundamental strategy for the more effective management of conflict, is worth noticing, despite its out-of-context generalized perception. Regardless of their size, the steps to be taken towards this direction should always have a positive sign, so that the parties to the conflict will be increasingly convinced that the line of cooperative action should be consistently pursued. Therefore, the prescriptive transformative model rightly rejects from the beginning the strategies reduced to the alternative use of positive inducements ("carrots") or negative sanctions ("whips"). For their combination is not only unable to overcome the deficit of trust but it may instead further feed this deficit with new negative "images" and "attitudes" and, at the same time, confirm it with the "presentiation" of the initially perceived – and elusive – certainty.[38]

More specifically, the starting point of this strategy is the initiative by one of the parties to the conflict to break the ice of distrust and to build up confidence, signalling unilaterally "a surplus trust" as to the other party so that the latter will be given the opportunity to respond positively. Since this unilateral initiative certainly involves certain risks – the party who takes the initiative has to behave as if it were to trust the other party – it should be organized in the spirit and on the basis of the variables or grouping of factors analysed earlier. Thus, such a unilateral initiative should be organized step-by-step and each step should be kept "small" so as to maintain a safety margin just in case the other side does not respond favourably. Going to the next step is conditional upon a positive response from the other side.

[38] Note that the use of any negative action in the framework of the "carrot-or-whip" strategy "presentiates" the existing suspicions, residual negative impressions, or convictions, as well as the negative experiences of one party in relation to the other, to the effect that it upgrades and reinforces their one-sided interpretations that "colour" the collapse rather than the consolidation of the development of cooperation.

Ideally, the source of unilateral initiative should be multilateral and associated with different issues.

The strategy of building confidence and trust, in its generalized approach, seems to incorporate the following elements:

Responsiveness. For a realistic building of confidence between the parties, where the lack of trust runs through their divergent and conflicting interests, the primary relational criterion is "responsiveness": mutual responsive action signals the development of a level of trust that, in turn, feeds further progress in the negotiating process. Responsiveness to the initial unilateral initiative taken by one party is of determining importance. It is the one that activates the confidence-building process. If there is no positive response, it is clear that the lack of confidence will permeate all the following options of the party who took the initiative, at least for the immediate time. It is worth noting here that the response of the other side may be manifested either in the same thematic field in which the unilateral initiative was expressed or in a different one, since, after all, the focus of the negotiation is ultimately on the wider scope of the relationship between the parties.

Positivity. The positivity criterion is directly related to that of responsiveness: responsive actions should have steadily and consistently a positive content creating positive incentives on the other side. Whether they are about individual actions or about determining the package of the issues to be negotiated, such actions should be perceived positively. Any deviation to actions with negative content – or to any coupling of issues that may be perceived as forming a coercive package – and the adoption of a hard-line stance from a party aimed at forcing the other party to negotiations can easily lead to deadlocks and, in effect, irreparably damage the confidence-building process. It is clear that the building of confidence and trust is fundamentally associated with the complex reality of the particular relationship and not with its abstract and "anthropocentrically discrete" consideration. Hence, the recourse to actions with a view "to wise up" the other side constitutes a serious interpretative and strategic mistake that may dissolve any attempt to jointly transform a conflict situation into a cooperative one.

Temporality. The temporality criterion seems to create a valuable margin for relational strength within which the responsiveness and positivity of actions retain their "edge" despite the inherent uncertainties. The actions that the negotiating parties undertake should have, as far as possible, a long-term perspective (sustainability) and be firmly oriented to values, principles, and institutional and normative solutions so that, at any given time, the particular negotiation process will be effectively supported and the parties will be assisted in overcoming possible deadlocks. The persistence in actions that express values of the international community and serve established principles, regulations and standards, accepted practices, and institutional governance structures of international relations within the time frame are not only internationally more appealing to the effort of building confidence and trust but they may also allow a calculated articulation of harsh political criticism without posing a direct threat to the negotiating process.

2

International Creative Negotiation

A Relational Theoretical Framework

1 INTERNATIONAL NEGOTIATION AS A HOLISTIC THEORETICAL APPROACH: INTERNATIONAL CREATIVE NEGOTIATION AS GOVERNANCE OF INTERNATIONAL COMMON INTEREST

This chapter addresses a holistic theoretical approach to the international negotiating process, considering it as fundamental intersubjective process instrumentation for preparing, constituting, and expanding relational regimes performing ICI in correlation with their constantly unveiling context. It discusses an approach encompassing the distinctive aspects of international negotiation that make it a structure-based process of creating and governing patterns of relations of ICI, thus "conventionalizing" the way of approaching and managing them in a continuous interaction with its context. Under this approach, international negotiation is "relational," "contextual," "subjective," "phase-structured," and "textual" – creative characteristics that involve divergent thinking towards ICI construction, and that are ignored or underestimated or inadequately approached by the autonomous prescriptive theoretical models discussed in Chapter 1. Thus perceived, the international negotiation process is creative of ICI governance in a world of relations. ICI exists and develops relationally, in negotiably produced relations among international participants set up to govern various, complex, and interrelated aspects of international life that are in flux and only intersubjectively determinable.

ICI creative negotiation is:

- **Relational.** It is an interactive process of collective governance constructing relations of ICI based on continuous intersubjective consensus development. It is interwoven with the treaty process, punctuating the preparation, constitution, and revision of treaty relations as regimes of ICI (relational regimes). "Negotiation" and "treaty" are complementary in the process of establishing and governing ICI relational regimes and unveiling the world of international ordering intersubjectively.

- **Contextual.** It is dependent on a generic context operating in two interrelated dimensions: the subjectively induced context, reflected in the idiomorphic international "societas" of sovereign states, interstate institutional entities, and transnational and national non-state entities; and the objectively induced context, the public international legal order reflected in the horizontality of normativity of international ordering.
- **Phased-Structured.** It is a structured relational governance process of three distinct phases, the Prenegotiation, the Constitutive Negotiation, and the Renegotiation, where the transition from one phase to the other is nonlinear because it depends on the subjective perceptions of the parties with respect to the better protection and promotion of their common interest. The Prenegotiation phase refers to a transformative relational governance, attempting to collectively transform a seemingly zero-sum or distributive situation into a policy-based relational pattern of ICI action reflecting a "non-zero-sum" or "integrative" situation. The Constitutive Negotiation phase refers to a relational constitutive governance, focusing on the process of establishing a treaty regime performing ICI and taking into consideration the outcome and practice of the Prenegotiation phase applying, mutatis mutandis, aspects of its diagnostic management. The Renegotiation phase refers to a revisionary treaty governance that, providing its continuous adjustment and adaptation to its context of operation, external and internal, and having its own structural and functional characteristics, builds upon the structural, procedural, patternment, and technique characteristics of the Constitutive Negotiation phase and applies, mutatis mutandis, aspects of the diagnostic management of the Prenegotiation phase.
- **Textual.** The basic instrument for negotiating the development relational regimes of ICI is the text of negotiation ("textual negotiation"). The instrumentation of all phases of negotiation is a text of collective wills that governs their relational outcomes. Irrespective of the form of the negotiating textual instrument (treaty, decision of an international organization, declarative instrument), the gradation of their normativity is pragmatically and not formalistically determined in the light of their negotiability. The adoption of a working language in textual negotiation is an important "shaper" of the event or the textual situation of negotiating process.
- **Subjective.** It is an authoritatively formed intra- and inter-subjective decision-making process permeating all aspect of governance. It is shaped as a governance activity among endogenously organized negotiating teams of international participants, internally deciding in terms of procedure and process and externally operating in authoritative conferential fora interactively generating relational ICI regimes. It brings about an intersubjective

construction of ICI by collectively generating instruments "conventionalizing" its protection and promotion as a shared endeavour and in correlation with its surrounding world (context).

2 "DANCING IN A RELATIONSHIP," OR, ON THE RELATIONAL NATURE OF INTERNATIONAL CREATIVE NEGOTIATIONS

Perhaps one of the most comprehensive and insightful determinations of the negotiating process derives from the field of industrial relations. Walton and McKersie, conceiving labour negotiations as an example of social negotiations, proceed to determine them as "a deliberate interaction of two or more complex social units which are attempting to define or redefine the terms of their interdependence."[1] And such labour negotiations are social negotiations because, as Walton and McKersie further explain, this process has two fundamental aspects, "attitudinal and organizational aspects," that are not "present in many other instances of commercial negotiations," unless, of course, I may add, they themselves form aspects of continuous relations or have a relational character.[2]

Such a relational (the terms of their interdependence), intersubjective (the deliberate interaction of two or more complex social units), and organizational (define or redefine these terms) approach to labour negotiations points out that collective bargaining in labour relations displays two important structural and catalytic features that are also specific to international creative negotiations and that seem to escape the attention of international theorists, lawyers, and political scientists alike.

First, the collective bargaining process constitutes a central construct in the continuous protection and promotion of common interest in industrial relations, punctuating them through a process of collective agreements. The common interest in industrial relations is constructed as a pluralistically evolving unity reflected in the regime of collectively bargained agreements, continuously developing and adapting labour relations within a context of public interest ordering.[3] And they do so, in view of: the recognition of the diversity of interests between employers (the management) and trade unions (representatives of workers) in a world of variably protected public interest by the government; the legitimacy of their expectations; and the predominant need to maintain the constancy of their interdependence relationship serving

[1] R. E. Walton and R. B. McKersie, *A Behavioral Theory of Labor Negotiations: An Analysis of a Social Interaction System*, McGraw-Hill, 1965, 3.

[2] Ibid.

[3] The term *industrial relations* is used interchangeably with the term *labour relations* to describe the system of governance of work relationships referring to the continuous interactions between management, trade unions, and, indirectly or directly, the government, searching for relationally optimum solutions at various levels. See A. Trebilcock, "Labour Resources and Human Resources Management," in *ILO Encyclopaedia of Occupational Health and Safety* (4th edn), part III, chapter 21 – available at: www.ilocis.org/documents/chpt21e.htm.

common interests (maintenance of industrial peace for the management, and the establishment and maintenance of certain labour standards, standards for wages, and job stability for the workforce), the level of which is intersubjectively specified and, hence, dynamically delimited. In fact, the collective labour agreements constitute, simultaneously, a relational regime and a relational process. This is well reflected in the subtle determination of collective agreements eloquently articulated by Otto Kahn-Freund:

> A Collective Agreement is an industrial peace treaty and at the same time a source of rules for terms and conditions of employment, for the distribution of work and for the stability of jobs. Its two functions express the principal expectations of the two sides, and it is through reconciling their expectations that a system of industrial relations is able to achieve that balance of power which is one of its main objectives.[4]

Second, the collective bargaining process, more specifically, operatively determines the terms and conditions that define and redefine, in a continuous, unceasing process, the level of industrial relations in conventional frameworks (collective agreements) and in correlation with their special context of reference (regulatory/legislative realm of labour relations, labour practices, and customs). Viewed this way, collective agreements, as activities rather than as completed/concluded projects, have a creative, constitutive character that actually explains the nature of their legality. The negotiable consensus building of their constitution (their consensus foundation) embraces the implementation of the broader "legislative purpose" of this collective bargaining process and its correlation to the context of reference. It focuses on the process of the negotiably operative specification of the terms and conditions of labour that have a subject-related thematic status (labour rights, obligations, procedures, and established practices). It is evident, therefore, that it is not actually the substance of the theme that is determined on the basis of the consensus-reached agreement between the two collectively bargaining entities (management – trade unions) with the indirect or direct involvement of the government, but the appropriate specifications and applications of the subject-related theme in accordance with the perceived requirements and progress of its socially related purpose. At the same time, it is the recognition of the diversity of interests between management and trade unions, occurring within a framework of governmental protection and promotion of public interests, and the legitimacy of their expectations that, in fact, converts the successively bargained collective labour agreements into a valid "instrument of social engineering."[5] Their effectiveness, as a continuous interplay between compliance, contextual requirements, and problem-solving, obviously does not depend upon the oversimplistic application of

[4] O. Kahn-Freund, *Labour and the Law*, Stevens & Sons, 1977, 122.

[5] For a general philosophical construction of law as continuously efficient social engineering, see R. Pound, *An Introduction to the Philosophy of Law*, Yale University Press, 1954, 47.

legal sanctions. It is embedded into the credibility of the creative negotiating process constructing common interest in the context of the government protection of labour relations, which is variably "structured" within the complex governance reality of labour relations (mechanism of negotiation or arbitration, state voluntary mediation services). In the last analysis, it is this characteristic that decisively influences the law and governance of labour relations.[6]

Similar, but considerably more complex – due to the special nature of the multiple entities involved and the intense contextuality of their relational interactions unveiled in a horizontally structured and operating international order – is the international negotiation process that is instrumental in creating ICI relations. An attempt to proceed to a generic determination of the ICI creative negotiation might be illuminating at this stage. Thus:

International Creative Negotiation is a structured process of a potentially advantageous interaction between two or, usually, more interdependent states, with the variable participation of relevant international institutional entities and other stakeholders, where they attempt to construct a relational response to their historically perceived reality of conflicting, diverging, or merely unbridged interests and associated knowledge by shaping, formulating, and reformulating a relational ICI regime based on consensus building and continuously harmonized with its context.

Such determination of the ICI creative negotiation captures, in a holistic manner, all its five elements mentioned earlier (relational, contextual, phase-structured, textual, and subjective). Nevertheless, the predominant underpinning characteristic is the missing theoretical link between "international negotiation" and "treaty" and their amalgamated contribution to the understanding, construction, and operation of ICI relational regimes. The creative negotiation process is interwoven with treaty situation, preparing, constituting, and adapting treaty relations as regimes of ICI. "Treaty" and "Negotiation" are complementary in the process of creating and governing relations of ICI.

Considering this theoretically neglected complementarity, the one-dimensional "contract view" of treaties that entails their understanding as "completed" agreements on the analogy of private law contracts is a methodologically rooted approach of the prevailing theory of positivist international law that is defied in practice,[7] because it

6 Ibid., 323.

7 The Vienna Convention on the Law of Treaties, 1969, under the catalytic methodological influence of the Second Special Rapporteur of the ILC, Sir Hersch Lauterpacht (Reports 1953 and 1954), followed by the Third and the Fourth ILC Special Rapporteurs (Gerald Fitzmaurice, Reports 1956–1960, and Humphrey Waldock, Reports 1962–1966), methodologically adopts the private contract view analogy in the law of treaties. Even so, however, the hard core of the private law contract and analogous rules enshrined in the Convention (definition of treaties {Art. 2(1)(a)}, the "consent to be bound" approach to the means of "concluding" it {Arts. 13–17}, invalidity of treaties {Arts. 46–53}, and termination of treaties {esp. Arts. 60–64}) have not an immediate substantive legal effect, like private law contracts,

basically ignores the public law nature of treaties.[8] Conceptualizing treaties as contracts, as legally "concluded" agreements formed by "consent" (rather than constituted by "consensus") to which international law attaches specific legal consequences analogous to private law contracts, is a misleading methodological construct. The process element, so important for a public interest conceptualization of normativity and fundamentally associated with a "legislator's view" – rather than a "lawyer's view" – of normativity, is methodologically placed outside the purview of the contract view of treaties. In effect, the negotiating aspect of treaties is entirely subdued to the transposed logic and exclusive application of "objective contract rules": it is externalized and it may only emerge under the mantle of the general obligation to negotiate in good faith or to conduct meaningful negotiations or as an external, first-step procedure to peacefully settle an international dispute.[9] Interestingly, the externalization of negotiation and its conceptualization as a separate political process of a generic character make their appearance in a resolution adopted by the UN General Assembly in December 1998, entitled "Principles and Guidelines for International Negotiations,"[10] where the prescriptive logic of international relations theories is superficially extended to its international law treatment. The resolution makes legally recognizable international negotiations generically ("all negotiations") by indicating "a general, non-exhaustive frame of reference for negotiations" resting, on the one hand, on the enumeration of principles of international law of relevance to international negotiations and, on the other hand, on the description of a few prescriptive guidelines for the conduct of negotiations in accordance with international law.[11]

However, the concept of treaties is intrinsically relational. Being in a complementary relationship with the negotiation, treaties create and serve regimes of a continuously evolving ICI. Hence, they should be conceived as *collective normative activities* that constitute, simultaneously, conventionally established patterns of ICI relations between and among international participants *and relational processes managing the governance of these conventional relations as ICI regimes through a structured negotiating process.*[12] And since treaties "conventionalize" a very

but a distinctive procedural effect, closer to a legislation effect, leading to an intersubjective and relational solution (Procedural rules {Arts. 65–66}, rules on the consequences of invalidity, termination, and suspension of treaties {Arts. 69–72}). See E. Raftopoulos, *The Inadequacy of the Contractual Analogy in the Law of Treaties*, 1990, op. cit., *passim*.

8 P. Allott, *Eunomia: New Order for a New World*, Oxford University Press, 1990, 296ff.

9 As pronounced by the International Court of Justice (ICJ) in *the North Sea Continental Shelf* case (Federal Republic of Germany/Denmark; Federal Republic of Germany/Netherlands), Judgment, I.C.J. Reports 1969, 47, para. 85.

10 UNGA Res. 53/101 (20 January 1999) UN Doc. A/RES/53/101.

11 Ibid.

12 Operating between the treaty parties but also affecting the non-parties, guiding them to negotiate the adoption of similar treaty relations (I would call this the "treaty-patternment effect"). The treaty-patternment effect is conspicuous in the successive negotiation of regional treaty regimes governing the same subject (e.g., conventional environmental regimes governing the protection of regional seas) or of bilateral treaty regimes governing a particular subject (e.g., extradition treaties or treaties on

complex, multifactorial, and constantly evolving international reality by making it relationally understood and governable, their origination is also in relation to the process of this reality and in interaction with it. Or, to put it otherwise, their constitution is relational and not merely contractual; it is process-related and intersubjective, conventionalizing ICI, and, as such, it emerges as a step beyond action or policy declarative instruments negotiated at an earlier stage (prenegotiated instruments).

Equally one-dimensional and equally inadequate is the theoretical model of international negotiations and its different versions developed by international relations, as was demonstrated in Chapter 1. International relations theories on negotiation and, especially, the two basic competitive prescriptive models, the distributive or positional negotiation model and the integrative negotiation model, are methodologically trapped by their fundamental theoretical presupposition: they are geared to produce a prevailing generic theory of negotiation. Moving on their familiar track of political science, both theoretical prescriptive models are completely dissociated from the endogenous to international negotiation process of international law and, in consequence, they squarely ignore the nature and function of the complementarity relationship between "negotiation" and "treaty." Instead, they generically refer to negotiations either as autonomous processes of intersubjective competitive manipulation distributing benefits and losses, or as discrete intersubjective processes integrating all interests involved building common benefit, or as combinations of the two where necessary. In doing so, both basic prescriptive theoretical models provide autonomous generalized approaches to the negotiation process with a completely different final aim: prevalence or predominance over the other side – a "positive solution for all" or a "commonly accepted solution," each elaborating a description and analysis of all those theoretically identified elements that axiomatically lead to the attainment of their different final purpose.

Sailing through and beyond these two methodologically limiting, generalizing, and mono-disciplinary approaches to "treaties as contracts" and to "negotiations as autonomous prescriptive models" the conceptualization of creative international negotiation reinforces the relational link between treaty and negotiation and provides, on the basis of their complementarity, a holistic understanding of the reality of ICI governance enshrined in the continuity construction of ICI treaty regimes. Such an instrumental approach, animated by the operative complementarity between treaty and negotiation, effectively accommodates the management of the inherent uncertainties and the learning possibilities of ICI treaty regimes that exist and operate as normative patterns of collective negotiation governance of particular types of relations protecting and promoting ICI. It is worth stressing that the

double taxation), but also in the negotiation of regional treaty regimes related to a pre-established global treaty regime on a particular subject (e.g., regional protocols governing the transboundary movement of hazardous wastes in Africa and the Mediterranean negotiated in relation to the global Basel Convention on this subject).

collective negotiation governance flowing from the operative complementarity between treaty and negotiation has naturally an incomplete and attemptive character and it carries with it its own dynamic that promotes the continuous negotiating process within the treaty regime.[13] As a result, it allows a constant political, social, and economic evaluation of its context and a fresh assessment of the level of relevant knowledge and practice, thus forging the relational bond of its participating subjects in pragmatic terms.

3 ON THE TEXTUALITY OF INTERNATIONAL CREATIVE NEGOTIATION

International creative negotiation is textual. The basic instrument for negotiating the preparation, constitution, and operative adaptation of an ICI treaty regime is the "negotiating text" that "frames" the negotiable relational outcome of the negotiating process. The patterned structure of this text, the gradation of normativity attributed to it and the language used for the articulation of its successive drafts are the elements of this textual framing and largely determine the style and the course of the international negotiating process.

Irrespective of the particular form of the negotiating text – whether it be the negotiation of a treaty, whether it be the negotiation of decision/resolution of an international organization, whether it be the negotiation of any other declarative instrument taking the form of declaration, strategy, action plan, statement, guidelines, agenda for action, code of conduct, or memorandum of understanding – the starting point is the same. Their negotiation refers to the construction of patterned textual instruments constituting aspects of relations governing ICI. On the other hand, their particular, standardized structural characteristics, clearly differentiating them *ex ante* between "conventional/treaty" and "declarative" instruments, and the different legal flavour associated with such differentiation, significantly determine the architecture of the related negotiation process.

Attention, however, here. In pragmatic terms, such *ex ante* legal differentiation may be relative because it is substantially relational and dependent on the context. Thus, it is far more complex than the well-known, simplistic positivistic dichotomy between "hard law" and "soft law." In fact, the gradation of their normativity is effectively determined by the reality of their negotiability: the hardening or the softening of their content is pragmatically related to the perceived effectiveness of the negotiated construction of ICI.

The adoption of a working language in the negotiation of patterned textual instruments is important as "a shaper" of the event or the textual situation of the

[13] On the nature of negotiation governance in the framework of environmental treaty regimes, see E. Raftopoulos, "International Environmental Negotiation as a Governance Technique," in E. Raftopoulos and M. L. McConnell (eds.), *Contributions to International Environmental Negotiation in the Mediterranean Context*, MEPIELAN Studies in International Environmental Law and Negotiation-2, Nomiki Bibliothiki SA – Bruylant, 2014, 1–5.

negotiating process. It does not merely facilitate communication among the negotiating participants, but it fundamentally guides them, through its distinctive pattern system, in the collective construction of an ICI relational regime. English is established as the preeminent common diplomatic language for the drafting of the negotiating text and the conduct of negotiation – although, in some decreasing cases, French may be used, where appropriate, as a residuary working language, especially when it comes to the question of defining delicate key concepts or terms having a distinctive cultural load associated with the pattern system of the particular language.[14] Thus, the drafting of the negotiating patterned textual instrument, the negotiation of its consensus-building foundation properly articulated in the evolving versions of its draft, and the discussion on reaching agreed attribution of meaning to concepts or terms within the framework of the various conferential negotiating bodies are to be conducted in the working language, most commonly in English. And, in fact, the use of a common working language during both the designing of the draft textual instrument and the conduct of its negotiated construction, which is foreign to the vast majority of the negotiating participants, appears to have a more subtle and rather unconscious dimension. Following the recent findings of psychological research,[15] it is notable that the use of such language facilitates their pursuance of a more common benefit-oriented and less emotionally connected individualistic approach to the issues under negotiation and, in effect, it contributes to building collective decisions on evaluations and assessments ultimately serving the construction of an ICI relational regime. Relatedly, the use of such language at agreed neutral loci, the various international negotiating fora, generally promotes the necessary creative psychological distance from the issues under negotiation. It imperceptibly directs the negotiating participants to collectively determine situations in a more abstract framework and in a deeper working relationship with the context of the negotiating issues and, hence, it enhances their ability to shape common interest options in more pragmatic terms.

In addition, a deep knowledge of the working language in the negotiating process is obviously important in view of the legislative role of the negotiating parties. It is

14 As influential linguist Benjamin Lee Whorf has most insightfully and eloquently put it, "every language is a vast pattern-system, different from others, in which are culturally ordained the forms and categories by which the personality not only communicates, but also analyses nature, notices or neglects types of relationship and phenomena, channels his reasoning and builds the house of his consciousness." B. L. Whorf, "Language, Mind and Reality," in J. B. Carroll (ed.), *Language, Thought and Reality: Selected Writings of Benjamin Lee Whorf*, MIT Press, 1956, 246, 252.

15 See A. Costa et al., "Your Morals Depend on Language," *Plos One*, 23 April 2014, available at: www.plosone.org/article/info%3Adoi%2F10.1371%2Fjournal.pone.0094842. Also see B. Keysar, S. L. Hayakawa, and S. G. An, "The Foreign-Language Effect: Thinking in a Foreign Tongue Reduces Decision Biases," 23 *Psychological Science* (2012), 661–668. As Costa observes, "deliberations at places like the United Nations, the EU, large international corporations or investment firms can be better explained or made more predictable by this discovery," and Keysar points out that "[p]eople are less afraid of losses, more willing to take risks and much less emotionally-connected when thinking in a foreign language," *Business Standard*, 6 June 2014.

necessary for the effective understanding and adequate assessment of the standard verbs, words, phrases, and their manner of use in the text determining the regulatory and normative scope, force, and contextuality of the negotiated instrument. Thus, the appropriate introduction of standard phrases into the treaty text having a mitigating (softening) effect on the prescription of obligations or duties, contextualizing their content, and achieving, as a result, an acceptable accommodation of interests (e.g., "as appropriate," "where necessary," "as far as/to the extent possible"), or the appropriate formulation of legal nuances determining the regulatory (more rule/standard-oriented) and normative (more governance-oriented) scope of the power-rights and duties-obligations of the treaty regime as well as indicating the operative complementarity of international and domestic order in the treaty text (e.g., by the proper use of the verbs "may," "shall," "should," "might," "must"),[16] or, even, wording combinations intensely – and usefully – contextualizing treaty undertakings,[17] plainly give the tone – and the depth of the difficulties – of textual negotiation. It may further concern the search for the selection of appropriate verbs entailing, generally and in varying degrees, a "water-down effect" in regard to the undertaking of regime duties-obligations and collective actions, thus achieving the integration of key disagreements between the negotiators into the treaty text and contextualizing their application (such verbs with general watering-down force are, e.g., "endorse," "encourage," "take into account," "reaffirm," "acknowledge," "promote," "call upon"). It may also refer to the articulation of the perception, weight, and function of concepts and procedures derived from the relevant context of economic, legal, political, social, and cultural reference, structuring the reality and organizing a value-based experience of constructing ICI (e.g., "the Parties shall take into account/into consideration the special conditions/the specific needs of" or "the agreement will be implemented to reflect equity ... in light of different national circumstances"[18]).

Furthermore, the communicative force of the working language in the negotiating process, ranging from the use of aggressive argumentation and labelling – supporting conflicting, or diverging groupings of interest or countervailing scientific

[16] Relatedly, the choice of formulating a verb in simple present tense (e.g., "constitutes an agreement") denotes a powerful consensus underlying the particular duty-obligation/power-right and a generally accepted understanding of its content.

[17] E.g., the phrase "(may) include, as appropriate, inter alia," granting considerable discretionary power to the parties on the implementation of particular national undertakings or national contributions. See Art. 10 (4) (National Action Programmes) of the *UN Convention to Combat Desertification, 1994*; Art. 6(8) on the implementation of the nationally determined contributions (NDCs) of the *Paris Agreement on Climate Change, 2016*.

[18] Thus, in the framework of the Paris Agreement on Climate Change (Art. 2(2)), the negotiation-built contextualization of the implementation of the principle of common but differentiated responsibility in the established climate change regime was the key step towards bringing all countries together in a constructive ICI climate governance ("This Agreement will be implemented to reflect equity and the principle of common but differentiated responsibilities and respective capabilities, *in the light of different national circumstances*").

approaches – to the overt and covert employment of language metaphors, may have an indicative value for the progress of the negotiation process. Aggressive argumentation and labelling implicate an imprudent hardening of positions, counterproductive polarization that may raise suspicion and degrade cooperative effort, and, ultimately, it may lead to a dangerous misorientation of the negotiation process, initially geared for the attainment of an efficient, effective, and socially acceptable relational ICI regime of conventional governance. The linguistic veiling of conflicting attitudes and views with aggressive terminology and polarized labelling constructs, before and during the negotiation process, seriously undermines and may ultimately have a crippling effect upon the negotiation process and far-reaching consequences. A striking example is the pervasive impact of aggressive terminology on the progress of the climate change negotiating process and on the shaping of its relational regime outcome. The deep division of the scientific and policy debate on climate change, by using polarized labels, such as "deniers" or "sceptics" and "alarmists,"[19] places the negotiating process in an antagonistic and combative field and, as a result, it may seriously weaken its ICI creative function: it undercuts its relational aspect by feeding isolationism, exclusion, and dismissal of ICI constructive consensus building, it accentuates division, and it is compelled to underestimate aspects of the context dynamics favouring, under the pressure of polarized labels, conservative but inefficient solutions.[20] In fact, the very creation and application of such polarized labels generate increasingly static views and attitudes, focusing on in-group cohesion at the expense of a constructive dialogue and a genuine relational consensus building.[21] And even the use of milder labels, like "convinced" and "unconvinced," may, despite their more neutral connotation, entail similar crippling effects. Important, such polarized labels suggest that the context is

[19] In pragmatic terms, such a use of the term "sceptic" is clearly problematic. All scientists are "sceptics," in the sense that any hypothesis must be supported by reliable and consistent evidence in order to be accepted by them, and other alternatives must be rejected. In broader terms, "scepticism" is the starting point for any progressive scientific quest and the necessary substratum for any scientific development. On the other hand, the projected use of the term "sceptic" as a label to describe an opposing group who hold views disputing prevailing scientific views and attitudes, has a distorting connotation, in the light of the dynamic development of scientific knowledge and the uncertainties surrounding it, and it is troublesome.

[20] It is characteristic that the Intergovernmental Panel on Climate Change's (IPCC) past five Reports since 1990, feeding the various phases of the climate change negotiation with fundamental knowledge and determinative evidence on climate impacts, turned out to be more likely to underestimate (twenty times more likely) than to exaggerate climate impacts because of its tendency to be conservative in its predictions, being worried about being accused of alarmism, and most of the data points to this effect. See K. Suenemann, Tendency to Underestimate Climate Impacts, video-lecture, UQx DENIAL 101x 4.4.6.1. Available at: www.edx.org/course/making-sense-climate-science-denial-uqx-denial101x-4.

[21] On the multifarious impact of the use and application of polarized labels in the climate change debate and the highly problematic implications of climate labels as constructed in the academic literature and as applied in the science policy debate see C. C. Howarth and A. G. Sharman, "Labeling Opinions in the Climate Debate: A Critical Review," *WIREs Climate Change*, 6, 239–254. doi:10.1002/wcc.332.

inadequately considered and the breadth of public opinion is not captured.[22] On the other hand, a meaningful public participation in the development of an effective ICI treaty regime requires an integrative understanding and a multitude of perspectives on climate change issues, while strengthening the social consensus around climate change policies.

Of particular interest with regard to the communicative force of the negotiating language is the frequent use of "negotiation metaphors." Lichtenberg's perceptive saying that "a good metaphor is something even the police should keep an eye on" directly points to the subtle function that metaphors may have: they map conscious and unconscious figurative uses of language, mirroring perceptions, approaches, or perspectives of the negotiating parties (collaborative or combative), and, for this reason, require much attention for the role they serve and an effective response.[23] Metaphors operate, in fact, as conceptual tools for navigating negotiations: they operate "covertly to gain tacit agreement on direction, means, and ends without full description or rationale."[24] In fact, their use by one side during the negotiating process, in order to generally characterize international negotiation, or to describe a specific problematical aspect of international negotiation or the way to approach and handle it, can provide a useful field of introspection for the other side. Metaphor awareness by the negotiating parties enhances the possibilities for mutual understanding and the effective search for constructing an ICI treaty relation. It may reveal how the side using it perceives the situation, implicitly evaluates it, and is led to build its possible responses in the course of the negotiation process. It indicates, in sum, a subjective approach to the relation under negotiation illuminating ICI areas as well as the central problem. Awareness of the metaphors' penumbra of assumptions may help the negotiating party not only in the subjective but, importantly, also in the relational uncertain aspects of the negotiating process.

On the other hand, it is noteworthy that the use of negotiation metaphors by the media, which follow a negotiation process and inform the public about it, may transmit a debatable picture of the nature and purpose of the negotiating process. The media's frequent use of the game metaphor for the characterization of an international negotiation as a "chessboard" reveals their misguided attitude that negotiation is like a game of chess, where, by the rules of the game, the final result is zero-sum, win or defeat, rather than collective pursuance of the progressive construction of a relational common interest.[25] Apart from this obvious and

[22] Ibid.

[23] Quoted in the famous Notebooks of Georg Christoph Lichtenberg (1742–1799) entitled *Waste Books* (*Sudelbücher*) (transl. with an intro. by R. J. Hollingdale), NYBR Classics, 2000. This work of the eighteenth-century polymath (an experimental physicist, an astronomer, a mathematician, and a practicing critic of art and literature) was much admired by later eminent writers and philosophers.

[24] T. H. Smith, "Metaphors for Navigating Negotiations," 21(3) *Negotiation Journal* (2005), 343–364.

[25] Besides, the possibility of a draw in chess is a resulting solution emanating from the ruled or agreed final inability of each side to win the game: a draw is not the aim of the two sides who struggle to be victorious. In the wider audiences of the media, chess is generally perceived as a game of planning and

fundamental difference, there is more to it: international negotiation, unlike chess, is multidimensional (no fixed rules but constraints arising from international, regional, and national contexts, combined with dynamic creativity in an uncertain world, not a balanced situation where parties stand on entirely equal footing); international negotiation, unlike chess, is not a game of logic but a process of collective management of possibilities for constituting a relational governance of common interest, thus having an intense subjective dimension. Equating international negotiation with a game of chess, the media imperceptibly transmit the chess war perception of international negotiation to their audience, which, in effect, becomes accustomed to zero-sum evaluations that may have a destabilizing influence on turning points of the negotiating process.

Negotiation metaphors, however, clustering a semantic and, more importantly, a pragmatic component,[26] may be effectively deployed in a much more subtle way. In fact, metaphors have a multifaceted communicative force: they entail the "connotational penumbra" of the expressions involved, they tend to substitute concrete for abstract terms allowing a creative ambiguity, and they transmit a factual perception of the constraining context.[27] As a result, they provide a – more or less successful – powerful analogical reasoning to intricate aspects of the building of a negotiating process through parallelisms of indefinite depths. This may well happen in cases where the immense complexity of the negotiating process of a treaty regime, fraught with uncertainties and risks, may invite metaphorical approaches where the communicative force of analogical thinking points to parallelisms with familiar human experience. The recent deployment of metaphors at the beginning of the Brexit negotiations provides a notable illustration, although to its extreme. "Relation-deconstructing" negotiation metaphors were extensively used by the British negotiators and commentators and the European Union (EU) negotiators, respectively, to offer figurative explanations and views, converging or diverging, on the Brexit negotiations ahead: "soft" Brexit (continued membership of the single market or customs union) vs. "hard" Brexit (give up full access to the single market and the customs union, giving Britain full control over its borders); or "a marital separation" allowing a distinction between Britain's immediate exit from the EU – "the divorce" – and its longer-term trading relations.[28] And the British foreign secretary declared that he wanted Britain to "have its cake and eat it." Equally colourful was the metaphor response by the EU: that "cherry picking" the best bits of the EU would not be tolerated; or that, according to the European Commission president, Jean-Claude Juncker, the EU was "not a golf club that could be easily

applying a strategy and tactics to win a war against an opponent, where the possibility of a draw is ignored.

26 See S. C. Levinson, *Pragmatics*, Cambridge University Press, 1983, 147–162.

27 Ibid., 150.

28 In fact, the British prime minister dismissed the use of the word "divorce": "I prefer not to use that term with regard to the European Union because often, when people get divorced, they do not have a good relationship afterwards."

joined or left"; it was a family, and Brexit should be treated as divorce; or that, according the European Parliament's Brexit negotiator, Guy Verhofstadt, "it would be wrong for EU taxpayers to be asked to pay Britain's bar bill." Perhaps the most successful EU relation-deconstructing negotiation metaphor was unfolded by the EU's chief negotiator, Michel Barnier, at a news conference:

> If you like walking in the mountains you have to learn a number of rules. You have to learn to put one foot in front of the other because sometimes you are on a steep and rocky path. You also have to look [at] what accidents might befall you – falling rocks . . . You have to be very careful to keep your breath. You have to have stamina because it could be a lengthy path and you have to keep looking at the summit.

4 ON THE PHASED STRUCTURE OF INTERNATIONAL CREATIVE NEGOTIATION

International creative negotiation is a phased-structured relational governance process. It is not simply a generic technique to reach agreement *in abstracto*. It is a context-dependent relational governance process preparing, constituting, and revising, by continuous consensus building, a treaty regime serving ICI (ICI treaty regime). It is, more specifically, a relational governance process structured in three distinct phases, Prenegotiation (preparing), Constitutive Negotiation, and Renegotiation (revising), where the transition from one phase to the other is nonlinear because it depends on subjective and contextual considerations gradually unfolding the developing aspects of ICI. In this process, particular attention should be paid to the relational feature of ICI conceptualization: it is progressively constructed "in treaty" (in relation to the negotiating parties) and, at the same time, "in relation to the international order" providing "an added value" in coherence with it.

Each negotiation phase is a life phase of a treaty regime. It is properly structured, generating patterned aspects of ICI, it has a referential character, and it is performed as a multilateral governance process.

Each negotiation phase encapsulates a dual referentiality. It functions "in relation" to a polycentric and dynamically developing international order, where the overall coherence and stabilization of the generated treaty regimes or regime arrangements and actions are ensured in terms of governing their relational interdependence.[29] It functions in relation to the multilateral "otherness" of the negotiating participants, reflected in the multiplicity of their national orders,

[29] Polycentricity is a fundamental feature of international legal order, implying its organization and function as a complex and endless "web" of interdependent relational normative processes of a conventional or declarative form, complementing each other, which interactively serve ICI, the full extent of which cannot be described. In general, a polycentric situation was famously described by Lon Fuller as one that comprises a large and complicated web of interdependent relationships, such that a change to one factor produces an incalculable series of changes to other factors. L. L. Fuller, "The Forms and Limits of Adjudication," 92 *Harvard Law Review* (1978–1979), 353.

political systems, traditions, culture, and roles. It also functions "in relation" to the particular characteristics of the resulting relational order associated with the generation of a declarative or conventional regime (regime action or treaty regime, respectively). Prenegotiation generates a declarative regime of collectively determined ICI goals and actions, building a collective identity and knowledge platform for the governance of collective/individual interests between the participants with a view to transforming the existing problematic situation and preparing the possibility of a prospective treaty regime. Constitutive Negotiation generates a relational treaty regime, determining and pursuing ICI by consensus building, configuring the "contractualization" of its scope of application, and institutionalizing the normative domain for its collective governance. Renegotiation generates the revision of an established treaty regime, determining and pursuing a collective governance of change in the relation underlying the treaty regime in response to external or esoteric contextual developments.

Each phase is performed as a distinct multilateral governance process: as a transformative governance in Prenegotiation, as constitutive governance in Constitutive Negotiation, and as relational governance in Renegotiation. All three negotiation phases aim at constructing an ICI relational regime of a declarative or conventional character. They are largely structured collective governance processes determining, protecting, and promoting ICI relations in context and in interactive continuity, punctuated by declarative or treaty instruments.[30] In this process, they develop a *relational governance structure*: each consecutive negotiation phase builds upon certain appropriate elements of the previous one. Thus, Constitutive Negotiation takes into account the Prenegotiation result and applies, mutatis mutandis, certain of its methodical elements, whereas Renegotiation operates largely using, mutatis mutandis, the methodical elements of Constitutive Negotiation. Each phase produces its "patterned" textual outcome (a declarative instrument in Prenegotiation and a treaty instrument in Constitutive Negotiation and Renegotiation), reflecting a particular stage of development of an ICI relational regime, or its textual instances. And it does so operating in context. The negotiation of the texts of ICI relational instruments is essentially linked with their context and is

30 International negotiation as a structured multilateral governance process constructing ICI regime relations in interactive continuity – and, thus, containing strong empirical elements – proposes a functional approach to governance. Of special interest, in this regard, is the model of governance developed by Peters and Pierre, who, going beyond the traditional state-centric models of governance, focus on the underlying processes of governance and identify the five major functions of governance to be performed in a reasonably integrated manner (decision-making, goal setting, resource mobilization, implementation, and evaluation and learning), see B. G. Peters and J. Pierre, *Comparative Governance: Rediscovering the Functional Dimension of Governing*, Cambridge University Press, 2016, 29–57. More generally, a functional approach to governance was depicted by the Commission on Global Governance as follows: "the sum of the many ways individuals and institutions, public and private, manage their common affairs . . . a continuing process through which conflicting or diverse interests may be accommodated and cooperative action may be taken." Commission on Global Governance, *Our Global Neighborhood*, Oxford University Press, 1995, 2.

guided, as I explain in more detail in the analysis of each negotiation phase, by three *reference configuration conditions* that fashion, in their totality, this fundamental interrelationship and perform, respectively, three functions: identification of the context, compatibility or coherence with the context, and "added value" in relation to the context. On the other hand, the transition from one negotiation phase to another is nonlinear. It is not the result of a logical transition resulting from an objectively determined completion of the preparatory negotiating phase that automatically leads to the constitutive negotiating phase, or from an objectively determined need for change of the constituted treaty regime that leads to the renegotiation phase and its revision. In fact, the phase transition is "intersubjectively" constructed. Each subsequent phase is essentially embarked on by the negotiating parties depending on how they more generally perceive, progressively understand, and pragmatically evaluate the challenges of, and changes in, the context in relation to the relational instrument of the previous phase.

It is therefore pertinent to stress at this stage that international creative negotiation cannot be pragmatically and effectively understood, if not approached as a structured relational governance process of three distinct phases in the framework of which a consensus configuration of an ICI relational regime is attempted, achieving and sustaining a dynamic harmony with the context. Each of these three phases may be further outlined as follows.

The Prenegotiation phase refers to a multilaterally pursued transformative governance process attempting to collectively transform a seemingly zero-sum or distributive situation into a policy-based relational pattern of ICI action reflecting a non-zero-sum or integrative situation and visibly preparing the *possibility* of establishing an ICI treaty regime. It constitutes a dynamically structured negotiating process where states play a central role, increasingly supported or coordinated by competent or authoritative international organizations, while other international entities (e.g., Secretariats of treaty regimes) or non-state actors (e.g., NGOs, private sector, and organized or local communities) may also appropriately contribute to this process. As is explained in Chapter 3, Prenegotiation, as a dynamically structured negotiation process, is constructed in two interrelated levels. First, the diagnostic level, where the leading role of the initiator and its instrumental leadership is showcased and an all-encompassing approach to the identification of the negotiable issues and the subjectivities of the participants is constructed with a view to serve ICI in coherence with the identifiable context. Second, the level of multilateral governance, where the structure and function of an appropriate multilateral conferential framework is set up to perform the relational management of the Prenegotiation process (e.g. ad hoc multilateral conferences). At this level, the techniques and procedural devices are constructed that lead to a collective constitution and the adoption of a formal instrument having, from a normative point of view, a declarative and programmatic character (declaration, strategy, action plan, statement, guidelines, agendas, or goal-setting instruments recently developed at the UN level, like the

Millennium Development Goals, 2000–2002, and the Sustainable Development Goals, 2015). These declarative programmatic instruments reflect the political commitment of the negotiating parties to a common framework or agenda of collective identification and determination of elements of individual and collective management of the issues involved with a view to progressively specify and serve their common interest in context. They provide a specific programme of common action and/or a specific determination of issues from a normative, policy, scientific, or socioeconomic perspective, creating the dynamic platform for a possible future negotiation of a relevant ICI treaty regime.

The Constitutive Negotiation phase refers to a multilateral constitutive governance process pursuing the establishment of a treaty regime performing ICI in context, while appropriately recognizing the complementary link with the declarative outcome of the Prenegotiation phase applying, mutatis mutandis, some methodical elements of its diagnostic level. It also refers to the expansion of an existing treaty regime through the establishment of new related Protocols (expansive constitutive negotiation). Relevant contextual factors (e.g., mobilization of non-state actors or the scientific community, effective communication of the progress of relevant scientific knowledge, policy stabilization or change, or impact of relevant socioeconomic and environmental conditions) may effectively contribute to the transition from the Prenegotiation phase to the Constitutive Negotiation phase. Correspondingly, the collective evaluation of internal and external contextual developments of the treaty regime, carried out by the treaty parties, may contribute to its institutional and normative expansion. Constitutive Negotiation is a structure-based process through which a collective consensus is built in a "patterned" treaty framework and, as a result, a relational treaty regime is constituted serving ICI and governing the treaty relation effectively and in continuity. This ICI treaty regime is negotiably created in coherence and in compatibility with the external context of reference (related treaties, relevant decisions of international organizations and international declarative instruments, internationally established practice) and in response to the reality of the international political, economic, social, scientific, and technological conditions and trends as perceived by the negotiating parties – or "sliced up" by the negotiating process. It is also created in view of the internal context of reference (domestic legal orders and political systems of the negotiating parties) considering the reality of national political, economic, social, and technological conditions and trends as perceived by each negotiating party at the time of negotiation. The transition from the Prenegotiation to a Constitutive Negotiation process is associated with a distinct political initiative undertaken either by a group of states (independently or in cooperation with a competent international organization and the possible participation of other relevant international institutional entities and bodies, including relevant NGOs) or by a competent international organization (in cooperation with states and the possible participation of other international organizations and other international institutional entities and bodies, including relevant

NGOs). In the case of expansion of a treaty regime, the Constitutive Negotiation process is initiated by a decision of the plenary organ of the parties to the treaty.

Constitutive Negotiation is performed periodically by a multilaterally established special body of conferential negotiation, the so-called Ad Hoc Working Group of Legal and Technical Experts or Intergovernmental Negotiating Committee (INC), depending on the nature of the relational treaty to be negotiated. It consists of state representatives and of representatives of competent international organizations in which a number of the negotiating states have a special membership status (e.g., the EU) ("the negotiating participants"), while the representatives of other relevant international organizations or international institutional entities as well as related stakeholders are also invited to participate as observers and contribute to the negotiating process ("the negotiation-contributing participants"). In the case of the expansive constitutive negotiating process, the Ad Hoc Working Group of Legal and Technical Experts or the INC embraces the representatives of treaty parties and the representatives of entities holding an institutionalized observer status in the framework of the treaty regime. Being oriented towards the negotiating construction of textual pattern of an ICI treaty relation, Constitutive Negotiation is effectively guided by the adopted Rules of Procedure and may be decisively assisted by the use of special techniques and good practices associated with the shaping of consensus in any treaty text negotiation (constitutive negotiation or renegotiation). The Secretariat plays a central role in the constitutive negotiation process. It operates as an administering body and a creative facilitator of the negotiating process, when the Secretariat's role is assigned ad hoc to the Secretariat of a relevant international organization or of an international institutional entity. It may also, and in addition, operate as an initiator and a guardian of the negotiating process, when the Secretariat's role is carried out by the Secretariat of a competent or relevant international organization that initiated the negotiating process. In the expansive constitutive negotiating process, the Secretariat operates mutatis mutandis in the light of its established institutional functions and role. All in all, the Secretariat, apart from its necessary administrative and supportive functions, may undertake an important creative role in the progress of negotiation and the drafting process of the treaty text to be adopted.

The Renegotiation phase takes the form of a structure-based, collective exercise of revisionary governance of the conventional regime pursuing its continuous and effective adjustment and adaptation to the developing context of reference, internal – which refers to the normative, policy, technical, and institutional developments of the treaty regime in the framework of its application – and external – which refers to its interactions with related legal, political, scientific/technological, and economic developments and new situations that influence or have an immediate impact upon the quality and the scope of application of the treaty regime. It builds on the structural and procedural treaty-patternment characteristics of Constitutive Negotiation, employing the same techniques, while it properly integrates some methodical elements of the diagnostic level of Prenegotiation. It may be formulated as a limited or an extensive amendment of the treaty instrument or take the form of replacing the treaty instrument by a new one. It is an intra-regime negotiating process and rests on a distinct regime action: its initiation and, generally, the stages of its operation and legal effects are procedurally provided in the amendment clause of the treaty, which is decisively and largely supplemented by an extensively consolidated relational regime practice. Thus, any party or group of parties may take the initiative to propose the amendment of the treaty, and the supreme governing organ of the treaty regime (Conference/Meeting of the Contracting Parties (MOP/COP) or Assembly, etc., of the Members of an International Organization) decides upon the commencement of the procedure to amend the treaty mandating the Secretariat to prepare, convene, and coordinate an "ad hoc" body of conferential negotiation, the Ad Hoc Working Group of Legal and Technical Experts. This negotiating body consists of the representatives of the Contracting Parties or members of the conventional regime as well as the representatives of those international organizations, international institutional entities, or international bodies that are granted the status of observers. Relatedly, the role of the Secretariat, in many respects, resembles that of the Secretariat in the Constitutive Negotiation; however, it displays certain more empowering characteristics that emanate from the distinguishing features of the Renegotiation phase. Thus it plays a central and crucial role precisely because of its established institutional function and central managing role in the continuous ICI operation and implementation of the treaty regime. As an institutionally established relational (not an intergovernmental) organ, the Secretariat is able to undertake an even more creative role in the development of the revisionary negotiation and the drafting of its textual outcome (the amended or the replacing treaty instrument). Its multifaceted, well-established, and broadly implicated creative role is involved in the consensus identification of the external context of reference, the determination of the morphology of Renegotiation (amendment or replacement of the treaty instrument – a negotiated option), as well as of the patternment of such morphology (the textual negotiating technique applied to the treaty revision), and it is effectively carried out by the employment of specific procedural, organizational, and negotiating techniques.

5 ON THE CONTEXTUALITY OF INTERNATIONAL CREATIVE NEGOTIATION

Nothing exists outside context and there are many contexts – however, the context is never entirely determinable; it is open-ended.

International creative negotiation is contextual. It takes place in the peculiar international society of collectivities (sovereign states, interstate institutional entities, and nongovernmental entities), having its own structure system, and it is decisively determined by the nature of this society. It is also determined by the purposive nature of the field of international ordering in relation to which it operates: namely the pursuance of a collective construction of ICI relations based on the progressive formation of "patterned" relational instruments of common action (declarative instruments) and consensus (treaties) ensuring polycentric ICI governance in creative continuity.

More specifically, international creative negotiation operates "in relation" to a generic context that is articulated on the basis of two interrelated components: the *subjectively-induced context*, reflected in the idiomorphic international "societas" of sovereign states, interstate institutional entities and transnational and national non-state entities, and *the ordering-induced context*, the public international legal order reflected in the horizontality of normativity of the international ordering. Both exert a determinative influence on international creative negotiation, and it is pertinent to illustrate, at this stage, their basic characteristics.

The subjectively induced context centres around the nature of the international society, its unending function and evolution through nonlinear, partially controlled transitions in different historical phases associated with a constant proliferation of issue areas and accommodating the common, converging, and diverging interests of its "members." As Allot stated insightfully, "international society, like any other society, is a process, a process of a struggle, a becoming, a structure-system constructing itself through the operation of its own structure-system."[31] International society, as a process endowed with its own structure system, is a relational society serving ICI: it functions for the continuous, and contextually relevant, construction and achievement of the common interest of its members in terms of law and political order relationship and accommodating a plurality of interests and visions. *Ubi societas, ibi jus*.[32] And vice versa.[33] The ever-expanding and increasingly complex relationship between international society and ICI construction and achievement tying law and political order is fundamental, because the reality of international society is sliced up as a relation

31 Allott, *Eunomia*, *supra* note 8, para. 13.96, 239.

32 This famous legal maxim is attributed to Cicero (*De Legibus*, 1, 42). Most interestingly, however, it seems that Aristotle's philosophical conceptualization of this mutually dependent relationship is perceptively well beyond this maxim, pointing to the nature of the relational society serving common interest: "*και η πολιτική δε κοινωνία του συμφέροντος χάριν δοκεί και εξ αρχής συνελθείν και διαμένειν· τούτου γαρ και οι νομοθέται στοχάζονται, και δίκαιόν φασιν είναι το κοινή συμφέρον* – and the political society, it is believed, was originally constituted and maintained for the interest of its members; because of this, the lawgivers contemplate the good of the society pronouncing that justice is their common interest" (transl. mine). Aristotle, *Nicomachean Ethics*, Loeb Classical Library, Harvard University Press (transl. by H. Rackham), 1926 (reprinted 1999), Vol. XIX, Bk VIII. ix. 4–5.

33 As John Westlake has put it, "the maxim *ubi societas, ibi jus est* correctly puts before us society and law as mutually dependent . . . Without society no law, and without law no society. When we assert that there is such a thing as international law, we assert that there is a society of states: when we recognize that there is a society of states, we recognize that there is international law." L. Oppenheim (ed.), *The Collected Papers of John Westlake on Public International Law*, Cambridge University Press, 1914 (Paperback edition 2014), 3.

clustering the governance (management) of this fundamental relationship. Such a conceptualization and understanding of the relational international society serving ICI goes well beyond any positivist construction, "objectifying" and, in effect, distorting the complementary (mutually dependent) relationship between international society and international law, by transforming it into one-way movement and by envisaging the possibility of its reversal as a problematic situation.[34] In fact, such a construction perpetuates the "lawyer's" rather than the "legislator's" approach to international law. As a result, it seems to overlook the intricacies and the interdisciplinarity of the international lawmaking process crafting ICI and that international lawmaking is predominantly a relational process, accommodating common, converging, and diverging interests of the "members" of international society and reflecting political, social, economic, ecological, or technological pressures. And that it is always in coherence with the international order and its heuristic power refers to the construction of ICI. International creative negotiation is an illustration of this complex process.

In this historical phase, international creative negotiation is shaped within the realm of international society, which is composed of:

- A concrete number of sovereign states (194) and one sovereign entity (the Holy See) which are, simultaneously, the constitutive members of the international society and its organs.[35] They are "collectivities rather than individuals" already having their legislatures or,[36] equally insightfully, they are "typically state-societies in the narrow sense," forming "essentially public realm societies."[37] States, as collectivities or public realm societies, have their own legislative, executive (governmental), and judicial power, ingraining into their systems their particular cultural condition and historical, social, and legal tradition. They have a continuous existence, without life span, and they are dramatically

[34] As proposed by Crawford who, discussing the development of communitarian norms entailing *erga omnes* obligations and their potential impact on the areas of the protection of human rights, of environmental law, and arms control, makes the following general assertion: "It has been a commonplace since Roman times that it is society that requires and generates law … Nowadays it seems that international law develops more rapidly than international society does, seeking to serve as a tractor rather than a trailer, reversing Cicero's scheme of society and law." And he concludes that this reverse movement, recasting Cicero's maxim, needs to be put to the test "whether one has good reason to assert *ibi jus gentium, ubi societas.*" J. Crawford, "Responsibility for Breaches of Communitarian Norms: An Appraisal of Article 48 of the ILC Articles on Responsibility of States for Internationally Wrongful Acts," in U. Fastenrath, R. Geiger, D.-E. Khan, A. Paulus, S. von Schorlemer, and C. Vedder (eds.), *From Bilateralism to Community Interest: Essays in Honour of Judge Bruno Simma*, Oxford University Press, 2011, 224, 240.

[35] This total includes the 193 sovereign states that are members of the United Nations and the State of Palestine, which is a de jure sovereign state, having the status of a nonmember observer state in the United Nations (like the Holy See), and a member of a number of international organizations, recognized by 136 states since 2012.

[36] C. Parry, *The Sources and Evidences of International Law*, Manchester University Press-Oceana Publications Inc., 1965, 8–9.

[37] Allott, *Eunomia*, *supra* note 8, para. 13.94, 238.

unequal in terms of power distribution and roles. They have territorial existence (their territory is themselves), endowed with progressively and variably expanding jurisdiction. And their international conduct, as collectivities or public realm societies, is determinable by the interactive convergence of all these special features but also by the substantial impact of international society, which is in continuous creative interaction with them. In this very complex process, states constitute "the parties" that legitimate, by collective consensus, the conventional (treaty) construction of ICI relations. Or, more broadly, they constitute the facts in relation to which international society is built and develops and its law is conceived. States operate as "rulers" as well as "ruled"[38] securing the protection and promotion of their common interest, governing the public realm of international society while governed by it. They have a dominant position because of this relational existence.

- An ever-increasing number of collective institutional entities that are cast in varying institutional forms and endowed with widely differing roles, performing activities having a direct impact upon the legal and political transformation of international ordering. As such, they act as collective institutional agents of the international society: they themselves constitute autonomous relational regimes serving the continuous and dynamic performance of their constitutive purpose while contributing, in various degrees to the understanding, preparation, construction, and development of conventional (treaty) ICI regimes. Collective institutional entities are variably shaped. They are structurally scaled according to the context-dependent – and hence changing – evaluations of their founders in their pursuit of collective institutionalized governance at global or regional levels in pragmatic terms. Relatedly, neither their founders nor their constituent instruments are uniformly defined. Most of them are created by states, and some may encompass other collective institutional entities (like the WTO, which has the EU as one of its founding members), let alone the famous Joint Vienna Institute (JVI) set up in 1992 as a cooperative venture of six collective institutional entities in their own right.[39] As far as their constituent instruments are concerned, the resistance to uniform solutions is aptly

[38] In the Aristotelian sense: "*Αλλά μην επαινείται γε το δύνασθαι άρχειν και άρχεσθαι, και πολίτου δοκεί που η αρετή είναι το δύνασθαι και άρχειν και άρχεσθαι καλώς* – Another point is that we praise the ability to rule and to be ruled, and it is doubtless held that the goodness of a citizen consists in ability both to rule and to be ruled." Aristotle, *Politics*, Loeb Classical Library, Harvard University Press (transl. by H. Rackham), 1932 (reprinted 1998), Vol. XXI, Bk III, 2, 1277a.25.

[39] The original sponsoring collective institutional entities of the JVI were the Bank for International Settlements (until 2004), the European Bank for Reconstruction and Development, the International Bank for Reconstruction and Development, the International Monetary Fund, and the Organization for Economic Cooperation and Development. The WTO became a sponsoring organization in 1998, the European Investment Bank joined as a Contributing Member in 2013, while the EU has had observer status since 2007. Its original purpose – to provide training to officials and managers from former centrally planned economies to assist them with the transition to market-based systems – was

denoted. Thus, collective institutional entities are usually established by treaties. But they are also set up by resolution, like those (e.g., UNDP, UNITAR or UNEP, and IEA or NEA) generated by the decisions of their founding collective institutional entities (the UN and IAEA, respectively), by parallel decisions of states, like the Nordic Council,[40] not to mention the foundational instruments of the OSCE (the Helsinki Final Act, 1973, the Charter of Paris for a New Europe, 1990, and the Charter for European Security, 1999) considered something less than a treaty or the milestone declarative instruments constituting APEC, 1989,[41] setting up a dynamic institutional entity of cooperative commitments and open dialogue between its members ("member-economies"). Correspondingly, of particular interest is the collective institutional entities established as self-governing, ad hoc, autonomous institutional structures within the framework of treaty regimes, especially in environmental treaty regimes,[42] which consist of the various COPs and MOPs and their Secretariats (normally the Secretariats of competent or relevant collective institutional entities) and exercise ICI governance of the treaty regime displaying an evolving degree of internal and external subjectivity vis-à-vis the Contracting Parties.[43] All these collective institutional entities, depending on the nature of the negotiable issues, their established competence or relevance, and their perceived role, may authoritatively contribute to the negotiated construction and evolution of ICI relations. And they do so by serving their own ICI purposes and performing their mostly abstract functions which, in effect, variably enhance the degree and depth of their involvement.[44] Most importantly, they may constitute

subject to a sunset clause, and it was gradually transformed: the JVI was turned into a permanent training institution to support and supplement the national efforts of JVI-eligible countries.

40 The Nordic Council was set up in 1952 as a formal interparliamentary entity promoting cooperation between the five Nordic countries. It consists of eighty-seven members from Denmark, Finland, Iceland, Norway, and Sweden, as well as from the autonomous areas of the Faroe Islands, Greenland, and the Åland Islands.

41 APEC has as its primary goal to support sustainable economic growth and prosperity in the Asia-Pacific region and consists of twenty-one member states called "member-economies" because the APEC cooperative process is predominantly concerned with trade and economic issues and, as a result, its members participate as economic entities. APEC is constituted by a series of milestone declarative instruments that are agreed each year and include goals statements, action agendas, strategies, vision documents, commitment documents, action plans, accords, and declarations.

42 R. R. Churchill and G. Ufstein, "Autonomous Institutional Arrangements in Multilateral Environmental Agreements: A Little-Noticed Phenomenon in International Law,"94 *AJIL* (2000), 623–659.

43 E. Raftopoulos, "Conventional Environmental Governance in the Mediterranean and Its Evolving Institutional and Fiduciary Aspects in a Pragmatic Perspective," 30 *Ocean Yearbook* (2016), 129, 141–155.

44 As Klabbers rightly observes, one of the remarkable features of international organizations is that in almost all of them, "the function is not very specific and arguably only exists on a high level of abstraction." J. Klabbers, "The EJIL Foreword: The Transformation of International Organizations Law," 26 *EJIL* (2015), 9–82, 32.

parts of the institutional structure of the negotiably established ICI treaty regimes: they may undertake the Secretariat role and, vested with its multifarious and open-ended functions, they may initiate a negotiating process for the construction of ICI treaty regimes on issues within their competence (as, e.g., the UN, the IMO, the Council of Europe, or UNECE do), and, in some cases, they may become either parties to an ICI treaty regime (like the EU in global or regional environmental treaty regimes or in a particular human rights treaty regime[45]) or members to another collective institutional entity, as stated earlier.

- An ever-increasing and undetermined number of nongovernmental entities, NGOs, and other non-state actors (public entities, territorial communities, epistemic communities, private sector), also encompassing their partnerships, collective formations, or networks. They form the social, economic, and cognitive reality of civil society, playing widely differing but, overall, expanding roles, variably transposing their perspectives in the creative negotiating process and making the governance of ICI treaty regimes a more transparent, more legitimate, and more fruitfully iterative process revealing a wealth of critically exposed alternatives. The increasing need for transparency, comparability, expert knowledge, and best practices if "numbers" are unavailable or problematic, has decisively paved the way for a governance voice of nongovernmental entities in the international ordering.[46] In this context, they consistently and variably contribute to all phases of the international negotiation process that prepares, establishes, and revises ICI treaty regimes, but also to the periods of the institutional life of the created treaty relational regimes, reinforcing the social, political, and knowledge-based dimensions of their governance. In fact, their role and influence may be considerable.[47] Being information sources in all aspects of the creative negotiation process, exposing the accountability of

45 *The Convention on the Rights of Persons with Disabilities*, 2006, is the first human rights treaty regime in which the EU was actively involved in negotiating and signing, alongside the EU Member States, and the EU became party to it on 23 December 2010. The Convention, adopted on 13 December 2006 at the United Nations Headquarters in New York and opened for signature on 30 March 2007, had the highest number of signatories (eighty-two) in history to a UN Convention on its opening day and its entry into force was extremely swift (3 May 2008).

46 F. Kratochwil, *The Status of Law in World Society: Meditations on the Role of the Rule of Law*, Cambridge Studies in International Relations, Cambridge University Press, 2014, 105–106.

47 Despite the debate on their legitimacy in international society, see, e.g., V. Collingwood, "Non-Governmental Organisations, Power and Legitimacy in International Society," 32 *Review of International Studies* (2006), 439–454; E. Roucounas, "Facteurs Privès et Droit International Public," 299 *Recueil des Cours de l' Académie de Droit International de la Haye* (2002), 1–419. However, as is perceptively pointed out, "the glory of the organizations of civil society is not democratic legitimacy, but the ability to be a pressure group," and they are not a substitute for democracy because they "do not share a common vision of the good," they do not "need [to] concern themselves with the common good in a holistic fashion," and they have "particular agendas and particular issues and particular constituencies." K. Anderson, "The Ottawa Convention Banning

governments' officials in their implementation of their obligations under treaty regimes,[48] not to mention their partnership involvement in the performance of certain international policies (e.g., humanitarian aid, landmines), illustrate well their multifaceted role and influence. Most interestingly, in the negotiation of certain relational patterns of treaty regimes, relevant nongovernmental entities may go beyond their normal contributing role and undertake an active drafting role because of their expertise and recognized experience on the issues involved, which correspondingly is lacking from state delegations. Thus, the Convention on the Rights of Persons with Disabilities, 2006, notably featured the fact that it was drafted "with a high degree of participation" by relevant nongovernmental entities representing individuals with disabilities and national human rights entities "rather than only or mainly by states," because of the importance of their expertise and experience on issues of disability and the lack of expertise, knowledge, and understanding by the negotiating states predominantly represented by foreign ministry officials and diplomats.[49] This development was inspired by the Ottawa Convention Banning Landmines, 1997, in which civil society had been substantially involved. Thus the international campaign to ban landmines, with its simple and powerful message for a complete and comprehensive ban, was initiated by international NGOs shedding light on the problem. A conferential negotiating process was organized as a genuine partnership between NGOs, collective institutional entities (UN institutions), and "like-minded states" – a new approach to negotiate the constitution of the treaty regime among a core of like-minded states that has eventually grown to comprise the vast majority of states, accepting, in effect, as a starting point "the comprehensiveness of the international NGO's position and its refusal to compromise the essentials of the landmines ban."[50] In this context, the negotiating states viewed NGOs both as the voice of the world opinion and as their partners through

Landmines, the Role of International Non-governmental Organizations and the Idea of International Civil Society," 11 *EJIL* (2000), 91–120, 118, 119.

48 Kelley insightfully analyses the significant influence of NGOs (but also of collective institutional entities) "on a subtle type of power, namely the power to shape the reputation of states" related to the need of states to be socially recognized and to how their governments are viewed by their own citizens and the international community at large, and she calls the act of reputation monitoring and grading of states and the international publicity surrounding its reporting "scorecard diplomacy." J. G. Kelley, *Scorecard Diplomacy*, Cambridge University Press, 2017, 5–6.

49 G. De Burca, "The European Union in the Negotiation of the UN Disability Convention," 35(2) *European Law Review* (2010), 174–196. As a result, he observes, "the practical assistance of NGOs was therefore very useful for many of the national delegations, and there was less resistance to civil society participation than might normally be the case in relation to the drafting of human right instruments where there is a stronger official line or state policy." 189.

50 Anderson, "The Ottawa Convention Banning Landmines," *supra* note 47, 107.

various practical schemes, ranging from appointing them as members to state delegations to allowing them inside access to the negotiating table.[51]

The ordering-induced context refers to the particular nature, structure, and function of the public international legal order: the relational nature of its process-normativity, the polycentricity of its collective governance in the continuous protection and promotion of ICI within the realm of international society, and the horizontality of its orientation and development through legal, political, and practice-related means. International creative negotiation is moulded in relation to the distinguishing relational, polycentric, and horizontal features of the constantly expanding public international legal order. Aiming at the preparation, establishment, continuous implementation and development of a treaty regime of any relational type and being, as a result, associated with systematic conventional ICI governance, international creative negotiation is instrumental in advancing and achieving the public realm purposes of international society. It generates a treaty regime that, at each stage of development, instantiates "an aspect" of the process of international polycentric governance related to a multiplicity of other treaty regimes performing ICI at interacting global and regional levels, and, more generally, "an aspect" of the international public legal order. Any treaty regime embodies societal interest in its pursuance and performance of ICI. As is well pointed out, the "multilateral or bilateral relations among participants in a particular legal relation ... necessarily embody social interest."[52] This contextual referentiality functions horizontally and vertically. The negotiation of a treaty regime is related to the horizontal development of the international public order-in-process seeking ICI, contributing to its consolidation and/or to its enlargement requiring, more and more, a thick legitimating consensus emanating primarily from sovereign states with the participatory support of collective institutional entities and nongovernmental entities. Simultaneously, the negotiation of a treaty regime presupposes the internal public realms of the negotiating sovereign states and it is conceptually and practically related to the implementative function of their hierarchically structured domestic legal orders and their differentiations.

Being an aspect of the international polycentric governance process, an ICI treaty regime, through its phased-negotiation life, is specifically related to the multiplicity of relevant ICI treaty regimes, operating or being in the process of development globally or regionally, interacting with them on two interrelated levels: on the one hand, it consolidates certain of their aspects that may refer to

51 Ibid., 112.
52 Allott, *Eunomia*, *supra* note 8, para. 16.74, 326. "Even the most detailed legal relation between two parties is created by society through law and includes within it the relevant interest of society determined in and through the operation of the total social process of society." Ibid.

principles, concepts, standards, mechanisms, measures, power-rights and duties-obligations, or policies by integrating them into its own conventional realm; on the other hand, it adds a new dimension to, or further specifies, such aspects. As a result, the ordering balance is continuously attained through *a dynamic or shifting consistency* between the negotiably generated treaty regime (its constitution and revision) and the process of the plurality of the contextually relevant treaty regimes, which is driven by "the added normative and policy value" of the former and which progressively becomes mutually and interactively productive. And this is a pragmatic consequence of the international societal reality pointing to the contextual interdependence of its ordering process: a number or most of the negotiating parties to the particular ICI treaty regime are simultaneously parties to relevant treaty regimes or negotiating parties to relevant treaties under negotiation. Besides, it is of decisive importance that their treaty relations are "patterned": they are constitutive of conventional forms of governance serving ICI relations between state-societies, with the participation of collective institutional entities and nongovernmental entities – rather than simply discrete transactions concluding abstract contractual relations between individual-like states. They form, more specifically, relational patterns of purposive normative activity where the effective and efficient collective governance of ICI as a process that relies on the ascertainment and performance of consensus (rather than the execution of "contractual consent") between the participants is of catalytic importance. What, in effect, really matters for the purposes of international creative negotiation is the understanding of the normative morphology and its working impacts of the relational treaty pattern, within which the agreement of the participants occurs and develops, and the concomitant realization that its negotiation life is determinatively affected by its social character.[53]

Relatedly, an ICI treaty regime may also be specifically associated with various forms of relevant instruments of international declarative governance (declarations, decisions of international organizations, action plans, strategies, guidelines, vision or goals documents), having a global or regional character, which may directly and variably feed the framing of its purpose and the scope of the application of its substantive content. Communicating policies, plans, and goals negotiably shaped at different levels and fora of the polycentric international society and entailing collective and individual programmatic actions in response to its deficits and problems, they may be precursors and effectively guide the intensification of interactions between international participants for a later development of a treaty regime.

53 For an interesting treatment showcasing the relational character of contemporary contracts and the development of the relational contract law, see I. R. MacNeil, *The New Social Contract – An Inquiry into Modern Contractual Relations*, Yale University Press, 1980, *passim*. As he states clearly in his Introduction (xiii): "The New Social Contract is social in two important senses. It contains its own internal social relations, and it is society's basic socio-economic tool."

This aspect of the context creates "thematic indicators" and "platforms of change" directing the negotiating parties to the progressive institutional management of the sea of uncertainties ingrained in all kinds of international issues in terms of identifying ICI and building, more or less successfully, an advancement of relational commitment.

Overall, the contextuality of international creative negotiation illustrates the dynamic aspect of what may be called "a jigsaw configuration" of the horizontal international law order. Each ICI treaty regime is a piece in the jigsaw of the polycentric international legal ordering and its contextuality denotes the working coherence of their interdependence in the process of their creative interaction. In other words, the coherence of a particular ICI treaty regime as a piece in the jigsaw of the polycentric international legal ordering is not only "being" but also "becoming": it is shifting and dynamic and its understanding is continuously shaped as a constructive process of conventional and contextual performance of ICI. In this sense, it is a purposive or teleological coherence,[54] where the continuously revealed ICI in a treaty relation gives meaning and advances the existing international ordering. In terms of theory, such an approach points, more generally and clearly, to a legislator's view, looking for continuity in and effectiveness of treaty ICI governance, rather than a lawyer's view, looking for the finality of treaty solution conforming with the assumed ideal of an abstract vertical international legal order. At the same time, such an approach to contextuality questions the political scientist's popularized conception of an "umbrella approach" to negotiation, generalizing, in the pursuance of an agreed positive goal (an agreement) its methodological steps and its context. The theoretical effort to "decolour" the negotiating process and provide an "objective" methodology suitable for all contexts, having a "monistic" application permeating through all levels, national and international, is misleading. This deep-rooted theoretical attitude of "craving for generality," paying no heed to the fact that "things which look the same are really different" and refusing to look into the

[54] It creates, therefore, not only a "forward explanation" of the contextuality of a relational treaty regime, referring to the consistency with the existing context. It also creates a "backward explanation", referring to the "added value" related to the ICI purpose of the relational treaty regime, its distinctive "telos," which indicates that the latter is also created from the ordering future. It points to the potentiality of contextuality in constructing and advancing ICI in the relational treaty regime (or in other declarative forms of international cooperation), thus influencing the existing context and the understanding of consistency or compatibility with it. The Aristotelian conception of teleological causation, the most distinctive element of his causation scheme, is conceivable here. For an insightful general theoretical discussion on the question of the Aristotelian teleological causation and its quantum interpretation, see A. Wendt, *Quantum Mind and Social Science: Unifying Physical and Social Ontology*, Cambridge University Press, 2015, 177ff. For the Aristotelian teleological causation, see Aristotle, *Posterior Analytics*, Loeb Classical Library, Harvard University Press (transl. by H. Tredennick & E. S. Forster), 1960, Vol. II, 71 *b* 9–11. Cf. 94 a 20; *Physics*, Loeb Classical Library, Harvard University Press (transl. by P. H. Wicksteed & F. M. Cornford), 1957, Vol. IV, Bk. II 3; and *Metaphysics*, Loeb Classical Library, Harvard University Press (transl. by H. Tredennick), 1932, Vol. XVII, Bk V 5.

irreducible variety of things,[55] disengages, from the outset, from any observation and evaluation of the interrelated, complex, and dynamically evolving particular contexts of reference and their differing fundamental impact on the negotiating process at various levels.

6 ON THE SUBJECTIVITY OF INTERNATIONAL CREATIVE NEGOTIATION

International creative negotiation is an authoritatively formed intra-subjective and intersubjective decision-making process permeating all aspect of governance. It is shaped as a distinctive multilateral governance activity among endogenously organized Negotiating Teams of international participants pursuing a collective construction of relational ICI regimes within an authoritative process marked by conferential negotiation fora and related to appropriate social consultation. The setting up and function of a Negotiating Team, intra-subjectively and intersubjectively, is an important characteristic of the creative negotiation process. It directly touches on the subjective dimension of management (participative management) associated with the structuring and decision-making of a Negotiating Team, which clusters a multitude of views and considerations in *unum in processu*,[56] when participating in the multilateral shaping of the declarative or conventional textual outcomes of the three-phased negotiation process.

6.1 *The Setting Up of a Negotiation Team*

The authoritative role of a Negotiating Team may be effectively and legitimately enhanced, and, as a result, better integrated into the international creative negotiation, if its setting up ingrains and its function cross-fertilizes, at all stages of the negotiation process (Prenegotiation, Constitutive Negotiation, Renegotiation), three interrelated approaches to negotiation: the political approach, the legal approach, and the scientific/technical approach. In other words, an International Negotiating Team should be composed of an *unum in processu* out of a plurality of political, legal, and scientific/technical expertise represented by its core members, operating under the direction of the head of the Negotiation Team who will bear the political responsibility for its function. Being constituted as a multidisciplinary team and operating as an interdisciplinary team, the Negotiation Team should be necessarily structured hierarchically but in a framework of functional flexibility: the roles of the members

55 As is most insightfully stated and criticized by Wittgenstein. See R. Monk, *Ludwig Wittgenstein: The Duty of Genius*, Vintage, 1991, 537ff.

56 *Unum in processu* indicates an open-ended *unum* not only horizontally but also vertically: it may also embrace sharp differentiations within a Negotiating Team that may have an impact on the progress of negotiation and its final product.

should be kept distinct in the working of the *unum* when related to matters requiring expert knowledge related to legal, political, scientific, or technical issues (flexible hierarchy). In brief, the head of the Negotiating Team, the legal expert, and the technical-scientific expert should have their distinctive but complementary roles in the team in a framework of flexible hierarchy.

The Role of the Head of the Negotiating Team

The head of the Negotiation Team represents the official authoritative power centre responsible for the internal and external management of the decision-making process of the Negotiating Team. Having the appropriate level of seniority, he brings to the Negotiating Team the wealth of his knowledge and experience as an international negotiator, operating as a responsible manager as well as a creative facilitator in its decision-making process. Operating as the head of a Negotiating Team at the level of the international (intersubjective) decision-making process, he has the discretionary power to proceed, if he deems it necessary, to take decisions in spite of the lack of guidance or formulated positions from the governance/administration, or to properly elaborate the creative specification of an unclear or deficient guidance expressing views *ad referendum*, namely views subject to subsequent agreement by the government. He may also promote the development of various levels of informal contacts and links with the heads of other Negotiating Teams during the negotiation conference, which may also be usefully extended to between the formal negotiating sessions.

At the same time, it is necessary that the head of a Negotiating Team has a sufficient level of scientific-technical and legal political knowledge relevant to the subject under negotiation, and reliance only on general diplomatic skills may soon prove deficient. Contemporary creative negotiations address complex situations and issues, requiring a certain level of understanding not only as to their substance but also as to their functional interlinkages, so that he should be able to sufficiently evaluate and manage the formal as well as the informal progress of the negotiating process. Finally, the head of a Negotiating Team is the responsible centre for all external communications of the team, being its formal spokesman.

The Role of the Author of the Texts of Negotiation

Within the Negotiating Team, the role of the author of the texts proposed by the team during the negotiation process is comparable to the role of the legislator and, for this reason, it is multifaceted and central. In addition to the self-evident high-level linguistic competence and especially the competence in the working language of the negotiation, authoritative drafting requires that the author of texts produced within the Negotiating Team should effectively reconcile the views of the members of the team, including his own, and place them in a dynamic perspective: as a negotiable text prescribing the team's common positions in the light of the anticipated shaping of an ICI relation. At the same time, he should show the members of the team the real, often hidden meaning of the textual language. Operating, in other words, as a legislator, the author of the texts should merge the plurality of opinions, views, ideas, interests, and proposals discussed in the Negotiating Team into a single text of positions and proposals cast in a legal language and architecture. This, however, should be considered as sufficiently open to further construction in the process of negotiating the creation of a declarative or conventional instrument, identifying or constituting correspondingly an ICI relation.

Since the Negotiating Team is multidisciplinary and works interdisciplinarily, pursuing a holistic approach for the attainment of a common purpose – for which it is accountable – and producing, to this effect, single texts of legal architecture following an internal negotiation, the author of these texts should further act as "a link" with the specific international negotiation and legal ordering in general, instilling into the texts the necessary "negotiation persuasiveness." The drafting of the textual products of the Negotiating Team should have a relational value. Their formulation should be properly related to the requirements, certainties, and uncertainties of the particular negotiating process, as well as to the more general requirements of the dynamic international ordering. And it is within this context of understanding the reality of the overall textual negotiation process in which the national perspective should be properly embedded. In fact, the awareness of the more general conception of *e pluribus in unum*, guiding the construction of ICI relations, underlies the "legislativeness" of the textual products, as is reflected in their morphological and normative patternment at the three phases of the creative negotiating process. In the light of these observations, the need to select an expert in law and policy for carrying out this role, endowed with practical experience and communication skills, is more than obvious.

All in all, the parameter of law and its authoritative emergence in the international negotiation process associated with the concomitant legislative thinking and process understanding of normativity is of utmost importance for drafting the texts intra-subjectively (within the Negotiating Team) and intersubjectively (interactively, between the Negotiating Teams). Such an approach is necessary in view of a distorted, rather frozen attitude towards law, usually appearing in practice within Negotiation Teams, overwhelmed by no international law and policy experts, and usually imparted to the conferential negotiating forum, where drafting is usually left in the hands of technical-scientific experts or administrators. And if the necessity of this approach is clear in the Constitutive Negotiation and the Renegotiation processes dealing with the establishment or expansion and the revision of a relational treaty regime,[57] it appears to be less evident in the Prenegotiation process in view of the political commitment underlying its declarative outcome. As is shown in Chapter 3, however, the legislative legal involvement in Prenegotiation is more subtle, because it is associated with its contextuality: the evaluation of the relevant legal and institutional landscape surrounding the Prenegotiation process and actually determining the realm of its function as situation-transformer. It is also associated with its principled formulation of its declarative product and, even more, with the elaboration of normative nuances of the commitments emanating from the political undertakings prescribed therein. In this latter case, legislative legal involvement may effectively identify the area of commonality of action and the required degree of its stabilization in the sea of flexibility,[58] so that transformative policies will be sustained. And this is a distinctive problem of declarative ICI governance.

The Role of the Scientific-Technical Expert

The scientific-technical infrastructure of the negotiating team is an indispensable part of contemporary Negotiation Teams, and the role of the scientific-technical expert is crucial in the cognitive management of the creative negotiation process and in all its three phases. As a member of the Negotiating Team, the scientific-technical expert provides much-needed interpretation of scientific-technical proposals, concepts, criteria, or standards and a diligent assessment of their consequences for the particular negotiation, evaluating the "weight" of the underlying scientific consensus and, sometimes, pointing to its relativity. In doing so, he offers an authoritative input in the scientific imaging of the language of the negotiating text, produced either in the intra- or in the inter-negotiation process. And there is more to that from a more general perspective. The process of increasing "deformalization" of international law,[59] well reflected in the Prenegotiation, Constitutive Negotiation, and Renegotiation of treaty ICI regimes, basically calls for "a managerial mindset" working for functionally effective solutions and balancing of interests in the governance of the treaty negotiating process.[60] This implies an intense technocratic, expert-oriented dimension of such governance and, with it, the importance of the role of the participating scientific-technical experts in attaining effective and efficient ICI treaty governance and normative processes. In fact, structures of knowledge are

57 As Philip Allott has nicely put it, one of the "special arts" of international lawyers is "the drafting of the instrument known as a treaty, in which disagreement and misunderstandings and concealed intentions are gathered together in verbal formulas upon which all contracting parties are said to 'have agreed.'" P. Allott, "The International Lawyer in Government Service: Ontology and Deontology," 23 (1) *Wisconsin International Law* (2005), 17–18.

58 In fact, as Kratochwil perceptively stated, the type of "softness" instantiated by such commitments is relevant to "practical problems, such as retaining flexibility while still wanting to benefit from stabilization." Kratochwil, *supra* note 46, 112.

59 E.g., M. Koskenniemi, "The Fate of Public International Law," 70 *MLR* (2007), 1, at 9ff.

60 M. Koskenniemi, "Constitutionalism as a Mindset: Reflections on Kantian Themes about International Law and Globalisation," 8 *Theoretical Inquiries in Law* (2007), 9, at 13.

inseparable from any form of governance process and the question, in this regard, is the way of "doing knowledge" in law and politics.[61]

Generally speaking, the process of preparing, constituting, and revising particular treaty regimes of ICI, enshrined in Prenegotiation, Constitutive Negotiation, and Renegotiation, but also the continuous but covert interrelated process of internal negotiation, are catalytically influenced by the knowledge-supportive participation and interpretative function of internal or externally employed scientific-technical experts (nationally-designated experts) and, notably, of those who come with prestige and experience. In fact, a science-based approach, interactively using the best available scientific information and knowledge, variably pervades all aspects of the three-phase international negotiating process, including the reliability of its legal aspects. Such an approach is evolved with the variable contribution of the scientific-technical expertise of the observers: the participating international institutional entities (competent or relevant international organizations or Secretariats of treaty regimes) or relevant international nongovernmental entities (NGOs or international scientific bodies) or invited independent international experts.

Thus, at the Prenegotiation phase, scientific-technical experts may decisively contribute to the identification, understanding, and evaluation of the issues of negotiation, and provide the necessary scientific-technical foundation for its transformative function. In fact, their influence in Prenegotiation may be far-reaching. It is essentially facilitated by the wide flexibility and openness of this phase, which, because of its international policy-making and action-oriented character, allows considerable space for scientific-technical involvement in the construction of declarative ICI relation. During the usually long-evolving Constitutive Negotiation phase, the multilateral construction of a relational treaty ICI regime systematically allows a continuous influx of relevant scientific knowledge and evaluation by the scientific-technical experts of the negotiating parties. In consequence, the current requirements of the scientific dimension of the negotiating issues are detected, leading towards a clearer understanding and a more workable determination of the scope and normativity of the prospective treaty governance. In the light of this, the orientation towards more realistic policy options will be facilitated and the treaty textual wording will reflect a more realistic, more reliable, and more operable construction of ICI in a treaty relation – thus effectively marginalizing the possibility of arbitrary compromises. In the Renegotiation phase, a similar role is performed by the scientific-technical experts, although on a much more powerful institutional basis. In fact, the scientific-technical perspective is effectively embedded into

[61] This, of course, may have further consequences, including new ways of doing knowledge in law and politics, like "local knowledge," thus opening the window for greater public participation in apparatuses of knowledge production in the negotiating process (see R. Cooney and A. Lang, "Taking Uncertainty Seriously: Adaptive Governance, Alien Invasive Species and the WTO," 18 *EJIL* (2007), 523, at 538ff.).

the governance of the treaty regime stemming from the parties and the international entities assigned the status of observer, but also generated from distinct scientific-technical bodies or networks that may be set up as part of the institutional structure and process of the treaty. This institutionalized scientific-technical infrastructure of the treaty regime may decisively contribute to the determination of the extent and depth of the more efficient and effective adaptation of the treaty regime to the regime-related (internal context) and the external contextual developments and challenges.

6.2 *The Organizational and Decisional Configuration of the Negotiation Team*

The nature of the Negotiating Team as a collectivity is directly linked to the way in which it is organized and configures its decisions. As a whole, the Negotiating Team should be approached as a pluralistic and sufficiently inclusive team representing public interest, the members of which are in a periodic conference performing their complementary but distinctive roles. In parallel, the Negotiating Team may informally enlarge its internal functional realm by inviting, according to the judgment of its members, nongovernmental entities relevant to the issues under negotiation (NGOs, professional associations, academia, private sector, public entities) for internal consultations. The aim is to ingrain into the configuration of its decision-making process more social legitimacy and more expert knowledge. It is therefore evident that the configuration of the decision-making process of the Negotiating Team requires an integrated managerial approach. Because the Negotiating Team, operating as a state representative collectivity, is mandated to properly construct and organize the projection of public national interest in view of its participation in a multilateral negotiation shaping relational frames, conventional or declarative, of ICI, it is vested with special privileges and immunities safeguarding its effective function.[62] The head of the delegation (Negotiation Team) plays a key role, acting as a responsible manager and facilitator in the configuration of this decision-making process.

More specifically, the head of the Negotiation Team, operating as the responsible manager and facilitator, should determine from the outset the ground guidelines governing the configuration of the decision-making process of the Negotiating Team. In doing so, he secures transparency and supports his ability to perform a mediating and strategic role in the intra-team discussions and negotiations, directing them towards the most integrative approach to the issues under negotiation in view/as a result of the interaction with the other negotiation teams (intra- and inter-teams negotiating process), and facilitating the consensus configuration of decision. These ground guidelines may prove most conducive to the effective and efficient participation of the Negotiating

62 See, e.g. Convention on the Privileges and Immunities of the United Nations, 1946, Arts. IV–VI, 1 UNTS 19.

Team in the progressive construction of ICI and, more specifically, may refer to the following:

- All decisions of the Negotiating Team should be taken by the consensus of its members: the intra-team negotiation should exhaust the limits for the configuration of an integrated decision properly and efficiently encapsulating all expressed views – including those of nongovernmental entities – to the extent that no official objections are raised.
- During the intra-team discussions, any negative or nonconstructive criticism on the views, ideas, or proposals put on the table should be ruled out in any event, so that creative thinking but also confidence and trust will be forged between members, thus reinforcing the team's dynamic coherence.
- During the intra-team negotiation/discussion, no official minutes should be kept, so that the free and flexible projection and osmosis of ideas, views, and proposals between its members will be facilitated.
- During the intra-team negotiation/discussion, a seamless flow of relevant information (political, legal, scientific-technical), as well as its collective organization, elaboration, and management, should be ensured in an open and democratic way, so that a more effective multidisciplinary communication between members will be achieved and, in effect, a more solid interdisciplinarity in the views and proposals of the Negotiating Team will be forged. Thus, the communication barriers that may be raised from narrowly defined or perceived service dependencies and exclusivities represented by any member of the Negotiation Team, or even arising from the arrogance of expert knowledge of a certain member hiding behind personal obsessions and the available arsenal of incomprehensible expert language jargon, will be weakened and, eventually, overcome.
- Despite the exhaustiveness of the intra-team negotiation, it should be clear that the decisions taken should, in no event, imply "locking of positions" in view of the forthcoming inter-team negotiation process, being identified with strongly consolidated positions irrespective of and before the negotiated collective construction of a conventional or declarative ICI relation. On the contrary, it should be made clear from the outset that the decisions of the Negotiation Team should be conducive to constructing ICI and, as a result, remain realistically imperfect and incomplete beyond a primary reached core formulation. In fact, internal (intra-group) divergences or contrasts may not be completely lifted whereas the intra-group management of the various aspects of the issues under negotiation is by no means cut off from their inter-group negotiation. The decisions of the Negotiation Team set the prestage of international negotiation process, generated at the national level, and their function as well as their further development should be considered *aggregative* for they are linked

to the negotiation and consensus-developing stratification of an ICI relational regime.[63]

- Internal discussion papers put together by the negotiating team to aid the first steps of the inter-team negotiating process, evaluating options and clarifying the scope of creative compromises or frameworks, may be communicated openly, following an authorization or approval. On the other hand, their leakages may play a negative role because they may be perceived as clearly defying the expected level of trust and transparency required in the creative negotiating process, and it may throw its shadow on the conduct of negotiations.

In the intra-team negotiation, the head of the Negotiating Team should systematically and consistently exercise his manifold role as facilitator in the process of reaching a decision. His first primary task should be to ensure the completeness and the steady progress of the intra-group negotiation leading to a team decision. For this reason, he should operate as a "creative bridge-builder" of the intra-team negotiating process, remaining neutral on issues that, because of their significance and intensity, may cause divisions between the members of the Negotiating Team. Without sliding into controversies, he should ensure the observance of procedure enshrined in the ground guidelines, deal with the solution of emerging procedural matters, facilitate the team discussions by proper interventions that clarify, reinforce, or summarize the progress achieved, and capture the important points, propose constructive ideas and views, and set up, if required by the special nature of the particular issue, subgroups of preparatory work.

In the inter-team negotiation, the Negotiating Team should be showing outwards the necessary dynamic unity regarding its participatory actions in the creative negotiation process as well as in the building of its decisions. Certainly, in the inter-team negotiation, the building of the internal decisions of the Negotiation Team starts from where the intra-team negotiation stopped and proceeds interactively. It refers to the "negotiation testing" of the intra-team decisions in terms of a collective/multilateral construction of ICI, within the framework and under the authority of a particular conferential negotiating forum or session. In this process, what has been developed concerning the intra-team negotiation applies mutatis mutandis in respect to the inter-group negotiation. Besides, there is one more factor to which particular attention should be paid and which is directly related to the required flexible hierarchy within the Negotiation Team: the beneficial manageability of the number of its members. The setting up of a Negotiation Team composed of a large number of members may require, during the negotiation, ongoing internal coordinating meetings for the more clear determination or redetermination of roles so that internal

[63] For the distortive consequences for the negotiation process resulting from the configuration of strongly consolidated positions arrived at the intra-negotiation process, see W. I. Zartman and M. R. Berman, *The Practical Negotiator*, Yale University Press, 1982, 208.

frictions and alienation of some members will be avoided. The risk here is that the head of the Negotiating Team may be excessively engaged with internal operational problems at the expense of his appropriate devotion to the creative participation of his delegation in the developing negotiating process. In other words, the participation of the Negotiating Team degenerates into counterproductive internal competition and, inevitably, slides into a dysfunctional introversion that seriously weakens its authority and makes the conduct of its affairs artificially inflexible or rigid.

In addition to dynamic unity, ensuring stability in the composition of the members of the Negotiating Team – as well as its systematic, without gaps, engagement in the various stages of each phase of the international negotiation process (Prenegotiation, Constitutive Negotiation and Renegotiation) – is of particular importance. Stability and continuity, together with dynamic unity, enhance the authority of the Negotiating Team in the creative negotiation process, create the space for enlightening its perception and understanding of the subtle nuances and the most delicate aspects of the issues related to the construction of an ICI relation, making it effectively proactive, and, eventually, build its central role, raising it to the inner circle of the inter-team negotiation influencing its orientation and progress. It is worth noting that a particularly useful tool in this aspect of the role of the Negotiating Team is the consistent involvement of its international lawyer member who can skilfully craft agreements and understands bridging differences.

Relatedly, the practice of consistently developing individual informal channels of communication and consultation either with certain delegations or with selected members of certain delegations is a further important step towards this direction. It indicates an important degree of self-organization of the Negotiation Team and marks its function in the construction of ICI during the inter-team negotiation process. Taking place on the sidelines of the formal negotiation, this practice enables the Negotiating Team to approach certain delegations informally in order to inform them about its views and concerns more widely and/or better understand their own positions and concerns. As a result, an appropriate side channel of communication is created between them with the aim of improving their negotiating perception and management of issues and developing, as far as possible, common approaches to better meet their particular interests and influence the outcome of textual negotiation.

While less attention seems to be paid, the participation message entailed by the actual composition and level of representation of the state Negotiating Team also needs to be addressed. Mirrored in the list of participants distributed to each negotiation session, they reveal the special "weight" of representation in the negotiating process that signals the degree of the concern and commitment of the negotiating party to work for a positive ICI outcome implementable in its domestic order while fuelling the development of appropriate internal policies. The special weight of representation may be scaled in three levels.

- As elementary state representation, where the negotiating state is typically represented by its permanent mission, often implying that it has no special concern on the issues of the negotiating session or of the negotiating process as a whole. It is present simply to "hold the flag" of its country, and its representation has a more information-transmitting character, providing complete information to the national competent authorities, and has no impact on the development of the negotiating process and its outcome. It sends an unclear message as regards its participation, especially in the establishment or the revision of a treaty regime, which becomes considerably cloudy for the effectiveness of its future participation and the degree of its compliance.
- As partial state representation, where the negotiating state has a limited representation entrusted to one or two delegates appointed by one competent national authority, paying no heed to the necessity of setting up a tripartite Negotiating Team in accordance with the three discipline-based approaches analysed earlier, and ignoring the participation of other relevant national authorities. Such a representation indicates the interest of the state in the negotiating process and may suggest the positive role of the delegation in the progress of the negotiating process. It may, however, raise doubts as to the degree of discretion with regard to its input and, in effect, as to the degree of implementation of the treaty outcome of the negotiation within its domestic order.
- As full state representation, comprising representatives of all competent, co-competent and relevant national authorities and, in some cases, even including relevant non-state actors. In such an integrated representation, there is a strong evidence that the negotiating state aims high: it intends to play an important role in the negotiating process, substantially contributing to the success of its negotiated treaty outcome and ensuring the effectiveness of its implementation and its appropriate integration into its domestic order. Of course, this level of mirroring state representation is not to be confused with the problem of beneficial manageability of the number of members of a Negotiating Team, which is an altogether different class of problem, as explained earlier.

All in all, the most effective combination of all these factors clearly contributes to the centralization of the role of the Negotiating Team. And to paraphrase a statement of fact derived from a broader political perspective, effective and efficient "organization" of its delegation will always be the most reliable and persuasive weapon of the weaker negotiating parties vis-à-vis the more powerful ones in their collective pursuance of constructing ICI.[64]

6.3 *The Accountability of the Negotiation Team*

The accountability of the Negotiating Team derives from its special relationship with the central governmental authority referred to the public power of international negotiating representation entrusted to the Negotiating Team. This little-noticed aspect of accountability, sailing through a sea of its typologies,[65] encapsulates a relational duty of public character, which has a trust foundation and contains certain aspects that determine its instrumental function, namely the trust negotiability of the process constructing ICI. It is a trustor–trustee accountability relationship characterized by the openness of standards and process discretion in negotiating ICI. It is marked by the expertise knowledge-in-negotiation of the trustee (the Negotiating Team) and the quality of its role performance. As a trustor–trustee accountability relationship, its modus operandi is formally institutionalized by a generally formulated decision of the competent central governmental authority appointing the members of the Negotiating Team, followed by the issuance of credentials delegating to the Negotiating Team the power to represent the country participating in a particular inter-team negotiating session. Members of the Negotiating Team may be removed, or the whole Negotiating Team may be replaced by another Negotiating Team, at the discretion of the central governmental authority.

It is therefore important to identify how far this accountability relationship can be "proceduralized" so that abuses are prevented and arbitrariness is blocked. And there is more to this proceduralization: it transforms the accountability relationship into a creative instrument itself. It may be used to improve the cognitive infrastructure of the central governmental authority, which becomes, more and more, better prepared to organize more qualitative Negotiating Teams, more informed in the configuration of coherence between international and national policies, and, eventually, more determined to critically evaluate the general function of its administration, finally opening the door for an appropriate, *ex post facto* involvement of the Negotiating Team in the future implementation of the negotiation product.

More specifically, the proceduralization of this accountability relationship has a *controlling-evaluative* dimension, which refers to the procedural duty of the Negotiating Team to inform the central governmental authority *ex post facto* by submitting a progress report, making an assessment of the performance of its role and of the negotiating session in which it has participated. It is true that a Negotiating

64 R. Michels, *Political Parties, Free Press*, New York, 1962, 61.

65 See generally M. W. Dowdle (ed.), *Public Accountability: Design, Dilemmas and Experiences*, Cambridge University Press, 2006, *passim*. Also see R. Keohane, "The Concept of Accountability in World Politics and the Use of Force," 24 *Michigan Journal of International Law* (2003), 1121–1141.

Team may have a relatively and variably high degree of discretionary power in deciding on the most effective exercise of its negotiating power. It is also true that a Negotiating Team is actually vested with the necessary autonomy that enables it to realistically contribute to the construction of common interest on a dynamically developing negotiation terrain entailing common understanding of the issues under negotiation, cognitive illumination through an expanding relevant scientific and technical knowledge, and, even, the deepening of inter-team trust expectation and reliability. On the other hand, it is within this context that the Negotiation Team is deemed to have its trust accountability to the appointing central governing authority, which is determined by a procedural minimum: the duty to submit a progress report at the end of the negotiating session. In view of the particular importance of these reports for the continuation and the future of the international negotiating process, as well as for their potential instrumental impact on the interlinked internal function of the state, they should take a comprehensive and standardized form so as to facilitate the carrying out of the necessary *ex post facto* evaluations and comparability.

Thus, after the end of each negotiation conference, the Negotiation Team should draw up a collective report capturing and explaining the level of consensus achieved, its negotiating context, and its perspective. Its accountability is placed in a specific temporal perspective: it is an *ex post facto* accounting that culminates in the process of its intra- and inter-team exercise of its power to negotiate. The report should present and explain comprehensively and from all angles (political, legal, scientific-technical) the process and stage of the negotiating process, the role of the Negotiating Team and its specific contribution to the international negotiation in relation to the positions, proposals, and directions of the intra-team negotiation. It should also illustrate the role and contribution of the other, or of the most influential Negotiating Teams, while evaluating, at the same time, the emerging main trends, results, and prospects. Of particular importance here is the often neglected or avoided specific reference and evaluation of its relationship with the internal administration during the international negotiating process, and especially of the level and quality of communication and response as well as the ascertained impact of technical or other barriers between them. It is evident that this latter reference may help create the platform for a broader evaluative control of the national operating context of the action of the Negotiating Team and the degree of effective and efficient responsiveness of the administrative support to its needs.

It is also pertinent that a collective report follows a standard form (a format) to the extent necessary, comprising a general framework of those elements that should be included therein, and, in effect, providing organized and potentially usable information. In this way, a collective report can further trigger an instrumental influence operating in at least two directions. First, it will facilitate the general checking and evaluative assessment of the quality and effectiveness of the performance of the Negotiating Team, thus ensuring appropriate accountability at all levels for its performance. Second, it will serve to identify all those elements that should be further considered, sufficiently elaborated, and evaluated by the state in a broader perspective, when designing a more encompassing, far-reaching, and multilevel exercise of its relevant policies at the international and internal-administrative levels, cultivating, in this way, a creative consistency between them. In other words, a collective report may perform a collateral advisory function that may provide the basis for future assessments, evaluations, and decisions in regard to approaching and managing the issues under negotiation, but they may also perceptively contribute to an endoscopic consideration of the related internal state functions.

In parallel to the collective report of the Negotiating Team, a special report may also be submitted by a member of the Negotiating Team, if necessary. Such an individual special report may only be submitted to the state authority represented by this member – in contrast to the collective report, which is to be submitted to all represented competent government agencies/ministries. It may refer to more detailed and necessary explanations, comments, or additional specific analysis concerning the collective report that may be of particular interest, scientific or operational, for this particular state authority.

6.4 *The Process Advisory Role of the Negotiation Team*

Finally, and in view of the quasi-legislative involvement of the Negotiating Team, special attention should be paid to the *ex post facto* advisory role of the Negotiating Team regarding the interpretation, translation, and implementation of the negotiated text of a treaty. Conceptually, this is a process advisory role based on the negotiating process knowledge and experience of the Negotiating Team, and this potential is usually underestimated or simply overlooked.

The members of the Negotiating Team, as parties to the quasi-legislative international conference that, after successive sessions, negotiably "co-legislated" the treaty text, as protagonists of the textual negotiation and co-authors of all intermediate drafts and of the final text, have no doubt the authority and the special knowledge required for undertaking the role of "natural advisor" in approaching, translating, and interpreting as well as implementing this text providing its opinion. In so acting, they point to the direction of avoiding misunderstandings, false dilemmas, or hesitations with respect to the spirit and the letter of the treaty, thus contributing to the better governance of the treaty regime.

A special word on the potential involvement of the Negotiation Team in the translation of the treaty text: the pursuit of engaging the Negotiation Team in the translation process of the treaty texts, especially where this is to be done in a non-official national language, namely in one of the languages that are not provided in the "Authentic Texts" clause or in the "Testimonium" of the treaty, has a particular significance. The text of the treaty, making "numerous implicit references to language . . . set out in other international instruments," being a product of countless other preparatory documents and translating a full circle of conversation taking place in the inter- and intra-team negotiation process, requires a more process approach to its translation.[66] It denotes, as a living relational legal instrument, encompassing a plurality of living views of protecting and promoting ICI in continuity, the necessity of leaning upon the Negotiation Team for its unique knowledge related to its living complex character. It is more than obvious that these negotiators, having a first-hand perception and deep knowledge of the balancing of interests and intentions reflected in the treaty text, of the significance of subtleties and the nuances of the language used and of certainties and uncertainties colouring the regime orientation, provide invaluable assistance and advice for the more authoritative translation of the treaty text into the particular non-official national language.

At the same time, no one should lose sight of the fundamental theoretical perspective of treaties, which is essentially associated with their relational public nature. They are not analogous to private law contracts (their legal effect does not merely derive from an objectified contract-like "perfect coincidence of wills" between the parties) but conventionally instantiated relational regimes governing ICI (their legal effect is associated with a multilateral legislative-like collective decision establishing and governing, in continuity and in reference to its context, conventional relations of ICI). In consequence, treaty texts always articulate a pluralistic unity of relational regime governance, where "*unum* does not abolish the plurality, nor is it insensitive to it."[67] As explained earlier in this chapter, *unum* exists *e pluribus*, and it remains open to it in the continuum constitution-implementation-evolution of a treaty text. This dynamic complexity, inherent in the treaty, needs to be very attentively considered during translation of its text with the assistance of the Negotiating Team.

66 See, e.g., A. Riles, "Models and Documents: Artifacts of International Legal Knowledge," 48 *ICLQ* (1999), 805, 813ff.

67 See generally on this point J. Waldron, "Legislators' Intentions and Unintentional Legislation," in E. Marmor (ed.), *Law and Interpretation: Essays in Legal Philosophy*, Clarendon Press, 1997, 329, 354. Under the legislative perspective, "it is one decision we need, not necessarily one personality, and so it is not merely as a matter of logic that we should refrain from attributing mental states to the legislature." Ibid., 354–355.

PART II

The Negotiation Phases in the Conventional Construction of International Common Interest

3

The Prenegotiation Phase as a Process of Transformative Governance

1 INTRODUCTORY CRITICAL REMARKS

The Prenegotiation phase of the international negotiation process refers to an international attempt to collectively transform a seemingly zero-sum or distributive situation into a negotiable relationship by shaping an ad hoc policy-based relational pattern reflecting a non-zero-sum or integrative situation serving international common interest. Such collective transformative governance has a relation-declarative character and serves as a precursor for the constitutive phase of international negotiation leading to the establishment of an ICI treaty regime.

More specifically, at the Prenegotiation phase, states, with the assistance of relevant international or transnational institutional entities or other stakeholders, make a collective attempt to determine the specific terms of a declarative kind of governance by shaping a political platform on which they will operate, collectively or individually, in order to transform a problematic or conflictual situation into a relational activity developing ICI. Declaring the identified deficiency or deficit of knowledge, policies, institutions, and norms with respect to the existing situation, the parties to Prenegotiation proceed to the recognition and adoption of common actions, goals, policies, principles, standards, criteria, measures, and, possibly, to the suggestion of specific actions directed to the negotiated construction of a future treaty regime or to the improvement of an already existing system of related treaty regimes. Prenegotiation then signifies a cooperative undertaking for establishing a relational framework of political commitment generating a transformative governance of a problem situation, which is *primae impressionis*, or inadequately dealt with, by the current international order, into a declarative (rather than legal) relation introducing ICI and preparing, in tune with its context of reference, the transition to new or revised relevant ICI treaty regimes. In fact, this transition is intertwined with the particular "ordering effect" produced by the Prenegotiation phase, which may operate either *precursorily*, in relation to the Constitutive Negotiation phase and the establishment of an ICI treaty regime, or *systemically*, paving the way for the development of the institutional governance of an existing ICI treaty regime,[1] or even forming the platform for a new generation of ICI treaty regimes and important declarative instruments.[2]

Prenegotiation is a structured negotiation, constructed in two interrelated levels: *the diagnostic level and the level of multilateral governance.* As a situation transformer, Prenegotiation operates horizontally and vertically. By its horizontal operation, Prenegotiation identifies the importance of relational governance of the problem situation, forging political commitment and action of the participants by communalizing it: that is, by bringing into relation the participants for its transformative management so that their declared common interest is served in a dynamic coherence with the community interest at large. In doing so, Prenegotiation raises leadership, specifies programme actions/work plans, sets targets, and consolidates the trust basis of political commitment. By its vertical operation, Prenegotiation orientates national policies and actions towards the promotion and implementation of the declared common interest objective, mobilizes nongovernmental entities and raises societal awareness. Overall, it creates a relational narrative of transformative ICI in the polycentric and dynamically developing international order, with a view to "build bridges" for a transition into more advanced normative and governance patterns, either by developing new treaty regimes (through future Constitutive Negotiation), or by causing the revision of existing ones (giving rise to Renegotiation).

On the other hand, it should be stressed that if Prenegotiation is launched within the framework of an International Organization, it is institutionalized, operating as part of its creative decision-making process. Initiated by a decision of its supreme organ (the Assembly), its negotiating process develops within the structure of the particular International Organization (an already institutionally established ICI relation) and in interaction with it (its main organs). It is carried out by an appointed ad hoc body (e.g., an Open-Ended Ad Hoc Working Group) that is mandated to provide, after negotiating sessions, a reporting or draft declarative

[1] A typical example of such systemic transition constitutes the catalytic influence of the Rio Declaration on Environment and Development and AGENDA 21: Programme of Action for Sustainable Development, 1992, upon the extensive revision of regional conventional regimes protecting the marine environment, incorporating its principles and integrating the sustainable development objective – thus creating an entirely new generation of environmental treaty regimes with distinctive governance, normative, and technical characteristics. It remains to be seen whether the more recently adopted Agenda 2030 and the seventeen carefully negotiated and crafted Sustainable Development Goals (SDGs) will generate such systemic transition: whether the declarative governance-through-goals will produce a more relational reform of conventional environmental regimes, effectively orchestrating the different levels and interlinkages of polycentric environmental governance.

[2] E.g., the Vienna Declaration and Programme of Action (UN World Conference on Human Rights, 25 June 1993), which marked a turning point for the "universalization" of human rights standards, including the right to development, after the end of the Cold War and, inter alia, staged the development of the Convention on the Rights of Persons with Disabilities, 2006, and the International Convention for the Protection of All Persons from Enforced Disappearance, 2007, or the United Nations Declaration on the Rights of Indigenous Peoples, 2007.

product to be adopted by the supreme organ (declarative outcome) and to be used as the necessary basis for the next level of the creative decision-making process: the initiation of Constitutive Negotiation within the Organization for the establishment of a treaty regime. As a result and despite its transformative direction and its declarative outcome, Prenegotiation here is structured and conducted similarly to Constitutive Negotiation because it is carried out against the structural and relational backdrop of an international organization. In this context, only the diagnostic level becomes relevant and strictly mutatis mutandis.

2 THE DIAGNOSTIC LEVEL

At the diagnostic level, Prenegotiation produces the field of the negotiation focus that encompasses the identification of the negotiable issues, the determination of the context of negotiation, and the evaluation of the best available alternative to Prenegotiation. In this process of distinctive esoteric dimensions, the role of the initiator-leader of Prenegotiation (normally a state or a small group of states with a common political platform but also an International Organization) is catalytic.

2.1 *Generating the Level of Negotiation Focus*

Prenegotiation has a particular distinctive value in the architecture of the negotiation constructing ICI because it "generates" the original field in which the collective transformation of a problem situation will be first attempted. It creates, in other words, the *field of negotiation focus,* exercising a powerful appeal in the initial attempt to identify the framework of a possible multilateral construction of a relational order serving ICI. More specifically, in situations of great uncertainty and strong dilemmas regarding the treatment of international problems, Prenegotiation forms the first necessary – and often theoretically underestimated – step in a nonlinear process of "conventionalizing" the reality of an ICI relation governing such situations. It delimits the focus of inquiry by a comprehensive determination of the negotiable issues, thus making the problem situation "communicative" between "subjects" (the negotiating participants). By its transformative effect, Prenegotiation "subjectifies" the focus of inquiry in terms of ICI performance: it is identified and managed within a structured relation between negotiating participants and their relation-generated interaction, properly "planted" in the surrounding political, legal-institutional, socio-economic, and scientific-technological world (specific context of reference). Prenegotiation brings about a relational platform for unfolding the possibility of further development of relational ICI through the next negotiation phase, the Constitutive Negotiation phase. This transition is nonlinear because it is contingent upon the advancement of further "subjective" orientations, like the additional development of special political actions in conjunction with a more adequate and pragmatic understanding of the context of reference.

Pursuing an initial "anchoring" in a declarative ICI relational regime, Prenegotiation exerts, from the beginning, influence on the way in which the negotiating participants would approach and negotiate the various sides and aspects of a dilemmatic or apparently zero-sum situation and change it by collectively transforming it. This is because Prenegotiation creates the proper framework managing the correlation between its object (declarative transformation of a problem situation) and subjects (negotiating participants) in a process of constructing ICI. Thus, Prenegotiation orientates towards the participatory construction of a declaratory regime, whereby the understanding of the problem and the issues related to it are commonly and interactively identified; the inadequacy and the shortcomings of the existing international and national institutional and regulatory regimes are commonly and interactively illuminated; the existing gaps in knowledge and the social repercussions are also commonly and interactively acknowledged (relational understanding), so that the possibility of commonly managing the protection and promotion of ICI (ICI governance) will be favoured and launched. In parallel, the relational trust is established: the relational understanding and the possibility of its ICI governance is correlated to the development of relational trust, which bridges the different interests, liberates creativity in negotiation, and legitimates its final product, its declarative instrument. As is shown in what follows, "engineering" ICI in the Prenegotiation phase, as well as in the other two phases of the negotiating process, is fundamentally relational and structurally patterned. And it has a further anticipatory effect: the raising of strong leadership among the participating governments to develop all those actions and initiatives that may be necessary for proceeding to the Constitutive Negotiation phase with a view to establish a relational treaty regime serving ICI.

2.2 *The Leading Role of the Initiator of Prenegotiation*

The launching of Prenegotiation assumes the political initiative by a state that seeks to build and promote a collective perception, trust, and programmatic synergy between *all* those involved in a particular problem situation through the Prenegotiation process, while, at the same time, it is willing to politically invest in its success, especially if the initiator is a state. In fact, the role of the initiator or leader of Prenegotiation is catalytic and its specific contribution to, and management of, the negotiation process has a determinative influence upon the negotiating parties and the outcome of negotiation. The initiator is vested with an important instrumental leadership role, encompassing transformational, transactional,[3] and ICI

[3] Instrumental leadership focuses on achieving goals and it is considered a valid extension of the transformational-transactional leadership paradigm, allowing for a more detailed and realistic description of the leadership phenomenon (J. Antonakis and R. J. House, "The Full-Range Leadership Theory:

features emanating from his authority, power, knowledge, and common interest-facilitating function. Instrumental leadership is a purposive interaction guiding a shared vision and continuous performance of ICI.[4]

Performing an instrumental leadership role in the Prenegotiation process, the initiator-leader provides the platform where Prenegotiation may reach a result that exceeds the lowest common denominator of the states involved in this process. The initiator-leader has the ability to design, organize, and "animate" the field of negotiation focus as close as possible to the attainment of the higher objectives and in the most pragmatic terms. In doing so, the initiator-leader imperceptibly builds his negotiating advantage, armoured with appropriate problem-related, well-documented knowledge and alternative proposals or options that may ultimately ensure the highest possible level of Prenegotiation outcome.

The initiator-leader of Prenegotiation may be a state, willing and able to undertake the instrumental leadership role – and this, of course, does not simply amount to a powerful state initiative. It may also be a competent International Organization, generally recognized for its knowledge-based animating role. More rarely, a group of states sharing a common political platform may undertake the initiator-leader role, but in such cases instrumental leadership may be less flexible and resilient, due to its multifarious formation. In practice, the state in which the competent international organization or the organization closely associated with the subject matter of Prenegotiation is seated usually undertakes the initiator-leader role, supported by the latter. There are some instances, however, where the state hosting the headquarters of an international organization may not be able to assume this role because of its weak position in the international system coupled with its problematic infrastructure (in this regard, Kenya's hosting of the headquarters of UNEP provides a characteristic example). On the other hand, if multiple "protagonists" appear during the Prenegotiation process, attempting to play a primary role in Prenegotiation has no significant impact upon the negotiating instrumental leadership of the initiator-leader. The latter, apart from the performance of the

The Way Forward," in B. Avolio and F. Yammarino (eds.), *Transformational and Charismatic Leadership: The Road Ahead*, Amsterdam: JAI Press, 2002, 3–34). According to the theory of transformational and transactional leadership, evolved since 1985, transformational leaders inspire their followers with a positive, value-based vision of the future, while transactional leaders rely on clearly defined *quid pro quo* transactions. The sufficiency of these two types of leadership behaviour has been challenged and the introduction of the construct of instrumental leadership fills the gap, "representing the strategic and follower work-facilitation leadership functions that are crucial for organizational and follower performance." J. Rowold, "Instrumental Leadership: Extending the Transformational-Transactional Leadership Paradigm," Zeitschrift für Personalforschung, 28(3) *German Journal of Research in Human Resource Management* (2014), 367–390.

4 In fact, this approach seems to keep pace with a more general view expressed by the UN Scientific Advisory Board: "Increasingly, leadership will mean interaction – the sharing of information and policymaking – the sharing of power." UNESCO: The Future of Scientific Advice to the United Nations – A Summary Report to the Secretary-General of the United Nations from the Scientific Advisory Board, September 2016, 19.

aforementioned functions related to the instrumental leadership, is vested with a decisive procedural power also associated with this role: his assumption of the undisputed role of president/chairman during the Prenegotiation process.

2.3 *The Determination of Negotiable Issues*

The initiator-leader of the Prenegotiation undertakes to identify, introduce, and document the negotiable issues on the basis of their *cognitive management*. Being the first and decisive step, the cognitive management of the issues in Prenegotiation refers to the diligently organized attempt to determine the negotiable issues in an integrated, relational, and instrumental methodical manner: knowledgeably (diagnostic thematic management), intersubjectively (management of "subjective framings"), and contextually (management of the special context of reference) aiming at building, in their interrelationship and interaction, a platform for possible development of ICI. The pursuit of cognitive management through these transformative methods reveals, in the most emphatic way, that the initial step for transforming an existing problem into a situation of collective-individual ICI management requires a deeper understanding and a systematic, interdisciplinary analysis of the interrelated domains of these transformative methods. In their combination, these transformative methods comprise a range of policy, scientific, and legal approaches that depict a bottom-up understanding in the design of the Prenegotiation framework and that can impact the generated process of transformative change.

2.3.1 Thematic Diagnostic Approach: The Management of Knowledge

The diagnostic approach to issues (diagnostic thematic management) is the first major task of the initiator-leader in his attempt to pave the way for the transformation of a newly arising or persisting problem situation into a multilateral, cooperative framework seeking the construction of ICI. More specifically, the initiator-leader should embark on a description of the basic causes, the extent, the results, and the significance of such a problem situation, as well as its possible interconnection with other issue areas in an effort to attain a comprehensive understanding of its nature and consequences. He should also proceed to a first assessment of the existing state of scientific and technical knowledge.

The development of the diagnostic approach should be carried out in the most objective manner so that it will be persuading and effective: it requires the use of the most objective criteria, appropriate procedures, and equitable assessments that are distinguished by their legitimacy, practicality, and open-ended determination, thus allowing adaptation and improvements during negotiation. Flexibility in the diagnostic approach is necessary because it keeps pace with the motivating role of the initiator-leader at the Prenegotiation: despite the initial pursuance of its best available objective foundation, the diagnostic approach should, in principle, remain "open" to critical improvements by each negotiating participant. After all, "objectivity" in a knowledge-based diagnostic approach is to be understood "intersubjectively" as an interrelated phenomenon constituted by a correlation of approaches and views between the participants integrating, through interaction and communication, past and present information and commonly projecting it for the management of the future. The initiator-leader actually aims at motivating a transformative Prenegotiation process rather than imposing his diagnostic approach on the negotiating participants because the latter becomes authoritative and eventually productive when it ultimately rests on common perceptions and approaches – when, in other words, it becomes properly "contextualized." It is, therefore, important that the initiator-leader develops his diagnostic thematic approach on a comprehensive relational platform. This would allow "a conventional space" of thematic building in relation to an instrumental management of knowledge and the management of its specific context of reference in pursuance of ICI.

As hinted earlier, the assessment of the level of development of the relevant scientific and technical knowledge at the Prenegotiation phase requires a "process-conscious" observational effort by the initiator-leader: in view of the delicate, sensitive, and open character of Prenegotiation and the intrinsically relational nature of (relevant) knowledge, he should provide a first authoritative, knowledgeably reliable, and realistically convincing assessment. This assessment is a core element in the transformative effort of the initiator-leader and it is properly materialized at the multilateral governance level organized and conducted by him. It is clearly reflected in the supporting report and appropriately ingrained in the first negotiating draft text of the declarative instrument to be submitted by him at the Ad Hoc Multilateral Conference, as is discussed later.

Furthermore, this assessment is a constant feature of all three phases of the ICI negotiation process, marking an important aspect of their relational governance structure, although to a varying degree.[5] It is a necessary condition for conventionally punctuating the pursuance of ICI and the proper understanding of the interconnection between scientific knowledge and ICI governance and the embedded uncertainty. This seems to require a deeper, more *quantum theoretical thinking* about the management of scientific knowledge: it refers more to the effective and efficient management of the crucial uncertainties of the problem situation so that a continuous relational construction and performance of ICI can be generated, rather than to "a steadily developing certainty of

[5] The interconnection between scientific knowledge and politics is a crucial aspect of negotiating issues of international environmental governance and in all three phases of the ICI negotiation process. See, e.g., M. L. McConnell, "The Relationship between Science and Politics in Environmental Negotiations," in E. Raftopoulos and M. L. McConnell (eds.), *Contributions to International Environmental* Negotiation *in the Mediterranean Context,* MEPIELAN Studies in International Environmental Law and Negotiation-2, Ant. N. Sakkoulas, Bruylant, 2004, Part II, 81–92; S. Andresen, T. Skodvin, A. Underal, and J. Wettestand, *Science and Politics in International Environmental Regimes: Between Integrity and Involvement,* Manchester University Press, 2000.

knowledge and control of the natural world"[6] with respect to the problem situation. The interconnection between scientific knowledge and ICI governance has an orientating function in very complex and interactively understood reality rather than a stabilizing function unveiling an objectively defined surrounding reality.[7] Hence, the assessment of the level of development of knowledge concerning the problem situation is to be understood as related not to its objective description, but to its instrumental function in conventionalizing and organizing the attainment of an ICI relational transformation of the situation under negotiation. It should be determined, in other words, in view of its instrumental function as *relational ICI engineering*: as contributing to negotiating the reconstructive organization and management of the problematic situation within the overall context of its existence (its social, economic, political, and cultural environment) and leading to its conventional transformation into an ICI relation.

In this process, and where required, the assessment of the level of development of knowledge as relational ICI engineering may be appropriately projected as "usable knowledge"[8] by the initiator-leader so that it will be perceived not only as credible but also as legitimate and salient.[9] These three criteria respectively refer to the scientific quality of the relevant knowledge, the quality of the institutions/individuals producing the relevant knowledge, and the contextual sensitivity of the relevant knowledge responding to the subjective understanding of its relevancy to the needs and requirements of the perceived reality of the situation. In their inextricably interwoven connection, these criteria indicate what is perceived as usable knowledge and clearly point to its important implications. Particularly in the Prenegotiation process, usable knowledge may decisively influence the initial effort to address the negotiable transformation of the perceived problematic situation, as well as the quality of its declarative outcome.

Approaching knowledge as relational ICI engineering projecting usable knowledge, the initiator-leader should operate on two interrelated levels integrating the three criteria and showcasing the following strategies.

6 On this point, but from a different perspective, see, e.g., S. O. Funtowicz and J. R. Ravetz, "Global Risk, Uncertainty, and Ignorance," in J. X Kasperson and R. E. Kasperson (eds.), *Global Environmental Risk*, United Nations University Press: Earthscan, 2001, 173, 178.

7 In fact, the relational nature of knowledge engineering ICI governance relations in an interactively revealed reality touches upon the province of quantum theory and its interpretation of reality. For a recent, fascinating, and insightfully clear treatise of quantum theory in this regard, see C. Rovelli, *Reality Is Not What It Seems: The Journey to Quantum Gravity* (transl. by S. Carnell and E. Serge), Allen Lane-Penguin Random House UK, 2016, esp. Part Four, 175–234.

8 On the importance of usable knowledge and its comprehensive and critical approach for the development of multilateral frameworks of environmental governance, see P. M. Haas, "Science Policy for Multilateral Environmental Governance," in N. Kanie and P. M. Haas (eds.), *Emerging Forces in Environmental Governance*, United Nations University Press, 2004, 115–136.

9 D. W. Cash, W. C. Clark, F. Alcock, N. M. Dickson, N. Eckley, D. H. Guston, J. Jager, and R. B. Mitchell, "Knowledge Systems for Sustainable Development," 100(14)*Proceedings of the National Academy of Sciences* (2003), 8086–8091.

The Contextual Approach and Management of Relevant Knowledge. This refers to an instrumental approach to knowledge (knowledge as relational ICI engineering), a tool of pursuing an interdisciplinary and contextual problem-management situation and contributing to the creation of a relational frame for ICI governance. In doing so, it provides a reliable cognitive basis for embarking on a pragmatic view of this relational frame, looking upon it as a correlation between its present and future overall interactions with its context. In fact, the conventionalization of the present interactions of the relational frame with its context is a way to "shape" the field, managing its future interactions in a process of clarifying and performing ICI. Relevant knowledge as relational ICI engineering should be therefore approached and managed along the lines of its quantum understanding – after all, "we have become physicists behind our backs."[10] The assessment of its level of development and the reality of its contextuality is complex, multidimensional, and process-related as it is run with uncertainties. As a result, the reality of the contextual approach to knowledge and its relevance cannot be known in all its details. It is fundamentally "constructed" in relation – and not independently of – to the current attainment level of participatory consensus of the scientific community and decision-making states or institutions with a view to a continuously efficient and effective performance of ICI. In effect, the assessment of the level of scientific knowledge as knowledge of an object is fundamentally relative, because it is a "constructed knowledge" based on the participatory consensus of the relevant actors, and instrumentally relevant, because it engineers their current conventional understanding and organization of the ICI relational performance. Relatedly, the quality of the "constructed knowledge"(the degree of its development, its effectiveness, its efficiency, and its social acceptance) is interrelated to the nature and quality of the collectively produced participatory consensus[11] (degree of representativeness, institutionalization of relational ICI governance). And it is also clear that uncertainties go all the way through to touch the matrix of such construction, because participatory consensus is built in relation to their historical perception regarding the application of their ICI or the conduct of their common values.

[10] As is eloquently stated by Lawrence Tribe, a prominent American constitutional scholar: "Like Moliere's gentleman who had been speaking prose all his life but did not know it, we have become physicists behind our backs," L. H. Tribe, "The Curvature of Constitutional Space: What Lawyers Can Learn from Modern Physics," 103 *Harvard Law Review* (1989), 1, 20. On the other hand, the superficial mention by leading political negotiators of quantum physics as a mystery field that we do not understand (see, e.g., the statement by I. Lövin, Deputy Prime Minister of Sweden, in *Our Oceans, Our Future Panel Discussion* – available at www.un.org/sustainabledevelopment/oceans) raises, at least, scepticism in view of the immense complexity of the negotiating endeavour (understanding and negotiating the correlation of things concerning the oceans in one Ocean Conference so that a collective action-oriented transformative ocean governance will be launched).

[11] Postulating the social aspects of knowledge and developing the social epistemology of scientific knowledge, Thomas Kuhn rightly declares that scientific knowledge "is an inherently collective product" and needs to be understood in reference to the specific nature of the group producing it. T. S. Kuhn, *The Essential Tension: Selected Studies in Scientific Tradition and Change*, University of Chicago Press, 1977, Part II Metahistorical Studies, chs. 10–14, 240–351.

In this framework, the assessment of the level of development of scientific knowledge, first to be attempted by the initiator-leader, may constitute a subjective probabilistic option: it may be configured in relation to different and competitive "cognitive constructions of participatory consensus" that are not fully comparable. In fact, they have incommensurable aspects that cannot be appropriately evaluated by common criteria.[12] And just as in the case of translation from one language to another, so these cognitive constructions, because they do not have identical theoretical and value-based contexts of reference, retain their specific generating contextuality: certain of their concepts and perceptions may function differently in their specific generating context to the effect that they cannot be measured commensurably.[13] Nevertheless they can be evaluated complementarily and understood interpretatively as add-ons optimizing, in the framework of the initiated negotiating process, the declarative (or conventional, in the case of constitutive negotiation phase) ICI performance.

Moreover, the contextual approach to knowledge as relational ICI engineering also encapsulates the knowing dimension: the knowledge inherent in the collective-individual practice development or in the collective-individual actions related to the application of ICI governance within a conventional or declarative structure. The management of contextual knowledge may then embrace "practical knowing" that operates complementarily to the level of scientific knowledge and in a relationship of their mutual activation. It emerges through the continuous application and progress of this structured ICI governance and constitutes the "epistemology action," leading, within this structured interaction, in the nonlinear development of knowledge.[14] And the effective transfer or sharing of this tacit knowledge requires the deepening of the structured ICI governance, its constant

12 As Webber observes, applying common measures to incommensurable options "would distort, transform or misrepresent the value, importance or quality" of these options and the common measure "would fail to capture adequately everything that matters" about these options, G. C. N. Webber, *The Negotiable Constitution: On the Limitation of Rights*, Cambridge University Press, 2009, 91.

13 T. S. Kuhn, "Objectivity, Value Judgment and Theory Choice," in *The Essential Tension*, op. cit., 320–339. Kuhn, in his latest work, separated the process of translation from the process of understanding between languages, introducing the concept of bilingual understanding. The learning process of bilinguals, on the one hand, relates to the acquisition of a second language without mediation by the first language, so understanding without translation is possible; on the other hand, a process of language add-on is practiced where a new lexical taxonomy is acquired that is separate from the native one, without being incorporated into it but enriching it by adding to it its new terms. T. S. Kuhn, "Dubbing and Redubbing: The Vulnerability of Rigid Designation," in C. Savage (ed.), *Scientific Theory*, University of Minnesota Press, 1990, 298–301.

14 See S. D. N. Cook and J. S. Brown, "Bridging Epistemologies: The Generative Dance between Organizational Knowledge and Organizational Knowing," 10(4)*Organization Science* (1999), 381–400. Edited version (2005) available at: www.sagepub.com/upm-data/9926_039585Ch03.pdf. As Polanyi perceptively declared, the knowledge of the practicing involves a tacit dimension that enables him to know more than "he can tell," a knowledge based on experience, a "tacit knowledge" or "tacit Knowing." M. Polanyi, *Personal Knowledge: Towards a Post-Critical Philosophy*, University of Chicago Press, 1958, *passim*; see also his *The Tacit Dimension*, University of Chicago Press, 1966, 4.

negotiating advancement, and the development of relational trust. So, the more relationally the declarative or conventional structured ICI governance applies, the more fundamentally the understanding or the perception of the undertaken or constituted relational ICI framework seems to change.[15]

The Procedural Approach and Management of Relevant Knowledge. Knowledge as relational ICI engineering also pertains to a legitimating procedural dimension. In fact, the procedural approach and management to relevant knowledge requires the reliability of the source of the scientific/technical knowledge, reflected in the level of its authoritative scientific consensus and the degree of its autonomy, so that its relational ICI engineering effect will draw a substantial political acceptability and support. As is aptly proved in practice, the greater the autonomy and independence of science from politics, the more powerful its influence.[16] This is particularly important at the sensitive Prenegotiation phase, where the attempt is being made to produce a diagnostic approach to the problematic situation with a view to establish confidence and trust for its transformative negotiation into an ICI relational framework. The initiator-leader should ensure that the communicated scientific and technical knowledge is best shielded so that it will attract an at least adequate political legitimation among the negotiating participants.

For this purpose, the initiator-leader should seek to establish the communicated scientific and technical knowledge on a recognized or recognizable institutional background. This can be generated in the framework of competent international organizations or other authoritative international institutional entities and their networks, where an adequate representation of non-state entities is ensured. Renowned international or national research institutes, enjoying a high degree of independence, and in particular their networks or "representative alliances" creating institutionalized synergies and developing interdisciplinary approaches – like the Earth League – may undoubtedly be resorted to as reliable sources of scientific information.[17] Besides, the use of multiple sources of this institutional background

15 Interesting, in this regard, is the observation of Lawrence Tribe, who, praising "the significant heuristic insights for legal analysis" offered by quantum theory using the quantum principle of uncertainty ("the more accurately you measure where a particle is, the less accurately you are able to measure where it's going"), notes that judges in particular cannot simply understand and resolve disputes between individuals "without permanently altering the legal and social space" and that "the very act of judging alters the context and relationships being judged." Tribe, "The Curvature of Constitutional Space," op. cit., 1–39.

16 Andresen, Skodvin, Underal, and Wettestand, *Science and Politics in International Environmental Regimes*, op. cit.

17 The Earth League (available at: www.the-earth-league.org/) is an interesting international voluntary network or alliance of prominent scientists and world-class scientific entities (a union of universities, institutions, and think tanks), from both hemispheres of the planet, dealing with planetary processes and sustainability issues, focusing on the application of knowledge for managing anthropogenic global change according to the principles of sustainable development. Operating beyond international panels, like the IPCC, national academies, and worldwide research programs, like the IGBP or the IHDP – which are either financially underfunded or ill connected across national boundaries or

may guide more appropriately the initiator-leader to secure a balanced approach to the reliability of scientific information and the concomitant policy response in the particular sensitive period of Prenegotiation. In fact, it feeds his supportive report to be submitted to the Ad Hoc Multilateral Conference with three catalytic and interrelated elements: demonstration of scientific/technical knowledge at a very high level, indications of possibly differentiating evidences, and corresponding configuration of the necessary options for a more effective and efficient construction of a declarative (or conventional) ICI relation.

Furthermore, of particular importance is the recently developed "institutionalization" in the management of scientific knowledge as ICI engineering in the framework of the UN, a flagship initiator-leader for the Prenegotiation of global issues, with the establishment of the Scientific Advisory Board (SAB).[18] The SAB was announced by the UN Secretary-General during the inaugural meeting of the UN High-Level Political Forum on Sustainable Development on 24 September 2013, during the 68th Session of the UN General Assembly. It provides advice to the UN Secretary-General and to executive heads of UN organizations on the science-policy -society interface for sustainable development, thus making a daring step: bringing together in a coherent manner the collective capacity of all relevant scientific fields, overcoming barriers between disciplines and methods, with due regard to the social and ethical dimensions of sustainable development. The inclusion of political scientists in the SAB signifies the increased awareness of the need for a holistic approach to international governance producing scientifically informed political leadership geared for innovative approaches to problem solving. Relatedly, the main functions of the SAB include the more effective and efficient integration of scientific results into the full spectrum of international governance, within and outside the negotiating process (global political discussions/consultations, negotiations, decision-making processes), but also identifying of knowledge gaps, advising on the public visibility and understanding of science and "offering insight on democratic global governance, focussed on sustainability and the responsible and ethical development of science."[19] Finally and in view of the special nature of the subject matter of negotiation, a scientific body may become de facto institutionalized in the management of scientific knowledge as ICI engineering. It may form an effective cognitive platform of generating expert knowledge catalytically influencing all stages of the negotiating process and progressively "thickening" the consensus towards the

even unable to do original research on emerging issues – the Earth League uses its autonomous resources to apply for national and transnational funding, to collaborate on setting and advancing research agendas, and to communicate to and discuss with decision makers as well as society at large providing credible advice and multiple choices.

18 The SAB (available at: https://en.unesco.org/un-sab/about/background) is composed of twenty-six high-level experts representing all geographical regions and many scientific disciplines relevant for sustainable development and gender, and the secretariat of its board is hosted by UNESCO at the request of the UN Secretary-General.

19 See Scientific Board of the UN Secretary-General: *Terms of Reference*, II (f, h, i).

development of a treaty regime. Thus, in the development of the climate change regime, the IPCC, through its five Assessment Reports (1990, 1995–1996, 2001, 2007, and 2013–2014), has played a catalytic role in making communicative solid expert knowledge decisively influencing the Prenegotiation, and led to the scaled development of the UN Framework Convention on Climate Change (1992), the Kyoto Protocol (1997), and the Paris Agreement (2015).

2.3.2 The Subjective Diagnostic Approach: The Management of Subjective Framings

The management of "subjective framings" constitutes a transformative method at a different level, interrelated to the transformative methods of the thematic diagnostic approach. Through this method, the initiator-leader of the Prenegotiation is able to proceed to the identification and management of the "subjective landscape" of the problem situation as is indicated by the world of the prospective delegates-negotiators. It is a particularly useful method of transformative negotiation when the initiator-leader is a state. From a broader perspective, it may be applied mutatis mutandis, and within the limits of structural requirements, to the other two negotiation phases.

Its particular importance lies in the fact that it has a complementary function to the diagnostic thematic management, enabling the initiator-leader to elaborate and organize, in pragmatic terms, the strategic management of the operative subjective framings characterizing the prospective delegates-negotiators with regard to the problem situation. These operative subjective framings depict the interpretative and operational identity and role of the prospective delegates-negotiators in the international field and in similar situations, and their systematic analysis gives the opportunity to the initiator-leader to effectively work on the working scope of transformative actions and the pragmatically available alternatives regarding the negotiability of the problem situation. Identifying, in a comprehensive and integrated manner, the "interpretative frames" of the prospective delegates-negotiators through which they, more or less consistently, shape their common, converging, or diverging individual attitudes or positions, and the "operational frames" through which they choose to carry them out, the initiator-leader is able to pave the way for the configuration of an adequate relational thematic understanding regarding the construction and management of the specific issues. In doing so, the initiator-leader acquires strategic advantage by better understanding the dynamic aspects of Prenegotiation and develops an informed understanding of the possibilities to collectively reframe the problem situation in a relational activity of ICI.

More specifically, the systematic identification and management of the operative subjective framings (interpretative and operational frames) may be performed in the following levels.

Identification of the Framing Entities. It is necessary that the full circle of the subjective framing entities is identified so that they will become participants in the Prenegotiation process. This circle may include, in addition to states, the entire spectrum of relevant non-state entities (competent or relevant international organizations, international institutional entities representing relevant treaty regimes, NGOs, private operators, professional associations, etc.). Their participation in the Prenegotiation process brings to the fore their characteristic framings-in-use of the problem situation emanating from their particular roles, so that a real "situation sense" of the dynamics of the transformation attempt and the need for alternative proposals becomes more visible and better understood.

Identification of the Subjective Framings. The identification of the framings-in-use of the full circle of participants in the Prenegotiation process is an essential tool in the strategy of gaining advantage in the transformative negotiation leading to the collective construction of an ICI relational regime. If classified, they refer to a series of specific framings related to the identity, values, policies, and actions of these participants that, in fact, determine the forming of their subjective perceptions and attitudes towards the understanding and management of particular situations and their specific context of reference. The management of the subjective framings-in-use may be specifically performed in two interrelated levels:

- At the level of determining the interpretative framings of the participants, where, depending on their nature and function, the following elements are mainly identified and evaluated as appropriate:
  - Their individual political, social, and economic orientation.
  - Their environmental orientation and their standing on sustainability governance issues.
  - Their preference for realistic or practical options or solutions, or conversely, for idealistic and impractical options or solutions.
  - Their orientation to scientific/technical information and its instrumental use in other complex cases of increased uncertainty.
  - Their common, converging, or diverging approaches to the understanding and the application of internal governance (interpretation of justice, the rights of citizens, effective public participation in the decision-making process, an assessment of the relationship of powers, the political basis of the decision-making process, effective legislation).
  - Their common, converging, or diverging approaches to the understanding and application of international governance for the protection and promotion of ICI in effective coherence with international context (their view of international law and the degree of its support and implementation, their perception and interpretation of the construction, protection, and promotion of ICI [systematic adoption of positive/non-zero-sum attitudes or, inclination to resort to distributive/zero-sum attitudes], their role orientation towards the

existing and developing international institutional organization, the level of support of synergies, polycentricity and multiplicity of organization, and creativity in the international governance system).

- Their different power bases in relation to the subject matter, featured in various combinations and in constant evolution (the degree of political and military power; the degree of economic and technological power; geopolitical power; the cultural/religious background; the degree of control of natural resources; the degree of organization, effectiveness, and efficiency of state power, but also of public protection and participation; effective role in the international decision-making process within the framework of international institutional entities; participation in powerful and authoritative international entities, partnerships, or groupings of economic, political, or military character; the undertaking of a leadership or protagonist role in international negotiations leading to treaties; recognition of international standing and trust by the international community at large).

- At the level of determining the performative framings of the participants, also depending on their nature and function, where the following elements are mainly identified and evaluated as appropriate:
  - The different fields of interaction (arenas) where the subjects of framings systematically project their common, converging, or diverging approaches and attitudes in relation to the management of international problems and the shaping and exercise of international governance (which may be referred to similar to the negotiation matters). They may vary from informal fields of interaction (unilateral incidental actions, competitive practices) to officially organized fields of interaction oriented towards the pursuance, protection, and promotion of ICI (diplomatic contacts, ad hoc conferences to negotiate frameworks of international cooperation or treaties, international organizations, recourse to the means of international dispute settlement). It is obvious that the latter lie at the top of the assessment of the performative framings.
  - The strategies systematically pursued by the participants, whereby they organize the projection of their common, converging, or diverging approaches and attitudes in relation to the general management of international problems and the search and configuration of their international governance. They refer either to strategies pursuing collective cooperation, carried out by the negotiated building of treaties or other forms of international cooperation (decisions of international organizations, international [multilateral or organizational] declarations, action plans, strategies, guidelines, etc.), or to strategies of adversarial competition, carried out by the systematic projection of particular national claims or demands and the use of particular means of power (geopolitical, economic, communicational) and options for attaining a distributive-sum effect on the negotiated issues (emphasis on zero-sum solutions).

– The outcomes of the performances of the participants: namely, how the analysed performances led to immediate effect, positive or negative, and what their specific implications are in the particular field of interaction in which they have been projected, evaluated in terms of their effectiveness in relation to the final result.
– The results of the performances of the participants: namely, how and to what extent they contributed to the overall improvement in the protection and promotion of ICI, evaluated on the basis of the wider implications in the context of ICI indicators, like the establishment of an effective and efficient international conventional regime (a treaty or an international institutional entity) related to the continuous, resilient, and evolving governance of the functional purposes of international community, the amelioration of the justice process, and the maintenance of international peace and security.

2.3.3 The Management of Contextuality of the Prenegotiation Transformation

Prenegotiation occurs within a context, and its advancement is basically related to its contextualization. An essential characteristic of the transformative Prenegotiation process prepared by the initiator-leader is the management of its special context of reference. It refers to a comprehensive identification of, and an effectively determined interrelationship with, the particular legal, political, and institutional "landscape" surrounding the Prenegotiation process. It is within the appropriately determined context that the textual negotiation process will be integrated and developed at this phase, aiming at the collective formulation of a declarative ICI instrument. In fact, the Prenegotiation process "enters the world" of the international order when embedded into its context, that is, the existing and continuously evolving legal and political field in relation to which its final product will acquire a compatible status and function. This is consistently required by the international public order pursuing the protection and advancement of ICI. The management of contextuality of the Prenegotiation constitutes a transformative method, through which the initiator-leader of the Prenegotiation is able to proceed to the instrumental identification and management of the "normative landscape" of the problem situation as it is unveiled by the related legal, political, and institutional contextual indicators. These contextual indicators inform about the scope of Prenegotiation, forming *the reference configuration conditions* that perform three methodically correlated but distinct functions: identifiability, compatibility, and heuristic. Correspondingly, three specific contextual indicators are qualified: context identification, contextual compatibility, and an "added-value" or constructive heuristic.

Context Identification. According to this contextual indicator, every draft text drawn up in view of Prenegotiation (by the initiator-leader) or during the

Prenegotiation process (by the negotiating participants) should make specific reference to all relevant treaty regimes, either in force or not, or even if they are still under negotiation. This also applies to transnational legislation generated at the regional level (EU legislation). It should also refer to the relevant decisions of international organizations or international institutional entities, as well as to the relevant international declarative instruments (guidelines, strategies, action plans, etc.) generated within the framework of global or regional conferential negotiations. Of course, context identification effectively ingrains the element of subjectivity into its reference: the negotiating participants may decide to restrict the instrumental identification of the context, where it appears that the omission (or even the relativization) of a certain reference may be required in order to reach a mutually acceptable outcome in the negotiations.

Contextual Consistency. Contextual consistency should ensure that the final declarative product of Prenegotiation stays in functional coherence with the context of reference. According to this contextual indicator, the declarative instrument of Prenegotiation should be in compatible relationship with the principles, rules, standards, policies, and actions of the relevant instruments of the context, building on them and going beyond them. In other words, it should be carefully constructed and operated in creative complementarity with them, so that ICI will be effectively served in the framework of the Prenegotiation declarative instrument. Although the latter is not formally a legal instrument, its collectively and multilaterally negotiated construction and its adequate understanding and application should be in functional consistency with its operative context: it should function as a compatible (non-conflicting or constructively deviating) declarative development in the process of broadening the ICI application to its special thematic field.[20]

If, on the other hand, the contextual consistency of a declarative instrument is deficiently approached and treated, then it may bring about "fragmentation effects" (resulting fragmentation) as regards the operation of the transformative governance of the problem situation in the polycentric international order,[21] causing isolation from the context of reference. Ignoring or overlooking normative

[20] Thus responding to the heuristic function, which is clustered in the ensuing "added value" contextual indicator. Such deviation, which has no negative meaning, is a direct reflection of the differing pursuits and interests that the negotiating parties have in a pluralistic international society producing polycentric ordering serving ICI; see Chapter 2.

[21] Note here that the proposed conceptualization of "resulting fragmentation" is strictly related to a specific dysfunctional aspect of the polycentricity in the governance of international ordering, and its corrective treatment in the transformative governance at the Pre-negotiation phase is instrumental in the more effective and holistic pursuance of ICI. Thus, it clearly goes beyond the long theoretical debate on "fragmentation of international law" and its opposing narratives on fragmentation/diversity, the rhetoric on fragmentation, its methodological presuppositions, and politics underlying the language of fragmentation as a powerful metaphor. See, e.g., A.-C. Martineau, "The Rhetoric of Fragmentation: Fear and Faith in International Law," 22 *Leiden Journal of International Law* (2009), 1–19.

and institutional actions and activities developed or developing in the context of reference may result in deviating, even conflicting, actions as regards the transformative governance of the particular problem situation causing dysfunctions in the constituted polycentricity, and, possibly, in blurring the overall perspective of such governance.

"Added Value" or Heuristic. The "added value" or heuristic contextual indicator should effectively determine the area of negotiable new or added-value actions, principles, and policies that may be necessary for the transformative management of the Prenegotiation theme into a declarative relation of ICI. It operates in complementary relationship with the other two contextual indicators encompassing all those "additional" common or special and innovative elements that are considered to effectively reinforce the transition from the existing problem situation to a relational framework declaring the pursuance of ICI. Operating as a spearhead for this transition, these additional elements form the core of transformative management.

As a result, they do not only offer the justificatory basis for the declarative relation pursuing ICI, but, more importantly, they also set the scene for a "staged" transition process: they fuel, in specific and pragmatic terms, the possibility of transcending to the Constitutive Negotiation phase for the establishment of a relevant treaty regime serving ICI or even accelerating and intensifying the process of negotiating and constituting relevant treaty/ies patterns. In doing so, they make contextual consistency meaningful: they unfold a purposive or teleological coherence where the continuous collective pursuance of ICI gives meaning and advances the existing international ordering. It is worth noting here that in certain bilateral Prenegotiation processes pervaded by the element of conflict, the "added value" or heuristic contextual indicator may be articulated as a declaration of common understanding of "areas of agreement" on specific issues, requiring coordinated and constructive common action, which effectuates the staged transition process and generates transformative results.[22]

[22] See, characteristically, the Joint Statement by the Union of Soviet Socialist Republics – United States at the Geneva Summit (21 November 1985), 25 ILM (1986), 102–104, where the declared areas of agreement (Security, Nuclear and Space Talks, Risk Reduction Centres, Nuclear Non-Proliferation, Chemical Weapons, Mutual and Balanced Force Reduction (MBFR), Confidence and Disarmament in Europe (CDE), Process of Dialogue, Northern Pacific Air Safety, Civil Aviation/Consulates, and Environmental Protection Exchange Initiatives and Research Fusion) embrace in full the staged transition process from the existing problematic situation, serving their relations "and the international situation as a whole," and pointing in the direction of developing treaty regimes (e.g., "an effective and verifiable" international convention on chemical weapons or an agreement on Northern Pacific air safety) or accelerating the negotiations in progress on certain agreements (e.g., the progress in the negotiation of the agreement on the reduction of nuclear arms led, in 1991, to the Strategic Arms Reduction Treaty (START I).

2.3.4 The Management of Alternative Solutions to Prenegotiation

The initiator-leader should, at the end of the diagnostic level of the Prenegotiation process, examine and assess the alternative solutions to Prenegotiation that appear to be open to the negotiating participants and place them in a pragmatic perspective. In this way, he will be able to better understand the underlying dynamic of the subjective framings of the negotiating participants because the quality and extent of their involvement would be directly related to the pragmatic weight and force of these alternative solutions.

More specifically, the initiator-leader should look into two interrelated factors that generally influence the weight and force of alternatives to Prenegotiation solutions: the nature of the subject matter of the Prenegotiation, and the nature of the binding force of the textual instrument resulting from the Prenegotiation. As regards the subject matter, it is evident that its effective and efficient management requires an overall coordinated and carefully designed response because of its complexity, its intensity, and its surrounding uncertainties, but also because of its communicative weight through its handling in the media. It requires the involvement, consensual assessment, and appropriate action of all relevant states, international organizations, and other institutional entities. As regards the binding force, the generated textual instrument of Prenegotiation, having a formally declarative nature, clearly implies a political commitment of a programmatic character and identifying effect. It is not imperative, but operates instrumentally: it lays down a framework of multilateral political cooperation for identifying, building, or reinforcing a common interest perspective in the collective management of the subject matter, entailing a normative orientation towards a possible establishment of a relevant ICI treaty regime.

In fact, both of the aforementioned factors catalytically weaken the force of the two possible alternative solutions to Prenegotiation open to the prospective negotiators, the direct negotiation of a treaty and abstaining from Prenegotiation. Pursuing the path of direct negotiation of a treaty, bypassing the Prenegotiation phase, may be least attractive to many – if not most – negotiators precisely because it may be considered premature and can either risk failure of the negotiations or, most possibly, lead to an unworkable agreement. Negotiating treaties prematurely suffers from a major drawback on its very basis. It produces solutions that are politically unstable because they produce "paper agreements" rather than a pragmatic and informed accommodation of interests constructing ICI and, hence, a resilient and effective relational treaty basis. It does not only ignore the importance of the relational foundation of the treaty and its pragmatic public law operation as an ICI treaty regime but it also generates solutions that are functionally unworkable and technically incorrect, especially in treaties strongly related to a process of new technological developments and a continuous flow of scientific information.[23] In fact, the Damoclean sword of the legally binding force of the directly negotiated treaty does not allow the negotiating participants to establish the necessary space for a creative elaboration and bridging of their divergent interests and views. As a result, it maintains the uncertainties in the drafting of the treaty text, inevitably leading to the formulation of general and abstract provisions rendering its legal regime, from a substantive and practical point of view, powerless and ineffectual. In addition, it should be underlined that there is always a high risk that negotiations would be led to a deadlock and, ultimately, to a negotiation wreck for all the reasons mentioned earlier.

Similarly, abstaining from Prenegotiation is, in fact, far from offering a genuine low-risk alternative solution. It is basically an alternative that induces a degree of isolation associated with a negative chain of effects. It entails downplaying the role of the abstaining state and the perception of its added-value image among state and non-state participants in the process of the transformative management of Prenegotiation. Unlike them, the abstaining state appears to adopt an uncooperative negative attitude, refusing to contribute to the effort for the necessary transformation of a problem situation into a relation of ICI under the terms of the Prenegotiation process by offering its perspective and particular views on the issues involved. Thus, it runs a high risk of inflicting damage to its reputation: it is exposed to the international community since it does not act in accordance with his expected role as an "active international partaker" demonstrating the necessary solidarity with the collective transformative Prenegotiation effort undertaken by states and supported by international organizations, NGOs, and the scientific community in the light of precipitating events requiring immediate action.[24] At the same time, it has lost the opportunity to directly influence and contribute to the consensus-building articulated in the declarative framework of Prenegotiation as well as to benefit from the coordinated programmatic actions emanating from it. Finally, the negative impact that abstention may have upon the domestic order of the state, at the political and social levels as well as at the level of publicity, should not be underestimated, especially when the situation under transformative Prenegotiation relates to an international problem of developmental, environmental, social, or legal character or a combination of these.

On the basis of this overall assessment of the alternative solutions to Prenegotiation, coupled with the analysed levels of diagnostic management for the

23 J. I. Charney elaborated this point early in regard to the negotiations at the Law of the Sea Conference, underlining the importance of resorting, first, to nonbinding fora that secure the necessary flexibility. See J. I. Charney, "Technology and International Negotiations," 76 *AJIL* (1982), 78, 84–92.

24 Forcibly and dramatically occurring events bringing about changes in relations, situations, knowledge, and technology and in the natural environment from within or outside the reaches of a paradigm. See, generally, M. J. Kirton, *Adaption-Innovation: In the Context of Diversity and Change, Routledge*, 2003 (repr. 2011), 323 ff.

determination of the negotiable issues, the initiator-leader would be able to better and more effectively prepare the function of the Prenegotiation forum and to build its expectation in a workable pragmatic perspective.

3 THE MULTILATERAL GOVERNANCE LEVEL

3.1 *Institutional Organization and Management of the Prenegotiation Process*

At the multilateral governance level, Prenegotiation develops as a multilateral conferential negotiation that, if the initiator-leader is a state, or even a small group of states, facing a *primae impressionis* or an inadequately dealt with problem situation, is normally structurally organized as an Ad Hoc Multilateral Conference. At this level, the responsible initiator leader should organize and conduct the negotiation of the declarative textual product of this phase within the framework of an appropriately structured Ad Hoc Multilateral Conference, ensuring the negotiation's completeness and effectiveness, as well as the necessary publicity of the outcome of the Prenegotiation (declarative text and process pursuing ICI). In doing so, the initiator-leader should employ specific management techniques of the Ad Hoc Multilateral Conference: drawing up a supporting report, drafting a single negotiating text, and preparing the agenda of its meetings.[25] On the other hand, Prenegotiation, at this level, may be scaled, because this is required by the nature of the subject, the complexity of the problem situation, the interactive operation of the context of reference, and the impact of the progressing scientific knowledge. Such a scaled Prenegotiation phase may consist of a series of Ad Hoc Multilateral Conferences on the particular subject matter, each of them producing its own, but interrelated, declarative instrument which may progressively build the bridge towards the Constitutive Negotiation phase.[26]

[25] A notable example is provided by the Multilateral Conference on the Environment on the Causes and Prevention of Damage to Forests and Waters by Air Pollution in Europe, organized by the Government of the Federal Republic of Germany in cooperation with the Executive Secretary of the UN/ECE (Munich, 24–27 June 1984), which dealt, for the first time, with the problem of acid rain.

[26] E.g., the scaled Prenegotiation process as reflected in the 1984 Bremen Ministerial Declaration, the 1987 London Ministerial Declaration, and the 1987 Hague Ministerial Declaration of the International Conferences on the Protection of the North Sea, which cumulatively led to the constitutive negotiation of the OSPAR Convention, 1992; see Ministerial Declarations: International Conferences on the Protection of the North Sea. Bremen, Germany, 1984, London, United Kingdom 1987, The Hague, The Netherlands, 1990, available at: www.ospar.org/site/assets/files/1239/declarations_compilation_1995.pdf. See, also, the multiple declarative instruments of the Prenegotiation phase of the Framework Convention on Climate Change (FCCC), 1992, that include the 1989 Hague Declaration on the Environment (the Hague Summit, 11 March 1989), the 1989 Noordijk Ministerial Declaration on Atmospheric Pollution and Climate Change (the Ministerial Conference on Atmospheric Pollution and Climate Change, Noordijk, 6–7 November 1989), and the 1990 Ministerial Declaration (the Second World Climate Conference, Geneva, Switzerland, 29 October–7 November 1990).

3.1.1 Structure and Function of Ad Hoc Multilateral Conference

The advantages of an Ad Hoc Multilateral Conference emanate from its three interrelated but distinct aspects: *its tiered structure, its comprehensive negotiating approach and management of the subject-matter*, and *the collective framing of its declarative product.*

Regarding its tiered structure, the Ad Hoc Multilateral Conference may be organized as a conferential negotiation of two steps: as a Preparatory Conference and as a Multilateral Conference. The Preparatory Conference constitutes a diplomatic conference preparing the Multilateral Conference: it is organized by the initiator-leader at an adequate diplomatic level of state representation (plenipotentiaries), with the participation of representatives of relevant international organizations, other international institutional entities (e.g., Secretariats of relevant conventional [treaty] regimes), or relevant nongovernmental entities (NGOs, socioeconomic actors, the scientific community, or public entities and territorial communities as appropriate), and it is responsible for negotiating the drawing up of the draft declarative text and the preparation of the formal Multilateral Conference. Thus, the necessary collective tone, embracing transparency and community perspectives, is set for the organization as well for the shared textual outcome of the Multilateral Conference that follows. The subject of the Preparatory Conference is usually simple and well defined. It specifically refers to:

- The establishment of a Drafting Group which is entrusted with the negotiating drafting of the text of the draft-declarative/decisional instrument of the Multilateral Conference.
- The preparation of the organizational matters and procedural issues of the Multilateral Conference in cooperation with the initiator-leader (e.g., creation of working groups, establishment of a drafting group for the preparation of the decisions of the Multilateral Conference, election of the bureau of the Multilateral Conference, report of the chair of the Drafting Group, determination of the original language/s of the conferences and of the working language).[27]
- The drawing-up of the draft provisional Agenda of the Multilateral Conference and of its Final Communiqué.

The Multilateral Conference is convened by the initiator-leader within a reasonable period of time (usually after the lapse of a few months after the Preparatory Conference) and at the highest possible level of representation of the participating states (e.g., ministerial level or director-general level in a government department),

[27] It would be quite useful if, from the outset, a distinction was made between the official/original languages of the Ad Hoc Multilateral Conference (Preparatory and Multilateral Conference) and the working language (normally English) of the Drafting Group in which the declarative text and other textual products of the Conference will be formulated.

International Organizations (General Secretaries, Executive Directors), international institutional entities (Secretaries /Coordinators of international conventional [treaty] regimes), and nongovernmental entities – stakeholders – Chief Executive Officers, Directors) that participated in the Preparatory Meeting. Organized on the platform already determined by the Preparatory Conference, it deals with:

- The adoption of the draft provisional agenda drawn up and proposed by the Preparatory Conference, which contains organizational and procedural matters, the draft-declarative/decisional textual outcome of the Conference, as well as social events organized by the initiator-leader.
- The confirmation of the established Drafting Group in order to continue and complete the negotiating drafting of the draft-declarative/decisional instrument to be submitted for adoption by the Multilateral Conference.
- The discussion and adoption of the draft-declarative/decisional instrument and of the draft of the Final Communiqué.

Through its two-tiered structure, the Ad Hoc Multilateral Conference ensures a comprehensive negotiating approach and management of the Prenegotiation subject as well as a collectively generated creative framing of its declarative outcome. Its importance lies in the fact that it embodies the interplay of three catalytic factors: the adequate political weight and, at the same time, the efficient expert examination of the scientific, legal, and policy issues involved at two successive and gradated negotiating levels; also, the appropriate relational modality provides an opportunity for a continuous and effective communication of attitudes and perceptions in a negotiation of low tones favouring the comprehensive and dialectical learning opportunity of the issues. The interplay of these factors may generate the construction of an ICI relation of declarative character.

Thus, since the Ad Hoc Multilateral Conference constitutes a forum for a Diplomatic Conference, it is plunged into the world of political reality. As is obvious, the participating high-level representatives of states, endowed with a pragmatic sense of the political conditions on which ICI may be pursued and constructed, are able to "communicate" the specific views and the related collective-individual interests of their states to the fullest possible extent. The community perspective is also brought into the negotiation process by the consideration of the views expressed by the participating international institutional entities and the relevant nongovernmental entities. Moreover, due to its two-tiered structure, the Ad Hoc Multilateral Conference directs all negotiating participants to deal with the same issues in two successive levels of different political intensity (from an initial lower to a negotiated higher level) and in a comprehensive and integrated manner. More specifically, at the Preparatory Conference, the lower political representation facilitates the focusing on the negotiating designing and integrated approach to the specific scientific-technical, legal, policy, and community issues that form the Prenegotiation subject. In doing so, it provides an adequate and appropriate space for the experts of all delegations to discuss, in a constructive, more informed, and less politically motivated atmosphere, the substantive aspects of the issues involved, which is not blind to the details. At the formal Multilateral Conference – run under the weight of the political responsibility of the high-level representatives of states, the authority and competence of international organizations/international institutional entities, and the socio-economic and technical weight of non-state entities – the textual negotiation process is completed in the framework of a pragmatic, transparent, and integrated interdisciplinary Prenegotiation designing while "fully-blooded" by the political acceptance of the high-level participants.

Furthermore, the Ad Hoc Multilateral Conference ensures a remarkable degree of appropriate relational modality: the opportunity for a gradated, continuous, comprehensive, and all-level communication of the common, converging, or diverging views of the negotiating participants in pursuance of a purposeful framing of the transformative management of the problem situation in terms of declaring an ICI relation. In other words, the degree of appropriate relational modality is determined by a structurally generated and context-dependent movement from "individualistic framings" of the problem situation to a "collective framing" of an elastic ICI relation. In this process, negotiation develops on a low-profile scale that favours the enlightenment and "dialectical learning" of the total set of issues constituting aspects of the pursued ICI relation. It provides the opportunity for a holistic approach to the multilateral construction of a transformative cooperative framework, where, from the outset, all relevant participants are substantially involved, including the scientific community, which may be vested a role resembling an ombudsman for the international community.[28] At the same time, it "transfuses blood" to an intermediate relational platform that "indicates" the possibility of transcending the established relation into a prospective ICI treaty regime within the specific context.[29]

3.1.2 The Techniques of Managing Ad Hoc Multilateral Conference

Convening the Ad Hoc Multilateral Conference, the initiator-leader of the Prenegotiation should operate on two interconnected levels:

[28] As it particularly happens to issues related to international environmental negotiations. See G. Sjostedt, "Negotiation on Trade and the Environment: Variation in the Multilateral Approach," in V. A. Kremenyuk (ed.), *International Negotiation: Analysis, Approaches, Issues*, 2nd edn, Jossey-Bass: A Wiley Company, 2002, 362, 372.

[29] E. Raftopoulos, "International Environmental Negotiation as a Governance Technique," in E. Raftopoulos and M. L. McConnell (eds.), *Contributions to International Environmental Negotiation in the Mediterranean Context*, 21. Generally, on the character of Prenegotiation as a learning opportunity, see P. T. Hopmann, *The Negotiation Process and the Resolution of International Conflicts*, University of Chicago Press, 1996, 179ff.; J. Cross, "Negotiation as Adaptive Learning," 1 *International Negotiation* (1996), 1ff.; B. I. Spector, *Negotiation as Learning: Pedagogy and Theory*. A paper in Honor of Bill Zartman. Presented at the Annual Conference of the International Studies Association, 2 March 2007, Chicago.

- At the substantive level, which refers to the *drafting of a supporting report* dealing with the issues under negotiation, as well as to the *drafting of a single negotiating text* setting out the negotiable elements of the intended declaration/ decision, etc.
- At the procedural level, which involves the systematic *drafting of the agenda* of the ad hoc multilateral conference.

Drafting a Supporting Report. The drafting of a supporting report regarding the problem situation and the issues of Prenegotiation represents the first exclusive task of the initiator-leader. The supporting report, based on the diagnostic thematic management that was analysed earlier, should be organized as a comprehensive, well-established, and well-structured study, so that all possible aspects of the issues under negotiation, including procedural issues, will be illuminated. The drafting of the report should be combined with the drafting of a single negotiating text of the negotiable declarative instrument. Thus, the recipient participants will be supplied with all the necessary information that would justify the need to negotiate the creation of a declarative instrument for collective action, highlighting the special field of ICI development.

More specifically, the supporting report may contain the following elements:

- An extensive analysis of the problem situation under negotiation, indicating the scope and importance of the problem situation, its causes and effects, the level of the relevant scientific knowledge and evidence, the current institutional and legal management of the problem situation at the national and international levels, the policy and science interface on the development of appropriate and adequate approaches to such management, or its potentially shaping trends.
- Suggestions for undertaking effective collective action, highlighting the need for developing international cooperation between state participants within a framework of ICI governance with the appropriate involvement of all relevant non-state actors, the systematization of information exchange so that the specific field of developing national and international actions will be determined, and procedures for the appropriate dissemination of scientific evidence and innovative research findings.

Drafting a Single Negotiating Text. At the same time, the task of drafting an adequately justified general draft instrument of a declarative character to provide a basis for negotiation, or, alternatively, a text containing the desirable elements to be included in such an instrument, requires particular care and attention since the choice of either of them is directly related to a proper political evaluation of the problem situation by the initiator-leader. In fact, the approach and application of a single negotiation text in the Prenegotiation process is an important procedural device for building and strengthening the necessary relational problem-solving attitude of the negotiating participants. All the way through the two-tiered Ad Hoc

Multilateral Conference, negotiation focuses on a single, open-ended negotiating declarative instrument that provides the basis for integrating the plurality of their interests and views of the negotiating participants into a progressively built text, procedurally or substantially, identifying their common interest. As a result, the destructive textual plurality is prevented and the procedure of inventing options is more focused and simplified, while a better opportunity is offered to the negotiating participants to realize their role as problem solvers. On the other hand, the choice of the form of the textual medium (a draft declarative instrument or, merely, drafting the elements for such an instrument) requires a careful and informed political decision by the initiator-leader, evaluating the reality of the Ad Hoc Multilateral Conference, the degree of its working flexibility, and the magnitude of the risks involved in such a choice.

The technical tool complementing the drafting of a single negotiating text, which enables its operation as an all-embracing process of continuously clarifying common interest, is the system of brackets. In practice, the single negotiating text procedure is linked with an initial paratactic formulation of the plurality of the interests involved "put in brackets," with a view to reach, through negotiated reductions and merging, a clear text of common interest, based on consensus and embodying plurality in a single accepted formulation. As is explained in the next chapter, the system of brackets signals the text gestation period related to the shaping and consolidating of its common interest formulation.

Drafting an Agenda. At the procedural level, the technique of drafting the agenda of the Ad Hoc Multilateral Conference provides those elements that, in their totality and in view of the nature of Prenegotiation, may effectively contribute to the successful operation of this conference. Reflecting its organizational basis and outlining the framework for a productive Prenegotiation process, the agenda needs to be drawn up in a manner specific to the nature of Prenegotiation and to ensure, to the greatest extent possible, the efficiency of its conferential conduct. The agenda may be accompanied by general information concerning the organizational details and the venue of the negotiating Conference.[30]

When drafting the agenda, the initiator-leader should carefully concentrate on the formulation of the following elements: the purpose of the Conference, its thematic design, the time period or the pace of the two conferential steps, and the personalities of the negotiating participants.[31] Thus, the determination and formulation of the purpose requires careful consideration because it should attract the largest possible number of negotiating participants holding subjective framings of

30 According to more recent practice, the initiator-leader may also send a concise message to the invited participants, adapted to the needs and perspectives of the particular Prenegotiation, which precedes the agenda.

31 Often referred to as the "4 Ps": Purpose, Plan, Pace, and the Personalities of the preparations for the launching of negotiations in general. See, e.g., B. Scott, *The Skills of Negotiating*, Wildwood House, 1986, 18ff.

the problem situation, so that they will be actively involved in the negotiable construction of the Prenegotiation product. Moving towards this direction, the initiator-leader should articulate the purpose clearly, in simple terms and as succinctly as possible. Organized in accordance with the particular requirements of the Preparatory and Multilateral Conferences and reflecting their realities, the thematic design refers to a limited number of issues, substantive and especially procedural as mentioned earlier, set out in the most neutral manner and in a determinate order and with the aim to be cumulatively conducive towards the successful outcome of Prenegotiation, thus opening a new window in the collective effort to transform the problem situation. In this way, negotiating the transformation or the ICI "reframing" of the problem situation becomes negotiably manageable. Both elements, the determination of the purpose and the thematic design, express the first step in shaping the Prenegotiation strategy of the initiator-leader, and for this reason their articulation requires the proper involvement of the legal and technical experts who would compose their own delegation. The time period for each of the two confer-ential steps of the Ad Hoc Multilateral Conference should be limited (two to three days for the Preparatory and two days for the Multilateral Conference – a vertical limitation) and the time between them should ideally range from three to five months (a horizontal limitation). In fact, an efficiently organized Prenegotiation is also related to a full assessment of the importance of its time horizon by the initiator-leader, that is, the appropriate synchronization of the effective negotiation of the thematic design with the programmed time limit, vertical and horizontal, of the two-tiered structure of the Ad Hoc Multilateral Conference.

Finally, the fourth and more delicate element, the personalities of the negotiating participants denoting the subjective aspect of the agenda, requires particular attention. An effective way to fruitfully deal with the subjective aspect of the agenda is to approach its drafting on the basis of Maslow's theory of hierarchy of needs, which is imperceptibly followed by international negotiating practice in this regard.[32] Thus, in order to motivate the active participation and creative contribution of in the Ad Hoc Multilateral Conference, the initiator-leader should diligently ensure that all five hierarchically successive layers of human needs of Maslow's pyramid are efficiently met, from the lowest to the highest. According to Maslow's theory, meeting the needs of a higher layer presupposes that the needs of the immediate lower layer are being effectively met. Starting from the satisfaction of the basic need of "survival" or "physiological need" which lies at the bottom of the hierarchical layers of needs, and proceeding through the satisfaction of the successive layers of the needs for "safety," "socialization-belonging," and "individuality-esteem," the fulfilment of the top need, that of "self-realization and creativity" or, more holistically, of "self-transcendence," may

[32] A. H. Maslow, *Motivation and Personality*, Harper, 1954.

be attained.[33] By transposing the logic of Maslow's hierarchy of needs onto the organizational handling of the Ad Hoc Multilateral Conference, the initiator-leader can reap more creativity from the negotiating participants. Creativity or self-transcendence (top need) requires that the former ensures that all underlying needs are effectively and efficiently being met. And it is obvious that the first three layers of needs (physiological needs, safety needs, and socialization-belonging needs, called "deficiency needs"), being of a purely organizational character, can easily be treated by the initiator-leader with a high degree of success. Taking steps regarding the best possible accommodation, security, transportation, and reception of the delegations as well as the organization of social events, side events, excursions, visits, educational tours, etc. constitutes adequate means of meeting the physiological needs, safety needs, and socialization-belonging needs, and may be clearly reflected, as programmatic actions, in the agenda or described in the general information accompanying the agenda.

On the other hand, meeting the top layer of needs (self-realization and creativity/self-transcendence), called "growth need," is not associated with the drafting of the agenda but with an individuality-informed management by the initiator-leader as a chairperson conducting the negotiation at the Ad Hoc Multilateral Conference. This requires taking care about the actual convergence of attitudes and practices related to the individuality of the participant in order to trigger his creative confidence. Thus, in view of the delicate, but also flexible, nature of the Prenegotiation process, the initiator-leader should operate at two interrelated levels: at the level of an overall respect for the individuality of the negotiating participants and at the level of providing for them all the necessary material and communication facilities.

At the level of respect for individuality, the initiator-leader should carefully deal with three aspects of respect: intra-negotiation respect (respect for the individual views, positions, or proposals of the negotiating participant as well as the possibility of a measure of their recognition), outer-negotiation hierarchical respect (respect shown to the negotiating participant by his hierarchical superiors or by a government or state agency – which independently influences the negotiation and to whom he is accountable – in relation to the degree to which the objectives set before the beginning of the conference have been achieved), and self-respect (the personal measure of achieving positive results in the negotiation). All three aspects of respect converge on the same result: the recognition of a space allowing him to achieve a "positive sign" in the pursuance of his individual objectives at the Prenegotiation – something that is desirable and feasible and, unlike the other two phases of negotiation process, can be much more easily accommodated in view of the political-programmatic character of the Conference outcome. At the level of the

[33] For an interesting notion of the top need, later developed by Maslow, which goes beyond his initial concept of "self-actualization" and embraces a more holistic level relating to the relational cosmos, see A. H. Maslow, *The Farther Reaches of Human Nature*, 1971, Viking Press, 269. In fact, the notion of "self-transcendence" clearly implies a space for developing an ICI consciousness.

material and communication facilities, the initiator-leader should consistently provide for the negotiating participant all those particular organizational facilities that are necessary for his creative involvement in the negotiating conference. Thus, the general information accompanying the agenda should list the venue for a press conference, an operational centre equipped with computers, Internet access, printers, and photocopy machines, and the allocation of rooms for bilateral or informal meetings.

All in all, the initiator-leader, by meeting the requirements of the self-realization and creativity of the individual negotiating participant and securing a positive sign in his negotiating function, effectively serves the advantages flowing from his instrumental role. That is, he exceeds the lowest common denominator of the states involved in this process and supports an overall creative momentum, but also unleashes individual transcendence (self-transcendence) towards developing ICI approaches, standards, and actions for the collective governance of the transformation of the problematic situation.

3.2 *The Patternment of the Content of Declarative Instruments*

The declarative outcome of the Prenegotiation process, generated by an Ad Hoc Multilateral Conference, displays pattern formation in its structure as well as in its content. The patternment of declarative instruments is a distillate of consistent international practice, it reflects the distinctive textuality aspect of Prenegotiation, and its knowledge is particularly useful for the negotiating participant.

The structure of declarations/decisions/action plans etc. of Prenegotiation is simple, consisting of two interrelated parts, the "considering part" and the "ordering part."[34] The "considering part" shapes the justificatory basis of the ordering part and comprises the negotiated referential context, the pragmatic and normative landscape within which the declarative instrument is generated and drawn. Its content is thematically standardized ad minimum, and its negotiation is focused on the agreed formulation of concrete "evaluative-justificatory" collective judgments, introduced in the form of the present participle indicating continuity.[35]

[34] The various declarative instruments may be indicatively formulated as a Conference Resolution (e.g., the Munich Resolution of 27 June 1984 of the Multilateral Conference on the Causes and Prevention of Damage to Forests and Waters by Air Pollution in Europe that led to the 1985 Helsinki Protocol on the Reduction of Sulphur Emissions or their Transboundary Fluxes by at least 30 percent), as a Ministerial Declaration (e.g., the 1989 Noordijk Ministerial Declaration on Climate Change that was a critical milestone on the road to the establishment of the FCCC regime, and the 1990 Ministerial Declaration of the Second World Climate Conference [Geneva, Switzerland, 29 October–7 November 1990] that called for the urgent negotiation of the FCCC), or as an Action Plan (e.g., the Mediterranean Action Plan, 1975, that provided the platform for the development of the 1976 Barcelona Convention for the Protection of the Mediterranean Against Pollution).

[35] The most commonly used such present participles include "recognizing," "acknowledging," "taking into account," "noting," "considering," "convinced," "recalling," "deeply concerned," "conscious," "welcoming," "aware of," etc.

These evaluative-justificatory collective judgments may basically refer to "precipitating events," the level of scientific/technological knowledge related to the theme of the declarative instrument, the existing relevant normative field, any existing or developing relevant international or national practice or actions, and the recognition of the special role of the negotiating participants in the management of this instrument.

More specifically, they may refer to:

- The recognition of the events occurring forcibly and dramatically and bringing about important changes in relations, situations, knowledge, technology, and nature within the realm of an existing paradigm or beyond it (precipitating events).
- The level of the existing scientific and technical knowledge related to the issues to be addressed by the declarative or decisional instrument and the need for its further advancement for better understanding of these issues and for developing, where suitable, more holistic, interdisciplinary, and sustainable approaches.
- The existing normative field of these issues usually consisting of: relevant treaties, in force or not yet in force or still under negotiation, decisions of international organizations, relevant international instruments of a declarative-programmatic character (Guidelines, Strategies, Principles, Codes of Conduct, Action Plans, Agendas, Goals, etc.) originating either from multilateral international conferences or from international organizations, and, possibly, relevant legislative instruments produced in advanced domestic orders currently in force.
- Any existing or developing international or national practices or actions related to the problematic issues (practices and actions in the framework of international organizations, among states or at the national level).
- The recognition of the special role of the participating states, international organizations, or other international institutional entities or non-state actors entities regarding the management of these issues.
- The recognition of developing states' need for assistance so that they can participate effectively and equitably in the transformative governance effort and future developments.

The "ordering part" constitutes the main body of the declarative instrument. It configures, through negotiation and consensus attainment, the specific application field of the considering part in the form of collective "performatives" indicating the different levels of collective (multilateral or organizational) as well as individual programmatic actions of the participants: more generally, the declarative governance of the subject of declaration for the protection and promotion of ICI. The negotiation at this level focuses on the determination of specific ordering terms of programmatic character introduced by typical, standardly used, verbs of performative force and formulated in present tense.[36] The ordering terms, the content of which is also thematically standardized ad minimum, refer to the need to take action at specifically determined levels such as:

- Intensification of international cooperation through specific horizontal actions so that the common management of the issues will be launched or improved (consultations, elaboration and development of common strategies, taking of interim measures, exchange of information, further involvement of relevant international organizations or other international institutional entities for appropriate action, promotion and reinforcement of means of international control of issues contained in the declarative instrument or/and of the declarative instrument itself, acceleration of ratification of relevant international agreements or pursuance of their more effective and efficient implementation).
- Intensification and improvement – or undertaking – of specific vertical actions at the domestic level relating to procedures, legal or administrative measures and technical standards that promote the purpose of the declarative instrument and concur or are compatible with related horizontal actions of international cooperation enhancing their application.
- Application of general principles and of the relevant guiding approaches (like, e.g., the ecosystem approach, the integrated approach, and, more recently, the science-based approach, using the best available scientific information and knowledge, including traditional knowledge).
- Cooperation in research and technology.
- Identification of linkages with other topics of international governance for a more integrated, efficient, and socially supported operation of the declarative instrument.
- Systematization of integrated governance in the framework of the declarative instrument, ensuring coordination of all competent international organizations in the field of its operation and development of cooperative structures with relevant stakeholders, especially with those who are influential, and submission of progress reports.
- Organization of information and communication regarding the scientific community and media for the broader scientific discussion and promotion of the purpose and object of the declarative instrument and the effective dissemination of the relevant information to the public (international scientific conferences, academic symposia or workshops, open discussions in the media), or

[36] The standardly used performative verbs include "adopt," "request," "note," "invite," "decide," "encourage," "develop," "recommend," "support," "propose," "take effective action," etc.

even the promotion of translated versions of relevant innovative legislative instruments.[37]

- An assessment of the value and significance of establishing a relevant conventional regime (a treaty) performing ICI in the future, covering the issues of the declarative instrument, in the light of other voluntary rather than legally binding options, while affirming a contextual coherence and complementarity with regard to existing relevant international ordering.

Thematically, the borderline between the considering part and the ordering part is thin and flexible. Depending on the particular nature of the subject of the declarative instrument and the intricacies of its negotiation, some aspects of either part may cross the negotiating line and join the ordering part (like the special role of the participating states or international organizations) or the considering part (like the identification of linkages with other topics of international governance or the significance of establishing a relevant treaty regime), respectively. Or, in certain contexts, the declarative instrument may take a simple form integrating both parts into a comprehensive narrative text of causes, approaches, judgments, actions and commitments[38]

If the initiator-leader of the Prenegotiation is an international organization, the content of the declarative instrument may be adapted to the special requirements of the organization. Thus, the declaration may be incorporated as an annex to the decision or resolution of the international organization adopting it. In this case, the decision and the annexed declaration constitute an integral whole to the effect that both the evaluative-justificatory collective judgments and the collective performatives associated with the purpose of the declaration are stratified, apart from the annexed declaration, into the considering and ordering parts of the decision. Moreover, such decisions or resolutions are addressed to the member states and, also, to the whole system of collective institutional entities and nongovernmental entities considered relevant for the launching of transformative declarative governance and a meaningful engineering of ICI with respect to a particular international problem.

37 As was the unofficial translation of the US Foreign Corrupt Practices Act, 1977, into forty-nine languages (including Greek), accessed via the electronic links of the website of the US Department of Justice, with a view to broadening general information on this subject. This law, the first of its kind, was the background to the development, step by step, of major international arrangements on the subject. This last point is also well reflected in the impact of the UK Climate Change Act, 2008, a pioneering piece of comprehensive legislation that "offered lessons" on how climate change legislation should be best structured to be effective, and helped the United Kingdom to create a sustained international campaign on climate change and play a leadership role in the negotiating process that has progressively led to the Paris Agreement on Climate Change, 2015, while inspiring other states.

38 See, e.g., The Ilulissat Declaration, Arctic Ocean Conference, Ilulissat, Greenland, 27–29 May 2008. Arctic Council (2008), Ilulissat Declaration.

A characteristic example is the UN Declaration against Corruption and Bribery in International Commercial Transactions annexed to its Resolution 51/191 of 16 December 1996. The Resolution invites member states to take appropriate measures and cooperate at all levels; requests the Economic and Social Council and its subsidiary bodies, in particular the Commission on Crime Prevention and Criminal Justice, to examine ways, including through binding international instruments, to further the implementation of the Declaration; invites other bodies of the UN system, including UNCTAD, to take appropriate action and promote the objectives of the Resolution and the Declaration; and encourages private and public corporations, including transnational corporations, to cooperate in the effective implementation of the Declaration.[39] Regarding the ordering part of the Decision, emphasis is given to the progress report to be prepared by the Secretary-General of the UN concerning the application of the Declaration and the measures taken by the member states, the organization itself, and other relevant international organizations or institutional entities. Relatedly, the ordering part of the annexed Declaration takes a more organizational-governance-specific turn, focusing on specific actions between the member states of the UN and on the limits of these actions, but also on the determination of the key concepts and principles of the Declaration.[40] Importantly, this Declaration provided the relational platform and the ordering effect for the transition to the UN Convention against Corruption, 2003.[41] And it had a general transition systemic effect in regard to the development of the OECD Convention on Combating Bribery of Foreign Public Officials in International Business Transactions, 1997.[42]

Finally, if the negotiating participants consider that a more form-specific application of the declaration is desirable and necessary, in order to instil a more official performative commitment into the programmatic realm of the declarative instrument, then they may proceed a step further: by incorporating detailed

39 Ibid.

40 Ibid.

41 Together with the International Code of Conduct of Public Officials adopted by UN Resolution 51/59 of 12 December 1996 and annexed to it, GA Res. 51/59, UN Doc. A/RES/51/59 (12 December 1996).

42 Among numerous examples of declarative instruments generated by international institutional entities and producing such transition effects, worth mentioning are the UNEP Guidelines on Environmental Impact Assessment, 1987, (UNEP/GC14/25 [1987]) endorsed by GA Res. 42/184 (UN GAOR, 42nd Sess., UN Doc. A/Res/42/184 [1987]) ("UNEP EIA Goals and Principles"), which were subsequently incorporated in the ECE Convention on Environmental Impact Assessment in a Transboundary Context, 1991; or the Cairo Guidelines and Principles for the Environmentally Sound Management of Hazardous Wastes, 1987, adopted by UNEP Governing Council by decision 14/30 of 17 June 1987, which provided the basis for the constitutive negotiation of the Basel Convention on the Control of Transboundary Movements of Hazardous Wastes and Their Disposal, 1989; or the UN/ECE Guidelines on Access to Environmental Information and Public Participation in Environmental Decision-Making, endorsed at the Third Ministerial Conference "Environment for Europe" in Sofia, Bulgaria, 1995 (ECE/CEP/24), and on which the Aarhus Convention on Access to Information, Public Participation in Decision-Making and Access to Justice in Environmental Matters, 1998, was built in the framework of the UNECE.

implementative annexes,[43] programme of action/strategy[44] or by linking the declarative instrument with a Memorandum of Understanding (MOU). In the latter case, the attached MOU embodies the common declarative will of the participants in the declarative instrument, vested in the form of a "performative political agreement," appropriately patterned,[45] which may include the following elements:

- Purpose and scope of cooperation.
- Basic arrangements: statement of principles, cooperative activities, interim management measures, authorities/national contact points for the purposes of the MOU, review activities, availability of resources – which can be further and variably specified in attached annexes.
- Entry of application and denunciation.
- Settlement of disputes by negotiation.

It is worth noting that the MOU is to be signed separately from the declaration.

4 THE OUTCOME OF PRENEGOTIATION

The finalized text of the declarative instrument is adopted by the Ad Hoc Multilateral Conference by consensus. To reach this concluding stage, the chair of the drafting group reports to the plenary session of the conference on the final version of the negotiated draft text of the declarative instrument, and if the text is "clear" without any "bracketed" wording, then the conference proceeds to confirm its finalization and declare its formal adoption. If, on the other hand, the submitted draft text, despite its meticulous negotiation at the drafting group level, retains a term or phrases in brackets due to their perceived important political connotations and implications requiring, as a result, an authoritative decision at the level of the conference plenary, then the conference undertakes to negotiate their treatment in the draft text in order to adopt it by consensus. Together with the draft declarative instrument, the conference approves the draft of the final communiqué, drawn up by the Preparatory Conference, to which the former is to be annexed. The final communiqué has a similar function to the final act to which a treaty is attached that is adopted by a diplomatic conference, culminating in the completion of the

43 E.g., the 1984 Bremen Ministerial Declaration and the 1987 London Ministerial Declaration of the International Conferences on the Protection of the North Sea, which provided an evolving platform for the constitutive negotiation of the OSPAR Convention 1992, *Ministerial Declarations*, supra note 26.

44 E.g., the 1993 Vienna Declaration and Programme of Action. Also, the 1991 Rovaniemi Declaration on the Protection of Arctic Environment and Arctic Environmental Protection Strategy.

45 Generally, for the nature, use, and importance of MOUs in international practice and their diverse status in international law, see A. Aust, *Modern Treaty Law and Practice* (3rd edn), Cambridge University Press, 2013, 28–54. An example of such a performative political arrangement is the Adoption of Agreements on Environment and Development – Non-Legally Binding Authoritative Statement of Principles for a Global Consensus on the Management, Conservation and Sustainable Development of all Types of Forests, adopted in 1992 by the UN Conference on Environment and Development.

constituent negotiating process while opening the period of treaty signature. Like the final act of the treaty, the final communiqué of the declarative instrument contains a succinct narration of the conferential negotiation process and its decisions. It records the organization of the Ad Hoc Multilateral Conference and the substance of the discussions within its framework, and it makes specific reference to the general political positions expressed by the ministers or other high-level representatives of the participating states, the views supported by international organizations or other stakeholders, but also the common approaches and positions adopted by the conference as a whole. According to international practice, the final communiqué is signed by the ministers or other high-level representatives of the participating states, but also by the participating international organizations.

On the other hand, the final communiqué of a declarative instrument should be clearly differentiated from the various communiqués that constitute the periodic decisions taken in the framework of certain international institutional groupings pursuing their collective interest, such as the Commonwealth, the G8 Summits or the G20 Summits. Being organized at the highest level of representation (state leaders) for attaining the highest possible policy coherence between them and a more general communicative impact on selectively prioritized international issues, these international institutional entities or groupings operate as distinct frameworks of powerful unincorporated associations projecting the undertaking of regularly reviewed political commitments. As a result, the generated communiqués reflect policy decisions based on collective evaluations and expressing the common positions, the principles, and the concrete steps of action that the leaders commit themselves to pursue for a specific period of time.[46]

And a last point. If the declarative instrument is adopted in the framework of an international organization acting as the initiator-leader of the Prenegotiation process, then the procedure is differentiated. It is the organization's full representation and highest authority organ, the conference or the assembly of its members, which takes by consensus a special decision or resolution on the adoption of the declarative instrument (declaration, code of conduct, etc.) that is attached to it as an annex.

46 For instance, the Commonwealth Heads of Government Meeting (CHGM) Communiqué, 17 November 2013, refers to the confirmation of the basic values of the Commonwealth, the common positions, and the steps to be followed, in a framework of promoting ICI, with regard to a wide range of interrelated issues concerning sustainable development, biodiversity, and international trade and investment vis-à-vis the G20, and to the confirmation of their political commitment to listed political values, to listed areas of global threats and challenges, and to areas of cooperation and organization of the Commonwealth. Also the G8 Final Communiqué, Lough Erne, 17–18 June 2013, refers to the selection of three specific areas on which the G8 will take specific actions (trade, tax systems, transparency), but also to actions on broader issues, such as food security and nutrition, climate change, terrorism, and foreign policy, whereas a summary declaration of ten points with concrete actions is linked with this communiqué.

4

The Constitutive Negotiation Phase as a Process of Constructing Treaties of International Common Interest

1 OVERVIEW

The Constitutive phase of the international negotiation process refers to the inter-subjective establishment of an international conventional (treaty) regime of ICI or to the new protocol expansion of such a conventional regime in an operative consistency with the context of polycentric international ordering. It is the negotiating process whereby a new treaty or a new protocol related to it are "constituted" as normative activities pursuing the protection and promotion of ICI on a consensual basis and by reference to their context. The product generated by Prenegotiation is part of this context; however, the transition from the Prenegotiation phase to the Constitutive Negotiation phase is unfailingly nonlinear: it is further linked to the efficient management of a variety of contextual factors (e.g., effective communication of the advancing relevant scientific knowledge, integrating technological progress, maturation in the applicability of certain relevant legal concepts, proper mobilization of non-state actors, effective dissemination of information) that need to be related to the declarative governance platform produced by Prenegotiation. Constitutive Negotiation systematically unfolds from more institutive processes of constituting ICI treaty regimes (initiating processes, consensus procedure, rules of procedure) to the more legislative constructive processes of constituting ICI treaty regimes that refer to their textual patternment (referential patternment, morphological patternment, and normative patternment). On the other hand, Constitutive Negotiation may properly make use of certain methodical elements of the diagnostic level of Prenegotiation, especially those referring to the management of knowledge and the management of subjective framings (relational governance structure), which were analysed in the previous chapter. Furthermore, distinctive techniques and practices of textual negotiation, which may be variably applied to all phases of negotiation, creatively contribute to the progress of negotiation and the consensus-building of the ICI treaty relation, exhibiting either an organizational character (opening statements, brainstorming sessions, inter-sessional workshops or meetings, side-events) or a textual one (the system of brackets, the recording of the names of participants in the reports of the meetings or conferences, non-negotiation texts, or non-papers).

2 INITIATION AND INSTITUTIONAL ORGANIZATION OF CONSTITUTIVE NEGOTIATION

2.1 *The Political Initiative*

The initiation of the Constitutive Negotiation phase is the result of a distinct international political initiative emanating from a multilateral action expressed by a declaration of a group of states, from an institutional action expressed by a decision of an international organization, or from a conventional regime action expressed in a decision of its supreme organ. More specifically:

- It may be undertaken by a group of states in which the state that acted as initiator-leader in the Prenegotiation phase, galvanizing the transition to the Constitutive Negotiation phase, is normally included. This multilateral action may also involve cooperation with a competent international organization, and possibly includes the participation of other relevant institutional entities. It rests on a co-decision that takes the form of a declaration and refers to the formal launching of the negotiation process leading to the creation of a treaty regime.
- It may also be undertaken by an international organization that enjoys a generally recognized global prestige and is vested with competence on the matter under negotiation, and that may also have acted as initiator-leader in the Prenegotiation phase. This organizational action may also involve cooperation with states, and possibly includes the participation of other relevant international organizations. It rests on a decision taken by the plenary organ exercising the highest authoritative governance in the international organization, mandating its secretariat to organize the relevant negotiating body.
- Finally, when an expansion of the treaty regime is to be carried out through specifying protocols, anticipated (as specifications of framework provisions of the treaty) or implied (as generated from the purpose of the treaty or from principled approaches formulated in the treaty), the launching of Constitutive Negotiation stems from an inner-regime action. It rests on a decision of the ad hoc plenary organ exercising the highest authoritative governance in the treaty regime, mandating the secretariat of the treaty regime to organize the relevant negotiating body for the possible establishment of a new related protocol.

2.2 *The Negotiation-Generating Decision*

As indicated earlier, all three aspects of political initiative rest on a collective decision generating the formal launch of Constitutive Negotiation, the negotiation-generating decision, which is structured on three distinctive elements:

- *Referential elements*: The negotiation-generating decision may make reference to previous "declarative" instruments collectively reached in the Prenegotiation phase and ranging from declarations and decisions to action plans, strategies, or guidelines. These declarative outcomes provide the first political-programmatic platform on which this decision draws its treaty-constitutive direction. It may also make a reference to related treaty regimes or declarative instruments forming the external, and horizontally evolving, context of reference (decisions, declarations, or statements of relevant international organizations, including the *travaux préparatoires*, or of relevant global or regional conferences) and, possibly, to precipitating events.
- *Methodological elements*: The negotiation-generating decision may further mention the morphological patternment of the ICI treaty regime to be negotiated (framework convention specified by the scaled development of performative protocols, integrative convention specified by the scaled development of annexes or regulations operating on a compulsory or voluntary basis). It may also refer to the general delineation of the scope of application of the prospective ICI treaty regime, if this is considered necessary (introduction of "without prejudice" proposals).
- *Procedural elements*: The negotiation-generating decision normally contains certain procedural elements: the time horizon of Constitutive Negotiation, indicating the time span in which the negotiation process should be started and completed; the locus of Constitutive Negotiation, responding to the specific political, economic, and administrative aspects of the particular negotiation process; and the mandate to the secretariat (the ad hoc secretariat of the negotiation forum or the secretariat of the international organization, or the ad hoc secretariat of the particular treaty regime) to prepare, convene, and coordinate the appropriate body of conferential negotiation.

2.3 *The Ad Hoc Body of Conferential Negotiation*

On the basis of the negotiation-constituting decision, a special body of conferential negotiation is established, the so-called Ad Hoc Working Group of Legal and Technical Experts or Intergovernmental Negotiating Committee, depending on the nature of the treaty to be negotiated. This special body is authorized to carry out, under the coordination of the secretariat and after a series of sessions, the textual negotiation process leading to the consensus-based finalization of the draft of the treaty. The ad hoc body of conferential negotiation is composed by two categories of participants: the negotiating participants, consisting of the delegates representing states, as well as representatives of competent international organizations having a special institutional relationship with the negotiating states (e.g., the EU); and the negotiation-contributing participants, consisting of representatives of competent or relevant international organizations, relevant international institutional entities (e.g., secretariats of treaty regimes), and NGOs, which are invited as observers and contribute to the negotiation process and consensus-building, taking influential part.[1]

When the initiation of Constitutive Negotiation emanates from a regime action, the ad hoc body of conferential negotiation consists of the representatives of the contracting parties to the treaty regime (negotiating participants) supported by the observers assigned their status by a decision of the meeting or conference of the contracting parties (negotiation-contributing participants).

It is worth stressing that the influential role of the negotiation-contributing participants at the conferential negotiation forum may be potentially catalytic in the very process of Constitutive Negotiation. And, mutatis mutandis, this is true in regard to the Prenegotiation and Renegotiation processes. Thus, the negotiation-contributing participants may provide information, ideas, and special scientific knowledge as well as practical knowledge,[2] thus ingraining into the negotiation the necessary social, economic, and scientific-technological dimensions and perspectives of the issues under negotiation and shedding light onto their linkages and limits. And they may do so, not only by negotiating, formally (in the conferential forum) or informally (lobbying with the delegates) but also –and quite interestingly – academically, through the recently established practice of side-events that provide an additional, dialectical platform, thematically associated with the negotiating process for an important knowledge-sharing, innovative approaches showcase, communication, networking, capacity building, and options exploration with negotiating parties and other participants, including mass media. Significantly, as was pointed out earlier,[3] they may undertake an active drafting role in the Constitutive Negotiation of certain treaty regimes, like the Convention on the Rights of Persons with Disabilities, 2006, or the Ottawa Convention Banning Landmines, 1997, because of their expertise and recognized experience in the issues involved, which correspondingly is lacking from states' delegations.

2.4 *The Role of the Secretariat as a Guardian of the Constitutive Negotiation Process*

Irrespective of the source of its mandate, the secretariat plays a key role in the Constitutive Negotiation process, operating as its guardian. If the source of its

1 See, e.g., J. E. Alvarez, "The New Treaty Makers," 25 *Boston College International and Comparative Law Review* (2002), 213.

2 See Chapter 3.

3 See Chapter 2.

mandate is a multilateral action, then the secretariat's role is usually undertaken by the secretariat of an international organization or of an international institutional entity that, in view of its generally recognized role combined with its competence on the issues under negotiation, is commonly regarded as able to operate as guardians of the consensus-building process: it does so, by organizing, administering, and contributing to it but also by protecting it from possible breaks, drawing from its organizational experience and culture.[4] If the source of the secretariat's mandate is organizational action or inner-regime action, then the secretariat of the mandating international organization or of the institutional entity of the treaty regime, respectively, is always vested with the role of the institutional guardian of the consensus-building process; in addition, however, it effectively secures the coherence and consistency of the constitutive negotiating process to the function and practices of the mandating international organization or of the institutional entity.

Exercising its administrative duties, the secretariat organizes and convenes the negotiating sessions of the special body of conferential negotiation, providing the necessary administrative support and drawing up the provisional agendas of these sessions. At the same time, it facilitates the negotiating parties to adopt the rules of procedure of the negotiation conference, taking into account the existing standardized rules of procedure applied by other treaty regimes, by the mandating international organization, or by the institutional entity of the treaty regime, and it draws up a draft of these rules that is approved by the special body of the negotiating forum.

Of particular importance is the potentially creative role of the secretariat, which may be exercised not only at the various stages of the negotiation sessions but also during the periods between them. Providing the basis for a textual negotiation, the secretariat prepares the first meeting of the body of conferential negotiation and sets out its material field: it introduces either a first draft or the elements of the treaty to be negotiated, thus framing the terms of the Constitutive Negotiation. These are accompanied by a report on the subject matter (the purpose, the object and, the issues of the negotiation), supplemented by a list of documents referring to relevant

[4] The case of the UNEP is characteristic in this regard. As an ad hoc secretariat, the UNEP played a catalytic role in the Constitutive Negotiation processes that led to the establishment of a number of regional and global conventional environmental regimes, and was finally assigned by the contracting parties the function of the secretariat (e.g., the Barcelona Convention for the Protection of the Marine Environment and the Coastal Region of the Mediterranean, 1976; the Cartagena Convention for the Protection and Development of the Marine Environment of the Wider Caribbean Region, 1983; the Nairobi Convention for the Protection, Management and Development of the Marine and Coastal Environment of the Eastern African Region, 1985; the Abidjan Convention for Co-operation in the Protection and Development of the Marine and Coastal Environment of the West and Central African Region, 1981; the Convention on Biological Diversity, 1992; and the Basel Convention on the Control of Transboundary Movements of Hazardous Wastes and Their Disposal, 1989). On the other hand, the Noumea Convention for the Protection of the Natural Resources and Environment of the South Pacific Region, 1986, was associated with, and assigned the secretariat's function to the South Pacific Commission, and the Lima Convention for the Protection of the Marine Environment and Coastal Area of the South-East Pacific, 1981, to the Permanent Commission of the South Pacific.

international instruments (treaties, decisions of international organizations, international declarations, actions plans or guidelines, etc.) and to relevant scientific or technical reports or papers produced in the framework of competent international organizations (supporting documents). For the configuration and appropriate formulation of this material package, the secretariat usually consults with competent international organizations or other international institutional entities, and it may be assisted by external experts of international reputation. In this way, the secretariat manages to build the material scope of the negotiating process on a sustainable and knowledgeable basis, which is indispensable for the operation of the determinative single negotiating text procedure.

The creative role of the secretariat is also dynamically enmeshed in the "legislative activity" of the textual negotiating process. During the negotiations, it produces explanatory notes or other supportive documents, proceeds to a careful formulation of concrete new proposals responding to developments or events having an impact on the substance of the negotiating text, and constructively contributes to the drafting of the text by producing compilation texts or package texts capturing the spirit and the gist of the proposals of the negotiating parties.[5] At the same time, the creative role of the secretariat may take a more diplomatic flair: the secretariat may operate as the guardian of the Constitutive Negotiation process, leading to the conventional (treaty) construction of ICI within the reality of the status order of international society – that is, the dynamic asymmetry in the distribution of power between the negotiating states, specifically instantiated in the multilateral or in the institutional (organizational or inner-regime institutional) basis of the ad hoc body of conferential negotiation. Thus, the secretariat, being the undisputed central contact point between the participants in the negotiating forum, may exercise a mediating and constructive role on the problematic aspects of the negotiating process and its looming prospects, positive and negative. Maintaining the overall supervisory function of the negotiating process in the periods between the negotiating sessions, it may undertake important initiatives for unofficial deliberations, explaining the difficult parts of the draft text, investigating the interests behind the views associated with these parts, and seeking to promote a convergence of the views and attitudes of the parties and clarification of ICI in the framework of the negotiated treaty.

At the final stage of the Constitutive Negotiation process, the role of the secretariat is a mix of administrative, creative, and diplomatic functions. When the Constitutive Negotiation process is completed within the ad hoc body of

[5] The compilation text incorporates the textual proposals of the negotiating parties on a particular issue or point, streamlining them by merging or eliminating the overlapping aspects. Note that compilation texts may also refer to texts that contain a "compromise solution," but they are based on an agreement *ad referendum*. The package text contains the alternative specific textual proposals of the negotiating parties on a particular issue or point that are comparable, capturing the scope or the horizon of the interests involved.

conferential negotiation and the draft of the treaty is finalized and adopted, the secretariat is mandated to organize and convene a diplomatic conference (or a conference of plenipotentiaries) for the official adoption and signature of the produced treaty text and of the Final Act to which the treaty is annexed. Even within the limited finalizing frame of the diplomatic conference, the secretariat may be very constructive and directive by working on the finishing touches of the text to be signed, and play a determining role in the drafting of the patterned decisions (resolutions) of the conference concerning issues of implementation of the treaty that are contained in the Final Act and are approved by the plenipotentiaries.

Concluding, reference should be made to the legal flavour of the creative role of the secretariat related to the textual negotiation process. All preparatory and explanatory documents drawn up by the secretariat, linked to the production of the package of the material field for the initiation of the Constitutive Negotiation process (textual framing) as well as to its legislative activity during this process (textual constructing), have, in their interrelationship, an interpretative value. They form the "preparatory work" and the "circumstances" that caused the establishment of the treaty and, as such, according to Article 32 of the Vienna Convention on the Law of Treaties, 1969,[6] they constitute "supplementary means" of treaty interpretation having either a "confirmatory" function regarding the otherwise clear meaning of the terms of the treaty reached according to Article 31 of the Vienna Convention, or a "determinative" function when the interpretation afforded by Article 31 is "ambiguous or obscure," or leads to a "manifestly absurd or unreasonable" result. And if their "confirmatory" function, although a potentially powerful base for resorting to them,[7] may practically raise questions, there is, however, a rather ample space for recourse to their "determinative" function, especially in view of the fact that Article 31(2) adopts a very limited approach to context in line with its inadequate contract view of treaties.[8]

6 Vienna Convention on the Law of Treaties, 1969, 1155 UNTS 331, Art. 32.

7 In fact, it considerably limits the circle of the circumstances in which these supplementary means of interpretation cannot be resorted to.

8 A relational approach to the context of a treaty, instrumental in performing ICI, is powerfully enshrined in the famous decision of the ICJ in the *Case Concerning the Gabčikovo-Nagymaros Project (Hungary* v. *Slovakia)*, Judgement, I.C.J. Reports 1997, 7 at 78: 140.

> Owing to new scientific insights and to a growing awareness of the risks for mankind – for present and future generations – of pursuit of such interventions at an unconsidered and unabated pace, new norms and standards have been developed, set forth in a great number of instruments during the last two decades. Such new norms have to be taken into consideration, and such new standards given proper weight, not only when States contemplate new activities but also when continuing with activities begun in the past. This need to reconcile economic development with protection of the environment is aptly expressed in the concept of sustainable development. For the purposes of the present case, this means that the Parties together should look afresh at the effects on the environment of the operation of the Gabčikovo power plant [140] . . . It is not for the Court to determine what shall be the final result of these negotiations to be conducted by the Parties. It is for the Parties themselves to find an agreed solution that takes account of the objectives of the Treaty, which must be pursued

3 THE CONSENSUS PROCEDURE AS A NEGOTIATING PRACTICE OF CONSTRUCTING COMMON INTEREST

3.1 *The Two Aspects of the Consensus Procedure*

The adoption of the consensus procedure at the beginning of the Constitutive Negotiation process denotes the basic procedural safeguard that the final product of the negotiation, the treaty outcome, will establish a conventional relation of ICI in newly emerged or disputed international issue areas. Encompassing varying degrees of conflicting interests, these issue areas require the consensual development of a comprehensive approach and integrated management in a framework assuring that each state delegation, ultimately, will not be forced to accept disadvantageous conditions in matters that, according to its assessment, are of major or particular importance. Being consolidated as the basic devise for legitimating such framework, the consensus procedure provides the necessary negotiation space for forming decisions constituting a relational treaty regime in pragmatic terms. International consensus is reached when the absence of any formal objection is recorded following an exhaustive textual negotiation of the issue so that no further compromise is possible. Thus, although established as a standard practice in many important negotiating conferences since the 1970s, its determination is shaped as a generic agreement process performing ICI, which should be considered in its two complementary aspects: a "resulting-normative" aspect and a "constructing-negotiating" aspect. This complementarity is crucial to understand the full-fledged role of consensus in building ICI.

Traditionally, the resulting-normative aspect of consensus procedure is conventionally recognized and may be found in a number of important treaty regimes as a no-formal-objection procedure.[9] It is noteworthy, however, that the rules of procedure adopted in the framework of treaty regimes, when introducing the consensus procedure for decision-making, are not explanatory: they do not define "consensus."[10] On the other hand, the constructing-negotiating aspect of

in a joint and integrated way, as well as the norms of international environmental law and the principles of the law of international watercourses [141]. What is required in the present case by the rule *pacta sunt servanda*, as reflected in Article 26 of the Vienna Convention of 1969 on the Law of Treaties, is that the Parties find an agreed solution within the cooperative context of the Treaty [142].

9 A characteristic definition of "consensus" is provided in Art. 161(8) of the UNCLOS regarding the decision-making of the Council of the International Seabed Authority, where "'consensus' means the absence of any formal objection," thus being restricted to the resulting aspect of the consensus procedure. Similarly, the Agreement Establishing the World Trade Organization, 1994, repeats the same restrictive definition in an explanatory note of Article IX regarding the decision-making of the WTO by consensus: "The body concerned shall be deemed to have decided by consensus on a matter submitted for its consideration, if no Member, present at the meeting when the decision is taken, formally objects to the proposed decision."

10 Even the recently amended Rules of Procedure of the General Assembly of the United Nations, 2008, simply refer to the consensus procedure without any further explanation or regulation (UN Doc A/520, Annex IV, VII.D.3, para. 104). Such a lack of explanation or regulation of "consensus" is

consensus procedure, whereby the negotiating process takes the driver's seat in order to attain the resulting-normative consensus effect in terms of pragmatic performance of ICI and to shed light on its emergence (a micro approach to consensus), is often neglected. Or, at the most, it is considered in a simply technical, not relational, manner. Yet the consensus procedure is much more than a mere decision-making rule – it is constructive of ICI. The practical consensus-building requirement for prior full and exhaustive negotiations does not immediately reveal the richness of process that generates consensus serving ICI. It is the constructing-negotiating aspect of consensus procedure that embraces this process and that appears to be structured in three interrelated levels: relational, strategic, and organizational management.

3.2 *The Consensus Relational Level*

The adoption of the consensus procedure in the Constitutive Negotiation process occurs in an intersubjective context characterized by three interacting relational factors: the symbolic equality of the negotiating states, the symbiotic participation of relevant non-state actors (international organizations, NGOs), and the underlying distinct and dynamically operating asymmetry in the distribution of power (status order). The equality of the negotiating states is not real, but it is instructive in consensus-building, so that the underlying dynamic asymmetry of power between them (status order) becomes broadly relational, with the contributing role of the relevant non-state actors effectively and legitimately performing ICI. In other words, the adoption of the consensus procedure provides the platform that ensures that the aforementioned interacting relational factors generate a relational pattern serving ICI.

As an anchoring practice in the Constitutive Negotiation process, the consensus procedure embodies in its understanding an indiscernible amalgamation of all three interacting factors, which, in fact, operate in and through the consensus procedure. The anchoring effect of the consensus procedure articulated as an ultimate procedural safeguard that the emerged consensus embraces at least – or does not vitiate – the major interests of the negotiating states, initially and interactively assessed as such by them, is dynamic. And it instantiates a relational pattern where the reality of the underlying asymmetric power of the negotiating states (status order), their symbolic equality, and the increasingly influential symbiotic participation of powerful stakeholders, are inextricably intertwined in a synthesis of delicate and open-ended balance of perceived common interest.

commonly featured in all rules of procedure of treaty regimes introducing "consensus," which are analysed later in this chapter.

The relational pattern generated by the consensus procedure rests on:

- The ultimate procedural safeguard that ensures that the achieved consensus performs ICI, and hence is operable, when it adequately and appropriately accommodates the major interests of the negotiating parties.
- The practice of coupling the consensus procedure with the package deal procedure.
- The procedure of not equating an individual objection to the negotiated realm of consensus with a veto.

Thus, the ultimate procedural safeguard lays the foundation for creative trust. In the end, the final conventional product of the Constitutive Negotiation process will be able to stand up if it adequately serves, or, at least, is not considered to have a vitiating effect on, issues of particular or major significance for every negotiating participant. As a result, trust is initiated from the beginning of the negotiating process by establishing not simply a meeting for drawing up a treaty, but a problem-solving conference for constituting a relational treaty regime. Such a conference embraces a multilateral negotiating effort to produce a comprehensive and balanced relational framework dynamically performing ICI and to withstand any individual attempt to "break up" the conventional ICI relationship thereby instantiated by consensus.

The practice of coupling the consensus procedure with the package deal procedure lies at the heart of the fluid relational pattern generated by the consensus procedure. The package deal procedure comprises an overall horizontal and vertical negotiated arrangement of the issues: all issues are bundled and discussed together (a horizontal agreement on all the issues of the package is required) and all issues are simultaneously accepted or rejected (a vertical positive or negative treatment of the package of issues as a whole). "Nothing is agreed until everything is agreed" is the negotiating principle permeating the coupling consensus with package deal. And this raises the prospect that if a particular round of the Constitutive Negotiation process (or of Renegotiation) runs into trouble, then the unravelling of what has been achieved so far by consensus and intensive negotiation could be an unavoidable consequence. It should be stressed here that the very construction of the package deal, many times, does not reflect a logical interconnection between the issues of which it is composed. It is rather the product of political evaluations and options, but also of common perceptions about the feasible scope of negotiations allowing an expansion or a reduction of the packaged issues where consensus can realistically be achieved. The package deal procedure and the consensus procedure complement and reinforce each other so that, on the one hand, they generate a relational pattern in the negotiation process (negotiating participants procedurally safeguard their role as problem solvers in establishing a relational conventional regime continuously performing ICI) and, on the other hand, they produce particular practices regarding the strategic and organizational management of this process.

The relational pattern is further and finally stabilized by the procedural protection of the negotiated realm of consensus-shaping from an individual objection and its eventual operation as a veto. This procedure clearly implies that the exhaustively negotiated and shaped realm of consensus already forms a pattern constituting a relation of ICI that basically embodies an effective accommodation of the three interacting relational factors mentioned earlier.[11] Thus, it is above and beyond the individual wills of the negotiating parties and, as a result, once finalized, it cannot be broken up by an individual perpetually objecting will. Conversely, consensus-shaping would require a concluding, carefully carried out attempt to achieve an acceptable integration of the isolated individual objection into the realm of consensus, by reasonably expanding the negotiation process. This is in tune with the ultimate solidarity encapsulated in the ethos of consensus. If this attempt fails, two procedural ways are open to the negotiating parties, both serving the consensus-shaping requirement:

- Recourse to the voting procedure: In this case, the rules of procedure will be residually applied, which refer to decisions on substantive issues and require a qualified majority (two-thirds, three-quarters, or other) of the parties, unless otherwise provided for by the Convention, as explained later in this chapter. It should be stressed here that the decision of the president or chairperson of the negotiating conference to resort to voting may effectively result in the withdrawal of the objection and the finalization of consensus.
- Decision to complete the consensus procedure, bypassing the objection. In such cases, the options open to the objecting negotiating state range from differentiation within the treaty regime to deviation from it. Thus, the objecting state may decide, displaying a spirit of solidarity, to join the consensus by organizing the space of its differentiating position: starting from the recording of its objecting position in the report of the negotiating conference it may also pursue that objection's inclusion in the preamble of the treaty endowing it with an interpretative value,[12] or it may later decide (at the time of the signature or ratification of the treaty) to cast it under the mantle of reservation to certain articles of the treaty, provided of course that the treaty, generally or specifically, does not prohibit such reservation or it is not considered incompatible with the object and purpose of the treaty by a decision of the supreme institutional organ

[11] Accordingly, any generalization that consensus does not deliver a veto power to every negotiating state because this might be abusive (e.g., L. B. Sohn, "United National Decision-Making: Confrontation or Consensus?" 1 *Harvard International Law Journal* [1974], 438) should be effectively and pragmatically viewed in relation to these three interacting relational factors. For some critical considerations on this issue concerning Bolivia's objection to the "open-textured" consensus on the Cancun Agreements building, in the FCCC process, the legal platform for a new climate change regime, see L. Rajamani, "The Cancun Climate Agreements: Reading the Text, Subtext and Tea Leaves," 60 *ICLQ* (2011), 499, 515.

[12] On this point see later in this chapter.

of the treaty.[13] On the other hand, the objecting negotiating state may finally decide not to participate in the treaty and, also, to go a step further by using the bypassing of its objection as a basis for challenging the validity of the achieved consensus. Undoubtedly, such a claim would be theoretically and practically untenable, because, otherwise, it would equate the individual objection, persisting after the exhaustive completion of the negotiating process, with a veto. Attention, however, should be drawn, here, to an abusive negotiation practice to create an appearance of consensus: in some cases, the president/chairperson of the negotiating conference may, abusing their office, deny a state or states the right to take the floor and express their objections to the text, thus forcing and forging an illusory consensus. In fact, the resort to such practice clearly implies that the president/chairperson (or any other officer applying it) is himself aware of a lack of consensus.

3.3 *The Strategic Management Level*

The practice of coupling the consensus procedure with the package deal procedure and their combined effect inevitably prolongs the negotiation process. But, as international practice shows, this structured broadening of the time horizon of consensus-building is conducive to a strong consensus status that forms the spine of a treaty regime, legitimating a more effective, efficient, and socially acceptable performance of ICI. On the other hand, the prolongation of negotiations may also work in the opposite direction. It opens up the dimension of projecting power-based extreme positions at the early stage of the negotiating process, feeding a competitive approach. The negotiating parties, having secured the consensus outcome of the Constitutive Negotiation process, tend to adopt extreme positions at the beginning of the negotiation in order to achieve, at the end, a satisfactory accommodation of their interests in the ICI order of the treaty regime. Such a strategic practice may be adopted by a powerful negotiating state or by a determinate group of negotiating states and resembles the strategy of "brinkmanship" related to zero-sum negotiations, but the key element of threat is contextualized and relativized, eventually subdued to the process of consensus-building.[14]

[13] See generally Article 19 of the Vienna Convention on the Law of Treaties rendering unauthorized reservations within its meaning as invalid *ab initio*, regardless of the positions other parties may take to the treaty. It is noteworthy that the ILC Guide's interpretation of Article 19, expressed in Guideline 4.5.3.4, establishes a presumption of elimination of the institutionally assessed impermissible reservation in case of silence of the reserving state "within a period of twelve months from the date at which the treaty monitoring body made its assessment." It suggests, however, that this Guideline "largely corresponds to the progressive development of international law" and "it would seem expedient to let practice evolve, although different circumstances might call for different solutions" (Report of the International Law Commission, sixty-third session (A/66/10/Add.1), 2011, para. 55, 542), thus recognizing the complexity of the domestic procedures and the entrenched contextuality of the operability of the presumption prescribed earlier in the domestic orders.

[14] The "brinkmanship-style" negotiator employs an extreme type of the hard-nut approach by pushing the other side to the edge of a precipice. See A. Goldman and J. Rojot, *Negotiation: Theory and*

More specifically, it is true that any determined group of states or even a single powerful state may, by adopting extreme positions, capture the consensus procedure and slow down the progress of the negotiating process by systematically projecting negative positions. And the practice of coupling the consensus procedure with the package deal procedure seems to favour the exercise of this strategic practice. However, this strategic practice is subject, from the beginning, to two basic and interrelated initial limitations: first, that the state or the group of states applying this strategic practice is of catalytic importance for the effective and efficient implementation of the negotiably constructed treaty regime of ICI; second, that the concessions they offer in exchange for the abandonment of their "hold-out position" provide a real possibility for creating a pragmatic ICI accommodation and, thus, effectively applying such a treaty regime. In addition, there are the distinctive limitations that develop and operate through the consensus procedure (operational limitations), which further weaken this strategic practice and make it increasingly vulnerable as long as the consensus stratification is progressively built. Thus, the more consolidated the stratification of consensus becomes on certain aspects of the negotiating package to which the negative strategic practice refers, the more vulnerable and open to criticism and pressures the negative position becomes. And this emanates not only from the negotiating states that have, from the beginning, opposed to this strategy, but also – and more catalytically – from those negotiating states that, though they initially were committed to this strategy, have later (in the process) and variably become part of the consolidated aspects of consensus. In consequence, they cannot accept or tolerate the continuance of this negative strategic practice any longer and they constructively support the furtherance of the consensus-building, isolating and, in effect, deactivating the hold-out position, which is now perceived as a practice signalling the potential risk of dismantling what has been already – and painstakingly – achieved.

3.4 *The Organizational Management Level*

The practice of coupling the consensus procedure with the package deal procedure and the resulting prolongation of the negotiation process is also intrinsically associated with the application of organizational management negotiating techniques and practices that are instrumental in facilitating consensus-building. The degree of workability and applicability of these techniques and practices is directly related to the degree that the consensus procedure, as an ICI activity, effectively embodies the three interacting relational factors mentioned earlier (the symbolic equality of the negotiating states, the symbiotic participation of relevant non-state actors, and

Practice, Kluwer Law International, 2002, 111–129. For a framework analysing the role of threat in the negotiation process and the strategy of brinkmanship, see M. Schwarz and K. Sonin, "A Theory of Brinkmanship, Conflicts, and Commitments," 24(1) *Journal of Law, Economics & Organization* (2008), 163–183.

the dynamically operating asymmetry [status order] in the distribution of power between the negotiating states).

3.4.1 The Procedural Techniques of Lateral Expansion and Fragmentation of Issues

More specifically, the organizational management of the consensus-building process comprises the application of two alternative instrumental negotiating techniques regarding the thematic pliability of the collectively determined package of issues: the procedural technique of a lateral expansion of the issues under negotiation on other related issues and the procedural technique of fragmenting certain issues under negotiation into smaller and more manageable issues or subtracting them. The application of each of these two alternative techniques is legitimated, during the course of the negotiating process, by a reformative consensus of the negotiating parties, which reinforces the relational dimension of common benefit by appropriately expanding or subtracting issues. Both techniques are equally applied to the Renegotiation phase.

The procedural technique of a lateral expansion of the issues under negotiation on other issues (related or unrelated) aims at enhancing the relational horizon of the negotiating parties, thus creating for them an additional fountain for drawing new elements of ICI. The broadening effect of this procedural technique touches on the revelation of the more general complementarity of issues in the negotiation process and its potential importance for securing consensus-building and eventually becoming part of it. At the same time, it decisively weakens or diminishes any possible alternative to the practice of coupling the consensus procedure with the package deal procedure that might be held by a negotiating party (the risk of reversing the agreement on this coupling). Conversely, it increases alternatives, strengthening the road to consensus and creating an additional margin for pay-offs between the negotiating participants (the addition of a more or less related, or unrelated, issue may lead to a compromise on a dispute over an issue or issues included in the package deal).[15] The broadening effect uncovers additional values for the negotiating parties as "associates" pursuing the conventional establishment of an ICI regime. The addition of potentially related issues from interconnected fields of international relations (international security, economic development, technological applications, international trade, international financial relations, or energy security) is indicative of the expanding manageability of the package deal. As a result, the development of multiple synergies on more or less related, or unrelated, issues of common interest will be put in the scene, highlighting the determinative importance of "complementarity" of issues as a basis for a more solid, more effective, and more relational consensus-building performing ICI.

[15] On this point, see, e.g., J. K. Sebenius, "Negotiating Arithmetic: Adding and Subtracting Issues and Parties," 37 *International Organization* (1983), 281–316.

The procedural technique of fragmenting certain issues under negotiation into smaller and more manageable issues or subtracting them aims at securing more consistency in the package of issues and increased relational coherence. The initially agreed comprehensiveness of the package is held back in the name of functionality, so that a real possibility of building ICI consensus will be ensured and relational trust will not be put at risk. It should be stressed, however, that both procedural techniques should be used with the utmost care: on the road to consensus-building, the possibility of the thematic pliability of the collectively determined package of issues should not weaken or jeopardize the already consolidated common benefits,[16] or even disturb the practicality of the package of issues.[17]

3.4.2 The Conference-Scaling Practices: Sub-fora and Miniaturization of Conferences

The conference-scaling practices, related to the management of certain slippery aspects of consensus-building in the Constitutive Negotiation and surrounded by many uncertainties, may be carried out by the creation of sub-fora or by the scaled miniaturization of the negotiating group in the conference.

More specifically, managing the process of consensus-building by creating appropriate and flexible sub-fora of negotiation is well established in international practice. This managing practice seems particularly apt in global Constitutive Negotiation because the number and weight of the issues under negotiation may require their allocation to different negotiating sub-fora, provided, of course, that their outcomes will be recast in the package deal linkages to form a workable integral whole.[18] These sub-fora channel negotiation into specific issues forming part of the negotiating agenda and are set up by the plenary of the negotiating conference on the proposal of the chairperson/president of the conference or in cooperation with the secretariat. Having a "subjective" foundation, the effectiveness of these sub-fora is related to their exclusive-inclusive character: they are formed as smaller open-ended groups of negotiating parties that are simultaneously inclusive, encapsulating, at least, an adequate representation of the basic interests involved in the particular subject under negotiation. However, the practice of establishing negotiating sub-fora should be viewed and organized as a process rather than as a state and be further

16 See L. E. Susskind, *Environmental Diplomacy: Negotiating More Effective Global Agreements* (1994), op. cit., 87ff.

17 For a more general approach to the policy of practicality in the linkage of issues and the risk of the nonpractical addition of issues, see, characteristically, A. E. David, *The Strategy of Treaty Termination: Lawful Breaches and Retaliations* (1975), op. cit., 149–151.

18 As was pointed out by Tommy Koh, the president of the third UNCLOS, one of the productive features of the negotiating process of this conference was its decision that "the package deal approach did not preclude it from allocating the 25 different subjects and issues to different negotiating forums, so long as the results were brought together to form an integral whole." T. Koh, "A Constitution for the Oceans," Remarks, available at: www.un.org/depts/los/convention_agreements/texts/koh_english.pdf.

endowed with workable relational overtones. In fact, the same practical reasons that necessitate the creation of sub-fora make equally indispensable an appropriate "inner-communication system" for those negotiating parties whose actual presence in the particular sub-forum is practically impossible (because their delegation is undermanned), so as to ensure an open line of communication with them.

This inner-communication system would allow absent delegations the opportunity to participate by proxy who would represent their expressed interests in the sub-forum. Thus, a friendly negotiating state or a negotiating state belonging to the same regional or interest group, or the representative of a regional grouping to which the non-present state belongs, or even a member of the bureau of the negotiating conference may effectively undertake this proxy role. In substantive terms, the elaboration of the inner-communication system would allow the non-present delegations to follow, and contribute to, the development stages of the part of the text that is negotiated within the sub-forum. They will be provided with all relevant drafts and documents discussed in the sub-forum by their proxy, they will examine them, and they will intervene in the negotiation through their proxy who will present their views and specifically formulated points. Besides, the psychological impact resulting from the operation of the inner-communication scheme should not be underestimated: it develops a sense of non-exclusion to the absent negotiating state and, more positively, it armours it with the feeling of constructiveness in this particular negotiating process, even from a distance.

Similar logic and considerations apply to the scaled miniaturization of the negotiating participants in the conference. This practice, however, clusters additional management layers, securing a well-balanced outcome through a reverse pyramid process (miniaturization process). Thus, in global negotiations, and especially in the UN framework, the perceived impossibility of reaching consensus on a thorny issue run by knowledge gaps, lack of practice, and controversial assumptions may generate the rise of a scaling process of miniaturization of the negotiating group so that a workable consensus will be progressively and flexibly built and finally legitimated. The scaled miniaturization process may be initiated, as in the case of sub-fora creation, by proposal of the chairperson/president of the conference or in cooperation with the secretariat to the plenary of the conference to transfer the negotiation of the issue to a smaller, intermediary open-ended group the composition of which will be left in the hands of the negotiating participants, and especially in their various regional interest groupings. The negotiated outcome at this minimized level can be transferred, by initiative of the chairperson and with the assistance of the secretariat, to a further minimized very small negotiating group, which may be composed of representatives of the regional interest groupings. When agreement is reached at this minimal, but leading, level, and after the regional interest groupings have examined it and agree with it, the final product of the scaling miniaturization process, based on diligent consensus-building, is presented at the plenary session of the negotiating conference for its well-expected adoption.[19]

It is evident that the initiation and effective implementation of the scaling miniaturization process in a negotiating conference requires the catalytic, special role performance of the chairperson/president of the conference. In view of the delicate nature of this undertaking and its top-down operation, it requires the transition to a peculiar conferential leadership role, based on the conference trust in the chairperson/president coupled with his ability to convince the conference of the need for applying this process in order to achieve progress in the negotiation, and his commitment to oversee this process so that its final result will be brought back to the conference for discussion and endorsement.

4 RULES OF PROCEDURE AND PRACTICES

The adoption of the rules of procedure constitutes the first important step in the Constitutive Negotiation process. The rules of procedure set up the organizational and functional framework of the negotiating forum. They are of determinative importance, because they "structure" the conduct of the negotiating process, ensuring its orderly and controlled progress. Through their knowledge and proper use, the weaker negotiating parties become able to build and exercise individual countervailing influence on negotiations, and this, without disturbing the reality of the catalytic importance of emerging or existing coalitions between the negotiating parties – which may appear in the particular negotiating forum or in the framework of an international organization where negotiation takes place – which may promote the collective use of these rules. At the other end, the rules of procedure may be abused when used as an instrument of obstructing tactics or strategies in order to delay the start of negotiations on substantive issues.[20]

19 The scaled miniaturization of conference practice was effectively employed by Ambassador T. Koh, chairman of the UNCLOS III negotiations (1981–1982), when chairing negotiations on the financial terms of contracts to mine the mineral resources on the deep seabed. In view of the many challenges posed by the negotiation of this particular issue ("non-existence of industry," "many unknown hypotheses," but, at the same time, "insistence by the conference on arriving at a consensus," as stated by him) he used this practice diligently. He asked the plenary permission to minimize the negotiating group of 152 delegations by convening a smaller, intermediary group of financial experts, which turned out to include thirty negotiating participants, which after several weeks of negotiation reached a deal. He then further minimized the negotiating group by organizing a very small group of four negotiating participants, asking the Group of 77 to name three representatives from Asia, Africa, and Latin America and the developed countries to name one representative (USA). The agreement reached was *ad referendum*: they were asked by the chairman to present it to their respective regional groupings for examination and final approval. Finally, the outcome was presented at the plenary that endorsed it (see Ambassador Tommy Koh on the Negotiating Process of UNCLOS III, United Nations Audiovisual Library of International Law, 12 January 2009. Available at: http://webtv.un.org/watch/amb.-tommy-koh-on-the-negotiating-process-of-unclos-iii/2600833510001).

20 See, e.g., R. E. Benedick, "Perspectives of a Negotiation Practitioner," in G. Sjosted (ed.), *International Environmental Negotiations*, SAGE Publications, 1993, 219, 237.

According to international practice, the negotiating parties mandate the secretariat of the negotiating forum to draft and present for adoption the appropriate rules of procedure. For this purpose, the secretariat may proceed to their drafting directly, usually convening and coordinating a small informal working group for the finalization of the draft and taking into account the existing standard rules of procedure applicable to other international treaty regimes or to international institutional entities. It may also simply import the rules of procedure adopted by the international organization to which it belongs, when the negotiation of the treaty regime takes place within the framework of a competent international organization, e.g., IMO, UNESCO, or it may properly adapt them to the specific requirements of the particular Constitutive Negotiation process carried out in the framework of an ad hoc negotiating forum.[21] The rules of procedure, being always placed as the first item of the agenda, are discussed and adopted at the beginning of the first meeting or session of the special body of conferential negotiation (the Ad Hoc Working Group of Legal and Technical Experts or the Intergovernmental Negotiating Committee).

In general, the rules of procedure of every negotiating forum of Constitutive Negotiation, following the logic of legislative drafting, are patterned, composed of standardized elements, while they are fruitfully supplemented, in certain respects, by procedures drawn from international practice.

4.1 *Purpose and Definitions*

The rules of procedure generally provide their scope of application in the framework of the related treaty regime. Certain key terms used in the rules of procedure are also defined, such as "parties present and voting" – which has a decisive effect in the voting procedure – "regional economic integration organization" – which usually concerns the participation of the EU prescribing the conditions of its participation in the negotiation process – or terms referring to "observers," "subsidiary body," "meeting," "secretariat," or "president."[22]

[21] Thus, for instance, the Rules of Procedure for the Meetings and Conferences of the Contracting Parties to the Barcelona Convention for the Protection of the Marine Environment and Coastal Region of the Mediterranean and its Protocols incorporate, after appropriate adaptation, the Rules of Procedure of the Governing Council of UNEP, having been introduced and properly developed by the UNEP/MAP Secretariat of the Barcelona Convention and adopted by decision of the Contracting Parties according to Art. 24(1) of the Convention. Similarly, the Rules of Procedure for the Meetings and Conferences of the Parties to the Basel Convention on the Control of Transboundary Movement of Dangerous Wastes and Their Disposal, have also been introduced in the same manner and adopted by decision of the parties according to Art. 15 of the Convention.

[22] When included in the rules of procedure, the phrase "parties present and voting" means the parties present and casting a (valid) affirmative or negative vote, whereas the parties that abstain from voting are considered as not voting. See, e.g., Rules of Procedure of the Conference of the States Parties to the Organisation for the Prohibition of Chemical Weapons, Rule 71; Rules of Procedure of the Conference of the States Parties to the Stockholm Convention on Persistent Organic Pollutants, Rule 2(i).

4.2 *Place and Time of Meetings*

This section determines the power of the negotiating forum to decide about the preferred or different venues of the negotiating sessions, their periodicity, the terms of convening them, the dates, and their duration, as well as the terms of convening extraordinary negotiating sessions.

4.3 *Invitation of Observers*

The rules of procedure provide the conditions for the invitation and participation of observers in the negotiating forum. As observers in the Constitutive Negotiation process, such non-state actors as intergovernmental organizations, other international institutional entities (e.g., secretariats of international conventional [treaty] regimes), NGOs, and third states (in cases where Constitutive Negotiation refers to a regional conventional regime) may be admitted, but also the private sector, labour organizations, or groups of indigenous people depending on the nature of the treaty regime under negotiation. Thus, Constitutive Negotiation may be constantly enriched by the social, economic, and scientific-technological perspectives contributed by the invited relevant stakeholders.

4.4 *Public and Private Sessions of the Meetings*

This section may provide that the negotiating sessions of a meeting or conference will be held in public, so that access to the sessions is allowed to observers and mass media. Thus, the plenary sessions of the ad hoc body of conferential negotiation or the meetings of the subsidiary bodies established by it are normally held in public, unless the ad hoc body of conferential negotiation decides otherwise, to the effect that their sessions are to be held in private and only their decisions made public. It should be noticed, however, that the decision on private sessions has a strategic significance for the progress of negotiation: it may facilitate the negotiation conduct of certain parties. In fact, the sessions of drafting groups operating as open-ended groups in relation to the negotiating parties and coordinated by the secretariat normally are private. The delicate process of multilateral treaty drafting and the initial textual accommodation of interests in pursuance of ICI require that participation in these groups is both inclusive and exclusive: at the plenary of the ad hoc body of conferential negotiation, the necessary core of the negotiating parties is usually indicated, which, because of their importance in the drafting of the text, should participate in these groups, while the participation of any other interested party is left open. The drafting groups present to the plenary the outcome of their internal negotiation, that is, an agreed draft of the treaty text.

4.5 *Agenda Setting*

The special section on agenda establishes the procedure for the preparation, structuring, and distribution of the provisional agenda, normally accompanied by the annotated provisional agenda that contains detailed information about the items of the provisional agenda and about the negotiating process. The provisional agenda is prepared by the secretariat and it may contain items proposed by the secretariat, items proposed by the negotiating parties or the participating international organizations and properly received by the secretariat, or even items introduced by the previous negotiating session. Particularly useful is the inclusion of a list of documents in every item of the agenda. It is also provided that the agenda, together with the supporting documents, should be distributed in the official languages normally "at least six weeks before the opening" of the negotiating conference or meeting, so that adequate time will be given for the preparation of the representatives of the negotiating parties.[23]

The section on agenda further refers to the terms of adoption of the agenda, where the ad hoc body of conferential negotiation may decide, after examining the provisional agenda, to revise it by adding (especially items considered urgent), deleting, deferring, or amending items. The agenda is adopted by consensus of the ad hoc body. It is worth noticing here that, if, during the adoption procedure, there is no consensus as to an item of the provisional agenda, then, according to international practice, this item is put aside but is held "in abeyance" so that the rest of the provisional agenda will be adopted and the negotiation will start. If at the end of the negotiating session the item is still pending, then a common practice is to be followed: the item will be automatically included in the agenda of the next negotiating session. This practice is based on the rule of procedure that provides that, if the consideration of an item has not been completed at a particular negotiating session, it will be automatically included in the agenda of the next negotiating session – unless the negotiating parties decide differently.[24] Finally, the agenda section also provides the obligation of the secretariat to report to the ad hoc body of conferential negotiation on the administrative and financial implications of all substantive items of the agenda.

[23] In the event that an additional item has been proposed by a negotiating party and received by the secretariat after the provisional agenda for the negotiating meeting or conference has been produced, but before the opening of the negotiating meeting or conference, the rules of procedure normally provide that the secretariat, in agreement either with the bureau (Rules of Procedure for Meetings and Conferences of the Contracting Parties to the Convention for the Protection of the Mediterranean Sea Against Pollution and Its Related Protocols, Rule 13) or with the president of the negotiating meeting or conference (Rules of Procedure for the Conference of the Parties to the Basel Convention on the Control of Transboundary Movements of Hazardous Wastes and Their Disposal, Rule 11), may include this item in a supplementary provisional agenda, which will be examined by the ad hoc body of conferential negotiation together with the provisional agenda.

[24] E.g., UNFCCC, Rules of Procedure of the Conference of the Parties and Its Subsidiary Bodies, Rule 16.

4.6 *Representation*

The rules of procedure provide the conditions for representation concerning the composition and credentials of delegations. The credentials, submitted to the ad hoc secretariat of the negotiating conference or meeting, are examined by a credentials committee, appointed at the beginning of each negotiating session, coordinated by the secretariat, and normally consisting of the members of the bureau of this session. The credentials committee submits its report to the plenary of the negotiating conference or meeting, which decides on their approval. With respect to the composition of delegations, the procedure is permissive and open-ended: it does not intervene with the sovereign right of states to decide on the quantity and quality (the required expertise) of their representation and it provides the general standard that each negotiating state will be represented by a delegation "consisting of a head of delegation and such other accredited representatives, alternate representatives and advisers as it may require."[25] The credentials are issued by the head of state or government or by the minister of foreign affairs of the member concerned, or by any other authority acting on their behalf or, in the case of a regional economic integration organization, by the competent authority of that organization. In practice, the credentials refer to the activities and actions to be carried out by a delegate at the negotiating session ("to negotiate," "to vote," or "to sign," in the case of a diplomatic conference aiming at the signature of the text of a treaty). Finally, according to international practice, representatives may provisionally participate in the negotiating session, pending a decision of the ad hoc body of conferential negotiation upon their credentials or upon its admission objected by any negotiating party.

4.7 *The Bureau of the Negotiating Meeting or Conference*

The rules of procedure provide the organization and function of the bureau of the meeting or conference of the ad hoc body of conferential negotiation that leads and controls the negotiating process. The bureau is composed of three levels of officers: the chairperson or president, who runs the proceedings and applies the rules of procedure; the rapporteur, who is responsible for the preparation of the sessional report of the meeting or conference, aided substantially by the secretariat; and the vice-chairpersons or vice presidents, who are elected to assume the post of the chairperson or president if he is temporarily absent (temporary replacement) or leaves for any reason (permanent replacement). The chairperson and the rapporteur

[25] E.g., Rules of Procedure for Meetings of the Conference of the Parties to the Convention on Biological Diversity, Rule 16; Rules of Procedure for Meetings of the Conference of the Parties to the Stockholm Convention on Persistent Organic Pollutants, Rule 17; Rules of Procedure for Meetings of the Conference of the Parties to the Organization for the Prohibition of Chemical Weapons, Rule 23. Note that this discretion ultimately works in favour of the developed countries, since the economic cost of a large representation coupled with the limited capacities at the national level substantially affect the choices of the developing countries, which, as a result, are represented by small delegations composed of one or two representatives.

sit, together with the head of the secretariat, at the pontium of the plenary, whereas the vice-chairpersons sit with their delegations. The officers of the bureau are elected by the ad hoc body of conferential negotiation for the whole duration of its meeting or conference on the basis of the principle of equitable geographical representation. However, the most recent trend specifically provides that, for reasons of greater efficacy, the election of the officers of the bureau takes place, at the second and subsequent meetings, before the end of the meeting, and they serve until the closure of the following meeting or conference.[26] In other words, their term of office begins with the closure of the session in which they were elected and lasts until the closure of the next session. In this way, the preparation of the next negotiating meeting or conference is substantially, and sometimes catalytically, facilitated by the active engagement of the bureau elected for it.

To ensure the greatest possible efficiency of the bureau and the effective implementation of the principle of equitable geographical distribution for its construction, the practice of a prior systematic deliberation is followed between the representatives of the negotiating parties under the guidance of the secretariat, taking into account the expected political potentiality of the bureau, as a body of conferential negotiation, in the consensual solidification of common interest in the negotiated treaty. In this context, the chairperson/president of the bureau, on the basis of the impartiality required for his role in the negotiating process, does not exercise his rights as a representative of his state (and in the case of voting he does not vote). Moreover, the bureau may be benefited by the *ex officio* participation of the chairpersons/presidents of special committees, if established during the negotiating process. The meetings of the bureau are convened at regular intervals by its chairperson/president to consider the proper function and progress of the negotiating process and decide upon its actions so that negotiation will be expedited and acquire a more constructive character. The secretariat participates in these meetings and its role is definitive. One final word touching on an important aspect of common interest construction in treaty negotiation – it concerns the contemporary discussion regarding the discretion of the bureau to invite a representative of the participating non-state actors (especially NGOs) to attend its meetings as an observer. Such a development, already prescribed in the rules of procedure of certain conventional environmental regimes,[27] will allow a more integrated engagement of non-state

[26] See, e.g., Rules of Procedure for the Conference of the Parties to the Basel Convention on the Control of Transboundary Movements of Hazardous Wastes and Their Disposal, Rule 21(2); Rules of Procedure for the Conference of the Parties to the Rotterdam Convention on the Prior Informed Consent Procedure for Certain Hazardous Chemicals and Pesticides in International Trade, Rule 22(2); Rules of Procedure for the Conference of the Parties to the Stockholm Convention on Persistent Organic Pollutants, Rule 22(1); Rules of Procedure for the Meeting of the Parties to the Convention on Access to Information, Public Participation in Decision-Making and Access to Justice in Environmental Matters, Rule 22(5).

[27] See, e.g., Rules of Procedure for the Meeting of the Parties to the Convention on Access to Information, Public Participation in Decision-Making and Access to Justice in Environmental Matters, Rule 22(2).

actors in the negotiating process at the advantage of the social, economic, and political basis of the conventionally constituted regime of ICI governance.

4.8 The Organization of the Negotiating Meeting or Conference

The rules of procedure also provide the rules for the setting up, organizing, and functioning of the necessary subsidiary organs as well as the rules defining the multifarious functions of the secretariat of the ad hoc body of conferential negotiation. The secretariat is primarily responsible for the administrative, logistic, and technical aspects of the negotiating process: the arrangements concerning the staff and services required by the negotiating meeting or conference within the framework of the available resources; the provision of adequate support and advice to the bureau and to subsidiary bodies; the arrangements for translation and interpretation services; the collection, translation, reproduction, and circulation of documents produced during negotiation at the ad hoc body of conferential negotiation and its subsidiary organs or of any other relevant documentation; the regularization of the sound recording of the negotiating session; arrangements for the custody and conservation of documents produced during the negotiation; and, generally, performance of any other task assigned to it by the ad hoc body.[28] Of course, the secretariat may furthermore exercise a constructive political function during the negotiating meeting or conference. Its head may proceed to oral or written statements to the MOPs/COPs plenary sessions or to the sessions of their subsidiary bodies on any matter of negotiation and, even, generally express views on the progress and prospects of the negotiating process. Special mention should be made of the potential creative role of the secretariat during the negotiated conventional construction of ICI – elaborated in other parts of this book – signified by its consistent formulation of special proposals regarding the development or adaptation of the negotiated text in view of the development occurred or occurring in the external context of reference, or by its production of compilation or package texts, or even by carrying out its invaluable institutional diplomacy, thus firmly maintaining its role at the core of the negotiating process, formally and informally.

The rules of procedure confer upon the ad hoc body of conferential negotiation the power to establish the committees and working groups that may be required for the specific performance of its functions. The ad hoc body may decide that these committees or working groups may be convened during the period between the negotiating meetings or conferences, elects the chairperson of each of these subsidiary bodies, and determines the specific issues to be discussed by each of them. These subsidiary organs elect their officers on the basis of the principle of equitable geographical distribution, thus ensuring that a balance of interests is represented at the level of the official management of their work. This is particularly useful when

[28] See, e.g., the latest formulation of rules of procedure in the framework of the UNEP: Rules of Procedure of the United Nations Environment Assembly of the UNEP, Rules 30 and 31.

a subsidiary body is created for the specific negotiation of contentious and complex technical, scientific, or legal issues with strong political dimensions.

Two kinds of subsidiary bodies are commonly created in response to the needs of the Constitutive Negotiation process. The drafting working groups or committees are instructed by the ad hoc body of conferential negotiation to discuss and proceed to the negotiated articulation of a certain part or certain complex and contentious draft article/s of the text of the treaty under negotiation. Also, the specialized working groups or committees are instructed by the ad hoc body to deliberate on thorny and bracketed scientific, technical, or legal aspects of negotiation (such as technical or scientific definitions, technical annexes, science-based special or exceptional regulations, or formulation of policy and technical matters in a proper legal form) and to produce an unbracketed text. According to international practice, the subsidiary bodies are created as open-ended groups; nevertheless, the participation of certain states playing a central and constructive role in the negotiation of the particular issue related to the creation of a subsidiary body (core states) is usually secured through their direct nomination by the ad hoc body of conferential negotiation. It goes without saying that the participation of these core states guarantees that the special negotiating platform producing the outcome to be reported reflects a pragmatic accommodation of interests on a powerful legitimating basis.

4.9 *Conduct of Business*

This section of the rules of procedure strictly refers to the procedural management of the Constitutive Negotiation process. It specifies the procedures providing when a negotiating session may be declared public or private, and when a quorum is constituted at the plenary sessions of the meetings or conferences. It also prescribes in detail the particular powers vested with the chairperson/president, the exercise of which remains under the broader authority of the negotiating parties. Relatedly, and beyond these specific procedural rules, there are good practices that may be definitive of the effective role of the chairperson/president. These include the development of a close working relationship with the secretariat of the negotiating conference embracing the negotiation of all related procedural, substantive, and policy issues. These practices also include transparency in the function of the chairperson/president: he/she should retain a clean image throughout the negotiating process and should not jeopardize his integrity or the trust of the negotiating parties by becoming part of secret negotiations developing on the sidelines of the negotiating conference.

This section of the rules of procedure also regulates all relevant aspects of formal negotiation by setting out rules that relate to the conduct of the oral procedure at the negotiating session,[29] and the submission of procedural and substantive proposals, as

[29] E.g., a "point of order" that may be raised exclusively in relation to a procedural matter and its invocation may interrupt a speaker; a "point of inquiry" that may be raised in relation to any

well as the conditions for withdrawals, amendments, or reconsideration of these proposals, but also the conditions for suspension, adjournment, or closure of the negotiating meeting or conference, or of the debate on an item under negotiation, which may affect the progress of the negotiating process. Note here that in the event of deadlock, taking usually the form of a stalemate or more rarely an extended delay because of the strongly opposed and firmly held attitudes and underlying interests of the negotiating parties, the decision to suspend the negotiating process may have a positive impact on the negotiating process.[30] Unlike the closure of the negotiating meeting or conference, which signals their failure and may have a serious negative impact on the negotiating process, the suspension of the meeting or conference, achieving the provisional "freezing" of the negotiating process, maintains, during the suspension period, the operation of the dynamics to achieve consensus, allowing the most creative forces to play a constructive role for a more efficient and effective resumption of the suspended meeting or conference. Overall, the handling of these matters may seriously affect the progress of the negotiating process.

4.10 *Decision-Making*

This section contains detailed rules prescribing the decision-making procedure of the ad hoc body of conferential negotiation incorporating the standard system of voting procedure based on the distinction between issues characterized as substantive and procedural, despite the fact that international practice has firmly embraced consensus as the foundation of decision-making, which is in tune with the instrumental nature of the negotiating process in constructing ICI. On the other hand, certain recent formulations of the rules of procedure increasingly introduce, in regard to substantive issues, the creative consensus decision at the top of the decision-making process, thus reflecting what is constantly and consistently applied

clarification on the procedure required by a representative, however, cannot interrupt a speaker, as is also the case when a "point of information" is raised that is addressed to other representatives in relation to speeches or working documents. A "point of personal privilege" may be raised in relation to any personal discomfort (for instance, negotiation room temperature, audio failures, or bad translation services) and its invocation may interrupt a speaker. The raising of these points cannot be put up for debate or vote. A point of order is decided by the chairperson/president, while a procedural motion (like a motion not to discuss an item of the agenda, raised before the general discussion on this item and considered a motion for reconsideration, or a motion to refrain from making a decision or for postponement of consideration and considered a motion for adjournment of debate) is decided by vote. It is common practice that a point of order may be raised in order to submit a procedural motion to the negotiating conference.

30 Narlikar generally distinguishes between three types of deadlock, a stalemate-type, an extended delay-type, and a breakdown-type of deadlock, which do "not always exist as discrete alternatives," but may be transformed interchangeably. A. Narlikar (ed.), *Deadlocks in Multilateral Negotiations: Causes and Solutions, Introduction*, Cambridge University Press, 2010, 1, 3–5. Note, however, that, in the framework of Constitutive Negotiation governing the conventional construction of ICI, a deadlock is basically of a stalemate type and, very rarely, of an extended delay type since the negotiating parties are engaged in a consistent pursuance of establishing a treaty regime serving their common interest.

in international practice: to reach decisions by consensus before voting. Thus, the parties "shall make every effort to reach agreement on all matters of substance by consensus," and "if all efforts to reach consensus have been exhausted and no agreement has been reached, the decision shall, as a last resort, be taken by a two-thirds majority vote of the Parties present and voting, unless otherwise provided by the Convention."[31]

The voting system provides the fundamental rule that each party or member of an international organization "shall have one vote," and it may specifically set out the standard conditions for exercising the right to vote of regional economic integration organizations, in matters within their competence.[32] Decisions of the ad hoc body of conferential negotiation on matters of procedure are to be taken by a simple majority vote of the parties present and voting, while whether a matter is substantive or procedural in nature may be decided either by the body of conferential negotiation "by the majority required for a decision on matters of substance,"[33] or by the president/chairperson, who may be overruled by a simple or qualified majority of the parties present and voting following an appeal against this decision.[34] Moreover, the rules of procedure specify the different methods of voting in every detail (show of hands, roll-call vote, secret ballot) and the way they are carried out. All elections are provided to be held by secret ballot, unless otherwise decided by the ad hoc body of conferential negotiation.

4.11 *The Languages of the Negotiating Meeting or Conference*

The rules of procedure determine the official languages of the negotiating meetings or conferences. More specifically, they provide that statements made in an official

[31] See, e.g., Rules of Procedure for the Conference of the Parties to the Basel Convention on the Control of Transboundary Movements of Hazardous Wastes and Their Disposal, Art. 40(1); Rules of Procedure for the Conference of the Parties to the Rotterdam Convention on the Prior Informed Consent Procedure for Certain Hazardous Chemicals and Pesticides in International Trade, Art. 45(1); Rules of Procedure for the Conference of the Parties to the Stockholm Convention on Persistent Organic Pollutants, Art. 45(1); Rules of Procedure for Sessions of the Executive Body for the Convention on Long-Range Transboundary Air Pollution, Rule 29(1). Also Rules of Procedure of the Committee against Torture (UN Doc. CAT/C/3/Rev. 3) 1998. Rule 50(1); Rules of Procedure for Meetings of the Conference of the Parties to the Organization for the Prohibition of Chemical Weapons, Rule 69.

[32] As the rule provides, these regional economic integration organizations "shall exercise their right to vote with a number of votes equal to the number of their member States which are Parties [and] shall not exercise their right to vote if their member States exercise theirs, and vice versa." See, e.g., Rules of Procedure for Meetings of the Conference of the Parties to the Convention on Biological Diversity, Rule 39(2).

[33] E.g., Rules of Procedure for Meetings of the Conference of the Parties to the Organization for the Prohibition of Chemical Weapons, Rule 70.

[34] Rules of Procedure for Meetings of the Conference of the Parties to the Convention on Biological Diversity, Rule 40(3); Rules of Procedure of the United Nations Environment Assembly of the UNEP, Rule 45(3); Rules of Procedure for Sessions of the Executive Body for the Convention on Long-Range Transboundary Air Pollution, Rule 29(5).

language of the negotiating meeting or conference should be interpreted into the other official languages, while official documents of the meetings or conferences should be drawn up in one of the official languages and translated into the other official languages. A representative of a party may speak in a language other than an official language, provided that the party makes arrangements for interpretation into one such official language. Moreover, the secretariat should maintain a set of official records in the official languages of the negotiating meeting or conference.

On the other hand, the rules of procedure indirectly introduce the concept of working language as the negotiating language used in practice without specifying it. The relevant provision, usually incorporated in the rules of procedure, provides that "official documents of the meetings shall be drawn up in one of the official languages and translated into the other official languages."[35] In international practice, the English language is established as the working language of the negotiation for the drafting of the text of the treaty as well as of the deliberations of the subsidiary bodies of the negotiating meeting/conference.[36] This is in harmony with the "single negotiating text technique" on which all negotiation phases (Prenegotiation, Constitutive Negotiation, and Renegotiation) are based. In consequence of this working linkage between working language and the single negotiating text technique, English, as the working language for the conventional construction of ICI, carries, in actuality, greater weight compared to the other official languages of the particular treaty when a question of interpretation arises.[37]

35 Rules of Procedure for the Conference of the Parties to the Rotterdam Convention on the Prior Informed Consent Procedure for Certain Hazardous Chemicals and Pesticides in International Trade, Rule 57; Rules of Procedure for the Conference of the Parties to the Stockholm Convention on Persistent Organic Pollutants, Rule 57; Rules of Procedure for Sessions of the Executive Body for the Convention on Long-Range Transboundary Air Pollution, Rule 32; Rules of Procedure for the Conference of the Parties to the Basel Convention on the Control of Transboundary Movements of Hazardous Wastes and Their Disposal, Rule 54.

36 Sometimes with the occasional concurrence of French, associated with the linguistic clarification of certain concepts or phrases in the drafted text.

37 As Polloux (a pseudonym for Edvard Hambro) rightly and eloquently observed in relation to the UN Charter, "[i]t may be said, with all due respect to the five versions, that, English and French being the working languages, the versions in those languages carry more weight than the remaining three. It should therefore be clear that any interpretation ought to stress particularly the French and English texts, and if there should be any variance between these two texts, the safest guiding rule would be, to base the interpretation not on the text which is most restrictive, but on that in the language in which the particular point in question was drafted." Polloux, *The Interpretation of the Charter*, 23 *BYBIL* (1946), 54, at 79. The particular significance of the interpretation rule giving priority to the original language used in the negotiation and drafting of the treaty was recognized by the International Law Commission, and, though not codified in the Vienna Convention on the Law of Treaties, it was supported, during the ILC discussions, by Verdross suggesting that a provision be added to the effect that if it was impossible to find a meaning that reconciled the texts, the language to be considered should be that in which the treaty had been drawn up (YBILC [1966-I, Part 2], 874th Meeting, 21 June 1966, para. 5). Besides, the application of this interpretation rule is not incompatible with the interpretation rule of 33(4) on the interpretation of treaties authenticated in two or more languages of the Vienna Convention: as Aust remarks, "if the treaty was negotiated and drafted in only one of the authentic languages, it is natural to place more reliance on that text, particularly if it is unambiguous.

In the regional negotiating meetings or conferences, the official and the working languages are determined on the basis of the practical needs and cultural reality of the particular region. In the Mediterranean region, the rules of procedure and the practice followed at the meetings and conferences of the Barcelona Convention for the Protection of the Marine Environment and Coastal Region of the Mediterranean and Its Protocols provide an interesting example. Thus, the rules of procedure, after defining Arabic, English, French, and Spanish as the official languages of the negotiating meetings and conferences of the Barcelona Convention system, contain the standard that all working documents of these meetings and conferences, as well as all reports and collective decisions or recommendations, "shall be drawn up in one of the official languages and translated into the other three official languages."[38] Articulating, even in general terms, the principle of establishing the negotiating language for the drafting of the texts generated in the negotiating meetings and conferences, the rules of procedure signify that the establishment of one negotiating language (the working language), inextricably interwoven with the single text negotiating technique, is of catalytic importance for the effective textual building of the treaty regime. The use of English as the negotiating (working) language for drafting the treaty text may be complemented by a later authoritative harmonization of the French version of the negotiated text,[39] following an informal procedure not provided by the rules of procedure. Thus, in the Barcelona Convention system, the drafting of the texts of its new Protocols (the Hazardous Waste Protocol, 1996, and the ICZM Protocol, 2008), as well as of the texts amending the Convention and amending or replacing its existing Protocols, was formulated in English, with a sporadic obtrusion of French only in regard to the proper attribution of a very few terms. At the stage of the finalization of the text by the Ad Hoc Working Group of Legal and Technical Experts, an authoritative

This approach is not incompatible with paragraph 4 (of Article 33) and the jurisprudence of the ICJ would seem to support it in suitable cases." A. Aust, *Modern Treaty Law and Practice*, op. cit., 226.

38 Rules of Procedure for Meetings and Conferences of the Contracting Parties to the Convention for the Protection of the Mediterranean Sea against Pollution and Its Related Protocols, Rules 27, 29. It is possible, though rare, that the rules of procedure may explicitly define English as the working language of the negotiating meetings and conferences. See Arctic Council Rules of Procedure, 1998 as revised in 2013, sec. 41.

39 Note here that this authentic harmonization of the French text (one of the official languages) with the negotiated English text (official and working language) relies on the – conscious or not – broader theoretical perception that the multilingual textual origination of a treaty is context-dependent. This language contextuality in multilingual treaty texts surfaces especially in relation to the appropriate attribution of the meaning of certain legal concepts or terms that have a relational foundation, reflecting the "otherness-subjectivity" of the contexts of reference of the domestic legal orders (particular traditions, cultural values, socioeconomic conditions, connection to public interest); see E. Raftopoulos, *The Inadequacy of the Contractual Analogy in the Law of Treaties*, Publications of the Hellenic Institute of International and Foreign Law, Athens, 1990, Part Four, 257–361. Also see A. Peters, *Universalist Assumptions and Implications of Comparative Law: Should They Be Deconstructed? Proceedings of the 93rd Annual Meeting of the American Society of International Law*, 1999, 366–369, generally pointing to the importance of the "otherness-subjectivity" of the contexts of reference in different legal systems and the limitations of the comparative method of law.

harmonization of the French versions was carried out by a special informal procedure. An open-ended informal deliberation group was set up and coordinated by the secretariat, consisting of a very limited number of representatives of the contracting parties – mainly of legal background, in order to facilitate the consolidation of the definitive formulation of the negotiated English text and, consequently, to secure the authentic harmonization of the French text with systematic reference to the English text.

4.12 *Amendments: Relationship to the Conventional Regime*

Finally, the rules of procedure provide for the possibility of their amendment (or, in some instances, suspension) on the basis of a decision of the meeting or conference of the parties or by the established organ of full representation of the parties, commonly taken by consensus, or, if consensus is not attainable, by a qualified two-thirds majority of its members, considered a substantive issue,[40] or in some international organizations by a majority vote.[41] Particularly in the case of international organizations, an additional procedural rule may be contained: that the rules of procedure cannot be amended until the organ of full representation (assembly, conference) has received a report on the proposed amendment from a committee established for that purpose, and, in some cases, they may be suspended provided that twenty-four hours' notice of the proposal for the suspension has been given.[42]

The final rule usually incorporated in the rules of procedure refers to the overriding authority (relationship of primacy) of the treaty regime over its rules of procedure: in the event of a conflict between any rule of the rules of procedure and any provision of the treaty regime system (convention and its related protocols), the latter "shall prevail."[43]

40 E.g., Rules of Procedure for Meetings of the Conference of the Parties to the Organization for the Prohibition of Chemical Weapons, Rules 93, 94; Rules of Procedure for Meetings of the Conference of the Parties to the Convention on Biological Diversity, Rule 56; Rules of Procedure for the Conference of the Parties to the Rotterdam Convention on the Prior Informed Consent for Certain Hazardous Chemicals and Pesticides in International Trade, Rule 59; Rules of Procedure of the United Nations Environment Assembly of the UNEP, Rules 71 and 72; Rules of Procedure for the Conference of the Parties to the Basel Convention on the Control of Transboundary Movements of Hazardous Wastes and Their Disposal, Rule 57.

41 E.g., Rules of Procedure of the Assembly of the IMO, Rule 57; Rules of Procedure for the General Conference of the IAEA, Rules 101 (amendment: simple majority of the members present and voting), 102 (suspension: a qualified majority).

42 E.g., Rules of Procedure of the United Nations Environment Assembly of the UNEP, Rules 72, 73. See also Rules of Procedure for Meetings of the Conference of the Parties to the Organization for the Prohibition of Chemical Weapons, Rules 93 (applied only to amendments).

43 E.g., Rules of Procedure for Sessions of the Executive Body for the Convention on Long-Range Transboundary Air Pollution, Rule 34; Rules of Procedure for Meetings of the Conference of the Parties to the Convention on Biological Diversity, Rule 57; Rules of Procedure for the Conference of the Parties to the Rotterdam Convention on the Prior Informed Consent for Certain Hazardous Chemicals and Pesticides in International Trade, Rule 60.

5 NEGOTIATION OF THE TEXTUAL PATTERN OF INTERNATIONAL AGREEMENTS

The essential dividing line between the Prenegotiation and Constitutive Negotiation processes is the quality of the generated relational regime perception of the negotiating parties: it lies in the determinative value of the legal force of the textual outcome of the negotiation. Whereas Prenegotiation produces a text of declarative form and force or a text of an interim international commitment (a declaration-oriented negotiation), the Constitutive Negotiation creates an agreement of ICI, i.e. a text endowed with a legal status that conventionally establishes a relational regime of ICI (a treaty-oriented negotiation). The treaty text is "conventionally" constituted by the negotiating parties by reference to the existing and evolving relevant order of international law and policies (international context) and the state of development of domestic orders (domestic context) and in pursuance of a collective legislative purpose.

The negotiation of the textual pattern of the treaty instrument takes centre stage in the Constitutive Negotiation process. The proposed term "Constitutive Negotiation" essentially emanates from the very constitutive character of the resulting agreement of ICI (ICI agreement). In fact, the legality of its text is not to be sought solely on the alleged "consensual objectivity" of its terms, because it clearly goes beyond the exclusive legality of an objectively reached contract-like consent. It is to be sought in the nature of the creatively developing ICI relationship, which is established by a treaty and is punctuated by it.[44]

This complexity of a relational approach to treaty/international agreement that is directed to the future, protecting and advancing ICI in terms of evolving creative consensus, collective trust governance, and dynamic compatibility with the context of relevant international conventional or declarative regimes and practices requires, for exactly these reasons, the "patternment" of the negotiated constitution of treaty/international agreement. Thus, irrespective of the object of negotiation, the negotiation process for the establishment of a treaty is patterned in the three interrelated levels:

- at the level of referential patternment;
- at the level of morphological patternment; and
- at the level of normative patternment.

44 For the attribution of a "constitutive character" to treaties, see, generally, Raftopoulos, *The Inadequacy of the Contractual Analogy in the Law of Treaties*, *supra* note 39. The theory of the "constitutive act" was perceptively developed by eminent German legal philosopher Otto von Gierke (*Die Genossenschaftstheorie und die Deutsche Rechtsprechung*, Berlin, 1887, 114 *et. seq.*) and, somehow, was followed by the Realist School of New Haven (or the Yale Law School Realist School) heralding the "policy approach" – as opposed to the "rule approach" – to law, confined, however, to the limits of its strict methodological programme (e.g., M. McDougal and W. M. Reisman, "The Prescribing Function in World Constitutive Process: How International Law Is Made" (1980). Faculty Scholarship Series. Paper 2661. Available at: http://digitalcommons.law.yale.edu/fss_papers/2661). See E. Raftopoulos, *Course, Theory and Language of International Law: "Objectivism" or International Common Interest?* op. cit., 41ff.

5.1 *Patternment at the Level of Context of Reference (Referential Patternment)*

The first step to Constitutive Negotiation is the determination of the overall context of the treaty/international agreement under negotiation. "In the beginning was the context" – "the context" signifying the relational interconnection of the negotiated incubation of the treaty regime and the existing and evolving international order of law (order *in processu*): the former is to be appropriately integrated into the latter, adding a new facet to the background of a horizontally developing, open-ended order of normative relation patterns serving ICI. In fact, such integration has a legitimating effect on the treaty under negotiation, because it supplements the will of the negotiating parties with its indispensable relational foundation.

Since Constitutive Negotiation occurs in context, it is necessary to identify the reference configuration conditions that fashion this fundamental interrelationship and guide the negotiation process. A careful look into the law and practice of conventionally constructing ICI unveils that the reference configuration conditions are constantly associated with the performance of three interrelated but distinct functions: identifiability, compatibility, and heuristic. Correspondingly, like the Prenegotiation phase, a set of three specific contextual indicators of reference configuration is shaped that perceptively provides a holistic balancing-in-innovation approach as a first step towards the negotiated conventional construction of ICI and guides the negotiation process. These are: context identification, contextual compatibility, and added value or constructive heuristic.

5.1.1 Identifiability of the Context of Reference (Context Identification)

By the use of this criterion, the negotiating parties expressly recognize the scope of the interrelationship between the treaty under negotiation and its context and they negotiate its identifiability. The identification of the context of reference is intersubjective, holistic, and dynamic. It refers to the totality of international normative instruments, generated either as treaty regimes, or as decisions of international institutional entities, or as international declarative instruments, which express, to a varying quality and extent, a normative relationship with the thematicality of the treaty under negotiation (relational order).

More specifically, such a relational order may be identified by reference not only to the treaty regimes in force but also to those not yet in force or those that have never entered into force and have become inactive.[45] Moreover, the negotiating parties

45 A characteristic example of such an inactive treaty regime is the Lugano Convention on Civil Liability for Damage Resulting from Activities Dangerous to the Environment, 1993 (27 ILM [1993] 1228), adopted in the framework of the Council of Europe, which, because of its advanced normative quality and the insightful comprehensiveness of its approach to the issue of environmental civil liability, has been systematically taken into account during the Constitutive Negotiation of subsequent related conventional regimes or during the negotiation of related guidelines as "context of reference," thus exerting a determinative impact on the basic normative structure and the substantive

evaluate the related importance of relevant decisions of international institutional entities as well as of relevant international declarative instruments (declarations of principles, guidelines, strategies, goals action plans) produced either in the framework of global or regional institutional entities or as outcomes of global or regional conferential negotiations. In this process, it may be agreed that, for reasons directly connected with the possibility of establishing the treaty under negotiation and of securing its internal consistency, the identifiability of the context of reference may be "subjectified." This subjectification may be carried out *ratione materiae*: by agreeing that a particular or certain international normative instruments should be excluded from the scope of the context of reference because they are considered beyond the purpose of the treaty under negotiation.[46] It may also be expressed *ratione personae*: by providing a generic individuating application of an important treaty regime forming an indispensable part of the context of reference where one or more negotiating parties that do not participate in this treaty regime are generally exempted.[47] On the other hand, note that the inclusion of a general reference to international law as a context of reference to a treaty under negotiation may exert a balancing effect in this latter case since it would allow the nonconventional implementation of many commonly accepted regulatory and normative arrangements contained in this treaty regime.

content of these instruments. See, e.g., Basel Protocol on Liability and Compensation for Damage Resulting from Transboundary Movements of Hazardous Wastes and Their Disposal, 1999, and also {I}Guidelines on Liability and Compensation for Damage Resulting from Pollution of the Marine Environment in the Mediterranean Sea Area, 2008, {/I}adopted by Decision 17/4 of the 15th Meeting of the Contracting Parties to the Barcelona Convention, Almeria, Spain (UNEP[DEPI]/MED IG.17/10 Annex V, 133–140).

46 Thus, during the negotiations of the Nagoya Protocol on Access to Genetic Resources and the Fair and Equitable Sharing of Benefits Arising from Their Utilization to the Convention on Biological Diversity, 2010, the negotiating parties agreed to exclude from its context of reference the ILO Convention 169 – Indigenous and Tribal Peoples Convention, 1989, which, promoting the rights of indigenous and tribal people, incorporates their rights over natural resources embracing the genetic resources. Its particular direction to advance the rights of indigenous and tribal peoples over their natural resources in a conventional legal framework, also touching on the governance of genetic resources, was considered as going beyond the balance pursued in the framework of the Nagoya Protocol, and, as a result, it was excluded from its context. According to the formulation of the Preamble of the Nagoya Protocol, the legal instruments agreed to compose its context are the FAO International Treaty on Plant Genetic Resources for Food and Agriculture, 2001, the WHO International Health Regulations, 2005, and the United Nations Declaration on the Rights of Indigenous Peoples, 2007 (UNGAR 61/295).

47 Characteristically, the reference to the UNCLOS is generically individuated in the framework of the Barcelona Convention, 1976, in its Preamble ("Bearing in mind the relevant provisions of the United Nations Convention on the Law of the Sea, done at Montego Bay on 10 December 1982 and *signed by many Contracting Parties*") as well as in the disclaimer clause of Article 3(3) ("Nothing in this Convention and its Protocols shall prejudice the rights and positions of any State concerning the United Nations Convention on the Law of the Sea of 1982").

5.1.2 Consistency with the Context of Reference (Contextual Consistency)

On the basis of the criterion of contextual consistency, the negotiating parties proceed to secure the compatibility of the treaty under negotiation with its identified context of reference and, in effect, the inter-regimes consistency. This inter-regimes consistency has a *functional* and a *quasi-legislative* character.

The functional consistency generally refers to the appropriate and effective coordination between the treaty under negotiation and the normative instruments of the identified context of reference. The negotiating parties should assure that the powers and duties contained in the treaty under negotiation are not in conflict with those of the related treaty regimes. They should also assure that the provided powers and duties do not constitute regression or excessive restriction of the basic regulatory arrangements attained by the related treaty regimes. Instead, they should ensure that their interconnection works in compatible continuity: the diversity of the treaty under negotiation should creatively and comprehensively contribute (either by specialization or by expansion in view of its particular context of reference) to the protection and promotion of ICI governance. In fact, the need to ensure inter-regimes consistency is expressly stated in those treaty regimes that provide their future conventional specialization. A cardinal example is the UNCLOS in relation to other special Conventions for the Protection and Preservation of the Marine Environment. Thus, Article 237(2) sets forth an "inter-regimes consistency" relational norm providing that these special Conventions "should be carried out in a manner consistent with the general principles and objectives of this Convention." Conventional environmental regimes normally contain an "inter-regimes consistency" relational norm.[48] And in certain cases, the inter-regimes consistency relational norm may take the form of a "mutual supportiveness" relational norm when it refers to existing related conventional environmental regimes that govern – or may provide the frame for governing of – only certain aspects or elements of the conventional environmental regime under negotiation. The constitutive negotiation of the Minimata Convention on Mercury, 2013, provides a characteristic example of developing and incorporating the mutual supportiveness relational norm in view of the existing special conventional regimes. Thus, in its Preamble, the Minimata

48 See, e.g., the "inter-regimes consistency" relational norm as set forth in Article 11 of the Basel Convention on the Control of Transboundary Movements of Hazardous Wastes and Their Disposal, 1989, which stipulates that the Parties to the Convention may "enter into any bilateral, multilateral or regional agreements or arrangements" provided that "these agreements or arrangements shall stipulate provisions which are not less environmentally sound than those provided for by this Convention in particular taking into account the interests of developing countries," and that, for those such agreements or arrangements entered into force prior to the Convention, the Convention will not affect them "provided that such agreements are compatible with the environmentally sound management of hazardous wastes and other wastes as required by this Convention." At the regional level, the Barcelona Convention, 1976, typically contains an inter-regime consistency relational norm in Article 3(2) setting out that the contracting parties may establish related "bilateral or multilateral agreements, including regional or sub-regional agreements … provided that such agreements are consistent with this Convention and the Protocols and conform to international law."

Convention recognizes its mutually supportive function with the relevant environmental treaty regimes (especially mentioning the Basel Convention on the Control of Transboundary Movements of Hazardous Wastes and Their Disposal and the Rotterdam Convention on the Prior Informed Consent Procedure for Certain Hazardous Chemicals and Pesticides in International Trade) while stating the general qualifying parameters of this mutually supportive relational norm: no impact effect of this Convention on the rights and obligations of any party deriving from any existing treaty regime, and no hierarchy between this Convention and other related treaty regimes is created by the foregoing recital.[49]

The quasi-legislative consistency, on the other hand, refers to the process of "conflation" between aspects of the treaty under negotiation and aspects of the related treaty regimes carried out through negotiation. More specifically, it involves the appropriate incorporation of "definitions," "principles," "obligation-duties," "power-rights," "technical/scientific standards," or "objects," contained in the texts of the related treaties, into the draft of the treaty under negotiation. It may also involve the appropriate incorporation of extensive technical annexes that are conventionally consolidated in the related treaty regimes and for which the negotiation may be only marginal. And it may further establish frames for creative cooperation with the relevant institutional organs of related treaty regimes with a view to develop certain common aspects – a constructive, legislative realization of the mutually supportive relational norm mentioned earlier. These levels of incorporation reflect a fundamental characteristic of the relational interconnection between relevant treaty regimes. More generally, they point to an aspect of the horizontal normativity of international law where the protection and promotion of ICI is carried out through a normative standardization process. In actuality, the specific determination of the scope of normative incorporation, a direct or an adjusted incorporation of the aforementioned elements, is part of the Constitutive Negotiation process.

On the other hand, a deficient or inadequate approach and management of contextual consistency of the treaty under negotiation may bring about serious "fragmentation effects" ("resulting fragmentation"), as in the negotiation of declarative instruments in the Prenegotiation phase, having, however, more far-reaching effects because of the legal nature and status of the treaty and its relational character. In treaty Constitutive Negotiation, gaps or shortcomings in relation to contextual

49 Minimata Convention on Mercury, 2013, Preamble, paras. 9–12. A characteristic formulation of the mutual supportiveness relational norm is included, e.g., in the UNESCO Convention on the Protection and Promotion of Diversity of Cultural Expressions, 2005, where Art. 20 establishes its relationship to other treaty regimes to which the parties to the Convention are also parties to them on the basis of mutual supportiveness, setting out the same qualifying parameters: non-subordination of the Convention to such other treaty, complementarity ("when interpreting and applying the other treaties to which they are parties or when entering into other international obligations, Parties shall take into account the relevant provisions of this Convention"), and no impact effect of this Convention ("Nothing in this Convention shall be interpreted as modifying rights and obligations of the Parties under any other treaties to which they are parties").

consistency with related or relevant treaty regimes or, even, declarative instruments (declared areas of normativity), stabilize normative or governance isolations from the working context of reference and the polycentricity of its ordering. Or they produce uncoordinated autonomies between treaty regimes, thus leading to an increasingly inefficient, diverging overdevelopment of the international legal order. In addition, it blurs the determination of the added value of the negotiated treaty on the basis of the next criterion.

The application of the contextual consistency criterion, in view of its enormous complexity of international legal ordering, should be basically directed by the legal experts of the negotiating participants. And there is one even more subtle reason for this. A legal expert is well equipped to assess the contextuality of the quasi-legislative character of the inter-regimes consistency: that normative incorporation is always purposive, serving the particular treaty ICI regime and, in effect, the application of the appropriately incorporated "definitions," "principles," "obligation-duties," "power-rights," "technical/scientific standards," or "objects" contained in the texts of the related treaties, might be different in the treaty under negotiation owing to the differences in their respective contexts and relational regimes.[50]

5.1.3 An Added Value or Constructive Heuristic Field

On the basis of the criterion of an added value or constructive heuristic field, the negotiating parties proceed to the scoping of the field of additional normative, regulatory, or institutional value to be covered by the negotiated treaty vis-à-vis its identified context of reference. They endeavour to answer the question about "what the additional or novel aspects of the treaty under negotiation would be, and, how its prospective emergence as a distinctive treaty regime in the relational international legal order would be justified."

The effective answer to this complex and far-reaching question is directly linked with the building of a creative common understanding of the negotiating parties as regards the constitution of the treaty regime, constructively supported by the specialized contribution of the participating international institutional entities (especially the representatives of competent international organizations or relevant treaty regimes) or NGOs granted observer status.

In the light of this, the added value or constructive heuristic field requires very attentive negotiation. It refers, more specifically, to the collective identification of

[50] It is characteristic that in the *MOX Plant* case, the arbitral tribunal, set up under Annex VII UNCLOS, discussing the British objection to its jurisdiction on account of the same matter being also pending before an OSPAR arbitral tribunal and the ECJ, observed: "even if the OSPAR Convention, the EC Treaty and the Euratom treaty contain rights or obligations similar to or identical with the rights set out in [the UNCLOS], the rights and obligations under these agreements have a separate existence from those under [the UNCLOS]." *MOX Plant* case, Request for Provisional Measures Order (*Ireland* v. the *United Kingdom*) (3 December 2001) International Tribunal for the Law of the Sea, 126 ILR (2005), 273, para. 50.

all those developing or innovative legal, political, economic, social, or technical-scientific aspects of the treaty regime under negotiation, or, if appropriate, of its regional particularities, the final purpose of which is the construction and advancement of ICI. Note that, in view of the catalytic importance of this process for the effective construction of consensus on the added value field, collective identification of these developing or innovative elements should take into account, and where possible embrace, the views and proposals of the widest possible spectrum of relevant groupings of interests liaised with legal, scientific technological, and socioeconomic stakeholders, but also with the regional approaches related to the multifactorial identification of the region under consideration. The latter is particularly characteristic in the case of the Mediterranean region and the negotiating construction of its marine environmental regime. Here, the cumulative evaluation of its special features, namely economic (developed-developing states – a microcosm of the North–South relationship, but also a region of economic and development action of the EU), political (international political competitions immediately connected with international peace and security, as well as a region of special political interest for the EU as a European regional sea), cultural (inter-cultural and inter-religious relations), legal (different and strikingly divergent legal and political systems), environmental-developmental (vulnerability of the Mediterranean environment, utmost need for sustainability of the resources of the Mediterranean Basin, protection of its marine and coastal ecosystem), or maritime sovereignty or jurisdiction (disputes concerning the delimitation of maritime boundaries in a semi-enclosed sea, strategic interests of third powerful states) shape a dynamic framework for the multifactorial identification of the region, which generates an added value field that, in actuality, determines all phases of the negotiating process and creates appropriate region-specific treaty arrangements.

5.2 *Morphological Patternment*

Since the interrelationship between the added value field of the treaty under negotiation and its context of reference is dynamic and complementary, the textual depiction of the treaty should be cast into pattern in order to secure a more resilient, adaptable, and effective governance of its purpose and the uncertainties surrounding it. As a result, the text of the treaty, in practice, is shaped following two methodical approaches: Framework Agreement – Performative Protocols *in processu* and Integrative Agreement – Executing Annexes *in processu*. Each methodical approach is related to the distinctive characteristics of the negotiated treaty relation as an ICI conventional relation, and to the continuous attainment of its legislative purpose, as required by the interrelationship mentioned earlier.

5.2.1 The Framework Agreement-Performative Protocols *in Processu* Approach

This morphological pattern, constituting a continuum of a scaled development and implementation of a treaty ICI regime, allows the prompt establishment of the treaty regime under negotiation despite the difficulties and uncertainties surrounding certain specific aspects of its operation and implementation. It points to a particular method of constituting a treaty regime as a progressively built continuum whereby the normative framework and the institutional structure of an ICI relation are conventionally established: the treaty regime is consolidated (framework convention/agreement) and, through the negotiably determined process of specification of the framework convention by its related protocols (performative protocols), the minimum acceptable field of specific operation and implementation of the treaty regime, scaled in time (*in processu*),[51] is attained. Of interest is also a different version of constituting treaty-performative protocols continuum of scaled development that may be found in the framework of the UN: a largely normatively developed framework treaty is supplemented by conventionally separate performative protocols that expand its regime operation in specific related areas, implying a more participation-oriented scaling.[52]

It is clear that this methodical approach demonstrates, in the most eloquent manner, the broader – and, surprisingly, long overlooked – theoretical conception that the negotiability of treaty and its generated ICI regime constitutes a determinative element of its normativity. The parties, being actually "in treaty relation,"[53] are bound fundamentally *relationally* (conventional constitution and

[51] A characteristic example of such functional interconnection between framework convention and performative protocols is found in Article 29 of the Barcelona Convention, 1976, which provides that the minimum acceptable field of specific operation and implementation of the Barcelona Convention system for a contracting party is that it will become a party to the Convention and, at the same time, a party "to at least one of its protocols," and vice versa.

[52] Thus, the United Nations Convention against Transnational Organized Crime, 2000, sets forth its functional interconnection with its performative protocols in Art. 37 (Relation with Protocols) as follows: "1. This Convention may be supplemented by one or more protocols. 2. In order to become a Party to a protocol, a State or a regional economic integration organization must also be a Party to this Convention. 3. A State Party to this Convention is not bound by a protocol unless it becomes a Party to the protocol in accordance with the provisions thereof. 4. Any protocol to this Convention shall be interpreted together with this Convention, taking into account the purpose of that protocol." So far, there are three such protocols: the Protocol to Prevent, Suppress and Punish Trafficking in Persons, Especially Women and Children, supplementing the United Nations Convention against Transnational Organized Crime, 2000; the Protocol against the Smuggling of Migrants by Land, Sea and Air, supplementing the United Nations Convention against Transnational Organized Crime, 2000; and the Protocol against the Illicit Manufacturing of and Trafficking in Firearms, Their Parts and Components and Ammunition, supplementing the United Nations Convention against Transnational Organized Crime, 2001.

[53] According to an insightful observation of Clive Parry, which is consistent with the proper etymological force/performance of the term and concept of "treaty," "to treat is but to negotiate and to be 'in treaty' is but to be in negotiation . . . An epoch such as the present in which 'consensus' and 'confrontation' are so often spoken of and as often achieved or effected, will not necessarily be out of sympathy with the view that the term and concept of a 'treaty' is not, and should not be, necessarily confined to

continuous development of a relation serving ICI progressively, in a multilevel manner and in terms of referential complementarity) rather than simply *contractually* (conclusion of a contract-like agreement producing legal results exclusively on the basis of an original perfect coincidence of the wills of the parties – *consensus ad idem* – according to the familiar – but inadequate – analogy of private law contract).[54] The negotiability of the treaty regime allows the negotiating parties, on the one hand, to proceed to the constitution of the treaty regime determining the "normative pacing" of its scaled specification and operation in time and, on the other hand, to eventually produce a more integrated and effective specific implementation at the minimum acceptable level. And they may achieve this negotiably through the continuous adjustment or adaptation of the performative protocols – but also of the framework convention itself – by means of their amendment or replacement, as well as through the establishment of new and additional performative protocols. In the latter case, these performative protocols either constitute a specified application of duties-obligations of the parties, cast in a framework form in the convention, or they are implied from the legislative purpose of the framework convention and its context of reference, in accordance with the consensual approach of the parties as is punctuated by their experience and knowledge in the relevant treaty regime. Overall, the framework agreement-performative protocols *in processu* approach offers, apart from the speed of implementation, the potential of a treaty regime specification as it is collectively developed – a realistic approach to ICI treaty governance in view of the underlying uncertainties surrounding its relational implementation.

On the other hand, a commendable "regime-working dimension" is generated, resulting from the pacing of the scaled application of the framework convention through its performative protocols. Thus, although this scaled application produces a contractual effect – as is expressly provided, each protocol is binding only to those parties that have ratified it, it constitutes, at the same time, a *relational platform* for the appropriate – more knowledgeable and more conscious – expansion of participation in the specification of the treaty regime. Since each protocol is a performative aspect of the scaled specific implementation of the content, or even the purpose, of the framework convention, it is open for participation, with the observer status, to those contracting parties that have not as yet become contracting parties to it, despite the fact that they have also participated in its Constitutive Negotiation but for various reasons have not proceeded to its ratification or even to its signature. This wider relational platform, where the functional application of the particular protocol is

a concluded agreement, binding in law." C. Parry, "Of Treaties," in A. Parry (ed.),*Collected Papers of Clive Parry*, Wildy, Simmonds and Hill Publishing, 2012, Volume II, 289.

54 For the inadequacy of the transfer of the analogy of the theory of private law contract into the law of treaties and for the theoretically neglected public law character of the latter, see, e.g., Raftopoulos, *The Inadequacy of the Contractual Analogy in the Law of Treaties, supra* note 39; *infra*, Allot., *Eunomia*, op. cit. *passim*.

operated at the meetings/conferences of the contracting parties, favours the creative interaction between parties and nonparties to the protocol (but, overall, contracting parties to the treaty regime), with the result that the progress of its ratification is expedited, a more balancing focus for its implementation is built, and more light is shed on its operational usefulness for its parties and for the treaty regime in general.

5.2.2 The Integrative Agreement-Executing Annexes *in Processu* Approach

This alternative morphological pattern is usually applicable where there is greater homogeneity among the negotiating participants or the negotiated treaty ICI regime is technical. In these cases, the continuum of a scaled development and implementation of a treaty regime is less evident for it operates in a more integral field of implementation: the treaty regime is constituted by an integrative convention/agreement and its executing annexes, which, being an integral part of the integrative convention/agreement, set out its specific field of implementation in a seemingly more comprehensive manner. The executing annexes are usually technical, formulating specifications of the duties-obligations and powers-rights constituting the integrative agreement. In some cases, they may constitute more complete elaborations of the duties-obligations, powers-rights or, even, institutional provisions of the integrative agreement required by complexities in their implementation or compliance,[55] or the need for additional details on mechanisms and procedures,[56] or by contextual particularities affecting their application.[57] This approach allows a clear and succinct drafting of the main body of the integrative agreement, channelling the technical, implementative, or procedural/institutional details to the annexes. As a result, the need for effective adaptability of such treaty details to contextual developments will be adequately served, because a more flexible, simplified amendment procedure is set out in the agreement governing the annexes, which has relational characteristics: when amendments to annexes or new annexes are adopted, they can automatically apply to all contracting parties or they can further provide an opt-in or opt-out regime.

On the other hand, such "comprehensiveness" in the integrative agreement-executing annexes approach – instead of the minimum acceptable level pursued by the previous morphological pattern – is actually relative: it is determined

55 See, e.g., the Stockholm Convention on Persistent Organic Pollutants, 2001, Annex A, Part II (how to implement measures on polychlorinated biphenyls) and Annex B, Part II (how to implement measures on DDT).

56 See, e.g., UNCLOS, Annexes II–IX.

57 See, e.g., the UN Convention to Combat Desertification, 1994, which includes four regional implementation Annexes (Annex I: Regional Implementation Annex for Africa; Annex II: Regional Implementation Annex for Asia; Annex III: Regional Implementation Annex for Latin American and the Caribbean; Annex IV: Regional Implementation Annex for the Northern Mediterranean), each establishing a region-specific approach to govern desertification that applies to all contracting parties, especially in regard to financial and technical assistance.

intersubjectively in process and in context, being complemented by the formulation of a framework clause providing for expanding the field of specific implementation, thus leaving an open gate for scaled implementation. And this goes parallel with the constant adaptation of the Annexes to the changing circumstances by following the procedure applicable to the convention/agreement. In sum, the negotiability of the treaty regime, as a continuum of scaled specification in its application, continues to function mutatis mutandis.

It is noteworthy that, under this alternative morphological pattern, the comprehensiveness of the specifying field of implementation associated with the executing annexes may also be "subjectified" through their negotiated differentiation between mandatory and optional annexes.[58] This form of negotiability may be usually agreed in cases of global Constitutive Negotiation of technical treaty regimes, where the diversity of interests among the negotiating parties and their heterogeneity, coupled with the need to ensure the widest possible participation for more effective and efficient protection and promotion (governance) of ICI, requires, from the outset, a recognition of the possibility of introducing a specifying field of implementation of "different speeds." At the same time, it has been observed that such negotiability of the treaty regime equally helps and facilitates, in practice, the mobility of the parties into this implementation field, thus relativizing and progressively containing, through the gradual enlargement of the participation in the optional annexes, the implications of different speeds.

5.3 *Normative Patternment or Patternment of Content*

The normative patternment lies at the heart of Constitutive Negotiation. Both the referential patternment and the morphological patternment are integrated into it. It is important to stress, by way of introduction, that the knowledge of the normative patternment of the treaty under negotiation, as well as its negotiable management regarding the nature of the issues, the force of the interests of the negotiating parties and their initial vague perception of ICI (importance, functionality, effectiveness, resilience, and permanence of the negotiated treaty regime), constitute the pillars around which the Constitutive Negotiation process is unveiled. The elements of the normative patternment are specified in what follows.

[58] It is characteristic here that the morphological pattern of the treaty regimes developed in the framework of IMO, e.g., the MARPOL 73/78 Convention that contains a series of very detailed technical Annexes, whose Annex I (Prevention of Pollution by Oil – in force 1984) and Annex II (Control of Pollution by Noxious Liquid Substances – in force 1987) are mandatory, whereas the rest of the Annexes are optional (Annex III, Prevention of Pollution by Harmful Substances in Packaged Form, in force 1992; Annex IV, Prevention of Pollution by Sewage from Ships, in force 2003; Annex V, Prevention of Pollution by Garbage from Ships, in force 1988; and Annex V, Prevention of Air Pollution from Ships, in force 2005).

5.3.1 The Preamble

Providing the introductory part of the treaty under negotiation, the preamble encompasses its negotiably determined context, sometimes points to its purpose, and forms its justificatory basis. As a result, the determinative criterion for its negotiation is how to design its coherence with the text of the main body of the treaty. Its negotiation should be conducted with the utmost care, particularly in view of the fact that this coherence has a determinative *legal effect*: the preamble constitutes the immediate context for the interpretation of the negotiated treaty and can be used for the future interpretation of its purpose and objective when a dispute about their application and interpretation may arise, according to Art. 31(2) of the Vienna Convention on the Law of Treaties, 1969. The general wording of the preamble may facilitate, in the event of any future dispute concerning the extent of the meaning of obligations-duties or powers-rights stipulated in the treaty, their broader interpretation or, at least, the avoidance of adopting their restrictive interpretation.[59] In some instances, and due to the particular nature and purpose of the treaty, such interpretative effect may be reinforced by the inclusion of a principle-related recital in the preamble containing an account of the canvass of principles in accordance with which the parties declare their determination to act.[60] This significant interpretative consequence requires that careful attention should be given to the negotiation of the preamble and the building of its coherence with the main text of the treaty.

Thus, after a first exploratory discussion of the content of its initial design, the negotiation of the draft of the preamble should be agreed (usually at the initiative of the chairperson of the negotiating session) to be transferred to the latest possible point in the negotiating process, when the main text of the treaty will be negotiably ripe. Otherwise, the choice to insist on embarking on its negotiation to the fullest possible extent and before negotiating the main text of the treaty will prove misleading and endanger the advancement of the negotiating conference. After all, the subsequent realization of its futile negotiation cannot rectify the crucial waste of time, and its side effects may hinder the development of the negotiating process.

Relatedly, the instrumental function of the preamble in the negotiating process should also be considered, for it can be employed by the negotiating parties as a final "negotiating storage." Thus, in cases where the negotiation has reached its final stage and is, nevertheless, bogged down over certain points persistently supported by a particular delegation (or by a very small number of delegations) but strongly

59 R. Cardiner, *Treaty Interpretation*, Oxford International Law Library, Oxford University Press, 2008, 187. It is noteworthy that, in regard to legislative instruments, the preamble is attributed a similar interpretative value since there is an established principle that it can be used to resolve problems of interpretation arising from provisions contained in the body of the legislative instrument.

60 For instance, the recently adopted Arms Trade Treaty, 2013, in its last preambular paragraph, makes a full account of the principles in accordance with which "The States Parties to this Treaty" are "determined to act."

rejected by the rest, then it may be proposed that these points may be transposed, after agreeing on their appropriate formulation, into the preamble. The usefulness of the function of the preamble as negotiating storage is obvious: on the one hand, it provides the possibility of a direct escape from an impasse and of a successful completion of the negotiation process and, on the other hand, it facilitates the retreat of the insisting delegation in a face-saving manner. Note, however, that the use of this negotiation function of the preamble should be evaluated very carefully, precisely because of its interpretative significance for the implementation of the treaty, as explained earlier.

At a more general level, one should not also underestimate the *referential power* of the preamble in regard to the evolving process of negotiating governance of a treaty regime. The formulation of phrases expressing concern about the continuous deterioration or the increasing frequency or severity of a particular situation, or recognizing the importance of certain developing policies or actions, may have a determinative effect in future negotiating governance: such phrases may provide the appropriate referential basis empowering future negotiations towards the development or expansion of the ICI treaty regime.

Finally, from a more technical point of view, the wording of the preamble is designed in a standard manner, integrating context-declarative and conventional elements. Thus, the recitals in the preamble, pinpointing the reasons for the establishment of the treaty ICI regime, are introduced by verbal participles commonly typified by standard verbs of diverging or graded emphasis, like "considering," "recognizing," "deeply concerned with," "noting," "affirming," "taking into account," "recalling," "being aware of," "bearing in mind," "convinced," "determined," "emphasizing," etc. The concluding paragraph introduces, in an identical manner ("have agreed as follows"), the conventional (consensus) foundation of the main body of the treaty.

5.3.2 Legislative Use of Terms: Legislative Definitions

This part of treaty negotiation is important in two respects, first, from the point of view of negotiating the text draft and, second, from the point of view of negotiating the treaty's legislating force.

From the point of view of text drafting, the "definitions" or the "use of terms" for the purposes of the agreement constitute part of the treaty pattern and, broadly, evidence of its legislative nature. Their inclusion, in fact, simplifies the structure of the text and their extent varies according to the nature of the treaty and the negotiating perception of the parties. More specifically, they refer to key terms, identified by the negotiating parties, which are formulated in various forms serving the purposes of the treaty – whence the standard phrase at the beginning of the relevant article "For the purposes of this Convention, {*term*} means . . .".

The key terms may be formulated positively ("The term means . . . ") or positively and negatively when it is necessary to exclude specified things ("The term means . . . " "The term does not mean . . . ") and, sometimes, they may take the "include" form because they refer to "areas of marginal uncertainty" and their usefulness lies in the fact that they may clarify open-textured aspects of the term's meaning.[61]

The key terms may be legal or technical and their meaning determination may be exclusive, closed,[62] or open-textured.[63] It is, however, noteworthy that in the case of open-textured definitions cast in the "include" form, a special *scaled-sourcing drafting* technique may be used whereby the meaning determination may contextually – and dynamically – derive. Thus, the indicative enumeration of the elements contained in the "include" form definition of the key terms may be designed relationally: to be complemented by annexes to the treaty that can be amended by a simple majority procedure, by other relevant international agreements or, even, by the national legislations of the state parties provided that such meaning determination does not deter normative progression.[64]

According to the international practice of treaty legislative drafting, the definitions of the key terms are usually grouped in one article (the first or the second). It is, however, also possible, particularly in cases where the text of a treaty is extensive and complex, addressing a broad spectrum of issues, to agree that the definitions of certain special key terms be incorporated in the thematic section or accompany the article to which they refer, thus facilitating the reading – and the understanding – of the treaty. A typical example of this last case is the UNCLOS, 1982, which, apart from Article 1, which sets out the "Use of Terms" of the Convention, contains a series

61 See *The Preparation of Legislation*, Report of the Renton Commission, London, Cmnd. 6053, 1973, 66ff.

62 Characteristic examples of exclusive or closed legal terms are the definitions contained in the UNCLOS and referring to "pollution of the marine environment" and "dumping" (Art. 1(4)(5)), to "passage" (Art. 18), to "warships" (Art. 29), to "archipelagic sea lanes passage" (Art. 53(3)), to "maritime casualty" (Art. 221(2)), or to "international organization" (Annex IX, Art. 1), whereas examples of exclusive or closed technical terms are the definition of "climate change" in Art. 1(2) of the UN Framework Convention on Climate Change, 1992, the definitions of "biological diversity," "biological resources," and "biotechnology") in Art. 2 of the Convention on Biological Diversity, 1992, or the definition of "chemical weapons" and "toxic chemicals" of Art. II(1)(2) in the Convention on the Prohibition of the Development, Production, Stockpiling and Use of Chemical Weapons and on Their Destruction, 1993.

63 As, for instance, in the definition of "underwater cultural heritage" in the UNESCO Convention on the Protection of the Underwater Cultural Heritage, 2001: "'Underwater cultural heritage' means all traces of human existence having a cultural, historical or archaeological character which have been partially or totally under water, periodically or continuously, for at least 100 years such as . . . " (Art. 1(1)(a)).

64 E.g., the definition of "disposal" in Art. 2(4) of the Basel Convention on the Control of Transboundary Movements of Hazardous Wastes and Their Disposal, 1989, provides that "'[d]isposal' means any operation specified in Annex IV to this Convention"; also, the legal definition of "torture" in the UN Convention against Torture and Other Cruel, Inhuman or Degrading Treatment or Punishment, 1984, which is stated in para. 1 of Art. 1, whereas para. 2 of the definitional Article stipulates that "[t]his article is without prejudice to any international instrument or national legislation which does or may contain provisions of wider application."

of articles where the definitions of special key terms are incorporated in the specific thematic section,[65] or in the special article,[66] to which they refer, or in a combination of the two.[67]

From the point of view of negotiating their legislating force, the definitions or the use of terms are attributed meaning instrumentally; their value lies in their purposive effects related to the operation and application of the purposes of the agreement. In view of the nature of treaty as a conventional regime governing ICI and the contextuality of its relational constitution and normativity, as explained earlier, its key terms are either created originally in the framework of the conferential negotiating process, being constructed on the basis of the most adequate and institutionally effective scientific and legal knowledge and evidence (*creative attribution of meaning*), or are transferred from other international agreements with or without modifications on the basis of a scientific and legal consensus (*transference of meaning*). Thus, through this multifarious determination of the key terms, the compatibility or coherence between the negotiated treaty and related international agreements is ensured and, in effect, better, more coordinated ICI governance is served.

Typical examples of a negotiated creative attribution of meaning of key terms are the definitions of "public authority" or of "environmental information" contained in the Aarhus Convention, 1998,[68] or the definitions of "Chemical Weapons Production Facility" or of "production capacity" included in the Convention on Chemical Weapons, 1993.[69] Further, an interesting example of transference of meaning, where the definition of a key term was initially constructed as an innovative and scientifically-institutionally adequate definition (through a declarative instrument), then was legally and institutionally completed and consolidated by treaty consensus and, thereafter, was directly transferred, negotiably untouched, to treaty instruments, is illustrated in the definition of "pollution of the marine environment." In this case, the definition was initially adopted in its contemporary and integrating form by the Group of Experts on Scientific Aspects of Marine Pollution (GESAMP) in 1969, then was embraced and enlarged by the Stockholm Conference on Human Development in 1972, where the word "energy" was added to the definition, and, finally, after a further negotiated elaboration and broadening of

65 Aust, citing the Convention on Chemical Weapons, 1993, considers the inclusion of specific definitions "for the purposes of Art. VI" in Art. II, where the definitions of key terms of the Convention are contained instead of the beginning of Art. VI, as an example of drafting to avoid. A. Aust, *Modern Treaty Law and Practice*, op. cit., 373.

66 E.g., Art. 18 (definition of "passage"), Art. 29 (definition of "warships"), Art. 38(2) (definition of "transit passage"), Art. 46 (definitions of "archipelagic state" and "archipelago"), Art. 70(2) (definition of "geographically disadvantaged states"), Art. 109(2) (definition of "unauthorized broadcasting"), Art. 122 (definition of "enclosed or semi-enclosed sea"), Art. 124 (definitions of "land-locked state," "transit state," "traffic in transit," and "means of transport"), or Art. 133(a) (definition of "resources").

67 Art. 221 (definition of "maritime casualty"), or Annex III, Art. 5(8) (definition of "technology").

68 See the Aarhus Convention on Access to Information, Public Participation in Decision Making and Access to Justice in Environmental Matters, 1998, Art. 2(2)(3).

69 Convention on Chemical Weapons, 1993, Art. II (8)(10).

the domain of its meaning attribution by the UN Conference on the Law of the Sea,[70] it was incorporated into the Convention on the Law of the Sea, 1982 (Part I, Introduction, Art. 1(1)(4) and was directly transferred to other regional conventional environmental regimes of sea governance.[71]

In sum, the negotiation of constructing the definitions of key terms of treaties is determined by two factors: the legislative purpose of the treaty and the relational character of these definitions, which may be developed and consolidated in the external context of reference (scientific field, institutional-declaratory field, related conventional-regime field). Through multilateral negotiation, it is identified to which degree and to what extent a relational key term is vested with its meaning either originally, by a creative attribution of meaning, thus becoming itself a reference point for other conventional regimes, or by transference of meaning from the context of reference. As a result, the legislative purpose of the treaty under negotiation, as well as the horizontal coherence of the polycentric ICI governance of the treaty regimes, are appropriately and adequately served. In view of its distinctive function, it is pertinent that the negotiation of the definitional part of the treaty should be pursued at a later state of the negotiation process, when both the need for its adoption and the extent of the meaning of the key terms would become evident.

5.3.3 Purpose and Scope of Application

This part of treaty negotiation refers to the *declaration or statement of the legislative purpose* of the treaty under negotiation. It also refers to *the material scope of its application* and, if the treaty has a regional character, it refers to the *geographical scope of its application*.

In regard to the declaration or statement of purpose and the material scope of application of the negotiated treaty, it should be stressed from the outset that their textual formulation as treaty articles makes them open to the procedure of amendment, laid down by the treaty, like any other article of the treaty. In fact, the general declaration of purpose and, even more, the specifically determined material scope of

70 The following additions were made to the domain of its meaning attribution – the reference to the "likelihood" of deleterious effects of pollution ("which results or is likely to result in such deleterious effects"), the extension of the harmful effects of pollution to "marine life" ("harm to living resources and marine life") – whereas an indicative reference to "other legitimate uses of the sea" was added to the description of the "hindrance to marine activities."

71 E.g., Barcelona Convention, 1976 (as amended), Art. 2(a), Bucharest Convention on the Protection of the Black Sea against Pollution, 1992, Art. II (1), Lima Convention for the Protection of the Marine Environment and Coastal Area of the South-East Pacific, 1981, Art. 2(a). Also see the Noumea Convention for the Protection of the Natural Resources and Environment of the South Pacific Region, 1986, Art. 2(f): "In applying this definition to the Convention obligations, the Parties shall use their best endeavours to comply with the appropriate standards and recommendations established by competent international organizations, including the International Atomic Energy Agency." See also the Helsinki Convention on the Protection of the Marine Environment of the Baltic Sea Area, 1992, Art. 2(1).

the treaty have, in view of their proper understanding as conventional activities of ICI, a dynamic rather than a static character and, as a result, they may be equally subjected to the legislative will of the parties in a future negotiation for their appropriate amendment.

It is noteworthy that the patternment of the scope of reference is related to the different techniques determining the "object" of the treaty and their complementarity. The diversity of these techniques is connected with the way in which the negotiating parties perceive their function to serve the effective and efficient operation of the legislative purpose of the treaty under negotiation in its continuous pursuance of ICI, something that may be feasible only in connection with the special context of reference of the treaty.

The statement of purpose enshrines the general determination of the legislative purpose of the treaty under negotiation. It sets out, in general and inclusive terms, the aims of the treaty and it is incorporated at the beginning of the text in most treaties, while it constitutes a standard provision of the constitutive instruments of all international organizations. It may also be interlinked with goals or objectives that set up specific, measurable targets, resting upon the broader and deeper platform of the purpose. Because of their specificity and measurability, goals may bring into a treaty regime significant implementation edge and signal a much-needed innovation in its operation.[72] The technique of formulating the statement of purpose may take two main directions: it may be typified as a specific provision of the treaty or it may coexist with the determination of the material scope of the treaty. The choice between these two techniques may be the subject of Constitutive Negotiation, even for the same type of treaties.[73] As noted earlier, the statement of purpose, however typified, may be modified in the future on the basis of the amendment procedure of the treaty.

In regard to the material scope of treaty application, negotiating parties endeavour to collectively identify the specific object of the treaty and in this process negotiation

[72] A notable example is provided by the Paris Agreement on Climate Change, 2015, which in Art. 2(a) sets out, for the first time in a treaty text – unlike the previous two treaty regimes on climate change (the UNFCCC, 1992, and the Kyoto Protocol 1997) – a specific quantified goal of utmost importance: the new climate change treaty regime specifies a target of a "well below 2°C above pre-industrial levels" increase in the global average temperature while pursuing a target of "1,5°C above pre-industrial levels." During the Constitutive Negotiation of the Paris Agreement, the previous target of 2°C circulated since 2009 and used in negotiations was finally abandoned, on the basis of more recent, solid scientific evidence and the prevalence of strong equitable considerations for the victim countries. For a perceptive general analysis, see J. Viñuales, "The Paris Climate Agreement: Less Is More." 59 *German Yearbook of International Law* (2017).

[73] E.g., the international conventional environmental regimes, which are closely interrelated, apply either the exclusive technique (Stockholm Convention on Persistent Organic Pollutants, 2001, Art. 1 – an objective – statement of purpose; The Rotterdam Convention on the Prior Informed Consent Procedure for Certain Hazardous Chemicals and Pesticides in International Trade, 1998, Art. 1 – an objective – statement of purpose) or the inclusive technique (Basel Convention on the Control of Transboundary Movements of Hazardous Wastes and Their Disposal, 1989, Art. 1 – scope of the Convention).

embraces all possible techniques for its specification. Depending on the nature of the treaty, and for reasons of consistency with its context of reference, the negotiating parties may employ a positive specification or, very often, a negative specification, or a combination of the two. Thus, the material scope of application, enshrined in a specific article of the treaty, may be articulated exclusively in positive terms.[74] It may also combine positive and negative specifications: it may positively delineate the normative extent of its application (e.g., "This Convention shall apply to . . .") but also of its non-application (e.g., "This Convention shall not apply to . . . ") as it may be necessary for reasons of compatibility or consistency of the negotiated treaty with relevant conventional instruments.[75] It is also possible that the delineation of the scope of application is articulated exclusively by reference to the existing or developing relevant conventional or jurisdictional regimes constituting the context of reference.[76]

Relatedly, the negotiating parties may directly proceed to a contextual determination of the scope of application by formulating a specific generic article ("General Provision"), where the relationship of consistency of the treaty with the existing or developing external context of reference is stipulated (like international law or its specific aspects, the UN Charter, established conventional regimes codifying international law – UNCLOS 1982 – or relevant bilateral or multilateral conventional regimes, existing or future).[77] Of direct relevance is also the inclusion of the so-called "without prejudice clauses" or "disclaimer clauses", which may prescribe the appropriate neutralization field of the scope of application of a treaty vis-à-vis related aspects of international law or existing special obligations of the parties in the framework of related international conventional regimes so that the appropriate compatibility and consistency between them will be ensured (as, for instance, the well-known and historically rooted standard clause providing "the sovereign immunity of warships or other ships owned or operated by a State," which is variably [due to the need for appropriately mitigating its effects] incorporated into conventional environmental regimes governing the protection of the marine environment).[78]

74 E.g., IAEA Conventions on Nuclear Accidents, 1986 (Convention on Early Notification of a Nuclear Accident, Art. 1.

75 See Rotterdam Convention on PIC Procedure, 1998, Art. 3, Helsinki Convention on the Transboundary Effects of Industrial Accidents, 1992, Art. 2. See also the Arms Trade Treaty, 2013, Art. 2.

76 E.g., United States–European Union Agreement on Extradition between the United States of America and the European Union, 2003, Art. 3 (Scope of Application of this Agreement in Relation to Bilateral Extradition Treaties with Member States), Convention on Biological Diversity, 1992, Art. 4 (Jurisdictional Scope).

77 E.g., Barcelona Convention, 1976 (as amended), Art. 3.

78 E.g., Barcelona Convention, 1976 (as amended), Art. 3(5), International Convention on Oil Pollution Preparedness, Response and Cooperation (OPRC Convention), 1990, Art. 1(3). The particular nature of the International Convention for Suppression of Acts of Nuclear Terrorism, 2005, is associated with the incorporation of a disclaimer clause of special interest stipulating that: "Nothing in this Convention shall affect other rights, obligations and responsibilities of States and individuals under

They may also embrace special consolidated positions or persistent claims of any negotiating party of a more general character.[79] In this last case, the technique of incorporating disclaimer clauses – sometimes formulated in exhaustive details[80] – is employed as a vehicle for ensuring the widest possible participation in the negotiating process; thus, they facilitate the Constitutive Negotiation by allowing "a negotiated margin of tolerance" for differentiations, avoiding, in effect, the opening of discussions on certain particularly sensitive situations or of issues of a more general nature that are related to the treaty under negotiation. Otherwise, such situations or issues will be raised as a significant obstacle, drowning the progress of negotiation,[81] or they would compel a state or states to cancel their participation in the negotiation of the treaty regime, thus limiting its potential normative and regulatory value.

Of special interest is the technique of *scaled specification of the scope of application* where, because of the special nature of the negotiated treaty, the construction of the scope of application is scaled. Thus, its framework formulation, cast in a positive (and negative) wording at the relevant article, explicitly stipulates its referential specification in the attached technical annex/es and, going further, in the recognition of the discretionary legal authority of the negotiating parties to proceed, in the context of their domestic legal orders, to an even broader, but compatible and impliedly progressive, legislative specification. The example of the Basel Convention on the Control of Transboundary Movements of Hazardous Wastes and Their Disposal, 1989, and its related regional conventional regimes in Africa (Bamako Convention on the Ban of the Import into Africa and the Control of Transboundary Movement and Management of Hazardous Wastes within Africa,

international law, in particular the purposes and principles of the Charter of the United Nations and international humanitarian law" (Art. 4(1)), but also that: "This Convention does not address, nor can it be interpreted as addressing, in any way, the issue of the legality of the use or threat of use of nuclear weapons by States." See also the formulation of the disclaimer clause contained in the Agreement on Trade Related Aspects of Intellectual Property Rights (TRIPS Agreement), 1994, which provides that "Nothing in Parts I to IV of this Agreement shall derogate from existing obligations that Members may have to each other under the Paris Convention, the Berne Convention, the Rome Convention and the Treaty on Intellectual Property in Respect of Integrated Circuits" (Art. 2(2)).

79 E.g., Barcelona Convention 1976 (as amended), Art. 3, Regional Cooperation Agreement on Combating Piracy and Armed Robbery against Ships in Asia, 2005, Art. 2.

80 Of particular interest is the disclaimer clause incorporated into the Protocol to the Barcelona Convention on Specially Protected Areas and Biodiversity, 1995, which, referring to the geographical coverage of the Protocol of the particularly politically sensitive Mediterranean Sea area and formulated after very intense negotiations, is set out as follows: "Article 2 . . . (2) Nothing in this Protocol nor any act adopted on the basis of this Protocol shall prejudice the rights, the present and future claims or legal views of any State relating to the law of the sea, in particular, the nature and the extent of marine areas, the delimitation of marine areas between States with opposite or adjacent coasts, freedom of navigation on the high seas, the right and the modalities of passage through straits used for international navigation and the right of innocent passage in territorial seas, as well as the nature and extent of the jurisdiction of the coastal State, the flag State and the port State. (3) No act or activity undertaken on the basis of this Protocol shall constitute grounds for claiming, contending or disputing any claim to national sovereignty or jurisdiction."

81 J. G. Merrills, *International Dispute Settlement* (3rd edn), Cambridge University Press, 1998, 13–14.

1991) and in the Mediterranean (Protocol to the Barcelona Convention on the Prevention of Pollution of the Mediterranean Sea by Transboundary Movements of Hazardous Wastes and Their Disposal, 1996) illustrates a clear manifestation of scaled specification of the scope of their application. In the relational conventional environmental regime established by these three treaty instruments, Article 1 sets out a positive and negative framework formulation of the scope of application, while it opens the window to two specification processes: it refers to technical Annexes I and II for the detailed – and dynamic – specification of its object ("hazardous wastes") and the criteria for its determination ("hazardous characteristics"), and, in addition, to the domestic legislation of the parties as a vehicle for the object specification beyond this relational conventional environmental regime. In regard to the latter process, Article 3 specifically provides the discretionary authority of each party to proceed individually, through its domestic legislation, to the extension of the conventionally determined scope of application, going beyond Annexes I and III, by following certain standard procedures.[82] It is noteworthy that the use of scaled specification for the determination of the scope of application of a treaty regime attains, simultaneously, two aims. First, it simplifies its amendability at the outer limits of its application: since it is generally established that technical annexes, in order to be effectively adapted to the dynamically developing new scientific data, follow a simplified amendment procedure, securing a faster result and more flexibility compared to that of the amendment of the main body of the treaty. Second, it effectively introduces an open-ended determination of the scope of application at the national level, provided that such determination is compatible with, and constitutes a progressive legislative construction going beyond, the already conventionally specified scope of application. After all, normative progression is embedded into the added value of the context of reference, associated here with the domestic order of the negotiating parties.

At the other extreme, the material scope of application of a treaty may be omitted when the nature of the treaty requires the concrete and comprehensive enumeration of the elements of its material objective. It is thus the particular nature of the treaty under negotiation that may orient the negotiating parties towards a definitional determination of its object "for the purposes of the convention," thus making it part of the "Definitions" of the treaty. A characteristic example is the Convention on Chemical Weapons, 1993, where the "Chemical Weapons" and the "Chemical Weapons Production Facility" are positively defined, whereas the "Purposes Not Prohibited Under this Convention" are negatively defined.[83] Interestingly, the UN Convention against Torture, 1984, immediately after positively defining the term "torture," introduces, through a disclaimer clause, an open-ended determination of

82 See also Bamako Convention, Arts. 2 and 3 and Annexes I, II, and Protocol to the Barcelona Convention on Hazardous Wastes Arts. 3 and 4 and Annexes I, II.

83 Convention on the Prohibition of the Development, Production, Stockpiling and Use of Chemical Weapons and on Their Destruction, 1993, Art. II (1), (8), (9).

the definition by recognizing the complementary and upward effect of provisions of wider application contained in international conventions or national legislations.[84]

In the case of regional treaties, the patternment of their geographical scope of application may arise in two levels: at the level of external delimitation and at the level of functional spatial determination of the treaty under negotiation. The external delimitation of the geographical scope of application is not identifiable objectively by resorting to a set of purely geographical or scientific criteria. On the contrary, it is normally determined by negotiation and intersubjectively, by using an amalgam of geographical, political, and functional criteria so that a feasible multilateral governance of the ICI regime in the region is effectively secured. It is, more specifically, established intersubjectively on the basis of an ICI conviction constructed among the negotiating parties in relation to the operation of the conventional regime. Once they have agreed, the external delimitation of the geographical scope is stabilized as the delimitation zone of the conventional regime. It is neither a geographical nor a scientifically determined region, but a region of multilateral governance serving ICI.[85] Of course, being part of the body of the treaty, it cannot be excluded from future amendment, however extreme this might be due to its foundational character. A vivid illustration is the geographical delimitation of the Mediterranean Sea region as formulated for the purposes of the Barcelona Convention in Article 1,[86] where it is clear that, in fact, political, social, and mainly cultural considerations have dominated its negotiated external delimitation.[87]

In contrast to the external delimitation, the functional spatial determination of the treaty under negotiation involves, from the beginning and in various modes of formulation, the seed of evolution since it is directly related to the dynamic

84 UN Convention against Torture and Other Cruel, Inhuman or Degrading Treatment or Punishment, 1984, in Art, 1(2) provides that: "This article is without prejudice to any international instrument or national legislation which does or may contain provisions of wider application."

85 The proposed notion of multilateral governance serving ICI illustrates a governance that is contextualized and relational, based on negotiation embracing a multilateral and multilevel process of building consensus of ICI. In some respects, it is more akin to the multilevel governance model as discussed by G. Peters and J. Pierre, *Comparative Governance: Rediscovering the Functional Dimension of Governing*, Cambridge University Press, 2016, 131ff.

86 "For the purposes of this Convention, the Mediterranean Sea Area shall mean the maritime waters of the Mediterranean Sea proper, including its gulfs and seas, bounded to the west by the meridian passing through Cape Spartel lighthouse, at the entrance of the Straits of Gibraltar, and to the east by the southern limits of the Straits of the Dardanelles between Mehmetcik and Kumkale lighthouses." Art. 1(1). See also the geographical delimitation of the North Sea "for the purposes" of the OSPAR Convention, 1992, encompassing the definition of "the maritime area" in Art. 1(a). In the same context, the geographical delimitation of the South Pacific "for the purposes" of the Noumea Convention for the Protection of the Natural Resources and Environment of the South Pacific Region, 1986, presents particular interest: thus, the "Convention Area" comprises the land and sea areas as defined in Art. 2(a) and complemented by Art. 3, which provides the power of each party, following a certain procedure, to "add areas under its jurisdiction within the Pacific Ocean between the Tropic of Cancer and 60 degrees South latitude and between 130 degrees East longitude and 120 degrees West longitude to the Convention Area."

87 See P. Haas, *Saving the Mediterranean: The Politics of International Environmental Cooperation*, Columbia University Press, 1990, 99.

effectiveness of the legislative purpose of the treaty. As a result, its intersubjectively, negotiably reached determination is inherently dynamic by virtue of the chronic normative quality of the treaty. It is fundamentally related to the needs of the progressively specified implementation of the treaty ICI regime unveiled by the scaling of its morphological patternment mentioned earlier (Framework Convention – Performative Protocols), and it marks a noticeable characteristic of the chronic operation of regional conventional environmental regimes. In this regard, the Barcelona Convention system presents a gripping narrative of functional spatial determination. Thus, the original framework convention ("Convention for the Protection of the Mediterranean Sea against Pollution"), although expressly providing in Art. 1(2) that the Mediterranean Sea Area "shall not include internal waters of the Contracting Parties," opened the window for its functional spatial determination by introducing it through the following disclaimer, "except as may be otherwise provided in any protocol to this Convention," clearly implying the dynamic of its chronic normative quality. The extensively amended framework convention proceeds, on the other hand, to a positive formulation of the functional spatial determination. After properly transforming its title ("Convention for the Protection of the Marine Environment and the Coastal Region of the Mediterranean"), it directly sets forth two general clauses generating its functional spatial determination and working more contextually and in complementarity with the geographical scope of application. Art. 1(2) provides that "the application of the Convention may be extended to coastal areas as defined by each Contracting Party within its own territory," while Art. 1(3) positively repeats the formulation of the initial Convention, setting out that "any Protocol to this Convention may extend the geographical coverage to which that particular Protocol applies." In this legitimating framework, the functional extension of the spatial application of the Protocols was effectively carried out.[88]

5.3.4 General Duties-Obligations

The negotiation of this part of the treaty is associated with " a fabric" of general commitments of the negotiating parties, which mainly refers to general duties-

[88] Characteristically, the new SPA and Biodiversity Protocol, 1995, sets out that its geographical coverage "also includes ... the terrestrial coastal areas designated by each of the Parties, including wetlands" (Art. 2(1)), and, in the case of the establishment of Specially Protected Areas of Mediterranean Importance (SPAMIs), it may also include, partially or wholly, the high sea provided that the procedure of Art. 9 of the Protocol is followed. Also, the extensively amended Land-Based Sources Protocol, 1980/1996, extends to "the hydrologic basin of the Mediterranean Sea Area" (Art. 3(b)), which is generally defined as "the entire watershed area within the territories of the Contracting Parties, draining into the Mediterranean Sea Area as defined in article 1 of the Convention" (Art. 2 (d)), whereas the ICZM Protocol, 2008, provides that its geographical coverage "is also defined by: (a) the seaward limit of the coastal zone, which shall be the external limit of the territorial sea of Parties; and (b) the landward limit of the coastal zone, which shall be the limit of the competent coastal units as defined by the Parties" (Art. 3(1)), which may, however, be differentiated in accordance with the terms and the criteria indicatively prescribed in Art. 3(2).

obligations, but it may also comprise the principles to be applied by the parties and certain powers-rights.

More specifically, the negotiating parties identify their basic duties-obligations, casting such duties-obligations in a framework language, which has a substantive or procedural character and a foundational function in regard to the construction of an ICI treaty relation, referring to its special thematic content (general relational duties-obligations). Quite limited and in a more standardized form are the general powers-rights, which may refer to the individual power-right of a party to maintain or adopt stricter or more advanced relevant domestic measures than those required by the negotiated treaty (a discretion to normative progression),[89] or to the power-right of each party to pursue the promotion of the application of the treaty to competent international organizations and, broadly, to international decision-making processes of relevant thematic orientation.[90]

It is also common that the negotiating parties may include in this part the principles governing the relation created by the treaty ICI regime, which will guide the parties, variably and in innumerable gradations, in the application of the treaty regime and in the continuous advancement of its purpose and objectives. Thus, there may be stipulated the general duty-obligation of the parties to apply substantive or procedural principles of specially related content – like "the precautionary principle," "the polluter pays principle," the undertaking of "environmental impact assessment" for proposed activities, "the principle of access to environmental information," or "the principle of sustainable development applicable to environmental treaty regimes)."[91] There may also be provided the general duty-obligation of the parties to apply substantive or procedural principles of general content properly introduced to the special treaty (like "the principle of the sovereign right of States to exploit their own resources, and the responsibility to ensure that activities within their jurisdiction or control do not cause damage to the environment of other States or of areas beyond the limits of national jurisdiction,"[92] or "the principles of adopting measures for the protection of public health and nutrition, and for the promotion of the public interest in sectors of vital importance to their socio-economic and technological development, and of preventing the abuse of intellectual property rights by right holders or the resort to practices which unreasonably restrain trade or adversely affect the international

[89] A typical formulation of this power-right is found in Art. 3(5) of the Aarhus Convention on Access to Information, Public Participation in Decision Making and Access to Justice in Environmental Matters, 1998: "The provisions of this Convention shall not affect the right of a Party to maintain or introduce measures providing for broader access to information, more extensive public participation in decision-making and wider access to justice in environmental matters than required by this Convention." See also the Convention on International Trade in Endangered Species of Wild Fauna and Flora (CITES), 1973, Art. XIV, OSPAR Convention, 1992, Art. 2(5).

[90] Aarhus Convention, 1998, Art. 3(7). Also, Barcelona Convention 1976, Art. 4(6).

[91] E.g., Barcelona Convention, 1976, Art. 4(3), Framework Convention for the Protection of the Marine Environment of the Caspian Sea, 2005, Art. 5, UN Framework Convention on Climate Change, 1992, Art. 3(1).

[92] Convention on Biological Diversity, 1992, Art. 3.

transfer of technology, provided that such measures are consistent with the provisions of this Agreement,"[93] or "the principle of equitable participation of developing states in the framework of special treaty regimes,"[94] or the principle of non-retroactivity of the special treaty regime [application *ex nunc*]).[95]

5.3.5 The System of Multilateral ICI Governance

The negotiation of this part of the treaty focuses on the construction of a patterned system of ICI multilateral governance that lies at the heart of the relational structure and function of the treaty under negotiation. The construction of this system is consistently patterned on five interrelated and interacting – though varying in their normative extent – levels:

- The level of thematization.
- The level of institutionality.
- The level of controllability.
- The level of transformability.
- The level of subjectivity.

5.3.5.1 THEMATIZATION

At the level of thematization, the negotiating parties determine the content and extent of the thematic regime of relational provisions, which may embrace principles, duties-obligations, and certain powers-rights emanating from the specification of the legislative purpose of the treaty protecting and promoting ICI. They are subjective provisions indicating the special thematic dimension of the "constitutive substance" of the treaty under negotiation and they are attributable to the conventionally distinctive collective-individual role to be assumed by the sovereign states – or by certain international organizations that may also become parties (most notably the EU). They operate as modalities of the thematic canvas articulating the application of the legislative purpose of the negotiated treaty (how the parties/the party should act or not act in order to implement the public purpose of the treaty). The negotiation here is focused on the "patterned" articulation of a particular system of thematic management whereby the continuous operation and implementation of the legislative purpose of the treaty is to be carried out through continuously working or developing terms and in creative interaction with the internal and external context of reference.

More specifically, thematization, encompassing principles, duties-obligations, and powers-rights, refers to the *conventional construction of normative indicators of thematic management*, which manifest the particular substantive and subjective

93 The TRIPS Agreement, 1994, Art. 8.
94 Framework Convention on Climate Change, 1992, Art. 3(2)(5).
95 E.g., Convention on Chemical Weapons, 1993, Art. III (2).

identity of a patterned treaty relation serving ICI. As conventional indicators of thematic management, these duties-obligations and powers-rights are articulated in a standardized form, capturing the particular thematic essence (substantive and subjective) of the treaty ICI regime, but they are also contractualized as regards their normative extent and quality, allowing context-consistent discretion, dynamic comparability (in time and context), and appropriate policy responsiveness. The knowledge of such standardization and, at the same time, of discretion in its management is of utmost importance for the negotiating parties and may decisively affect the organization of their negotiating conduct.

On the other hand, the inclusion of principles is closely related to the special nature and purpose of the treaty under negotiation but, more importantly, to the negotiating perception of the parties regarding the future interpretative function of principles in the framework of the implementation of the treaty ICI regime. It is, therefore, noticeable that the negotiating parties may avoid the inclusion of principles in the text of the treaty and prefer, instead, to exclusively confine the articulation of conventional indicators of thematic management to special duties-obligations and powers-rights. This may happen when the parties take the view that the principles, because of their nature,[96] may cause uncertainty or doubts as regards the application of the treaty and, consequently, lead to totally unforeseen or unanticipated results.

Depending on the nature of the ICI relation constructed by the treaty, and to a variable extent, the Constitutive Negotiation of these duties-obligations and powers-rights, as conventional indicators of thematic management, refers to the following themes.

General Duties-Obligations. As mentioned earlier, the negotiating parties formulate the foundational relational duties-obligations of the treaty regime, casting them in a framework language, which conventionalizes the application of the ICI relation constructed in the treaty under negotiation and refers to its special thematic content. This conventionalization of the treaty purpose by general relational duties-obligations is articulated in more or less standard introductory wording such as "The Contracting Parties undertake to/shall, in accordance with the provisions of the Convention, take/apply . . . " or "In pursuing the objective of this

[96] As Dworkin observes, in his prominent distinction between rules and principles, principles articulate "a reason that argues in one direction, but does not necessitate a particular decision" – they guide towards one direction but they do not determine the result – and they distinguish themselves from rules by "the dimension of weight or importance." R. M. Dworkin, "Is Law a System of Rules?" in R. M. Dworkin (ed.), *The Philosophy of Law*, Oxford Readings in Philosophy, Oxford University Press, 1977, 38, 47–48. As a result, "when principles intersect," it is the relative weight of each that should be evaluated for the resolution of the conflict, *but in context*, within the framework of the effective implementation of the ICI purpose of the treaty. As Twining and Miers rightly pointed out, both the generality of principles and their prescriptive status "in influencing a result" are "subject to innumerable gradations." W. Twining and D. Miers, *How to Do Things with Rules* (5th edn), Cambridge University Press, 2010, 83.

Convention, the Parties shall . . .," but their substantive prescription varies: it may simply be expressed in very general terms,[97] or it may be formulated as a cluster of specifying terms,[98] sometimes connected with relevant general principles,[99] or it may establish differentiations by reference to the distinctive role of the parties,[100] or it may contain related combinations of these.[101] On the other hand, such conventionalization of the treaty's purpose may be subsumed under "the purpose and object" clause of the treaty,[102] or may even disappear under the strong legislative design of the treaty expressed as a "statement of purpose clause" and thereby illuminating, in clearly legislative terms, the normative direction and effect of the treaty.[103] The latter cases may especially characterize treaties governing thematic relations of legal content.

Procedural and Substantive Duties Specifying Thematic Role Actions. The negotiation here is focused on the construction of a series of detailed procedural and/or substantive duties-obligations specifying the *thematic role actions* linked to

97 E.g., International Convention on Oil Pollution Preparedness, Response and Cooperation, 1990 (OPRC Convention 1990), Art. 1(1): "Parties undertake, individually or jointly, to take all appropriate measures in accordance with the provisions of this Convention and the Annex thereto to prepare for and respond to an oil pollution incident."

98 Convention on Chemical Weapons, 1993, Art. I: "1. Each State Party to this Convention undertakes never under any circumstances: (a) To develop, produce, otherwise acquire, stockpile or retain chemical weapons, or transfer, directly or indirectly, chemical weapons to anyone; (b) To use chemical weapons; (c) To engage in any military preparations to use chemical weapons; (d) To assist, encourage or induce, in any way, anyone to engage in any activity prohibited to a State Party under this Convention. 2. Each State Party undertakes to destroy chemical weapons it owns or possesses, or that are located in any place under its jurisdiction or control, in accordance with the provisions of this Convention. 3. Each State Party undertakes to destroy all chemical weapons it abandoned on the territory of another State Party, in accordance with the provisions of this Convention. 4. Each State Party undertakes to destroy any chemical weapons production facilities it owns or possesses, or that are located in any place under its jurisdiction or control, in accordance with the provisions of this Convention. 5. Each State Party undertakes not to use riot control agents as a method of warfare." See also Convention on the Prohibition of the Use, Stockpiling, Production and Transfer of Anti-Personnel Mines and Their Destruction (Landmines Convention), 1997, Art. 1.

99 E.g., Barcelona Convention, 1976, Art. 4; OSPAR Convention, 1992, Art. 2; Espoo Convention on Environmental Impact Assessment in a Transboundary Context, 1991, Art. 2.

100 E.g., UN Convention to Combat Desertification, 1994, Arts. 4 (General Obligation), 5 (Obligations of Affected Country Parties), 6 (Obligations of Developed Country Parties). Also, UN Comprehensive Test Ban Treaty, 1996, Art. I (Basic Obligations).

101 See the extensive Art. 4 of the UN Framework Convention on Climate Change, 1992.

102 E.g., United States–European Union Agreement on Extradition between the United States of America and the European Union, 2003, which only comprises Art. 1, "Object and Purpose," stating that "the Contracting Parties undertake, in accordance with the provisions of this Agreement, to provide for enhancements to cooperation in the context of applicable extradition relations between the Member States and the United States of America governing extradition of offenders."

103 E.g., UN Convention against Corruption, 2003, which contains Art. 1, "Statement of Purpose," providing, like a legislative instrument, that "[t]he purposes of this Convention are: (a) To promote and strengthen measures to prevent and combat corruption more efficiently and effectively; (b) To promote, facilitate and support international cooperation and technical assistance in the prevention of and fight against corruption, including in asset recovery; (c) To promote integrity, accountability and proper management of public affairs and public property."

the application of the particular ICI relation patterned in the treaty. These are, in other words, relational duties that encapsulate detailed substantive and procedural thematic role actions associated with state parties and bearing normative prescriptions for the application of the purpose of the treaty. The negotiation of these duties-obligations requires an adequate to a deep knowledge of the subject matter of the treaty and its management. Depending on the special purpose and the nature of the treaty as well as on the tone of negotiation, the procedural duties specifying thematic role actions for state parties may be articulated, to a varying normative extent and in a ranging degree of discretion, by measures and procedures referring to the determination-evaluation, prevention, protection, and management of the thematic objective. Two examples vividly illustrate such construction. The Aarhus Convention on Access to Information, Public Participation in Decision Making and Access to Justice in Environmental Matters, 1998, provides the detailed procedural duties of "each Party" to ensure "access to environmental information" (Art. 4), "collection and dissemination of environmental information" (Art. 5), "public participation in decisions on specific activities" (Art. 6), "public participation concerning plans, programmes and policies relating to the environment" (Art. 7), "public participation during the preparation of executive regulations and/or generally applicable legally binding normative instruments," and "access to justice" (Art. 9). The Chemical Weapons Convention, 1993, specifies the detailed procedural duties of "the State Parties" to submit to the Organization for the Prohibition of Chemical Weapons established by the Convention declarations with respect to chemical weapons and chemical weapons production facilities (Art. III), to provide access to stored or destroyed chemical weapons for the purpose of systematic verification (Art. IV), to proceed to the destruction of the chemical weapons productions facilities under detailed procedures and specific conditions, providing access for systematic verification (Art. V), and how to exercise chemical activities not prohibited under the Convention (Art. VI). Characteristic procedural duties specifying thematic role actions for the state parties abound in different types of treaty ICI regimes.[104] Furthermore, treaty patterns of a special legal character (like extradition treaties, treaties of mutual legal assistance, or treaties of civil liability and compensation) usually articulate a combination of procedural and substantive relational duties-obligations, cast in a legislative format and content but allowing a certain conventional discretion, which specify the thematic legal actions state parties should

[104] E.g., Helsinki Convention on the Transboundary Effects of Industrial Accidents, 1992, Arts. 4–8; Convention on Biological Diversity, 1992, Arts. 6–11, 14–16; Convention on the Law of the Non-Navigational Uses of International Watercourses, 1997, Arts. 11–28; Rotterdam Convention on PIC Procedure, 1998, Arts. 5–12; OPRC Convention, 1990, Arts. 3–6; IAEA Conventions on Nuclear Accidents, 1986, (Convention on Early Notification of a Nuclear Accident, Arts. 2–3, 6, 8, Convention on Assistance in the Case of Nuclear Accident or Radiological Emergency, Arts. 2–3, 7, 10–11); Regional Cooperation Agreement on Combating Piracy and Armed Robbery against Ships in Asia, 2005, Arts. 10–13, 16.

perform with due diligence within the framework of their regime.[105] Such a combination of procedural and substantive relational duties-obligations, marked by variable conventional discretion, may be further dictated by the special nature and objective of the treaty ICI regime.[106] In this context, reference should be made to a particular framework procedural power-right that appears in some treaty patterns and provides the legal platform for the "interested parties" to generally enhance their thematic role action: it prescribes the general conditions, under which they may, at the negotiating initiative of any of them, voluntarily extend the thematic application of the treaty regime by mutual agreement, employing, at their discretion, specified advisory mechanisms.[107]

Institutional Responsiveness. An important conventional indicator of thematic management signifying subjective identity is the party institutional responsiveness. It refers to the formulation of duties-obligations relating to the designation or development of competent national authorities and "national focal points,"[108] or to the development of national or regional systems of institutional responsiveness,[109] or to the development of cooperation between competent national authorities,[110] for the more effective implementation of the ICI relation constituted by the treaty.

Development of National Normative and Technical Measures of Implementation. This standard thematic management indicator of subjective identity refers to the duties-obligations of the parties to adopt national measures, legal or administrative, in accordance with the requirements of their domestic orders, on the content of which they have a wide discretion ("take the necessary

105 See European Convention on Extradition, 1957, Arts 2–24; United States–European Union Agreement on Extradition between the United States of America and the European Union, 2003, Arts. 4–14; United States–European Union Agreement on Mutual Legal Assistance, 2003, Arts. 4–10; International Convention on Civil Liability for Oil Pollution Damage, 1992, Arts. III–X; International Convention on the Establishment of an International Fund for Compensation for Oil Pollution Damage, 1992, Arts. 4–9; International Convention on Liability and Compensation for Damage in Connection with the Carriage of Hazardous and Noxious Substances by Sea (HNS Convention), 1996, Arts. 7–12, 37–44.

106 E.g., UN Convention against Corruption, 2003, Arts. 5–59; UN Convention against Torture and Other Cruel, Inhuman or Degrading Treatment or Punishment, 1984, Arts. 2–16.

107 See, e.g., the Helsinki Convention on the Transboundary Effects of Industrial Accidents, 1992, Art. 5.

108 See, e.g., the Helsinki Convention on the Transboundary Effects of Industrial Accidents, 1992, Art. 17; the Framework Convention for the Protection of the Marine Environment of the Caspian Sea, 2005, Art. 26(1); the Basel Convention on the Control of Transboundary Movements of Hazardous Wastes and Their Disposal, 1989, Art. 5; the Regional Cooperation Agreement on Combating Piracy and Armed Robbery against Ships in Asia, 2005, Art. 9(1)(3); the Rotterdam Convention on PIC Procedure, 1998, Art. 4; the IAEA Conventions on Nuclear Accidents, 1986 (Convention on Early Notification of a Nuclear Accident, Art. 7, Convention on Assistance in the Case of Nuclear Accident or Radiological Emergency, Art. 4); the UN Comprehensive Test Ban Treaty, 1996, Art. III(4).

109 E.g., OPRC Convention, 1990, Art. 6.

110 E.g., UN Convention against Corruption, 2003, Arts. 38, 39.

measures").[111] These may include appropriate policy and financial measures to provide a more effective and efficient participation of a state party in the implementation of the particular treaty, as is evidenced in environmental treaty regimes.[112] It is worth noting that this indicator may also refer to the constantly recognized power-right of the parties to progressive normative discretion: that is, the power to adopt and apply – or retain – stricter measures than those provided by the particular treaty regime, which features different types of treaty regimes,[113] constituting a framework clause that may fuel their transition to a more advanced implementation of the treaty purpose.

Relatedly, this standard thematic management indicator of subjective identity also refers to the articulation of special duties-obligations of the parties to adopt national implementative measures of a technical character. These may comprise the duty to establish a national programme for monitoring the factors considered to have, in time and context, a determinant impact on the implementation of the treaty regime – individual development of national monitoring programmes by each party, but also development of common or supplementary national monitoring programmes among the parties[114] or, in certain cases, the duty to create or strengthen observation mechanisms for the preparation and updating of national inventories related to the object of the treaty,[115] or the duty to develop

[111] Convention against Corruption, 2003, Arts. 27, 65(1); Convention on the Prohibition of the Use, Stockpiling, Production and Transfer of Anti-Personnel Mines and Their Destruction (Landmines Convention), 1997, Art. 9; Convention on Chemical Weapons, 1993, Art. VII; Aarhus Convention on Access to Information, Public Participation in Decision Making and Access to Justice in Environmental Matters, 1998, Art. 3(1); Convention against Torture and Other Cruel, Inhuman or Degrading Treatment or Punishment, 1984, Art. 2, where the nature of the treaty requires that "each State Party shall take effective legislative, administrative, judicial or other measures to prevent acts of torture in any territory under its jurisdiction." Also see the UN Comprehensive Test Ban Treaty, 1996, Art. III.

[112] See the Convention on Biological Diversity, 1992, Art. 19(1); the Helsinki Convention on the Transboundary Effects of Industrial Accidents, 1992, Art. 3(4); the Helsinki Convention on the Protection and Use of Transboundary Watercourses and International Lakes, 1992, Art. 3(1).

[113] See the Framework Convention for the Protection of the Marine Environment of the Caspian Sea, 2005, Art. 26(2); the Convention against Corruption, 2003, Art. 65(2); the Espoo Convention on Environmental Impact Assessment in a Transboundary Context, 1991, Art. 2(9); the Rotterdam Convention on PIC Procedure, 1998, Art. 15(4); the Convention against Torture and Other Cruel, Inhuman or Degrading Treatment or Punishment, 1984, Art. 1(2); the Aarhus Convention on Access to Information, Public Participation in Decision Making and Access to Justice in Environmental Matters, 1998, Art. 3(5); the Rotterdam Convention on PIC Procedure, 1998, Art. 15(4); and the Helsinki Convention on the Transboundary Effects of Industrial Accidents, 1992, Art. 24(2).

[114] E.g., Barcelona Convention, 1976, Art. 12; Bucharest Convention on the Protection of the Black Sea against Pollution, 1992, Art. XV; Framework Convention for the Protection of the Marine Environment of the Caspian Sea, 2005, Art. 19; Helsinki Convention on the Protection and Use of Transboundary Watercourses and International Lakes, 1992, Art. 4; Convention on Biological Diversity, 1992, Art. 7; UN Convention against Corruption, 2003, Art. 61(2)(3).

[115] As is characteristically provided in the Protocol of Integrated Coastal Zone Management in the Barcelona Convention, 2008, Art. 16.

national action programmes for the identification and management of such factors.[116]

Public Participation in Governance. This recently established subjective thematic indicator refers to the appropriate conventional incorporation into the treaty of the duty-obligation of each party to ensure public participation in the governance its ICI regime and, hence, to effectively and efficiently underpin the social dimension of such governance. More specifically, this duty-obligation sets out the framework for the appropriate involvement of the relevant non-state actors in treaty governance by securing their access to information, their participation in the decision-making process and their access to justice.[117] The incorporation of this duty, and especially the extent of its application, is strongly connected with the nature of the treaty and its special context of reference.[118] On the other hand, it is noteworthy in this context that the inclusion of such duty-obligation that manifests a strong relational turn opening the window for a progressing institutionalization of relationships with non-state actors for better governance does not, in fact, bring about any transformation of the legal nature of the treaty regimes. States continue to be the central actors, the "Parties," and the conventionality element of the treaty plays a pivotal role in its governance. States "negotiate their constitution and their consensus-establishment, the required level of their specific implementation, their progressive advancement and the scope of their revision in context," while the relevant non-state actors "contribute to this unceasing process as 'related actors' for the better, and potentially, more democratic, more socially acceptable and harmonized ICI governance."[119]

Cooperation in the Fields of Information, Scientific, and Educational Development. The articulation of these specific duties-obligations of cooperation is an almost constant feature of a particularly large part of treaties, denoting a key subjective thematic indicator of their constitutive construction. These standard duties-obligations specifically refer to the exchange of information related to the treaty

116 E.g., UN Convention to Combat Desertification, 1994, Art. 10.

117 See the Aarhus Convention on Access to Information, Public Participation in Decision Making and Access to Justice in Environmental Matters, 1998, *passim*. Also, Barcelona Convention, 1976, Art. 15 (of special interest in this regard is the integrated approach to public participation provided in its performative Protocol on Integrated Coastal Zone Management in the Mediterranean, 2008, Art. 14 (2–3)); Helsinki Convention on the Transboundary Effects of Industrial Accidents, 1992, Art. 9; UN Convention against Corruption, 2003, Arts. 10(a), 13; Stockholm Convention on Persistent Organic Pollutants, 2001, Art. 10.

118 Thus, the Framework Convention for the Protection of the Marine Environment of the Caspian Sea, 2005, Art. 21(2), as well as the Rotterdam Convention on PIC Procedure, 1998, Art. 15(2), limits the extent of this duty only to one aspect, the public access to information.

119 E. Raftopoulos, "Theorizing about Conventional Environmental Sea-Regimes as International Trusts: The Case of the Barcelona Convention System," 2015, op. cit., 263, 267–268. For the importance of a more general theoretical understanding of contemporary governance as a matter of transformation rather than elimination of state and as a need for making a deeper inquiry into the state apparatus to understand how other contingencies have changed the preconditions for governing, see Peters and Pierre, *Comparative Governance, supra* note 35, *passim*.

ICI regime and in accordance with its purposes either in general,[120] or in indicatively stated fields,[121] and/or even specifying restrictive conditions for certain kinds of sensitive information relating to the core of the treaty.[122] They may also refer to the establishment of research and development programmes serving the purposes of the treaty and promote its governance, either individually or collectively, and usually in conjunction with competent international organizations or with a network of research institutes,[123] and, where appropriate, guided by an interdisciplinary approach.[124] Further, they may create or promote programmes of educational or training character or programmes contributing to public awareness, which may take the form of technical assistance.[125]

Unilateral Duties: Assistance in Developing Countries, Transfer of Technology, Internal Capacity Building. These asymmetric standard duties, establishing unilateral obligations of the parties, signify subjective thematic indicators of the constitutive construction of a number of treaties and may be embodied according to the nature and purpose of the treaty. They may relate to the provision of financial resources to developing state parties,[126] or to the access and transfer of technology to them,[127] but also to the building of their internal capacity, usually coupled with

[120] E.g., Framework Convention for the Protection of the Marine Environment of the Caspian Sea, 2005, Art. 21; Convention on Chemical Weapons, 1993, Art. XI (1)(2.b); UN Framework Convention on Climate Change, 1992, Arts. 4(1)(h).

[121] E.g., Convention on Biological Diversity, 1992, Art. 17; Helsinki Convention on the Transboundary Effects of Industrial Accidents, 1992, Art. 15; Landmines Convention, 1997, Art. 6(6); Helsinki Convention on the Protection and Use of Transboundary Watercourses and International Lakes, 1992, Art. 13.

[122] See, e.g., the standard clause on "protection of information" in the Helsinki Convention on the Transboundary Effects of Industrial Accidents, 1992, Art. 22, and the Helsinki Convention on the Protection and Use of Transboundary Watercourses and International Lakes, 1992, Art. 8.

[123] E.g., OPRC Convention, 1990, Art. 8; UN Convention to Combat Desertification, 1994, Art. 17; OSPAR Convention, 1992, Art. 8; Convention on Chemical Weapons, 1993, Art. XI (1)(2.a).

[124] As is characteristically provided in Art. 15(3) of the Protocol to the Barcelona Convention on Integrated Coastal Management in the Mediterranean, 2008: "The Parties shall provide for interdisciplinary scientific research on integrated coastal zone management and on the interaction between activities and their impacts on coastal zones. To this end, they should establish or support specialized research centres. The purpose of this research is, in particular, to further knowledge of integrated coastal zone management, to contribute to public information and to facilitate public and private decision-making."

[125] E.g., Convention on Biological Diversity, 1992, Art. 13; Aarhus Convention on Access to Information, Public Participation in Decision Making and Access to Justice in Environmental Matters, 1998, Art. 3(3); Regional Cooperation Agreement on Combating Piracy and Armed Robbery against Ships in Asia, 2005, Art. 14(3); Convention against Torture and Other Cruel, Inhuman or Degrading Treatment or Punishment, 1984, Art. 10; UN Framework Convention on Climate Change, 1992, Arts. 4(1)(i), 6; Rotterdam Convention on PIC Procedure, 1998, Art. 16.

[126] E.g., Convention on Biological Diversity, 1992, Art. 20; UN Framework Convention on Climate Change, 1992, Art. 11; Stockholm Convention on Persistent Organic Pollutants, 2001, Art. 13.

[127] E.g., Convention on Biological Diversity, 1992, Art. 16; UN Framework Convention on Climate Change, 1992, Art. 4(8)(9); UN Convention to Combat Desertification, 1994, Art. 18.

certain of the aforementioned thematic indicators,[128] or to the provision of technical assistance,[129] also articulated in conjunction with these thematic indicators.[130]

Relationships with Other Conventional Regimes. The embodiment of duties-obligations that relate to prospective conventional actions of the parties to a treaty, building institutional interconnections beyond the treaty ICI regime with a view to pursue its more effective and more integrated implementation, signify a standard subjective indicator of thematic management. Formulated in a framework form, these duties-obligations may refer to the prospective development of relationships with other relevant international conventional regimes,[131] or to the possibility of entering into relevant bilateral, multilateral, or regional treaties compatible with, or not derogating from, this treaty,[132] with the aim of enhancing or reinforcing its overall or partial implementation. It is worth noting that, in some rare cases, where it appears that entering into new bilateral or multilateral treaties (or the continuation of existing such treaties) is envisaged as a strong performative aspect of the treaty regime, the relationship framework of duties-obligations may be connected with an appendix listing the elements on which such bilateral or multilateral agreements should be based.[133]

Financial Governance Regime. Depending upon the nature and purpose of the ICI relation established by a treaty, the negotiation for the creation of the particular financial regime governing the treaty and associated with the economic duties-obligations of the parties – when such negotiation is considered necessary at the constitutive negotiating phase – may be basically oriented towards two directions.[134] The first direction is articulated by clauses that merely focus either on the duty-

[128] E.g., UN Convention to Combat Desertification, 1994, Arts. 17(1), 19; UN Convention against Corruption, 2003, Art. 60.

[129] E.g., Rotterdam Convention on PIC Procedure, 1998, Art. 16; Stockholm Convention on Persistent Organic Pollutants, 2001, Art. 12; UN Convention against Corruption, 2003, Arts. 1(b), 60(2)(6)(7), 62(2).

[130] E.g., Minimata Convention on Mercury, 2013, Art. 14 (capacity-building, technical assistance, and technological transfer).

[131] E.g., Convention on Chemical Weapons, 1993, Art. XIII; OPRC Convention, 1990, Art. 10; IAEA Conventions on Nuclear Accidents, 1986 (Convention on Early Notification of a Nuclear Accident, Art. 9); UN Convention against Corruption, 2003, Art. 59; Helsinki Convention on the Transboundary Effects of Industrial Accidents, 1992, Art. 24(1).

[132] E.g., United States–European Union Agreement on Extradition between the United States of America and the European Union, 2003, Art. 18; Basel Convention on the Control of Transboundary Movements of Hazardous Wastes and Their Disposal, 1989, Art. 11; UN Convention against Corruption, 2003, Arts. 59, 62(4); OPRC Convention, 1990, Art. 10; United States–European Union Agreement on Mutual Legal Assistance, 2003, Art. 14.

[133] E.g., Espoo Convention on Environmental Impact Assessment in a Transboundary Context, 1991, Art. 8 (Bilateral and Multilateral Cooperation) and Appendix VI (Elements for Bilateral and Multilateral Cooperation).

[134] There are treaties that do not contain this thematic indicator, such as the Helsinki Convention on the Transboundary Effects of Industrial Accidents, 1992, the Framework Convention for the Protection of the Marine Environment of the Caspian Sea, 2005, or the United States–European Union Agreement on Extradition between the United States of America and the European Union, 2003.

obligation of the parties to collectively determine the regime of their economic participation in the treaty (*pactum de contrahendo*), mentioning, in some cases, the financial mechanism (e.g., trust fund),[135] or refer to the competence of the conference or meeting of the contracting parties to decide by consensus on the determination of the financial regime,[136] or provide the incorporation of the UN scale of assessment appropriately adjusted to take into account differences in participation between the UN and the particular treaty,[137] and further stipulate the treatment of a party that is in arrears in the payment of its financial contribution under the treaty.[138]

The second direction is articulated by clauses that may combine the equitable duty-obligation of each party to provide, in accordance with its capabilities, financial support and incentives for the attainment of the objective of the treaty, identifying at the same time the relevant roles of the developed and developing state parties, with the duty-obligation to establish a distinct financial mechanism for the effective support of the equitable financial regime, operating under the authority of the conference/meeting of the contracting parties that will decide on its institutional structure.[139] Moreover, the possibility of instituting an international fund either by a separate treaty so as to give effect to an interconnected special treaty regime,[140] or as part of such treaty,[141] further illustrates the multifaceted aspects of this direction that are open to negotiation.

135 E.g., Barcelona Convention, 1976, Art. 24(2), Bucharest Convention on the Protection of the Black Sea against Pollution, 1992, Art. XXIII.

136 E.g., Basel Convention on the Control of Transboundary Movements of Hazardous Wastes and Their Disposal, 1989, Art. 15(3); Rotterdam Convention on PIC Procedure, 1998, Art. 18(4); Regional Cooperation Agreement on Combating Piracy and Armed Robbery against Ships in Asia, 2005, Art. 6; Aarhus Convention on Access to Information, Public Participation in Decision Making and Access to Justice in Environmental Matters, 1998, Art. 10(3).

137 E.g., Landmines Convention, 1997, Art. 14.

138 E.g., Convention on Chemical Weapons, 1993, Art. VIII (7)(8).

139 This direction is particularly followed by global conventional environmental regimes; see, e.g., the Convention on Biological Diversity, 1992, Arts. 20, 21; the UN Framework Convention on Climate Change, 1992, Arts. 4(3–9), 11; the UN Convention to Combat Desertification, 1994, Arts. 20, 21; the Stockholm Convention on Persistent Organic Pollutants, 2001, Art. 13. It is noteworthy that the UN Framework Convention on Climate Change, 1992, proceeds to the formulation of an interim arrangement defining Global Environmental Facility (GEF) as "(the) international entity entrusted with the operation of the financial mechanism," which, in this connection, "should be appropriately restructured" (Art. 21(3)). A similar interim financial arrangement is contained in the Stockholm Convention on Persistent Organic Pollutants, 2001 (Art. 14). In fact, the GEF was progressively established as a financial mechanism in a number of other global conventional environmental regimes (Convention on Biological Diversity, 1992; UN Convention to Combat Desertification, 1994; Stockholm Convention on Persistent Organic Pollutants, 2001). In the recent Minimata Convention on Mercury, 2013, the inclusion of the GEF as a component of its financial mechanism is elaborated in Art. 13(6)(7).

140 See the International Convention on the Establishment of an International Fund for Compensation for Oil Pollution Damage, 1992; and the International Convention on Civil Liability for Oil Pollution Damage, 1992.

141 See the International Convention on Liability and Compensation for Damage in Connection with the Carriage of Hazardous and Noxious Substances by Sea (HNS Convention), 1996, Arts. 13–36, setting out the establishment, structure, and function of the HNS Fund.

5.3.5.2 INSTITUTIONALITY

At the level of institutionality, the negotiating parties determine the level of institutionalization of the treaty where the autonomous institutional will is to be developed. It refers to the setting up of ad hoc international institutional entities whose structure is variably patterned in accordance with the nature and purpose of the treaty ICI regime and its particular relationship with its context of reference.

On the other hand, it is noteworthy that institutionality may not arise as an autonomous structure in the event that the negotiation of a treaty is generated in the framework of a competent international organization, where the negotiating parties are its members and the treaty is integrated into the field of its special competence, being connected with the function of its organs. In such cases, the international organization provides the necessary institutional platform for the exercise of ICI governance by the generated treaties, which, in fact, constitute performative conventional regimes applying its object and purposes. The case of the IMO and of the more than fifty international agreements created in its framework is a characteristic and well-known example. As is provided by the Constitutive Convention of the IMO, one of the basic functions of the Organization for achieving its purposes is, inter alia, to provide for the drafting of conventions and agreements and to recommend them to governments and intergovernmental organizations, as well as to convene the necessary negotiating conferences.[142] It is also the performance of specific functions arising in connection with the aforementioned function, and particularly of those assigned to the IMO by international conventions or agreements "relating to maritime matters and the effect of shipping on the marine environment."[143] In this framework, its principal organs (the Assembly, the Council, the Secretariat, and its four committees [the Maritime Safety Committee, the Legal Committee, the Marine Environment Protection Committee, the Facilitation Committee, and the Technical Cooperation Committee]) are actively and effectively involved in all phases of the negotiating process of these agreements (Prenegotiation, Constitutive Negotiation, and Renegotiation), and in their application.

At this level, a particular interest presents the negotiation of conventional environmental regimes, which is systematically related to the establishment of a distinctive institutional structure for the exercise of autonomous collective ICI governance. It refers to the construction of *ad hoc international institutional entities* that may be differentiated as to the extent or degree of their institutionality. More specifically, Constitutive Negotiation on institutionality takes a twofold direction: towards the construction of the core institutional pattern, common to all environmental treaties, and towards the possibility of appropriate institutional deepening, performed by the creation of additional subsidiary (e.g., compliance committee or

142 Convention on the International Maritime Organization, 1948, as amended, Art. 2(b).
143 Ibid., Art. 2(d).

technical and scientific committee) or *sui generis* organs endowed with varying competences.[144]

The negotiation of the core institutional pattern refers to the establishment of the two principal organs of conventional environmental regimes, the Meetings or the Conferences of the Contracting Parties (MOPs or COPs), and the Secretariat. The MOPs or COPs constitute the supreme collective organ in which all contracting parties are represented, on the basis of the principle of equality, and decide on all issues relating to the governance of the particular conventional environmental regime (internal institutional issues, issues concerning the operation and implementation of the conventional regime, issues concerning the expansion or "deepening" of its interactively developing normative domain, or issues relating to external inter-regime ICI relations or relations with other states). Vested with the generally prescribed status of observer, which is a vital complementary feature of the core institutional structure, relevant intergovernmental institutional entities, NGOs, and other stakeholders may be admitted to participate in the COPs or MOPs, contributing to the negotiating process to reach decisions but without the right to vote. The Secretariat, on the other hand, constitutes the permanent administrative organ and its functions, though of an open-ended determination, vary.[145] They refer to activities regarding administrative support to the institutional structure of the conventional regime, information and submission of reports to the contracting parties related to the implementation of the conventional regime, and activities regarding liaison with other relevant intergovernmental organizations or international institutional entities of relevant conventional regimes. The Secretariat performs its functions under the authority and mandate of the MOPs or COPs and its designation is the outcome of a consensus reached by the negotiating parties: thus, its functions may be assigned to a competent intergovernmental organization,[146]

144 A characteristic, though rare, example of a *sui generis* organ is the Bureau established in the framework of the Barcelona Convention, under Art. 19: composed of representatives of six Contracting Parties, on the basis of the principle of equitable geographical distribution, the Bureau plays an important intermediary role in the advancement of the implementation of the Barcelona Convention system, whereas in emergency situations, it is vested with the power to decide with the secretariat on appropriate responses and take emergency measures. See E. Raftopoulos, "Conventional Environmental Governance in the Mediterranean and Its Evolving Institutional and Fiduciary Aspects in a Pragmatic Perspective." 30 *Ocean Yearbook* (2016), 129, at 140–141.

145 The clause setting out the functions of the secretariat most commonly includes a framework provision that the secretariat will perform "such other functions as may be determined by the Parties," or "by the Conference of the Parties." See, e.g., the Aarhus Convention, 1998, Art. 12(c); the Barcelona Convention, 1976, Art. 17(v)(vii); the Framework Convention for the Protection of the Marine Environment of the Caspian Sea, 2005, Art. 23(g)(i); the UN Framework Convention on Climate Change, 1992, Art. 8(g); the Convention on Biological Diversity, 1992, Art. 24(e).

146 As usually happens in cases where an international conventional regime is created in the framework of an international intergovernmental organization; see, e.g., the Aarhus Convention, 1998, Art. 12. Apart from this case of institutional interconnection, there are also cases where the negotiating states consider that the assignment of the secretariat functions to a competent intergovernmental organization is of utmost importance and, consequently, they agree to conduct the constitutive negotiation within its framework with the view to designate it as a secretariat of the prospective treaty regime.

and, in certain cases, to two intergovernmental organizations for better coordination and more effective governance,[147] while, in exceptional cases, the functions of the Secretariat may be performed by an international NGO of special status.[148] Besides, there are cases where the secretariat is established as an internal administrative body of the particular conventional regime operating under the exclusive authority and control of the MOPs or COPs,[149] or even simply as the administrative organ of the MOPs or COPs.[150] Finally, it is noteworthy that this two-level institutional structure may be adopted by other, non-environmental, international treaty regimes.[151]

The two-level core institutional structure of principal organs may be combined with the negotiable creation of various subsidiary organs that deepen the institutional structure and may contribute to the more effective, more efficient, more representative, and, indeed, more scientific governance of the treaty ICI regime. More specifically, the options for their negotiated construction vary. They may be established as part of the institutional structure during the constitutive negotiation or emerge during the Renegotiation, usually consolidating an existing informal practice. Their establishment may also take a framework form, generally prescribed as an aspect of the functions of the conference/meeting of the parties. They may even preexist the Constitutive Negotiation of a treaty ICI regime and be incorporated into it by a decision of the conference/meeting of the parties stating their appropriate adaptation. Basically, three types of subsidiary organs perform three distinct functions: the scientific-advisory,[152] the economic-

147 E.g., the Rotterdam Convention on the Prior Informed Consent Procedure for Certain Hazardous Chemicals and Pesticides in International Trade, 1998, Art. 19(3), provides that "the secretariat functions for this Convention shall be performed jointly by the Executive Director of UNEP and the Director-General of FAO, subject to such arrangements as shall be agreed between them and approved by the Conference of the Parties."

148 E.g., the Ramsar Convention on Wetlands of International Importance Especially as Waterfowl Habitat, 1971, Art. 8, provides that the Ramsar Secretariat Convention is carried out by the International Union for Conservation of Nature (IUCN) "until such time as another organization or government is appointed by a majority of two-thirds of all Contracting Parties." The Secretariat personnel are legally considered employees of the IUCN.

149 E.g., the Secretariat of the Framework Convention for the Protection of the Marine Environment of the Caspian Sea, 2005, Art. 23(1–3) or the permanent Secretariat of the Convention on the Protection of the Black Sea against Pollution, 1992, Art. XVII (6).

150 See the Helsinki Convention on the Protection of the Marine Environment of the Baltic Sea Area, 1992, Art. 21.

151 See, e.g., the UN Convention against Corruption, 2003, where a corresponding two-level institutional structure is stipulated, the Conference of States Parties and the secretariat provided by the secretary-general of the United Nations (Arts. 63, 64), while the Conference of the States Parties "shall establish, if it deems it necessary, any appropriate mechanism or body to assist in the effective implementation of the Convention" (Art. 63(7)).

152 E.g., the Subsidiary Body on Scientific, Technical and Technological Advice (SBSTTA) established under Art. 25 of the Convention on Biological Diversity, 1992; the Subsidiary Body for Scientific and Technological Advice provided in Art. 9 of the UN Framework Convention on Climate Change, 1992; the Scientific Advisory Board generally provided in Art. VIII (21)(h) of the Chemical Weapons Convention, 1993, or the Scientific Advisory Board (SAB), established in the framework of the UN, *supra* note 18, Chapter 3. It is worth noting that the Intergovernmental Panel on Climate Change

technological,[153] and the implementative-supervisory[154] organs. Participation in the first two types of subsidiary organs may be comparable to that of the COPs/MOPs, whereas in the implementative-supervisory subsidiary organs, participation is limited and more personally oriented, composed of legal and scientific experts serving in a personal capacity. It is noteworthy that the negotiable possibility of establishing *sui generis* subsidiary organs of a dualist character, being intergovernmental and of limited representation, vested with advisory-coordinating functions but, exceptionally, exercising a decisive competence in emergency situations. This rather rare case arises in the Barcelona Convention system through the establishment of the Bureau.[155] Constructed during the renegotiation of the Barcelona Convention in 1995, the Bureau, in view of its fruitfully dynamic operation, may be considered a potentially "incubated" executive organ that may evolve into a principal organ, corresponding to the councils of intergovernmental organizations.

On the other hand, the negotiation on the institutionality of treaty ICI regimes may, in certain cases, follow two different directions: it may refer to an even more complex and powerful level or, conversely, to a clearly weaker level of institutional structure. This is because the negotiation on institutionality, serving the subjectivity of the ICI relation encapsulated in the treaty pattern, may be moving selectively in both directions, shaping the most appropriate and feasible system of institutional ICI governance.

Thus, the construction of a three-level core international institutional structure corresponding to the institutional structure set up in intergovernmental organizations may also be pursued during the Constitutive Negotiation process. The Convention on Chemical Weapons, 1993, is characteristic in this regard: it establishes the Organization for the Prohibition of Chemical Weapons "to achieve the object and purpose of this Convention, to ensure the implementation of its provisions, including those for international verification of compliance with it, and to provide a forum for consultation and cooperation among States Parties" (Art. VIII (1)). The seat of the headquarters of the Organization is The Hague (Art. VIII (3)), and it sets up, as the organs of the Organization, the Conference of the States Parties, the Executive Council, and the Technical Secretariat, following a fully-fledged

(IPCC), a scientific and intergovernmental body jointly established by the UNEP and the WMO in 1988 to provide a clear scientific view on the current state of knowledge in climate change and its potential environmental and socioeconomic impacts, also serves the UN Framework Convention on Climate Change, 1992, feeding the function of the conventional regime with its Assessment Reports.

153 E.g., the Advisory Body on Administrative and Financial Matters established in the framework of the Convention on Chemical Weapons, 1993, or the GEF and its function in a number of international conventional environmental regimes, appropriately adapted to them, *supra* note 139.

154 The various Compliance Committees are provided or progressively established in the framework of conventional environmental regimes. Interesting, in this regard, is the Confidentiality Commission operating in the framework of the Chemical Weapons Convention, 1993, the main function of which is to settle any disputes between state parties related to confidentiality.

155 See *supra* note 94.

three-level core institutional structure of intergovernmental organization.[156] The Organization, like any intergovernmental organization, is presented as a legal entity of advanced subjectivity endowed with dynamic legal personality: "on the territory and in any other place under the jurisdiction or control of a State Party," it enjoys "such legal capacity and such privileges and immunities as are necessary for the exercise of its functions,"[157] while the Conference of the States Parties is vested with the general power to establish the necessary subsidiary organs.[158] On the other hand, the Regional Cooperation Agreement on Combating Piracy and Armed Robbery against Ships in Asia, 2005, establishes the Information Sharing Center "as an international organization whose members are the Contracting Parties to this Agreement," located in Singapore, and enjoying "such legal capacity, privileges and immunities in the Host State of the Center as are necessary for the fulfilment of its functions."[159] The Center features a two-level core institutional structure, consisting of the Governing Council, composed of one representative from each Contracting Party, and the Secretariat, headed by the Executive Director assisted by the staff, who is responsible for the administrative, operational, and financial matters of the Center and represents the Center.[160] Finally, in some types of treaty regimes, like the UN Convention against Torture and Other Cruel, Inhuman or Degrading Treatment or Punishment, 1984, the appropriate institutional structure of ICI governance is articulated with the establishment of an autonomous committee of experts. Under this Convention, the Committee against Tortures is set up, consisting of "ten experts of high moral standing and recognized competence in the field of human rights, who shall serve in their personal capacity," and its members are elected by the states parties to carry out the functions provided in the Convention.[161] The Committee may set up ad hoc conciliation commissions "when appropriate,"[162] and its members, as well the members of its ad hoc conciliation commissions, are entitled to "the facilities, privileges and immunities of experts on mission for the United Nations as laid down in the relevant sections of the Convention on the Privileges and Immunities of the United Nations."[163] The Committee is accountable to the State Parties and to the General Assembly of the United Nations, submitting an annual report on its activities under this Convention.[164] In this scheme, the Secretary-General of the United Nations undertakes some secretariat functions for the Convention, providing the necessary staff and facilities for the effective performance

156 Their composition, procedures, decision-making, function, and powers are set out in Art. VIII (B, C, D) of the Convention on Chemical Weapons, 1993.
157 Ibid., Art. VIII (E.48).
158 Ibid., Art. VIII (B.21.f).
159 Art. 5.
160 Art. 4.
161 UN Convention against Torture and Other Cruel, Inhuman or Degrading Treatment or Punishment, 1984, Arts. 17, 18–22.
162 Ibid., Art. 21(e).
163 Ibid., Art. 23.
164 Ibid., Art 24.

of the functions of the Committee under this Convention and transmitting the reports of the parties.[165]

5.3.5.3 CONTROLLABILITY

At the level of Controllability, the negotiating parties determine, through the formulation of largely standardized special clauses, the normative quality and extent of three interrelated procedures of treaty ICI regime controllability: accountability, compliance, and settlement of disputes. Through the operation of these procedures, the relational – rather contractual – nature of controllability is unveiled, for they provide specific duties-obligations and powers-rights-generating actions protecting and improving the ongoing function of the conventionally constituted ICI relation on the basis of a continuous consensus-building, and by no means pursuing the accurate application of an assumed original contractual consent of the parties. In other words, these procedures are primarily geared towards giving effect to a legislative intention in time and context, rather than enforcing an "objectively concluded" contractual will of the parties. Controllability is an activity serving a conventional ICI relation, rather than an end-state enforcing a contractually concluded discrete relation. It is worth noting that relational controllability may be further reinforced when certain types of treaties require, by their very nature, the incorporation of a special verification system as a determinative core element of their negotiation.[166] Much less powerful seems to be the negotiated inclusion of a verification clause in the form of a general procedural power-right.[167] Moreover, in certain types of treaties, the negotiation of relational controllability may also be associated with the articulation of collective review or evaluation clauses regarding the effectiveness of the treaty regime.[168] In perspective, relational controllability

165 Ibid., Arts. 18(3), 19.

166 Thus, the UN Comprehensive Test Ban Treaty, 1996, Art. IV, sets out a detailed special verification system consisting of four constitutive elements: (a) an international monitoring system; (b) consultation and clarification; (c) on-site inspections; and (d) confidence-building measures. Similarly, the Convention on Chemical Weapons, 1993, contains a detailed Annex on Implementation and Verification ("The Verification Annex") providing the general rules of verification (Part II), and elaborate specific provisions for verifications measures pursuant to the implementation of the core articles of the Convention. (Parts III–XI).

167 Thus, the Bamako Convention on the Ban of the Import into Africa and the Control of Transboundary Movement and Management of Hazardous Wastes within Africa, 1991, provides, in Art. 19, that "[a]ny Party which has reason to believe that another Party is acting or has acted in breach of its obligations under this Convention must inform the Secretariat thereof, and in such an event, shall simultaneously and immediately inform, directly or through the Secretariat, the Party against whom the allegations are made. The Secretariat shall carry out a verification, of the substance of the allegation and submit a report thereof to all the Parties to this Convention." This clause is transplanted into the Protocol to the Barcelona Convention on the Prevention of Pollution of the Mediterranean Sea by Transboundary Movements of Hazardous Wastes and Their Disposal, 1996, Art. 13.

168 E.g., United States–European Union Agreement on Extradition between the United States of America and the European Union, 2003, Art. 21; OPRC Convention, 1990, Art. 13.

may, under certain conditions, provide the appropriate material to build up the Renegotiation process.

Accountability

The negotiation concerning accountability refers to the drafting of largely standardized provisions prescribing the procedural duty-obligation of the contracting parties to submit to the secretariat periodic reports on the way in which they implement the treaty ICI regime (reporting procedures). In fact, the parties' duty-obligation to report on their treaty implementation is most commonly and consistently utilized as a tool for their public accountability in the governance of the treaty regime, safeguarding an adequate level of transparency and collective control.[169] In this context, the negotiating parties determine the normative scope of application of the standard duty-obligation to report: should the report be restricted only to the implementation of the Convention and its related protocols or should it be extended to cover also the implementation of the decisional or declarative instruments generated by the treaty regime, namely the decisions, recommendations, action plans, or regional/global strategies adopted by the institutional mechanism of the treaty regime? Negotiation may also refer to the core actions and their management to be contained in the reports (taking legal, administrative, or other measures, granting statistical or monitoring data, inventories, etc. relating to the implementation of the treaty regime, as well as assessing their effectiveness and the problems encountered in the implementation of defined instruments of the treaty regime), or to the form of the reports and the intervals of their submission. In regard to conventional environmental regimes, the standardization of the duty-obligation to report usually ranges, depending on their particular purpose and objective, from a simple reference,[170] to a limited,[171] or extensive,[172] formulation of this duty-obligation.

169 As Brown Weiss eloquently stated in regard to conventional environmental regimes, "reporting has become a primary monitoring instrument … Indeed there is almost a band-wagon effect among countries to include a provision on reporting in new agreements." E. Brown Weiss, "Strengthening National Compliance with International Environmental Agreements." 27(4) *Environmental Policy and Law* (1997), 297, at 299.

170 E.g., Helsinki Convention on the Transboundary Effects of Industrial Accidents, 1992, Art. 23.

171 E.g., Convention on Biological Diversity, 1992, Art. 26; Framework Convention for the Protection of the Marine Environment of the Caspian Sea, 2005, Art. 27; Nagoya Protocol on Access to Genetic Resources and the Fair and Equitable Sharing of Benefits Arising from Their Utilization to the Convention on Biological Diversity, 2010, Art. 29

172 E.g., Barcelona Convention, 1976, Art. 26; OSPAR Convention, 1992, Art. 22; Stockholm Convention on Persistent Organic Pollutants, 2001, Art. 15; Convention on International Trade in Endangered Species of Wild Fauna and Flora (CITES), 1973, Art. VIII (7–8). But also see the UN Convention against Torture and Other Cruel, Inhuman or Degrading Treatment or Punishment, 1984, Art. 19(1)(2).

Compliance

The negotiation on compliance refers to the setting up of a compliance procedure and mechanism, and it is closely related to the negotiation on accountability since its function is largely dependent on the procedural duty-obligation of the parties to submit reports. The negotiation on compliance procedure and mechanism aims at building appropriate compliance within the particular framework of the treaty ICI regime at both the individual level (capacity building of a party to comply, public participation in the compliance of a party) and the collective level, in pursuance of the systematic and more effective protection and coherent advancement of the ICI relation encapsulated in the treaty text. In actuality, the negotiation on compliance is a narration of a constructive normative reality that is entirely different from the positivist legal approach, which assumes that state parties are naturally endowed with the capacity to comply with the requirements of a treaty regime. Compliance cannot be measured in a snapshot. Such an approach stems from the inadequate theoretical application of the analogy of private law contract to treaties (the "contract view" of treaties), which requires that compliance should be objectively measured as an instantaneous legal consequence relating to the violation of "concluded" contact-like treaty obligations. However, compliance is a relational normative activity that is built with the treaty ICI regime. It is inextricably interwoven with its continuous function and development as well as with the different levels of pragmatic implementation of compliance by the parties. This latter requires, for its proper understanding, a focus on a multiplicity of interrelated factors: domestic institutional capacity, party-level economic and social development, public participation in governance, and interactive evaluation of the impact of the treaty regime on the party level and of the need for its improvement. The negotiation to set up such a system of creative compliance of the parties refers to an innovative process and, for this reason, it is a rather recent development.[173]

Depending on the nature of the treaty relation and the perception of its dynamic operation, the negotiation on setting up a compliance procedure and mechanism may be associated, more specifically, with the development of two alternative compliance patterns:

- The construction of a collective duty-obligation of *pactum de contrahendo*: the parties undertake to pursue future negotiations in good faith and dynamically with a view to build a procedure and mechanism of compliance and to achieve this specific result. In other words, to construct a collective twofold duty-obligation: to negotiate a specific issue in good faith and to attain a positive ICI result within the normative, relational, and contextual space

[173] For instance, a number of regional conventional environmental regimes do not contain a special clause on compliance control.

of the ICI conventional regime,[174] and in an evolutionary, purposive manner.[175]

- The establishment of a generally prescribed procedure controlling compliance in the framework of the institutionality of the treaty ICI regime.

The negotiation of the first pattern of compliance focuses on the degree of specification of the terms prescribing the twofold collective duty – the obligation to negotiate, and to attain a positive result, the actions of the parties, and the ICI legislative purpose of the treaty under negotiation. In other words, an effort is made to configure, through the formulation of this collective duty-obligation and in the most encompassing manner, the link between the future good faith negotiating conduct with the attainment of a relationally and contextually relevant positive result (procedure and mechanism of compliance). This is well depicted in the Aarhus Convention, 1998, where Art. 15 sets out the duty-obligation of the Meeting of the Parties to "establish, on a consensus basis, optional arrangements of a non-confrontational, non-judicial and consultative nature for reviewing compliance with the provisions of this Convention," while they will "allow for appropriate public involvement and may include the option of considering communications from members of the public on matters related to this Convention." Within this framework, the First Meeting of the Parties (2002), following the completion of the relevant negotiation carried out by a mandated ad hoc working group, proceeded to the adoption of Decision I/7, "Review of Compliance," which established the Compliance Committee and set out its structure and functions.[176] On the other hand, the more abstract formulation of

174 The ICJ moved in this direction in its advisory opinion on Legality of Nuclear Weapons (8 July 1996), ICJ Reports 1996, para. 99; interpreting the obligation of state Parties under Art. VI of the Treaty on the Non-Proliferation of Nuclear Weapons, 1968 ("Each of the Parties to the Treaty undertakes to pursue negotiations in good faith on effective measures relating to cessation of the nuclear arms race at an early date and to nuclear disarmament, and on a treaty on general and complete disarmament under strict and effective international control"), as a *pactum de contrahendo*, it pronounced that "the legal import of that obligation goes beyond that of a mere obligation of conduct; the obligation involved here is an obligation to achieve a precise result – nuclear disarmament in all its aspects – by adopting a particular course of conduct, namely, the pursuit of negotiations on the matter in good faith."

175 In the *Case Concerning Gabčikovo-Nagymaros Project* (25 September 1997), ICJ Reports 1997, para 112, the ICJ generally pronounced the evolutionary approach to the duty to negotiate for the implementation of certain articles of the 1977 Treaty Concerning the Construction and Operation of the Gabčikovo-Nagymaros System of Locks, Hungary and Czechoslovakia, 16 September 1977 (1109 U.N.T.S. 235).

176 ECE Report of the First Meeting of the Parties, Addendum (ECE/MP.PP/2/Add.8), Decision I/7, "Review of Compliance," adopted at the First Meeting of the Parties held in Lucca, Italy (21–23 October 2002). See also the similar Art. 18 of the Kyoto Protocol to the UN Framework Convention on Climate Change, 1997, and the establishment of the Compliance Committee by Decision 24/CMP.7, "Procedure and Mechanisms Relating to Compliance under the Kyoto Protocol," UNFCCC: Decisions Adopted by the Conference of the Parties Serving as the Meeting of the Parties to the Kyoto Protocol, Addendum (FCCC/KP/CMP/2005/8/Add. 3), p. 92.

this collective duty-obligation, without any further specifying terms, is also a frequent negotiating option.[177]

The negotiation of the second pattern of compliance focuses on the degree of the institutional depth in the articulation of the general procedure regarding compliance control within the framework of the treaty regime. Thus, the COPs or MOPs, as supreme institutional organs in which all contracting parties are equally represented, are attributed a central role, vested with the authority to assess compliance with the treaty regime. It is, however, through negotiation, that the general conditions of such authority are effectively determined, prescribing the normative scope of compliance control, the instruments activating compliance procedure, and the appropriate actions to achieve or enhance compliance. A characteristic illustration of this pattern of compliance is found in Art. 27 of the Barcelona Convention, 1976, stipulating that the Meetings of the Contracting Parties are assigned the power to assess the compliance with the Convention Protocols, but also with the measures and recommendations, adopted for their implementation, "on the basis of periodical reports referred to in Art. 26 and any other report submitted by the Contracting Parties," and to recommend, when it considers it appropriate, "the necessary steps to bring about full compliance with the Conventions and the Protocol and to promote the implementation of the decisions and recommendations."[178]

Such negotiating direction, determining the second pattern of compliance, encapsulates the seed for its development: it may develop into a more cohesive and integrated institutional structure, reflected in the future establishment of a compliance mechanism, thus reinforcing the institutionality level of the treaty regime. This two-step approach to the construction of an ad hoc mechanism of compliance as part of the institutional structure is well illustrated in the development of the regime of the Barcelona Convention, 1976. The 15th MOP, reframing the pattern of compliance provided in Article 27, decided to adopt the institutional product of the relevant negotiation carried out by its mandated "Ad Hoc Working Group on Implementation and Compliance under the Barcelona Convention" (2004–2007), and to establish the Compliance Committee as an advanced subsidiary organ, functioning in complementarity with the MOP, with a view to attain more efficient implementation of the Barcelona Convention system, taking into account the specific situation of each Contracting Party.[179]

177 See, e.g., Stockholm Convention on Persistent Organic Pollutants, 2001, Art. 17; Rotterdam Convention on PIC Procedure, 1998, Art. 17; Framework Convention for the Protection of the Marine Environment of the Caspian Sea, 2005, Art. 28.

178 See also OSPAR Convention, 1992, Art. 23.

179 MAP: Decision IG 17/2: Procedures and Mechanisms on Compliance under the Barcelona Convention and Its Protocols, Report of the 15th Ordinary Meeting of the Contracting Parties to the Convention for the Protection of the Marine Environment and the Coastal Region of the Mediterranean and Its Protocols, Almeria (Spain), 15–18 January 2008, UNEP(DEC)/MED IG. 17/10, Annex V, Decisions of the 15th Meeting of the Contracting Parties, 23–27.

On the other hand, it is a recent development that the construction of an ad hoc mechanism of compliance may be part of the Constitutive Negotiation of a treaty regime. The negotiation on the inclusion of the Compliance Committee in the institutional structure of a treaty regime (as a subsidiary organ of the Conference of the Parties) and on the specification of its general conditions of operation (purpose, competence, composition, procedure, and decision-making) in an open-ended manner (the Conference of the Parties is empowered to adopt further terms of reference for the Committee) marks, depending on the nature and context of the treaty under negotiation, a potentially constructive negotiating possibility.[180]

Finally, in certain types of treaty regimes, Constitutive Negotiation may require from the beginning the establishment of a very high level of procedural control of compliance in the framework of their advanced institutional structure. Thus, the Chemical Weapons Convention, 1993, which sets up the Organization for the Prohibition of Chemical Weapons with a three-level core institutional structure (the Conference of the States Parties, the Executive Council, and the Technical Secretariat),[181] like all intergovernmental organizations, provides a high level of procedural control of compliance relating to its institutional structure. It stipulates, in Art. XII, that the Conference of the States Parties "shall take the necessary measures" prescribed in this Article "to ensure compliance with this Convention and to redress and remedy any situation which contravenes the provisions of this Convention," taking into account all information and recommendations submitted by the Executive Council, and these measures may, in serious cases, take the form of "collective measures to States Parties in conformity with international law." At the same time, the Executive Council is empowered to request a State Party "to take measures to redress a situation raising problems with regard to its compliance," and, in case of failure, "within the specified time," to recommend to the Conference to proceed to sanctions, which may include inter alia restriction or suspension of the state party's rights and privileges under this Convention.[182] Similarly, the UN Comprehensive Test Ban Treaty, 1996, follows the same pattern of compliance in the framework of its corresponding advanced institutional structure. The Comprehensive Nuclear Test-Ban Treaty Organization, also having a three-level core institutional structure (the Conference of the States Parties, the Executive Council, and the Technical Secretariat),[183] provides, in Art. V of its treaty, that the Conference of the States Parties, "taking into account, inter alia, the recommendations of the Executive

180 Minimata Convention on Mercury, 2013, Art. 15. See also the recent Paris Agreement, 2015, which, in Art. 15, stipulates the establishment of "a mechanism to facilitate implementation of and promote compliance with the provisions of this Agreement," stating only the general characteristics of the Committee, while the modalities and procedures of its operation are provided to be adopted at the first session of the Conference of the Parties.

181 Chemical Weapons Convention, 1993, Art. VIII (A.4).

182 Ibid., Art. XII.

183 UN Comprehensive Test Ban Treaty, 1996, Art. II(4).

Council," is empowered to "take the necessary measures" prescribed in this Article "to ensure compliance with this Treaty and to redress and remedy any situation which contravenes the provisions of this Treaty," and these measures, in cases of noncompliance with the basic obligations of this Treaty, may take the form of "collective measures which are in conformity with international law." Similarly, the Executive Council may request a state party "to redress a situation raising problems with regard to its compliance," and, in case of failure, "within the specified time," to recommend the Conference proceed to sanctions, "which may include *inter alia* restriction or suspension of the State Party's rights and privileges under this Treaty."[184]

At the other end, the Constitutive Negotiation in most treaties establishing human rights regimes is directed towards the construction of a more simple pattern of compliance: the institution of a supervisory body (mechanism) of a relational character (a committee of experts) for monitoring compliance. This supervisory body, operating on the basis of the periodically submitted reports of the state parties, is empowered to initiate and facilitate "a constructive dialogue" with the state party, which "does not give effect to the provisions of the Convention" or violates them, and, in this framework, to undertake a certain investigatory action on its own initiative and in cooperation with the state, finally "publicising the case" by including it in its annual official report.[185]

Settlement of Disputes

The negotiation of the procedure of managing disputes refers to the drafting of largely standardized provisions determining the exercise of the duty-obligation of the parties to submit their disputes on the interpretation and application of the treaty regime to an "umbrella procedural system" incorporating political, legal, and mixed methods and institutions of dispute settlement.

Most of the treaty regimes employ the patterned clause "Settlement of Disputes" to serve as a restorative procedure of the ICI conventional relation. The umbrella procedural system enshrined in these regimes may vary in respect of its normative scope, and it may also be differentiated with respect to management of the

184 Ibid. Art. V.

185 UN Convention against Torture and Other Cruel, Inhuman or Degrading Treatment or Punishment, 1984, Arts. 17–24. It is interesting that the Optional Protocol to the Convention against Torture and Other Cruel, Inhuman or Degrading Treatment or Punishment, 2002, strengthens the simple pattern of compliance by establishing a two-pillar visiting mechanism: an international mechanism, the Sub-Committee on Prevention, complemented by a national mechanism, the National Preventive Mechanisms. Both of them build a constructive dialogue with the competent authorities of the state party, providing recommendations on effective measures (see Arts. 2–22). See also the Convention on the Rights of the Child, 1989, Arts. 43–45, establishing the Committee on the Rights of the Child, or the International Convention for the Protection of All Persons from Enforced Disappearance, 2006, Arts. 26–36, establishing the Committee of Enforced Disappearances, or the International Convention on the Protection of the Rights of All Migrant Workers and Members of their Families, 1990, Art. 72ff, establishing the Committee on the Protection of the Rights of All Migrant Workers and Members of Their Families.

combination of the methods and institutions involved. Here, the negotiating parties focus on a range of issues featuring the structure and the content of the patterned clause "Settlement of Disputes," which refer to:

- The choice of the approach to managing the system of methods and institutions of settlement of dispute: *horizontal management*, based on the free choice of methods and institutions, *or vertical management*, based on the provided successive function of methods and institutions, taking place within a determined time limit, until reaching a settlement.
- The choice of the scope of stratification of the most appropriate system of methods and institutions of settlement of dispute, which may range from the traditional means of international disputes settlement (political ["negotiation," "mediation," "good offices"], mixed ["conciliation," inquiry], or legal [arbitration, judicial settlement] means) to resorting to the institutional structure of the treaty regime or other innovative methods of dispute settlement.

The usual negotiating direction regarding the methods and institutions of dispute settlement is towards the construction of a combination of a horizontal management, where the system is run by the free choice of the parties, and a vertical management, where the system integrates, in ranging formats, voluntary and compulsory elements. The outcome is an umbrella procedural system operating horizontally and vertically where the parties may choose the appropriate combination of political, legal, or mixed means of dispute settlement to a varying extent. More specifically, this integrated umbrella procedural system may encompass a scaling management of dispute at two successive levels: at the first level, the parties to the dispute should seek to resolve their dispute "through negotiation or other peaceful means of their choice," while, at the second level, the method or institution of dispute settlement is specified, leaving to the parties certain choices for its activation. Thus, if the parties cannot settle their dispute at the first level, they should proceed to the second level and resort to an arbitration process (the rules and procedures of which may be specifically stated in a standardized manner in an annex or in the text of the respective provision), either "upon common agreement," coupled with the normative discretion of the parties, to declare "at any time" unilaterally the recognition of arbitration "as compulsory ipso facto and without special agreement" in relation to any other Party accepting the same obligation,[186] or "at the request" of one party to the dispute.[187] The first level may also be restricted to negotiation while the second level may be organized in two

[186] E.g., Barcelona Convention, 1976, Art. 28; Noumea Convention for the Protection of the Natural Resources and Environment of the South Pacific Region, 1986, Art. 26; Cartagena Convention for the Protection and Development of the Marine Environment of the Wider Caribbean Region, 1983, Art. 23.

[187] E.g., OSPAR Convention, 1992, Art. 32; MARPOL 73/78, Art. 10.

successive sublevels of dispute management formulated in different versions. Thus, if negotiation fails, the dispute, "within a reasonable time," should be submitted to arbitration "at the request" of one party to the dispute. And if, within a specified period, there is no agreement on the organization of the arbitration, any one of these parties "may refer the dispute to the International Court of Justice by request," allowing, however the discretion of each state party to declare "at the time of signature, ratification, acceptance or approval of or accession to this Convention" that it does not consider itself bound by the second level of dispute management.[188] Another version of the second level of the dispute management pattern refers to the declaration of a party, if the first level fails, for the compulsory submission of the dispute either to an arbitration procedure or to the ICJ or to both in relation to any party accepting the same obligation,[189] which may be supplemented by recourse to a conciliation procedure specifically determined, "unless the parties otherwise agree."[190]

Moreover, the integrated umbrella procedural system may be reinforced at both levels of dispute management by constructing an appropriate combination of methods, institutions, and the institutionality of a particular treaty regime. This is well illustrated in the Convention on the Law of the Non-Navigational Uses of International Watercourses, 1997, where the scaling management of the dispute is built on two multifaceted successive levels. The first level provides a consensual and expansive platform, encompassing a variety of methods and institutions, and reflects a two-step approach: the parties should seek a settlement of their dispute through "negotiation" and, if negotiation fails, they should jointly seek "good offices," "mediation," or "conciliation by a third party," or make use "of any joint watercourse institutions that may have been established by them," or agree "to submit the dispute

188 See the UN Convention against Corruption, 2003, Art. 66. This specific pattern of dispute management is generally adopted by most treaties establishing human rights regimes, e.g., the UN Convention against Torture and Other Cruel, Inhuman or Degrading Treatment or Punishment, 1984, Art. 30; the International Convention on the Protection of the Rights of All Migrant Workers and Members of Their Families, 1990 Art. 92; International Convention for the Protection of All Persons from Enforced Disappearance, 2006, Art. 42.

189 Aarhus Convention, 1992, Art. 16; Espoo Convention on Environmental Impact Assessment in a Transboundary Context, 1991, Art. 15; UN Convention on the Transboundary Effects of Industrial Accidents, 1992, Art. 21; Basel Convention on the Control of Transboundary Movements of Hazardous Wastes and Their Disposal, 1989, Art. 20, which in addition provides that failure to reach common agreement on the second level "shall not absolve the Parties from the responsibility of continuing to seek to resolve it by the means referred to" in the first level (Art. 20(2)). See also the IAEA Conventions on Nuclear Accidents, 1986 (Convention on Early Notification of a Nuclear Accident, Art. 11; Convention on Assistance in the Case of Nuclear Accident or Radiological Emergency, Art. 13), which combines the last two versions of the second level of the dispute management pattern mentioned earlier in this chapter.

190 Rotterdam Convention on PIC Procedure, 1998, Art. 20; Stockholm Convention on Persistent Organic Pollutants, 2001, Art. 18; UN Convention to Combat Desertification, 1994, Art. 28. Also, Convention on Biological Diversity, 1992, Art. 27, which proceeds to further specify the first level by stating, apart from negotiation, the duty of the parties to "jointly seek the good offices of, or request mediation by, a third party" (Art. 27(2)).

to arbitration or to the International Court of Justice." The second level, on the other hand, provides a compulsory platform for dispute management operating in two directions: if the first level fails to produce a consensual dispute settlement, the dispute should be submitted, at the request of any of the parties to it and within a specified period, to a specifically prescribed impartial fact-finding commission that generates recommendations for an equitable solution of the dispute, "unless the parties otherwise agree." Alternatively, it is provided that a party may declare, when entering the present Convention, or at any time thereafter, and in the case of failure of the first level, that it recognizes as compulsory *ipso facto* the submission of the dispute to the ICJ and/or to arbitration vis-à-vis any party accepting the same obligation.[191]

An interesting version of reinforcement of the integrated umbrella procedural system is associated with the high degree of institutionality of a treaty regime producing the enrichment of both levels of dispute management and a notable degree of verticality of the system. The Convention on Chemical Weapons, 1993, provides such a case: the Organization for the Prohibition of Chemical Weapons, established therein, is actively involved, through its organs, in both the horizontal and the vertical management of the dispute settlement system introducing certain vertical aspects of such management. As is stipulated, the first level of dispute settlement system provides a consensual expansive platform of methods and institutions referring to "negotiation" or "other peaceful means of the parties' choice," which include "recourse to appropriate organs of this Convention," as well as "referral to the International Court of Justice" by mutual consent.[192] Moreover, the Executive Council "may contribute to the settlement of a dispute by whatever means it deems appropriate, including offering its good offices."[193] The second level is introduced by the competence of the Conference to "consider questions related to disputes raised by States Parties or brought to its attention by the Executive Council," and, "as it finds necessary," to "establish or entrust organs with tasks related to the settlement of these disputes."[194] Moreover, the Conference and the Council "are separately empowered, subject to authorization from the General Assembly of the United Nations, to request the International Court of Justice to give an advisory opinion on any legal question arising within the scope of the activities of the Organization."[195]

At the other end, it may be agreed that the umbrella procedural system will be limited to the first level of dispute management, thus underlining the intersubjective, context-sensitive character of such management. The omission of the second level may be required by the contextuality of the Constitutive Negotiation of the

[191] Convention on the Law of the Non-Navigational Uses of International Watercourses, 1997, Art. 33.
[192] Convention on Chemical Weapons, 1993, Art. XIV(2).
[193] Ibid., Art. XIV(3).
[194] Ibid., Art. XIV(4).
[195] Ibid., Art. XIV(5).

particular treaty regime and the emanating historical perceptions of the negotiating parties of the particular region based on deeply rooted diverging political, legal, or cultural interests that allow only a consensual management of disputes.[196] An interesting version, also reflecting the contextuality of Constitutive Negotiation, is provided by treaty regimes fully "internalizing" the horizontal management of the dispute settlement system. Thus, the Landmines Convention, 1997, combining methods with the institutionality of its conventional regime, refers to the duty-obligation of the state parties to "consult and cooperate with each other to settle any dispute," as well as to their ability to "bring any such dispute before the Meeting of the States Parties." The latter may contribute to the dispute management "by whatever means it deems appropriate," indicatively mentioning the offering of its good services for the choice of an agreed settlement procedure and recommending a time limit.[197]

5.3.5.4 TRANSFORMABILITY

At the level of transformability, the negotiating parties determine the patterned structure and content of the revision procedure of the treaty regime, which is articulated in the standardized clauses on "Amendment." The significance of the construction of the amendment clause lies in the fact that it secures the consensually progressing articulation of the legislative purpose of the treaty regime, the coherence of its expansive specification, and, in effect, its balanced transformation, within a patterned normative platform arranging the procedure for the exercise of review governance of the contracting parties. This conventional transformability process, carried out through negotiation and consensus-building, engineers the resilience of the treaty regime and its feasible innovative adaptability to, and synchronization with, the internal and external contextual developments. For the purposes of the Constitutive Negotiation, the negotiating parties focus on two core issues:[198]

- The clear distinction between the amendment of the treaty/convention and its performative protocols and the amendment of their technical and implementative annexes,[199] associated with the generally recognized differentiated effects

196 See, e.g., Bucharest Convention on the Protection of the Black Sea against Pollution, 1992, Art. XXV; Framework Convention for the Protection of the Marine Environment of the Caspian Sea, 2005, Art. 30. See also Regional Cooperation Agreement on Combating Piracy and Armed Robbery against Ships in Asia, 2005, Art. 17.

197 Landmines Convention, 1997, Art. 10.

198 A full analysis of the revisionary negotiation process is presented in the next chapter, where the Renegotiation phase is examined.

199 As pointed out earlier, the implementative annexes specify the details on how to implement and comply with certain obligations-duties of the treaty regime, contextualizing them if required by the nature of the treaty (e.g., the UN Convention to Combat Desertification, 1994, Annexes I–IV), whereas the technical annexes have a merely descriptive content and scientific, or technical, character indicating the technical aspect of the implementation of a treaty regime. If, however, the annexes refer to significant additional details regarding institutional mechanisms or procedures of the treaty, it may be provided that their amendment regime may be that of the Convention and

generated, correspondingly, from the contractual or relational character of their operation.

- The problem of regime duality resulting from the contractual effect of the amendment of the treaty/convention and its performative protocols and the chronic coexistence and parallel application of the old and the new treaty regimes, but also the problem of "temporal inertia" caused by the temporality of the entry into force of its amendment, which may raise serious issues concerning its prompt and adequate implementation.

With respect to the first issue, it is a commonplace in all treaty regimes that the negotiation of the amendment clause is constantly and consistently differentiated between the construction of the amendment procedure of the treaty framework and their related performative protocols, and the construction of the amendment procedure of the technical and implementative annexes. Both amendment procedures are negotiably shaped in relation to the institutionality of the particular treaty regime and are embedded into its function. However, the former is formulated as a two-step process, creating a collective first level referring to the adoption of the amended text by a decision of a diplomatic conference of the contracting parties or the full representational organ of an international organization, based on an appropriately qualified majority vote, and a subsequent second level referring to the individuating acceptance of its implementation, which produces a relationally qualified contractual effect (the amended text enters into force only when a qualified number of individual acceptances is reached, and only for them). On the other hand, the latter simply operates at one single level: it requires the collective adoption by a decision of the full representation organ, based on a qualified majority vote, which produces a relational effect, applying to all parties within a specified time frame and allowing only a contractual opting out whereby a party may communicate its objection within a specified period and be exempted.

More specifically, most conventional environmental regimes, of a regional or global character, establish an identical pattern for the aforementioned differentiation of the amendment procedure, determining its normative scope as follows.

- Any contracting party may propose amendments to a convention, related protocols, and their annexes.

Protocols (e.g., the Barcelona Convention for the Protection of the Marine Environment and Coastal Region of the Mediterranean, 1976, Annex on Arbitration), or it may be open to both amendment regimes, yet prescribe important limiting conditions for the simplified procedure (e.g., UNCLOS, Arts. 312 and 313 – the simplified procedure of Article 313 dispenses with a negotiating conference, and the adoption of the proposed amendment relies on a non-objection procedure, provided that a state party does not object to it "within a period of 12 months from the date of the circulation of (its) communication." And however adopted, the amendment will enter into force if ratified or acceded to by at least sixty state parties and it will have a contractual effect: it will apply to those who have accepted it (Arts. 315, 316). On the other hand, other treaty regimes maintain the differentiated amendment regime for annexes detailing institutional mechanisms and procedures (e.g., Minimata Convention on Mercury, 2013, Annex E (Arbitration and Conciliation Procedures).

- A diplomatic conference of the contracting parties or the full representation organ (a meeting or a conference of the contracting parties, or the commission) adopts (by a qualified majority decision of three-fourths, by unanimous decision, or by consensus and by three-fourths majority if consensus cannot be reached) the text of the amendment to the convention and/or its performative protocols, which enters into force only between the contracting parties having individually notified the depositary of their acceptances and only when three-fourths (or two-thirds or a specified number) of them have done so.
- The meeting or the conference of the contracting parties adopts (by a qualified majority decision usually of three-fourths) the text of the amendment to the technical annexes which becomes effective for all contracting parties on the expiry of a period, determined ad hoc by the meeting or the conference or expressly stated in the Convention, while any party unable to approve it should notify in writing the depository of its objection within this period and thus be exempted.[200]

In this context, it is worth noticing that the small number of contracting parties, constituting a region, may have a special impact on the formulation of the decision to accept amendments associated with the harmonization of the procedural differentiation of the amendment clauses in favour of the relational effects. This is well illustrated in the Bucharest Convention on the Protection of the Black Sea against Pollution, 1992, which stipulates that the Diplomatic Conference and the Commission will adopt, "on the basis of consensus," the amendments to the Convention and/or the protocols and annexes correspondingly, and that, in both cases, the amendments will enter into force "after the depositary has received notifications of acceptance of these amendments from all Contracting Parties,"[201] thus indicating a *bifurcated comprehensive contractual acceptance.* Moving in a similar direction, the Kuwait Convention, 1978, prescribes a *bifurcated comprehensive relational acceptance.* It provides that a Diplomatic Conference and a Meeting of the Council (identical to MOPs) will adopt, by unanimous

[200] See the Barcelona Convention, 1976, Arts. 22, 23; the Cartagena Convention, 1983, Arts. 18, 19; the Noumea Convention, 1986, Arts. 24, 25; the Nairobi Convention for the Protection, Management and Development of the Marine and Coastal Environment of the Eastern African Region, 1985, Arts. 19, 20. See also the OSPAR Convention, 1992, Arts. 15–19; the Aarhus Convention, 1992, Art. 14; the UN Convention to Combat Desertification, 1994, Arts. 30, 31; the Espoo Convention on Environmental Impact Assessment in a Transboundary Context, 1991, Art. 14; the UN Framework Convention on Climate Change, 1992, Arts. 15, 16; Convention on Biological Diversity, 1992, Arts. 29, 30.

[201] Arts. XX and XXI. The Bucharest Convention on the Black Sea, 1992, consists of six contracting parties: Bulgaria, Georgia, Romania, Russia, Turkey, and Ukraine. A bifurcated comprehensive contractual acceptance based on unanimity is also provided in the Framework Convention for the Protection of the Marine Environment of the Caspian Sea, 2005, Arts. 25 and 34, consisting of five contracting parties: Azerbaijan, Iran, Kazakhstan, Russia, and Turkmenistan. Interestingly, the Helsinki Convention on the Protection of the Marine Environment of the Baltic Sea Area, 1992, Arts. 31 and 32, provides that the amendments to the Convention "recommended" by the Commission will enter into force "after the Depositary has received notifications of acceptance of that amendment from all Contracting Parties," whereas the amendments to the annexes "recommended" by the Commission follow the general pattern as described earlier.

vote, the amendments to the Convention and/or its protocols and annexes correspondingly and that, in both cases, the amendments will enter into force for all Contracting States, within a specified time, "except those which have notified the Depositary of a different intention."[202]

Furthermore, other patterns of contemporary treaty regimes constituting ICI relations establish a similar pattern of contractual and relational differentiation of the amendment procedure, embracing their specific terms as well as their variations. In addition, they may also designate as competent an Ad Hoc Review or Amendment Conference of the Parties,[203] whereas, in some types of treaty ICI regimes, the adopted amendment is provided to be laid down in a protocol requiring a minimum number of consenting instruments to enter into force,[204] or it is stipulated that any proposal for amendment by a state party requires the lapse of a certain period of time after the entry into force of the treaty concerned.[205]

Of particular interest are treaty regimes that enrich the pattern of contractual and relational differentiation of the amendment procedure by expanding it to the procedural management of the problem of temporal inertia associated with the entry into force of the treaty amendment. This is done by the introduction of the pattern of varying forms of "tacit amendment," which further reinforce the relational effect of amendment and appear in treaty regimes characterized by a high degree of institutionality in their structure and a distinctive technical content for the pursuance of their ICI purpose. Thus the Convention on Chemical Weapons, 1993, provides that the amendments to the Convention that are adopted by an Amendment Conference "enter into force for all States Parties" when they are ratified or accepted by all those State Parties that, constituting a simple majority, cast a positive vote at the Amendment Conference "with no State Party casting a negative vote" (consensus amendment).[206] Interestingly, a State Party that is not present at the Amendment Conference is bound by the amendment. Correspondingly, the amendments to the annexes related to "matters of an administrative or technical nature" will "be considered approved," if the positive recommendation of an executive organ, the Executive Council consisting of 41 members, meets with no objection by any State Party "within 90 days after receipt of the recommendation," and they will "be considered rejected," if the negative recommendation of the

202 Kuwait Regional Convention for Cooperation on the Protection of the Marine Environment from Pollution, 1978, Arts. XX and XXI consisting of eight contracting parties: Bahrain, Iran, Iraq, Kuwait, Oman, Qatar, Saudi Arabia, and the United Arab Emirates.

203 See the Landmines Convention, 1997, Art. 13; the International Convention for Suppression of Acts of Nuclear Terrorism, 2005, Art. 26. Also see the Rome Statute of the International Criminal Court, 1998, Arts. 121(1) and 123(1).

204 See the IAEA Conventions on Nuclear Accidents, 1986 (Convention on Early Notification of a Nuclear Accident, Art. 14; Convention on Assistance in the Case of Nuclear Accident or Radiological Emergency, Art. 16).

205 See the UN Convention against Corruption, 2003, Art. 69.

206 Convention on Chemical Weapons, 1993, Art. XV (2)(3).

Executive Council also meets with no objection by any State Party under the same conditions (opting-out amendments).[207]

Of similar interest is the treaty regimes constituted in the framework of the IMO, where the pattern of contractual and relational differentiation of the amendment is structured as a two-tier standard process of revisionary governance: the amendment procedure conducted in the framework of the Organization (the IMO) and the amendment procedure carried out in the framework of the Ad Hoc Conference of the Parties to the particular Convention. In both amendment procedures, amendments are adopted and enter into force following the same specified procedure. Thus, amendment by the Conference of the Parties or by the Organization is adopted by a two-thirds majority of the Parties to the Convention "present and voting," and, if it refers to the Convention, enters into force *contractually* (with respect to the two-thirds of the Parties notifying their acceptance) or *contractually with relational connotations* (the combined merchant fleets of two-thirds of the Parties "constitute not less than 50 per cent of the gross tonnage of the world's merchant fleet"). If it refers to technical annexes or appendices, it enters into force *relationally* (with respect to all Parties after the lapse of a defined period of time, except for any Party that has objected to the amendment or has announced its *contractualization* of the amendment – it will "enter into force for it only after a subsequent notification of its acceptance").[208] Besides, the consideration of the amendment in the framework of the organization is carried out by its appropriate organ as indicated in the procedure (e.g., the Marine Environment Protection Committee of the IMO, the Maritime Safety Committee or, generally, by an appropriate body of the Organization), which adopts the proposed amendments "of only the Parties to the Convention present and voting," while the amendments to technical annexes or appendices "are deemed to have been accepted" according to the aforementioned procedure, unless an objection is officially communicated by a blocking minority,[209] which entails their rejection. It is obvious that, within this two-tier standard process of revisionary governance, the provided opting-out power

[207] Ibid., Art. XV (4), (5)(d).

[208] See the OPRC Convention, 1990, Art. 14; the International Convention for the Control and Management of Ships' Ballast Water and Sediments (BWM Convention), 2004, Art. 19. For contractual effects with relational connotations, see MARPOL 73/78, Art. 16. Also see the International Convention for the Safety of Life at Sea (LIFE), 1974, Art. VIII; the International Convention on Standards of Training, Certification and Watchkeeping for Seafarers (STCW), 1978, Art. XII; the Convention on the International Regulations for Preventing Collisions at Sea (COLREG), 1972, Art. VI. Of interest is the more recent International Convention on Liability and Compensation for Damage in Connection with the Carriage of Hazardous and Noxious Substances by Sea (HNS Convention), 2010, Arts. 47 and 48, providing a special procedure for the amendment of the limits of liability laid down in Art. 9 of this Convention, which is submitted to the Legal Committee of the IMO for negotiation and adoption and enters into force relationally due to its intense technical flavour (Art. 48).

[209] As is provided, the blocking minority consists of "not less than one third of the Parties" within the determined period or in some Conventions, or it may be complemented by more relational criteria ("by the Parties the combined merchant fleets of which constitute not less than 50 per cent of the

allows tacit amendment in all stages of the amendment procedure for a party that chooses not to act.

5.3.5.5 SUBJECTIVITY

At the level of subjectivity, the negotiating parties determine a series of patterned clauses, composing the "Final Provisions" part of the treaty, whereby the constitution and the function of the treaty ICI regime is "subjectified" in a way that is consistent with the attainment of its legislative purpose. The scope of treaty subjectification covers a group of standard clauses referring to the expression of the will of the parties to legally participate in the treaty relation ("Signature," "Ratification, Acceptance, or Approval," "Accession," "Withdrawal"), the relational core of such participation for the operation of the treaty ("Entry into force"), the entrusting institutional framework of treaty subjectification ("Depository"), and the treaty's textual languages ("Authentic texts"). The scope of treaty subjectification may also be extended to contain, according to the choice of the negotiating parties and the special nature of the treaty regime, standard clauses referring to the differentiating aspects of the will of the parties to legally participate in the treaty relation ("Reservations," "Provisional Application," "Territorial Application").

Regarding these standard clauses on subjectivity, it is necessary to highlight two interrelated key aspects linked to their pragmatic importance as to the effectiveness of the function of the treaty ICI regimes. First, they play an essential role in the effort of the negotiating parties to construct a foundational legal platform of "plurality-in-treaty relation": they signify the modalities for the subjective stratification and effects of the constitution of the particular treaty regime in terms of the application of its ICI legislative purpose. They are not the mere means of expressing a contractual "consent to be bound," that is, of concluding a treaty in terms of an assumed contractual coincidence of wills, stemming from the theoretical perception perpetuating the inadequate private contract view of treaties.[210] In fact, these standard clauses identify, constantly and consistently in all treaty regimes, the sphere of subjective action of the "contracting parties" related to the constitution of a treaty ICI regime, where the subjectivity of the choice to become a party to it, and individual participation in it, are fundamentally associated with the continuous function of its ICI legislative purpose and the relational effect of its implementation.

Second, they signify the extent of the subjectivity domain recognized in a treaty ICI regime comprising a group of clauses, appropriately standardized and to a varying degree, which determine the possible instances of *subjectification of participation* in the treaty regime. The subjectification of participation refers to the possibility of the negotiating parties to introduce into the text of the treaty individuating clauses related to:

gross tonnage of the world's merchant fleet whichever condition is fulfilled"). See MARPOL 73/78, Art. 16(1.2.f.iii).

210 See Raftopoulos, *The Inadequacy of the Contractual Analogy in the Law of Treaties*, *supra* note 39, *passim*.

- The territorial, temporal, or material extent of treaty application, articulated in the form of the standardized clauses providing its "territorial application" or its "provisional application" or "interim arrangements" or the power of its stricter application at the level of national legal orders
- The legal integrity of participation, associated with the nature and purpose of the treaty but also with the weight of the package deal underlying the treaty, formulated by the standardized clauses prohibiting or allowing the inclusion of "reservation clauses" into the treaty, or silent on it.
- The individual repeal of participation, articulated in the form of standardized clauses regarding the "withdrawal" or the "denunciation" of the treaty.

Although often overlooked during the Constitutive Negotiation process, it is worth stressing that all the issues relating to the clauses that subjectify the constitution and function of treaty ICI regimes may pose, to a greater or lesser extent and precisely because of the public character of the treaty, sensitive political questions. For this reason, their management should be prudently integrated into the Constitutive Negotiation process. The practice of leaving their discussion until the final stage of Constitutive Negotiation, where the accumulated fatigue but also the enthusiasm for the finalization of the other parts of the treaty text dominates the minds and the behaviour of the negotiators, often relegates their late negotiation into a formalistic procedure that should be exclusively left in the hands of legal experts (or in the legal service of the secretariat of the international organization) as if it were a distinct issue of legal formality, somehow of negotiating interest.

More specifically, whereas the clauses relating to "Signature," "Ratification, Acceptance, or Approval," and "Accession" may have a more or less formal legal character,[211] the clause relating to the "entry into force" requires, because of its relational character, a purposive attainment of consensus that clusters a political balancing decision. As a result, it may require that a minimum number of states' participation is reached by the deposit of instruments of ratification, acceptance, approval, or accession, either exclusively,[212] or in combination with a minimum

[211] Note, however, that the possibility of ratification, especially when associated with domestic institutional problems or constraints, may have a general impact on the quality of Constitutive Negotiation. On the importance of different ratification requirements in the negotiation of certain treaty regimes having distinct political connotations, see, e.g., B. Starkey, M. A. Boyer, and J. Wilkenfeld, *International Negotiation in a Complex World*, Rowman & Littlefield, 2015, 65–66.

[212] E.g., Convention on Biological Diversity, 1992, Art. 36(1); UN Convention to Combat Desertification, 1994, Art. 36(1); Convention on the Law of the Non-Navigational Uses of International Watercourses, 1997, Art. 36(1); UN Convention against Corruption, 2003, Art. 68(1); UN Convention against Torture and Other Cruel, Inhuman or Degrading Treatment or Punishment, 1984, Art. 27(1); Landmines Convention, 1997, Art. 17(1). Certain treaty regimes may provide that the minimum arithmetic criterion may cover not only ratification, acceptance, approval, or accession, but also signature, "without reservation as to ratification, acceptance or approval." See the Convention for the Suppression of Unlawful Acts of Violence against the Safety of Maritime Navigation (SUA Convention), 1988, Art. 18(1); OPRC Convention, 1990, Art. 16(1).

qualitative participation,[213] while it is consistently provided that in the case of participation of "a regional economic integration organization," any instrument deposited by it "shall not be counted as additional to those deposited by States members of such an organization."[214] Note that when the number of the contracting parties is small, the clause on entry into force may, according to the agreement of the negotiating parties, have either a relational or a contractual character.[215]

Also, because of the nature and purpose of the treaty, the negotiating parties may introduce clauses on "territorial application,"[216] or its "provisional application,"[217] or "interim arrangements."[218]

The nature and purpose of the treaty, but also the special weight of the package deal enshrined in the consensus underlying the treaty, may determine the negotiating options concerning the management of the clauses on "reservations." Thus, it may be specifically stipulated that reservations to the treaty are prohibited, if the negotiating parties consider that the package deal on which the treaty is built and the effective pursuance and continuous attainment of its ICI purpose are inextricably interwoven with the legal integrity of the content of the treaty and the legal participation in it.[219] In other words, the inclusion of a clause expressly prohibiting

[213] E.g., MARPOL 73/78, Art. 15(1); LIFE Convention, 1974, Art. X(1); International Convention on Load Lines, 1966, Art. 28(1); BWM Convention, 2004, Art. 18(1).

[214] Aarhus Convention, 1992, Art. 20(2); Convention on Biological Diversity, 1992, Art. 33(5); Nagoya Protocol, 2010, Art. 33; Helsinki Convention on the Transboundary Effects of Industrial Accidents, 1992, Art. 30(2); Espoo Convention on Environmental Impact Assessment in a Transboundary Context, 1991, Art. 18(2); UN Convention to Combat Desertification, 1994, Art. 36(3); Convention on the Law of the Non-Navigational Uses of International Watercourses, 1997, Art. 36(3); UN Convention against Corruption, 2003, Art. 68(1).

[215] Thus, whereas the Bucharest Convention on the Protection of the Black Sea against Pollution, 1992, provides its entry into force after ratification by four out of six contracting parties (Art. XXIV), the Framework Convention for the Protection of the Marine Environment of the Caspian Sea, 2005, provides its entry into force only after ratification by all five contracting parties (Art. 33).

[216] E.g., United States–European Union Agreement on Extradition between the United States of America and the European Union, 2003, Art. 20; BWM Convention, 2004, Art. 17(4).

[217] E.g., IAEA Conventions on Nuclear Accidents, 1986 (Convention on Early Notification of a Nuclear Accident, Art. 13; Convention on Assistance in the Case of Nuclear Accident or Radiological Emergency, Art. 15); Landmines Convention, 1997, Art. 18.

[218] Like the Convention on Biological Diversity, 1992, stipulating the assignment of the secretariat function to the UNEP "on an interim basis for the period between the entry into force of this Convention and the first meeting of the Conference of the Parties" (Art. 40), or the UN Framework Convention on Climate Change, 1992, providing that the secretariat functions "will be carried out on an interim basis by the secretariat established by the General Assembly of the United Nations in its resolution 45/212 of 21 December 1990, until the completion of the first session of the Conference of the Parties," and also setting out that the GEF/UNDP, UNEP, and IBRD will be "entrusted with the operation of the financial mechanism referred to in Article 11 on an interim basis" (Art. 21), or the UN Convention to Combat Desertification, 1994, providing that the secretariat functions "will be carried out on an interim basis by the secretariat established by the General Assembly of the United Nations in its resolution 47/188 of 22 December 1992, until the completion of the first session of the Conference of the Parties"(Art. 35).

[219] E.g., Convention on Chemical Weapons, 1993, Art. XXII; UN Comprehensive Test Ban Treaty, 1996, Art. XV; UN Convention to Combat Desertification, 1994, Art. 37; Framework Convention on Climate Change, 1992, Art. 24; Convention on Biological Diversity, 1992, Art. 37; Framework

the submission of reservations may be regarded by the negotiating parties as constituting a crucial safeguard for the package deal achieved in the treaty while it prevents the corrosive effects and possible imbalances that would be caused by the permission and future use of reservations. On the other hand, if the negotiating parties consider that permitting the possibility of making reservations in general[220] or specified reservations[221] is compatible with the achieved package deal and contributes to the advancement of the purpose of the treaty regime by encompassing the domestic legal, political, economic, or social particularities of the proposing states (subjectivities) into its constructed framework, they may proceed to the formulation of a clause of permissibility of reservations, although such an option appears to be applied in rather limited cases. Finally, the omission of negotiating a reservation clause and the silence of the treaty on this matter, which may be due either to a conscious option of the negotiating parties or to their failure to deal with it, would leave the future interpretation and management of the permissibility of reservations to the application of the residual relevant provisions of the Vienna Convention on the Law of Treaties, 1969,[222] and, finally, to the intersubjective "compatibility test," laid down in Article 19(c) of the Vienna Convention,[223] with reference to the object and purpose of the treaty regime.

Convention for the Protection of the Marine Environment of the Caspian Sea, 2005, Art. 32; ICAO Convention on the Making of Plastic Explosives for the Purpose of Detection, 1991, Art. XII; OSPAR Convention, 1992, Art. 28; Bucharest Convention on the Protection of the Black Sea against Pollution, 1992, Art. XXVII; Landmines Convention, 1997, Art. 19; Minimata Convention on Mercury, 2013, Art. 32. Also, the Rome Statute of the International Criminal Court, 1998, Art. 120. Prominently, the UNCLOS, characterized as a Constitution of the Oceans, prohibits reservations in Article 309 ("unless expressly permitted by other articles of this Convention"), as it is based on an interlocking package deal – "its most significant quality" contributing most distinctly to its success – constituted by consensus, where its provisions form an integral whole. See United Nations, *The Law of the Sea: UN Convention on the Law of the Sea*, New York, 1983, Introduction, ixff.

220 E.g., International Convention on the Arrest of Ships, 1999, Art. 10.

221 E.g., International Convention for Suppression of Acts of Nuclear Terrorism, 2005, Art. 23(2); International Convention on the Arrest of Ships, 1999, Art. 10(1)(c). In certain treaty regimes, the reservation clause combines the prohibition of "general reservations" to the Convention with the permission of their entry into specified articles and the Annexes, e.g., the Convention on International Trade in Endangered Species of Wild Fauna and Flora, 1973, Art. XXIII; also see the Convention on Chemical Weapons, 1993, Art. XXII.

222 See Arts. 19–23.

223 For the application of the compatibility test provided in Article 19(c) of the Vienna Convention see Aust, *Modern Treaty Law and Practice*, op. cit., 110–112. It is noteworthy that the Conventions established under the IMO do not contain a clause on reservation, however, the power-right to make reservations, apart from its possible reliance on the relevant provisions of the Vienna Convention, 1969, may be directly implied from the standardized wording and facilitative spirit of their provision on "Signature, Ratification, Acceptance, Approval and Accession," where "States may become Parties to the Convention by: (a) signature not subject to ratification, acceptance, or approval; or (b) signature subject to ratification, acceptance, or approval, followed by ratification, acceptance or approval; or (c) accession." More recently, the IMO Legal Committee adopted the 2006 Reservation and Guidelines in order to facilitate the entry into force of the 2002 Protocol to the Athens Convention relating to the Carriage of Passengers and Their Luggage by Sea, 1974, recommending that states that

On the other hand, the inclusion of a "withdrawal" clause or of the much less appealing – and hence rather rare – "denunciation" clause raises three interrelated issues that should be illuminated and adequately discussed during the negotiation process. They concern the clarification of their legal significance, the formulation of the elements of their content, and the importance/consequences of their – rather rare – omission from the text of the treaty.

Regarding their legal significance, both "withdrawal" and "denunciation" constitute unilateral acts of a highly subjective basis leading to the same result: the termination of the participation of a party in a treaty regime. Both, in fact, articulate the public power-right of a party, relying on subjective criteria, to repeal the application of the treaty regime vis-à-vis itself individually and *ex nunc*, without affecting the continuation and the broader operation of the treaty regime. Since they entail the same legal consequences, the choice between them lies, at first sight, in the discretion of the negotiating parties. However, "withdrawal" is a better term, because it better depicts the repeal of individual participation in the treaty regime, providing a broader perspective compared to "denunciation," which is a term having a narrower legal connotation, and, for this reason, it may be taken, especially by non-lawyers, as further implying a condemnation of the treaty regime.

As far as their content is concerned, the negotiation is focused on the construction of the terms for the exercise of the power-right to withdraw or denounce the treaty regime as a relational exercise of national sovereignty connected with the protection and promotion of ICI. In consequence, the clauses on "withdrawal" or "denunciation" are patterned as to the steps of the procedure to follow for the exercise of the power to repeal individual state participation in terms of ICI, which, as such, operates *ex nunc* and in trust. More specifically, the construction of all clauses on "withdrawal" or "denunciation" refers to the determination of three basic conditions that compose the prescribed procedure: the point in time when the exercise of the relevant power-right is allowed, the form this exercise should take, and the time required to put it into effect. In addition to these basic conditions, other specific conditions may be included as appropriate, depending on the nature and the legislative purpose of the particular treaty regime. Thus, negotiation on a number of treaties exclusively concentrates on the specification and formulation of these three basic conditions: the point in time for the exercise of the "withdrawal" or "denunciation" may be determined either after the lapse of a certain time period following the entry into force of the treaty regime,[224] or at any

ratify, approve, or accede to the 2002 Protocol to the 1974 Athens Convention "should include a reservation or declaration to the same effect concerning a limitation of liability for carriers and a limitation for compulsory insurance for acts of terrorism, taking into account the current state of the insurance market." IMO/Legal Committee, 101st session, LEG 101/8/3, 12 March 2014, Annex 1, 1.

224 This time may vary from two to five years; see, e.g., Aarhus Convention, 1992, Art. 21 ("withdrawal"); UN Convention to Combat Desertification, 1994, Art. 38 ("withdrawal"); Bucharest Convention on the Protection of the Black Sea against Pollution, 1992, Art. XXX ("denunciation"); Lima Convention for the Protection of the Marine Environment and Coastal Area of the South-East Pacific, 1981, Art.

time;[225] the form of their exercise is always "in writing," and they are put into effect after the lapse of the time provided in the treaty. In many treaties, beyond these three elements, relational terms may be added that may be related to:

- The structural specificity of the treaty (morphological patternment) and the comprehensiveness of the effect of withdrawal to a treaty framework and its performative protocols.[226]
- The institutional management of the effects of "withdrawal."[227]
- The non-impact on a specific field of the treaty regime, in the framework of which the withdrawing party has undertaken a regime action applying it prior to the activation of its withdrawal,[228] or, more generally, the non-release of the state party from its duties-obligations under the treaty regime for any act or omission occurring "prior to the date at which the denunciation becomes effective" or for the continuation of the consideration of any matter that is already under institutional consideration "prior to the date at which the denunciation becomes effective."[229]
- The normative complementarity between the more relational management of the power-right of a state party to withdraw from the particular treaty regime and its non-impact on the interrelated context of reference of this treaty regime,

16 ("denunciation"). See also the IMO Conventions like MARPOL 73/78, Arts. 18 and 19 ("denunciation"), the OPRC Convention, 1990, Art. 17 ("denunciation"); the BWM Convention, 2004, Art. 20 ("denunciation"); the LIFE Convention, 1974, Art. XI ("denunciation"); the STCW Convention, 1978, Art. 13 ("denunciation").

225 IAEA Conventions on Nuclear Accidents, 1986 (Convention on Early Notification of a Nuclear Accident, Art. 15 [denunciation]; Convention on Assistance in the Case of Nuclear Accident or Radiological Emergency, Art. 17 ["denunciation"]); Regional Cooperation Agreement on Combating Piracy and Armed Robbery against Ships in Asia, 2005, Art. 20 ("withdrawal"); ICAO Convention on the Making of Plastic Explosives for the Purpose of Detection, 1991, Art. XV ("denunciation"); United States–European Union Agreement on Extradition between the United States of America and the European Union, 2003, Art. 22(2) ("termination" – a term used because of its bilateral character). The same direction is followed by the UN Convention against Corruption, 2003, Art. 70 ("denunciation"), providing, in addition, that a regional economic integration organization "shall cease to be a Party to this Convention when all of its member States have denounced it."

226 E.g., Framework Convention on Climate Change, 1992, Art. 25 ("withdrawal"); Convention on Biological Diversity, 1992, Art. 38 ("withdrawal");Barcelona Convention, 1976, Art. 34 ("withdrawal"); Noumea Convention, 1986, Art. 32 ("denunciation"); Cartagena Convention, 1983, Art. 29 ("denunciation"); Kuwait Convention, 1978, Art. XXIX ("withdrawal").

227 For instance, the Helsinki Convention on the Protection of the Marine Environment of the Baltic Sea Area, 1992, Art. 37(2) ("withdrawal") sets out the competence of the depositary to "convene a meeting of the Contracting Parties for the purpose of considering the effect of the withdrawal."

228 See the Helsinki Convention on the Transboundary Effects of Industrial Accidents, 1992, Art. 31, providing that withdrawal "shall not affect the application of Article 4 to an activity in respect of which a notification has been made pursuant to Article 4, paragraph 1, or a request for discussions has been made pursuant to Article 4, paragraph 2." A similar provision is contained in the Espoo Convention on Environmental Impact Assessment in a Transboundary Context, 1991, Art. 19.

229 UN Convention against Torture and Other Cruel, Inhuman or Degrading Treatment or Punishment, 1984, Art. 31(2) ("denunciation").

in view of the explicitly provided "unlimited duration" of the treaty regime stated at the beginning of the relevant clause.[230]

Finally, the negotiating choice of not incorporating a clause on "withdrawal" or "denunciation," reflected in some treaties,[231] evidently raises the question whether the right to withdraw or denounce the treaty regime may be appropriately implied from its legislative purpose and its nature. In such a case, the exercise of the power-right to withdraw from or denounce a silent treaty as a power to repeal individual state participation in terms of ICI, operating *ex nunc* and in trust, poses similar issues to those stated earlier, but their management takes place ad hoc within the framework of the function of the legislative purpose of the special treaty regime and is directly related to the determination of the "space of its implied operation." Characteristically, in the very few constitutive conventions of international organizations where a clause on withdrawal or denunciation is not embodied, it is considered that withdrawal may be properly implied,[232] while withdrawal from or denunciation of various other types of "silent" treaties is connected with their ad hoc regime management of the matter and/or the related weight of the relational and contextual factors and their multifaceted aspects (public nature of the treaty, ICI legislative purpose, domestic, regime-internal and -external context of reference, and the pragmatic circumstances surrounding the multilateral constitution of the treaty regime), which finally seem to determine in practice the possibility or the probability of the exercise of such a power-right.[233]

[230] Thus, the Landmines Convention, 1997, Art. 20 ("duration and withdrawal") provides that a State Party exercising its power-right to withdraw from this Convention is obliged to notify its withdrawal "to all other States Parties, to the Depositary and to the United Nations Security Council," stating "a full explanation of the reasons motivating its withdrawal," that the specified six-month period for the taking effect of withdrawal does not apply if the State Party "is engaged in an armed conflict" but only after the end of the conflict, and that the withdrawal "shall not in any way affect the duty of States to continue fulfilling the obligations assumed under any relevant rules of international law." Likewise, the Chemical Weapons Convention, Art. XVI ("duration and withdrawal") specifically lays down that a State Party has the power-right to withdraw from this Convention "in exercising its national sovereignty" when it decides that "extraordinary events, related to the subject-matter of this Convention, have jeopardized the supreme interests of its country," that it is obliged to give notice "to all other States Parties, the Executive Council, the Depositary and the United Nations Security Council," which should include "a statement of the extraordinary events it regards as having jeopardized its supreme interests," and that its withdrawal "shall not in any way affect" its duty "to continue fulfilling the obligations assumed under any relevant rules of international law, particularly the Geneva Protocol of 1925."

[231] E.g., Convention on the Law of the Non-Navigational Uses of International Watercourses, 1997; Framework Convention for the Protection of the Marine Environment of the Caspian Sea, 2005.

[232] Like in the case of the UN Charter and the "Interpretative Declaration" regarding withdrawal from the Charter, adopted by the First Committee at the San Francisco Conference and accepted at the plenary conference, according to which a withdrawal from the UN could be exercised in exceptional cases, indicatively referred to. see K. Widdows, "The Unilateral Denunciation of Treaties Containing No Denunciation Clause," 53 *BYBIL* (1982), 83, 98, 102.

[233] In certain treaties, the exercise of the power-right to withdrawal seems to be associated with the ad hoc regime management of this matter (e.g., Convention on the Law of the Non-

In the light of this, the perception that the negotiating choice of not incorporating a clause on withdrawal or denunciation opens the way for the residual or subsidiary application of the relevant Article 56 of the Vienna Convention on the Law of Treaties, 1969, seems rather unrealistic. This Article, basically articulating the inadequate private law contract view of treaties, on the one hand, lays down the generalizing rule that a treaty that does not contain a provision for withdrawal or denunciation is not subject to withdrawal or denunciation, and, on the other hand, provides for two exceptions to this rule that may allow withdrawal or denunciation: the contractual exception, when the intention of the parties to admit such possibility is established, and the relational exception, when such a possibility is implied from the nature of the treaty, while "a not less than twelve months' notice" should be given of the intention of the party to denounce or withdraw from a treaty. It is obvious that the residual or subsidiary application of Article 56 would lead to a series of problems unveiling its detachment from the international practice and its theoretical poverty. In sum:

- Article 56 conveys an individualistic, contractual logic: it establishes an objective, extra-contextual rule prohibiting the party from withdrawing or denouncing if such a power-right is not explicitly provided in the treaty, allowing only, in the first place, a contractually based and, in the second place, a relationally implied general exception.
- However, the issue of treaty silence on this matter is fundamentally and comprehensively a relational and contextually approached issue: it refers, from the beginning, to its ad hoc negotiated management as a treaty regime issue linked to the multifaceted aspects and weight of the relational and contextual factors that determine, in practice and in terms of ICI, the possibility of the exercise of withdrawal or denunciation.
- Article 56, through the provided exceptions to its generalized contractual rule, brings forward a restrictive procedure that can be hardly considered practically workable and theoretically tenable: first, it places the hard onus of proving the exceptions on the party invoking them so that it can support its claim for withdrawal or denunciation of the treaty vis-à-vis the other parties; second, this claim, in case of disagreement, basically activates the assumed "contractual bond" of the concluded treaty and may be turned into a dispute that will follow

Navigational Uses of International Watercourses, 1997), while, in most other treaties, the weight of the relational factor may determine the far-reaching consequences of such an ad hoc management (e.g., treaties establishing permanent territorial regimes, peace treaties, treaties on disarmament, treaties of alliance, or certain treaties protecting human rights, but also other types of treaties – e.g., commercial treaties – when they highlight the special importance of the relational bond – for instance, the pragmatic circumstances surrounding its negotiated establishment, like the Framework Convention for the Protection of the Marine Environment of the Caspian Sea, 2005).

the procedure of dispute settlement laid down in Articles 65 and 66 of the Vienna Convention on the Law of Treaties, a development that may well work only in the minds of positivist international lawyers.

6 SPECIAL TECHNIQUES AND PRACTICES OF CONSTITUTIVE TEXTUAL NEGOTIATION

The special techniques and practices, usually applied to Constitutive Negotiation (but also, mutatis mutandis, to the Renegotiation process), may be organized into two categories: organizational and textual techniques and practices.

6.1 Organizational Techniques and Practices

6.1.1 Opening Statements

The interactive orchestration of the negotiating process starts, mainly at this phase but also at the Renegotiation phase, with the opening statements of the heads of the negotiating delegations. Made at the beginning of the first session of conferential negotiation, the opening statements follow the presentation of the report by the secretariat. They offer a first response to the report and to the explanation provided by the secretariat of a first draft of the international agreement, drawn up by her, or of the treaty elements – if more flexibility is required as regards the form – that they should constitute the area of negotiating the agreement and be cast in a quasi-legislative language. Note that, whatever its form, the constitutive draft text of the treaty, provided by the secretariat, will contain those appropriate elements collectively adopted and embodied in the declarative instrument of Prenegotiation, since they reflect the initial framework of a consensual political and programmatic determination of ICI associated with the governance of the issues under negotiation.

A negotiating delegation may send a first substantial message of responsibility to the other delegations regarding its role in the negotiation process (a constructive role consistently contributing to a positive management of the issues under negotiation), should its opening statement contain the following basic elements.

- Its understanding of the negotiable issues and of the scope of their negotiation.
- The objectives of the negotiation – what ought to be achieved.
- The priorities to be established, underlining the more important aspects of the negotiation.
- Its intended contribution to the negotiating process (functional, political, scientific, material).
- Its attitude and evaluation (if relevant) regarding the negotiation of the same or similar issues in other international fora or frameworks or previous attempts at such negotiation.

- Its general positioning and remarks on the report and on the first draft instrument or on the elements provided by the secretariat.
- Its general positioning and remarks on the general institutional and normative landscape (legal, institutional, and institutional context at global, regional and national levels) related to the issues under negotiation.

Opening statements should be made first by the negotiating countries and after them by the relevant international organizations, NGOs, and other non-state actors (e.g., private sector, social actors, territorial communities, epistemic communities) that have been invited as observers. Attention should be paid to the length of the opening statement: it should be as succinct, balanced, and comprehensive as possible. Long opening statements, with unnecessary details and using complex and unclear language, that tediously repeat what has already been said by other delegations are usually not heard.

6.1.2 Brainstorming Sessions

The brainstorming session constitutes a potentially important creative technique facilitating the spontaneous unveiling of ideas by a group of negotiating participants in relation to a special issue or problem, separated from the mainstream negotiating process, with a view to collectively generate specific innovative, creative, or additional ideas advancing its effective management.[234] This creative technique embraces the quantitative production of possible seed ideas and their after-production critical evaluation, leading to a constructive selection among them, so that the best of them will be subsequently injected into the mainstream negotiating process. In this process, the brainstorming session enhances commitment to the generated solutions, because the participating group is intertwined with their generation, playing a creative role.

Thus, brainstorming sessions may be designed as a two-stage process: as a quantitative production of possible seed-ideas and as a post-production critical evaluation and selective decision. The organized facilitation of quantitative production of seed-ideas, in fact, feeds the ensuing reduction process whereby the most effective solution is reached through a qualitative promotion and selection of the best of these ideas, alone or in combination with others. Overall, their comprehensive management process starts with the encouragement of a flow of seed-ideas that are paratactically arranged and managed (a side-by-side compilation of ideas that may converge, diverge, or be completely unusual or original) and, progressively assume, by consecutive evaluations, a hypotactic arrangement (a hierarchy of the

[234] The idea was originally developed by A. F. Osborn, *Applied Imagination: Principles and Procedures of Creative Thinking*, New York, 1953, chap. 25, where he examines the procedure of creative cooperation within groups with a view to produce creative ideas. This idea was further developed by subsequent empirical research.

paratactically arranged ideas, including their synthesis, reached by collectively agreed evaluations and an eliminative reduction procedure).

More specifically, a brainstorming session may be initiated either by the conferential secretariat or by the chair of the bureau of the session, supported by the negotiating parties. In the framework of the two aforementioned stages, it may be organized in three consecutive levels on the basis of specific procedural guidelines. First, at the preparatory level, the following organizing procedural guidelines should be applied.

- A clear determination of the issue upon which the brainstorming session will be focused – a multiplicity of issues should be avoided because they may easily derail the function of the brainstorming session.
- An informal determination of the group of the brainstorming session that may be exclusive, comprising a limited number of negotiating parties with a strong presumption of competence or expertise for the issue under consideration, and, at the same time, inclusive, embracing all basic interests related to the issue and represented in the negotiating session – the conferential secretariat is also represented *ex officio*.
- A strict determination of the duration period of the brainstorming session for the delivery of its product in the negotiating session.
- Its distinctive separation from the formal negotiating session, projecting its own identity as a mandated facilitative procedure that clusters a collective production of creative ideas related to a thorny and sensitive issue and a selection of the best among them, thus contributing to the progress of the negotiating process.
- Its organization as an informal procedure, so that a creative collaboration between the members of the group will be facilitated, signalling their awareness of their distinctive role as a think tank aiming at a more cognitive, normative, and managerial specific problem-solving, dissociated from national interests.
- The choosing of a coordinator of the brainstorming session, who is usually a representative of the conferential secretariat but may also be the most influential member of the group, and who operates as facilitator of the group function: he directs the discussion, observes the procedure, and stimulates the paratactic and hypotactic building of creative solutions.

Second, at the level of paratactic management of ideas, the following operating procedural guidelines should be applied.

- Strict adherence to the basic procedural guideline of no negative criticism on the ideas put forward during the first stage of the session, so that a horizontal development of possible seed-ideas, approaching the specific issue from all possible angles and perspectives, will be encouraged and secured.
- No minutes during the session and no individuation of the ideas connecting them with the persons who generate them, otherwise, the brainstorming session

may easily degenerate into another negotiating session, entirely losing its special problem-solving identity – such an individuation of the generated ideas becomes counterproductive because it may inescapably be treated by the other members of the group as being identified with the positions supported by the member of the group in the formal conferential negotiation; relatedly, it may seriously hinder or even incapacitate the creative discretion of a member of the group to contribute to the special problem-solving without minutes recording its view and with no relation to the formal positions he may express during the formal conferential negotiation.

- A full recording of ideas, so that the collectivity of the problem-solving effort on the basis of ideas will be more effectively realized by the members of the group, while their dialectic productivity as well as their systematic transition to the next level of hypotactic management will be more effectively facilitated.

Third, at the level of hypotactic management of ideas, certain evaluative procedural guidelines should be applied.

- Filtering ideas on the basis of the group (collective) acceptance of their appeal to promising solutions to the problem, so that the group focuses only on those seed-ideas that are accepted by all and are considered capable of development into creative solutions.
- Collective elaboration of the filtered ideas, so that their strong elements will be identified and improved, to the largest possible extent, in terms of both approach and application, while exhausting the possibilities of their dialectic interconnection and pyramid-shaped formations where each member of the group can make creative additions to an array of ideas or to independent ideas.
- Final evaluation and ranking of the improved array of independent ideas, so that the final package of ideas will be decided that is considered to produce the most creative solution to the specific problem and contributes to the progress of the negotiation process.

6.1.3 Inter-Sessional Workshops

In complicated negotiations, where serious problems emerge with regard to the understanding of issues or new ideas of central importance to the progress of the negotiating process, the creation of inter-sessional workshops may be decided by the conferential negotiation forum for their study, documentation, clarification, and explanation. Inter-sessional workshops may decisively contribute to the progress of the work of the conferential negotiation facilitating its operation.[235]

[235] E.g., Inter-sessional workshops were effectively created in the framework of the Ad Hoc Open-Ended Informal Working Group to Study Issues Relating to the Conservation and Sustainable Use of

The conferential negotiation forum sets up the terms of reference of these inter-sessional workshops, leaving some practical questions to be decided by them, adopts their program of work,[236] and calls the secretariat to organize them. It may also require the secretariat to provide an estimate of the financial and other resources required to conduct an inter-sessional workshop,[237] assigning to it the responsibility for allocating the expenses of the inter-sessional workshop in a way that meets the needs of the conferential negotiation forum. Inter-sessional workshops, aiming at inclusivity in participation and, at the same time, pursuing direct and constructive communication between the participating delegates away from formal negotiating venues at the lowest possible cost, are held in one working language (English).

Their terms of reference may determine:

- Their character (informal, open-ended) and their direction (what officials of the secretariat or members of the bureau of the conferential negotiation forum will guide their work).
- Participation (it is open to all negotiating participants and observers).
- Their format (panels of experts selected in accordance with their personal capacity, while, at the same time, an equitable geographical representation and a balanced representation of all relevant scientific areas is secured so as to cover efficiently the issues dealt with by the group).
- The specific issues to be examined, included in an agreed program of work, and possibly their interlinkages with broader issues of environmental governance and sustainability at the international and national levels (coordination with related international conventional regimes, capacity-building, technology transfer – it is an open question whether scientific background papers should be prepared before the meeting of the group, addressing also the existing regulatory and management gaps).

Marine Biological Diversity beyond Areas of National Jurisdiction, which was established by a Decision of the General Assembly of the United Nations (UNGA Res. 66/231 [5 April 2012] UN Doc. A/RES/66/231, para. 167ff.) and held its fifth negotiating session from 7 to 11 May 2013 (UNGA: Report of the Ad Hoc Open-Ended Informal Working Group to Study Issues Relating to the Conservation and Sustainable Use of Marine Biological Diversity beyond Areas of National Jurisdiction and Co-Chairs' Summary of Discussions, Annex, A/67/95, 13 June 2012) and its sixth negotiating session from 19 to 23 August 2013 (UNGA: Intersessional Workshops Aimed at Improving Understanding of the Issues and Clarifying Key Questions As an Input to the Work of the Working Group in Accordance with the Terms of Reference Annexed to General Assembly Resolution 67/78 – Summary of Proceedings Prepared by the Co-Chairs of the Working Group, UNGA 67/78 (10 June 2013) UNDoc. A/AC.276/6).

236 The programme of work of an inter-sessional workshop may be included in an annex to the report of the conferential negotiation forum agreed to its formation. See, e.g., UNEP: Report of the Ad Hoc Open-ended Working Group on Mercury on the Work of Its First Meeting, UNEP(DTIE)/Hg/OEWG.1/6, 2007, Annex II.

237 The secretariat may provide an estimated total cost of the Inter-sessional Workshop, including direct costs, staff costs and the overhead percentage cost.

- The textual form of the outcome of their work (a summary presentation of the procedure – it is an open question whether recommendations will be produced or alternative options will be formulated in order to be examined by the negotiating forum).

6.1.4 Side-Events

This recently widely established international practice holds a particular interest because it adds a new dimension to the conferential negotiating forum by creating an open dialectical platform, outside the negotiation room and agenda, for an expert information and discussion on specific thematic aspects and related cross-cutting critical issues of the subject-matter under negotiation. Side-events may be organized, individually or jointly, by relevant international institutional entities (intergovernmental organizations, secretariats of treaty regimes), nongovernmental entities (NGOs and other non-state actors), but also by states,[238] operating individually or in cooperation with other negotiating participants or relevant actors and practitioners, while organizers are responsible for all logistical arrangements. Taking place in especially reserved conference rooms, they are open to all negotiating parties and other participants, as well as to the media, while accreditation is usually required.

Providing an additional dialectical platform for knowledge sharing, innovative ideas and approaches, robust evidence of practice, communication, networking, capacity building, and options exploration, side-events are thematically defined and variably organized, depending on the importance and the complexity of the issue to be discussed. Thus, they may simply contain succinct background information about the issue and a catalogue of speakers and moderators (panelists), often including a distinguished keynote speaker to make the event more attractive. At the other end, they may include extensive background information, discussion points or the scope of event, and the agenda or programme, comprising a panel of distinguished experts, often combined with government representatives (speakers), and sometimes linked to a special presentation of the particular issue.

In fact, the practice of side-events provides a learning opportunity for a dialectical comprehension and more integrative knowledge of the issues involved. It thus opens new windows into critical, more hidden aspects or innovative approaches related to the construction of ICI and, as a result, it may ingrain more technical, legal, and practical knowledge and promote synergy in the formal negotiating process. Taking

238 Negotiating states may host side-events at state pavilions, thus creating well-equipped spaces for information, exchange of views, and dialogue on specific issues showcasing feasible solutions. Of increasing importance is the more recent practice of video coverage of selected side-events, especially in negotiating processes taking place at the global level, like climate change negotiations. Being widely accessible, they become vehicles for a worldwide dissemination of comprehensive information from different angles, familiarizing the relevant world audiences, outside the negotiation, with the necessity for engaging in enlightened common interest governance of specific issues.

a more academic-dialectical turn and enhancing the areas of free and problem-managing-oriented dialogue at all levels, side-events may, for instance:

- Illuminate the correlation of relevant treaty regimes.
- Provide insights into innovative legal tools, governance frameworks, and potential legal actions.
- Showcase innovative or complementary approaches to a particular issue promoting concerted actions.
- Present a robust evidence of the risks involved or successful examples of projects promoting holistic and proactive management of the issues.
- Discuss transformative responses and actions, capacity-building activities and transparency frameworks experiences.
- Provide an account of the overall status and progress in developing technological, economic, social, and ethical dimensions of the issues under negotiation.
- Create special fora of dialogue between negotiating participants on a much broader interest-representational basis, bringing into them relevant but not negotiating socio-economic actors (e.g., indigenous people, the larger scientific community and the private sector, the church, etc.) and mobilizing public-private partnerships.
- Even celebrate relevant important international events (like the launching of a global declaration related to the subject matter of the negotiation) signalling important developments.

6.2 *Textual Techniques and Practices*

6.2.1 The System of Brackets

The system of brackets complements the single negotiating treaty text drafting operating horizontally and vertically as a vehicle towards an un-bracketed or clear consensus wording of the text. Its horizontal operation refers to the paratactic formulation of the diverse positions expressed, reflected in the side-by-side placement of the identified textual elements. Very often, there are initial drafts of articles or parts of draft articles consisting of several paratactically placed alternative proposals/views. Moreover, a paratactic formulation of draft texts may also emerge during the negotiation process, when new proposals are tabled and new draft articles are added in brackets, usually to provide the necessary space for a creative way out of a deadlocked situation or having an added value.[239] In all these cases, the paratactically formulated texts bear their own weight, they may be not very much related to each other and they are variably repetitive when referring to alternative formulations, and they are catalytic in facilitating the building of an *e pluribus unum* text

[239] In these latter cases, any added article is numbered in accordance with the UN-established practice by the following typified series of Latin numerical expressions: bis-2, ter-3, quarter-4, quinquies-5, sexies-6, septies-7, octies-8, novies-9, decies-10.

serving ICI. They are subject to negotiation for their collective evaluation, prioritization, bridging, and, eventually, reduction and constructive synthesis so that one unbracketed version of the text based on consensus is achieved.[240]

Its vertical operation refers to a single draft text wording that requires a negotiated determination of the depth and scope of its meaning. It usually concerns the wording of the draft text of a provision that has still to be agreed in detail. This may have a text-expansive or a text-mitigating effect. Depending on negotiation and the evolving intersubjective understanding of ICI, the wording of the text has to become more flexible in order to accommodate all interests involved by agreeing on its more "framework formulation" or by incorporating standard phrases having a mitigating (softening) effect on the prescription of duties-obligations, "contextualizing" its content.

All in all, the system of brackets signals "the text gestation period" pointing to a process of collective reductionist formulation of common interest in the treaty draft. In practice, the single negotiating text procedure is linked with an initial paratactic formulation of the plurality of the interests involved put in brackets, with a view to reach, through negotiated reductions and merging, a clear text of common interest. Through this tool of progressive minimization of *unum in pluribus*, a reliable relational management of uncertainties is attained, based on solid consensus and embodying the widest possible range of plurality of interests in a single accepted formulation.

6.2.2 Recording the Names of Negotiating Participants in the Reports of the Meetings and Conferences

When the negotiating delegations (states, international organizations, NGOs, and other non-state actors) take the floor to make their opening statement, or any other statement at a conferential negotiation, or at a distinctive platform associated with it (ministerial segment or high-level segment), then the name of the state or of the non-state entity they represent is recorded in the Report of the conferential meeting.[241]

At the substantive Constitutive Negotiations that follow, no names of countries or non-state entities are recorded in the report (instead, abstract references are made: "one delegate," "many/few/some delegates," "the delegates," etc.) in order to avoid

240 Note here that the paratactic formulation of alternative proposals/views may, in some cases, be indicated in footnotes in combination with brackets. In fact, the choice between brackets and footnotes is of no substance but merely a matter of drafting technique.

241 The high-level segment is more inclusive: it encompasses not only ministers but also senior officials. However, due to its strong political connotation, the name "ministerial segment" is adopted in a number of conferential negotiations encompassing ministers and senior officials of states, whereas the floor is also given to the representatives of international organizations, NGOs, and other non-state actors. See, e.g., UNEP/MAP: Report of the 19th Ordinary Meeting of the Contracting Parties to the Convention for the Protection of the Marine Environment and Coastal Region of the Mediterranean and Its Protocols, Athens, Greece (9–12 February 2016), UNEP(DEPI)/MED IG.22/28, VI Ministerial Segment, 23–32.

solidification of positions and, thus, safeguard the necessary flexibility in the negotiating process of consensus-building and of constructing ICI. Nevertheless, according to international practice, there are certain instances where, even in this context, the names of countries or non-state entities may be specified. These normally include:

- A special obligation is undertaken.
- A state exempts itself from an adopted action.
- A voluntary/special payment/contribution or technical support is offered.
- A state expresses its distinctive legal/political position/claim related to the issues under negotiation.

6.2.3 Non-Negotiation Text: "Non-Paper"

The technique of non-negotiation texts – "non-papers" is supportive of carrying out the textual negotiation, functioning as an informal, non-committing instrument for mapping the zone of consensus and the area of feasible focus of the negotiation, encouraging or assisting its progress. It may also assist in launching discussion on very sensitive issues or even in exploring the topic under negotiation, without committing the negotiating parties to express official positions, thus avoiding potential confrontations or conflicts. In fact, its value lies in its informal, non-attributable, non-committing, and negotiation-supportive character. Produced during the negotiating process, it is dissociated from the position of its drafter (secretariat, chair of the bureau of the negotiating session, international organization, or state) and serves as a working basis for the current or the next session of the negotiating conference. When prepared by negotiating parties, non-papers are designed to explain or unblock positions on the text under consideration and they are not regarded as part of the official record of the negotiating session.

Thus, at the ad hoc negotiating conference or meeting (Ad Hoc Working Group of Legal and Technical Experts or Intergovernmental Negotiating Committee), the chair may propose, or may prepare at the request of the negotiating parties, the lodging of a non-negotiation text. Under the authority and responsibility of the chair, the non-negotiation text, or the non-paper, may be distributed as a conference room paper (CRP) to the negotiating parties, providing them with the opinion of the bureau regarding the current status of the developing consensus as well as marking those areas requiring more documentation or convergence for consensus-building and, for this reason, orienting them towards more focused negotiations. The negotiating parties consider the non-negotiation text and the Chair may further proceed into a composition of the final version of the non-negotiation text by integrating their views without attribution. In certain contexts, non-papers may form the basis for negotiation of a draft package agreement: they may be developed by the Chair as an abridged version of an initial extensive version of a draft of a text to serve as a working basis during the next session of constitutive negotiation, and they often do not bear a document number.[242] Finally, in cases of a deadlocked negotiating session of a certain issue, the chair or co-chairs may formulate a non-negotiation text, or non-paper, not attributing it to the negotiating participants to serve as a working "textual bridge" for a future negotiation of this issue.

It should be noted, however, that the practice of Chairs' texts should be exercised with due care and in tune with the consensual construction of international common interest. And this may be doubted when, in cases where negotiated issues cause strong confrontation among the negotiating parties and it does not appear likely the negotiated consolidation of consensus, the Chair "takes top of" the composition of an alternative wording of the text and offers this text in the delegations for their consideration. Such exercise of the practice is likely to constitute the "Trojan Horse" for the introduction of uncontested language into the text and its imposition on the negotiating parties, something that would not happen in an open negotiating process. It may be a covered imposition – and not an ICI accommodation – of the status order on the emerging consensus. On the other hand, it should be underlined that, at the other end, the negotiating parties may, at an advanced stage of constitutive negotiation, agree to entrust the Chair to prepare a Chair's text as a compromise version of the negotiated draft treaty in order to bridge the remaining differences between their expressed interests.[243]

7 THE OUTCOME OF CONSTITUTIVE NEGOTIATION

When the conferential negotiation forum finally approves the negotiated draft text of the treaty or protocol, its work is completed. The Secretariat, then, according to its mandate, convenes and organizes a diplomatic conference or a conference of plenipotentiaries, a formal and highest-level conferential forum, for the official adoption of the draft text to be followed by its signature by those states deciding to do so. According to international practice, the Secretariat undertakes the

242 See Ad Hoc Working Group on the Durban Platform for Enhanced Action, ADP.2015.8. Informal Note, Non-Paper, Note by the Co-Chairs, 5 October 2015, Draft Agreement. Available at: http://unfccc.int/resource/docs/2015/adp2/eng/8infnot.pdf. It is worth noting that the non-paper, prepared by the ADP co-chairs at a request from negotiating countries, contained the draft Paris climate package in an abridged version and was produced by the co-chairs to serve as a working basis for the next session of negotiations (Bonn, Germany, 19–23 October 2015); it also contained a draft of the decision that will operationalize the agreement from 2020.

243 The constitutive negotiation of the Minimata Convention on Mercury 2013 provides a notable example in this regard. At its fourth session, the established Intergovernmental Negotiating Committee agreed that the Chair would prepare a text as a compromise and technically harmonized version of the draft mercury instrument for its fifth – and final – session. Prepared and considered at a full set of regional consultations in the inter-sessional period, the chair's text was very positively accepted by all negotiating parties as a sound basis for the advancement of the constitutive negotiation leading to the finalization of the text. See UNEP, Intergovernmental Negotiating Committee to Prepare a Global Legally Binding Instrument on Mercury, Fifth Session (Geneva, 13–18 January 2013), UNEP(DTIE)/Hg/INC.5/7.

preparation of the draft of the Final Act to be adopted by the diplomatic conference, which should contain certain standard elements relating to a brief narration of the particular Constitutive Negotiation process and a record of the diplomatic conference. It refers, more specifically, to a succinct description of the evolution of the Constitutive Negotiation process until its completion at the level of conferential negotiation forum, to the organizational elements of the diplomatic conference (place, participants, agenda, rules of procedure, election of the bureau), to the deliberations regarding the text of the treaty or protocol and its adoption, and to the adoption of implementing resolutions,[244] and the recording of possible reservations or declarations and statements. The texts of the resolutions, as well as the texts of declarations, statements, and reservations, if any, are appended to the Final Act. The text of the treaty or protocol, requiring a separate signature from the Final Act, constitutes an annex to the Final Act.

During the diplomatic conference, the representatives of the states participated in the treaty negotiation and those of international organizations who participated in the negotiation and are entitled to become parties to the treaty (e.g., EU), together with the president of the diplomatic conference and the head of the secretariat of the conferential negotiation forum (the executive director or the general secretary of the international organization who performed the duties of a secretariat at the conferential negotiation forum), adopt and sign the Final Act, separately from the text of the treaty. The Final Act testifies to the official completion of the Constitutive Negotiation process and the adoption of the text of the treaty attached to it as an annex, thereby opening the signature period of the treaty, which normally lasts one year. Both the Final Act and the Treaty are formulated, under the care and the constant supervision of the secretariat, in all the official languages provided in the treaty. The diplomatic conference inaugurates the opening of the signature period and the treaty is ceremonially signed by those representatives who are accredited to sign. The duration of the signature process is provided in the final provisions of the treaty and is normally one year. The signatories (or the signatory international organization) may become parties

[244] The implementing resolutions adopted by the Diplomatic Conference may refer to a wide range of issues. These usually include: matters related to the attainment of the timely entry into force of the treaty and the preparation for its effective application; the interim arrangements for the period between the signature and entry into force of the treaty, including the consideration of actions and measures and arrangements for financial and technical assistance, in order to facilitate its earliest possible entry into force and successful implementation of the treaty at all levels. They may refer to actions on issues that have not been efficiently addressed in the text of the treaty, or to the invocation and listing of the relevant international instruments that constitute the external context of the treaty. They may also refer to matters concerning the development of cooperation with states directly related to the implementation of the treaty (like Resolution 2 of the Final Act of the Bucharest Convention on the Protection of the Black Sea Against Pollution, 1992, stating the endeavour of the parties "to initiate cooperation including future meetings with [the Danube States] for the purposes of the Convention," XXXII [4] ILM [1993], 1107), or the development of cooperative schemes with relevant international organizations. Finally, they may refer to particular secretariat arrangements.

to the treaty by depositing the instruments of ratification, acceptance, or approval to the depositary provided by the treaty. If states (or a party-intended international organization) have not signed the treaty within the signature period, they may become parties to it only through a one-step action, by depositing the instrument of accession to the treaty depositary at any time.

5

The Renegotiation Phase as a Process of Revisionary Governance of Conventional Regimes

1 NEGOTIABLE TRANSFORMATION MUTATIS MUTANDIS

The Renegotiation phase instantiates the intra-institutional process of revisionary governance in the framework of an operating international conventional regime (treaty regime) aiming at making it more effective and efficient. In the framework of relational governance structure that characterizes all three phases of creative international negotiation, Renegotiation develops by extensively building on the structural and procedural (consensus procedure, rules of procedure) elements and the general treaty-patternment approach of Constitutive Negotiation, of course properly adapted to the structural requirements and particularities of revisionary governance of the treaty regime, and applies the same techniques and practices as analysed in the previous chapter. And it may also make use of certain methodical elements of the diagnostic level of Prenegotiation, especially those referring to the management of knowledge.

Moving on its own tracks as treaty revisionary governance, Renegotiation has, apart from its very special structural and functional characteristics, an important political significance. It reflects the parties' deeper understanding of the impact that the architectural structure and the textual formulation of a treaty pattern may have as a pragmatic framework protecting and promoting ICI. Renegotiation marks the ingrained "negotiability" of the normative force of the treaty regime in view of its relational nature, its ICI (public) purpose, and its dynamic character. The continuous responsiveness and functional upgrading of the treaty to the changing realities of its ICI implementation through Renegotiation is considered to safeguard the anticipated "stability-in-continuity" of the treaty regime. Otherwise, the treaty regime would develop an increasing degree of entropic tendencies disordering it and involving a high risk of uncertainty and instability that, eventually, degenerate it.

Particularly, Renegotiation reinforces the participatory trust of the parties because it confirms the "relational resilience" of the treaty pattern: as a dynamic resilience continuously specified at the implementation level, thus preventing or managing emerging instances of individual or partial alienation, maladjustment, increasingly insufficient, or even lack of, compliance, or recorded general dissatisfaction. Renegotiation, as a process of revisionary governance, secures and legitimizes the continuous creative relation between the treaty regime and its context. At the same time, it provides the appropriate and institutionally determined platform for a negotiably feasible intensification and optimization of the terms specifying the implementation of ICI in the treaty pattern, when this is considered necessary and realistic.

Such a specialization of the conventional ICI performance may refer either to the expansion/deepening of the legality of the conventional regime (treaty pattern) or to the reinforcement of the organic structure of its governance, or to both. It may result not only in the limited or extensive amendment of the original treaty text, which is the common case, but also in the more rare conventional recasting or replacement of the treaty, leaving the regime aspect intact by securing the terms of its operational and normative continuity. Since Renegotiation works in the framework of an already operating conventional regime, it is "more structured" compared to the other two phases of international negotiation while it repeats, mutatis mutandis, similar methods, practices, techniques, and procedures. In addition, and in contrast to the other two phases, it has a repetitive character, because it constitutes an indispensable part of the patterned system of ICI multilateral governance of the treaty regime. Operating at the level of transformability through a standard amendment procedure, as analysed in the previous chapter, Renegotiation engineers the resilience of the treaty regime, whenever institutionally feasible, and dynamically secures its most effective adaptability to contextual developments.

2 INITIATION AND INSTITUTIONAL ORGANIZATION OF RENEGOTIATION

2.1 *The Initiation of Renegotiation*

The initiation of the Renegotiation phase for the revision of an ICI treaty regime rests on a distinctive, institutionally provided, regime action enshrined in the amendment clause of the treaty: any party or group of parties may take the initiative to propose, at any time,[1] the amendment of the treaty, and the supreme governing organ of the treaty regime (conference/meeting of the contracting parties or assembly, etc., of the members of an international organization) will authorize by consensus, after appropriate internal consultation, the commencement of the procedure to amend the treaty. By its decision, the supreme governing organ mandates the Secretariat of the treaty regime to organize the opening and coordinate the amendment negotiating process, which will develop in accordance with the procedural

[1] Unless the amendment clause of the treaty stipulates the expiry of a certain number of years from its entry into force before the amendment procedure is set into motion by such initiative; see, e.g., UN Convention against Corruption, 2003, Art. 69(1).

stages generally prescribed by the patterned clauses on amendment constantly incorporated in the treaty regime. This decision, apart from setting out the time horizon within which the Secretariat should complete its mandated task of Renegotiation, is usually formulated in "probabilistic terms" as regards the final product: it refers to the "possibility" of the amendment of the treaty text, clearly implying the wide space for negotiating enquiry into the actual feasibility of the amendment, while, at the same time, leaving open the door for a more radical adaptation of the treaty regime through its recasting or replacement, as is explained in what follows.

More specifically, the Secretariat, as a recipient of the mandate, prepares and convenes a conferential Renegotiation body, an Ad Hoc Working Group of Legal and Technical Experts for negotiating the amendment of the treaty text, composed of the representatives of the parties and the non-state entities vested with the status of "observer" (international organizations, secretariats of international conventional [treaty] regimes, NGOs, the private sector, professional unions, etc.). Like in the Constitutive Negotiation process, the Secretariat lies at the core of the Renegotiation process and, in fact, plays an even more critical role in its development. Because of its prescribed institutional position in the framework of the treaty regime and its long and tested performance of special actions for its implementation, the Secretariat's role in the Renegotiation process is that of the efficient guardian of the treaty regime. As such, the Secretariat may play a particularly overall constructive part in the Renegotiation and the finalization of the draft text to be adopted, exercising what may be called *due institutional diligence*. Thus, the Secretariat, apart from securing an effective and efficient organization and coordination of the negotiating sessions of the Ad Hoc Working Group of Legal and Technical Experts, guiding them with the adopted Rules of Procedure and the established practices followed under the treaty regime, assumes, from the outset, a key creative role, preparing the Report of the Proposed Amendments that will serve as the authoritative basis for the development of the Renegotiation process.

2.2 *The Institutional Guardianship of the Secretariat in the Renegotiation Process*

An essential element of the *due institutional diligence* of the secretariat at the Renegotiation phase is its preparation and proper distribution of a Report on the Proposed Amendments, which is the result of its institutional experience and expertise, as well as of its creative institutional interaction with the parties to the treaty regime and the observers (mainly international organizations). Relatedly, the Secretariat is capable of including in the Report the more general scientific, technical, or legal justification/foundation of the proposed amendments, as indicators of their "added value," pointing to the evolving scientific consensus or its prevailing direction or even articulating the "usable knowledge."[2] This capability is the culmination of the secretariat's prior institutional function as a powerful "knowledge broker" acting on three interrelated levels: as a knowledge administrator, as an interface between those who produce and those who use the relevant knowledge, and as a capacity builder by enhancing the access to knowledge. More specifically, the Secretariat may facilitate and contribute to an effective communication, formal or informal, between the parties and those various bodies and networks (scientific institutes and communities, NGOs, and other non-state actors) that generate and manage knowledge relevant to the proposed amendments. Thus, it may take immediate steps by organizing and coordinating informal meetings, scientific conferences, or expert discussion panels, or by assigning to – usually – leading experts the task of writing scientific, legal, or technical reports or studies increasingly requiring the adoption of an interdisciplinary approach. In many instances, these steps should be effectively associated with the incorporation of "local knowledge perspectives" and expert findings need to be contextualized.[3] It may also care for the operation of more long-term actions associated with its role as knowledge broker by supporting the development of knowledge and skills through its organization of relevant interdisciplinary training courses, and, recently, through the development – rather limited, so far – of relevant educational programmes, substantiating the educational aspect of governance of the particular treaty regime. Finally, it may apply the existing level of knowledge to new areas of development of the treaty regime advancing ICI, thus facilitating the review of the relevant data and the consideration of appropriate treaty amendment.

The Report on the Proposed Amendments contains the specific amendment proposals elaborated by the Secretariat, formulated in a legal language and form and supported by concise and clear justification. It may also incorporate the separate specific amendment proposals of the parties or of the institutional partners or observers (international organizations or other international institutional entities), similarly formulated and justified. The latter should be submitted to the Secretariat within a determined period of time before the opening of the first session of the Renegotiation process in order to be presented in a single negotiating text and arranged in a paratactic form to the Secretariat's proposals in each article. Any other amendment proposal, submitted to the Secretariat outside this period, will be introduced as a supplement to the Report, according to practice. The Report will be properly distributed to the parties and the observers.

2 On the importance of the projection of "usable knowledge" in the negotiation process, see Chapter 3.

3 The importance of incorporating local knowledge perspectives into any phase of the international negotiating process, especially in environmental treaty regimes, has led to the broadening of the "expertise" concept (including the so-called traditional or indigenous knowledge holders or citizen experts, etc.) and the expansion of "science" into the broader "knowledge." See K. O'Neill, *The Environment and International Relations* (2nd edn), Cambridge University Press, 2017, 73.

The amendment proposals may take three concrete forms: as new and additional articles; as extended or limited amendments to the articles of the treaty, including complete redrafting; as deletion of the articles considered obsolete. During the successive sessions of the conferential Renegotiation process, but also in the periods between the negotiating sessions, the Secretariat exercises its organizational and creative role, mutatis mutandis, to the Constitutive Negotiation phase, yet endowed with more authority and power, precisely because of its institutional position and function within the treaty regime. In those cases in which the Secretariat incorporates two distinct institutional identities, that of the Secretariat of the treaty regime and that of the Secretariat of an international organization (institutional dualism), like the UNEP in a number of autonomous environmental treaty regimes,[4] then its impact on the process and the final formulation of the text produced at the Renegotiation phase may be undoubtedly catalytic.

At all stages of the Renegotiation process, the Secretariat is expected to properly conduct the negotiation of the single amendment text, and to highlight and effectively indicate, on the basis of its prescribed functions, the requirements and the prospects of the evolving operation and implementation of the treaty regime. Thus, a distinctive aspect of its due institutional diligence in this process is the observance and creative interpretation of the Rules of Procedure, as well as the supportive explanation of the practice or the tradition followed in the framework of the treaty regime. In the periods between the negotiating sessions, the secretariat is best placed, institutionally and politically, to take the initiative to exercise "institutional diplomacy" in order to facilitate, in a creative manner, the progress of Renegotiation. It may take informal visiting initiatives to provide a better explanation of specific proposed amendments for a party or parties having difficulties with them, or to better explain the underlying interests of the views of a party or parties objecting to them with or without alternative proposals.

Of particular importance is the fact that the Secretariat is further well placed, institutionally and politically, to convey to the negotiating sessions the reality of the

4 As already noted in the previous chapter (note 4), the UNEP is expressly assigned the Secretariat functions in a number of regional environmental treaty regimes (e.g., Barcelona Convention for the Protection of the Marine Environment and the Coastal Region of the Mediterranean, 1976, Art. 17; Abidjan Convention for Co-operation in the Protection and Development of the Marine and Coastal Environment of the West and Central African Region, 1981, Art. 16; Cartagena Convention for the Protection and Development of the Marine Environment of the Wider Caribbean Region, 1983, Art. 15; Nairobi Convention for the Protection, Management and Development of the Marine and Coastal Environment of the Eastern African Region, 1985, Art. 16), as well as in global treaty environmental regimes (e.g., Stockholm Convention on Persistent Organic Pollutants, 2001, Art. 20(3); Minimata Convention on Mercury, 2013, Art. 24(3)), or it has been defined as such at the First Conference of the Contracting Parties (Basel Convention on the Control of Transboundary Movements of Hazardous Wastes and Their Disposal, 1989, Art. 16(3); Convention on Biological Diversity, 1992, Art. 24(2)), or it is even prescribed that it constitutes, together with another co-competent international organization, the Secretariat of an environmental treaty regime (e.g., together with the FAO in the Rotterdam Convention on the Prior Informed Consent Procedure for Certain Hazardous Chemicals and Pesticides in International Trade, 1998, Art. 19(3)).

operation and implementation of the conventionally constituted ICI relation. Working on the location of the *Renegotiation zone*, on the basis of which the more stabilized aspects of the treaty text are separated from the more volatile ones, it opens up the negotiation with respect to the latter, to the extent and the degree decided by the parties. Locating the Renegotiation zone, the Secretariat functions constructively, and has a stabilizing effect on, the treaty regime, indicating the need to secure consensus on the compatibility of the zone of Renegotiation with the ICI operation of the original treaty regime: both the specific linkages with the external context of referential order and the extent of the specific revision of the treaty regime should safeguard the continuity of its operation and promote its purpose and the ICI governance. And it is in this framework that the final choice of the morphological pattern of Renegotiation (the possibility of amendment or replacement of the treaty text) is to be negotiably decided.

When the negotiating sessions of the Ad Hoc Working Group of Legal and Technical Experts are completed and the draft of the revised text is finalized, the Secretariat introduces it to the supreme governing organ of the treaty regime for its approval. The latter's approval is accompanied by a special mandate to the Secretariat to convene and organize a Diplomatic Conference or a Conference of Plenipotentiaries, the supreme negotiating forum, for the official adoption of the revised treaty text. Like in the Constitutive Negotiation, the Secretariat prepares the draft elements of the Final Act, which will be adopted by the conference and to which the amended text will be annexed.

3 RENEGOTIATION OF THE TEXTUAL PATTERN OF AN INTERNATIONAL AGREEMENT

3.1 *The Contextuality of Renegotiation*

Like the other two phases of negotiation, Renegotiation begins with its contextualization. The first step is the careful collective orientation of the revisionary negotiation of the ICI treaty regime towards the context of its referential order and to its appropriate and effective determination at the time of Renegotiation. As a result, the reference configuration conditions, fashioning the interrelationship between the Renegotiation of the treaty regime and its contextual order and guiding its determination, perform, mutatis mutandis, the same methodically correlated but distinct functions: identifiability, compatibility, and heuristic. Correspondingly, the three qualified contextual indicators of context identification, contextual compatibility, and "added value" or constructive heuristic are similarly operational. On the basis of these criteria, the zone of Renegotiation is shaped and legitimated in terms of protecting and promoting ICI within the framework of the relational stability of the treaty regime, giving effect to the legislative intent of the parties.

Furthermore, and in addition to what has already been said about the three standard criteria in Constitutive Negotiation, there is one important regime dimension of the contextual order that plays a determinative role in the zone of Renegotiation. In fact, at the Renegotiation phase, an important and particular internal context of reference is generated by the institutional life of the conventional regime and develops as a derivative context in interaction with the external and internal contexts (related treaty regimes, various forms of relevant declarative governance at the international level, development of knowledge, relevant law aspects developed in the framework of the international and domestic legal orders, or special political, economic, and social features or physical characteristics specific to the particular treaty regime). Unlike them, however, *the derivative context of reference* has a direct consensual basis, and, hence, a particular weight between the parties. It operates in complementarity to the treaty, as a performative aspect of the conventional regime, and is evidenced by a wide range of actions produced for the more effective, more efficient, and socially acceptable ICI governance of the treaty regime.

The derivative context comprises all kinds of decisions, actions, or practices collectively adopted and performed by the parties to the particular ICI treaty regime and pave the way for Renegotiation. It also comprises the management of scientific knowledge as ICI engineering within the conventional regime, which is progressively reflected in accepted scientific studies prepared within the institutional framework of the particular treaty regime either by the Secretariat or by the secondary scientific-technical organs of the conventional regime and in view of their pragmatic application in the microcosm of the treaty regime.[5] It may also be associated with the institutionally interconnected action plans, constituting a separate arm of technical and scientific development of the governance of the treaty regime, especially of environmental treaty regimes, systematically feeding the substratum of the declaratory governance exercised by the parties (decisions, recommendations, strategies, guidelines) in terms of an inner construction process of ICI.[6] In these cases, the institutionally-based management of the broadening of the usable knowledge, through concrete applications and assessments regarding the function of the treaty regime, inescapably feeds the field of Renegotiation.

Relatedly, the derivative context performs another little-noticed function: it forms a fountain from which the parties may draw and properly articulate their amendment proposals, evaluating their overall weight for the possible improvement of the conventional regime, as well as the desired scope of the revisionary renegotiation.

5 See Chapter 3.

6 A characteristic example is the Mediterranean Action Plan and its symbiotic relationship with the Barcelona Convention system whereby the active knowledge of the continuous evolution of this treaty regime is built. See E. Raftopoulos, *Barcelona Convention and Protocols: The Mediterranean Action Plan Regime*, Simmonds & Hill Publishing Ltd., 1993, *passim*. Also see Raftopoulos, *Conventional Environmental Governance and the Mediterranean or Plus Ultra* (in Greek), New Edition, Nomiki Bibliothiki, 2014, 40ff.

Any amendment proposal drawn from the derivative context should, more generally, satisfy the criteria of stability-in-continuity of the treaty regime, as well as of its permissible flexibility ranging from effective provision specifications or additions of annexes to its normative or policy expansion consistently with its purpose. More importantly, the feasibility of the proposed amendment should be carefully contemplated: whether it should be incorporated into the treaty text or remain as part of the derivative context. Should the revisionary proposal be cast in the form of an amendment and be adopted as such, expanding or properly adapting the normative implementation of the treaty regime, or should it be left to operate in the fluidity of the derivative context (scientific-technological, legal, political, socioeconomic, or their combination)? Would it be more effective and efficient if it continued to operate and develop in the declaratory form of the derivative context, thus avoiding the complications of the "contractual rigidity" resulting from the amendment procedure and, especially, the time element for its entry into force and its gradual application? Or, perhaps, would it be even more advisable to test it at the level of declaratory governance of the treaty regime – through decisions, recommendations, guidelines, and action plans – so that its resilience and the power of its normative added value in relation to the promotion of the ICI of the particular treaty regime will be more firmly established?

The answer to these questions signals the variety of considerations related to the nature of Renegotiation and the "living experience" of the treaty instantiating and performing ICI, and determines, in one direction or the other, the options of the parties to it. It will also work out the level and the quality of an equitable accommodation with the underlying "status order" entrenched into the particular treaty regime (notably, the dynamic asymmetry in the distribution of power between the negotiating states).

3.2 *The Morphological Patternment of Amendment*

The morphological patternment of Renegotiation refers to the textual negotiating technique applied to the amendment of the treaty concerned. In the Renegotiation process, all parts of the text pattern of the treaty, as analysed in the framework of the Constitutive Negotiation (preamble, definitions, purpose and scope of application, general duties-obligations, and the established system of multilateral governance of ICI, including its title), are open to amendment, and Renegotiation determines the extent and the depth of the pursued amendment. There is, however, an element of weakness in the textual formulation of the amendment outcome of Renegotiation. Thus, while the discussion in the Renegotiation process places amendment within the realm of the treaty regime, referring to its impact and function in relation to the original treaty text, as well as within its external and internal context of referential order, the textual outcome of Renegotiation strictly and exclusively refers to the text of the adopted amendments, without linking them with the rest of the treaty text (codification of amendment). In other words, despite its referential understanding and negotiating drafting, the amendment outcome of Renegotiation is technically drafted following an amendment-inclusive rather than an amendment- integrating approach. Thus, the formal amendment text only comprises the three forms of amendment mentioned earlier (new articles, extended or limited modifications of articles including complete redrafting, repealed articles), cast in a standard format (morphological patternment), usually indicated by the following pattern:

A. TITLE: The title of the Convention is amended as follows:

......

B. PREAMBULAR PARAGRAPHS:

- The (... third ...) preambular paragraph of the Convention is amended as follows:

  ....

- The following new paragraph/s are added to the Preamble:

  ....

C. ARTICLE 1: ....(title) .....

- Paragraph (a) / Paragraphs (a) and ... (d) is/are amended as follows:

  ....

D. ARTICLE 2: ....(title) .....

- Article 2 is amended as follows:

  ....

E. ARTICLE 3 and its **Title** are amended as follows:

....

F. The following **new Article 4A** is adopted:
ARTICLE 4A (renumbered as Article 5): ....(title) .....
....

G. ARTICLE 8 (renumbered as Article 9): ....(title) .....
Paragraphs 3 and 6 are deleted

H. .... to .... **X.** ....
Articles .... are renumbered as Articles .... respectively.

It is evident that this standard format of the amendment text, manifesting the amendment-inclusive approach and exclusively referring to the formulation of the accepted amendment, needs to be adequately and properly followed by its codification in a single treaty text and in all its officially provided languages. This will immensely facilitate the individual acceptances of the amendments – where required – and, relatedly, it will effectively support timely discussion of the overall picture presented by the amended treaty. Such codification of amendments requires authenticity, and this responsibility lies with the Secretariat, which should produce the formal consolidated text of the amended treaty in all its official languages. In many instances, particularly where the amendment of the treaty text is extensive, the Secretariat first proceeds, within a short time from the adoption of the amendment text, to the production of an informal consolidated text, formulated in the working language/s of the Renegotiation (English, in addition to French, or possibly another language used complementarily during the Renegotiation process),[7] in order to enhance the communicative effect of the amended treaty and give an impetus to expanding its individual acceptances by the parties. The secretariat's practice of preparing an informal consolidated text is particularly useful when it operates as a first step towards the formulation of the formal consolidated text, endowed with confirmed accuracy and meticulous attention to details, following appropriate deliberations with the parties. The formal consolidated text will be publicized by the Secretariat and will be formally distributed to the parties and the observers of the treaty regime, irrespective of the entry into force of the amended treaty. In fact, such a step-by-step Secretariat's practice imperceptibly expands its performative autonomy[8] in the framework of the treaty regime, building on its working relationship with the parties. On the other hand, each party, which individually accepts the amendment of the treaty, should adequately and quickly proceed to such codification into its own national language, thus making accessible to, and facilitating the enlightenment of, its administration.

3.3 *Amendment or Replacement? The Dynamic of the Renegotiation Process*

A determinative factor underlying the Renegotiation process and its final outcome, often overshadowed by political and legal discussions, is the element of subjectivity ingrained in the relational approach to, and management of, the revision of the treaty regime (relational subjectivity). The element of relational subjectivity may, under given circumstances, guide the negotiating parties to supersede the provided framework of the amendment procedure and their emanating procedural duty to negotiate and decide according to its terms. Thus, when certain factors concur, and if this is consistent with particular nature of the treaty regime and serves its ICI purpose, it is possible – and advisable – that the parties to the treaty may collectively decide, during the Renegotiation process, to adopt the replacement, instead of the amendment, of the treaty or of certain of its performative protocols. In doing so, they will generate their *conventional reconstitution or recasting* built upon the existing relational platform of the treaty regime. They will reestablish or recast the treaty or its performative protocol

7 See Raftopoulos, "International Environmental Negotiation as a Governance Technique," op. cit., 60.

8 For a succinct *tour d'horizon* of the *problematique* related to the expansion to new issue-linkages and autonomy as perceived by the staff of an international organization, see N. Hall, *Displacement, Development, and Climate Change: International Organizations Moving beyond Their Mandates*, Global Institutions Series, Rutledge, 2016, 8–10.

instrument, yet their legal force will have a contractual (consent) rather than a legislative (repeal) effect, similar to the effect of the amendment: the replacing treaty or related protocol instrument will apply only to the relations of those parties that are parties to the replaced and the replacing instrument.[9] Replacement, like amendment, has a contractual effect. It maintains the original conventional (treaty or protocol) links with regard to relations between those parties that are only parties to the original conventional instruments as well as to the latter's relations to the parties to the replacing instrument. Thus, the relational foundation of the treaty regime remains intact, while its adequate, conventionally determined reconstitution is timely promoted and set in operation. Unlike amendment, replacement has an important early time effect: for its entry into force, the replacing treaty instrument requires only the minimum number of ratifications required for its original establishment. At the same time, the progressive expansion of the replacing treaty into the relations with the remaining parties, which continue to be attached to the original treaty regime, accelerates because the application of the replacing treaty takes centre stage, punctuating a more advanced operation of the ICI treaty regime and, thus, pushing to an effective reduction, and ultimately elimination, of the area of the resulting dualistic governance within the treaty regime.

Since replacement instead of amendment is the result of negotiation, it may emerge either at an early stage or at the last stage of the Renegotiation process. The decision of the negotiating parties to proceed to a conventional reconstitution or recasting of the original treaty instrument, but also its timing, requires the concurrence of certain interrelated factors. It is based on a consensus generated from a multifactorial decision-making process reached by the renegotiating parties, in the light of a more effective, efficient, and coherent ICI governance in the framework of the treaty regime. It is worth noting that the Vienna Convention on the Law of Treaties, limited by the inadequate methodology of the "contract view" approach to treaty law it has adopted, does not even touch on this issue. Its methodological fortification around the static concept of contractual consent, based on the transfer of private law contractual analogy,[10] excludes any legal consideration of the process element of treaties and the element of decision associated with its relational foundation and operation as an instrument of protecting and promoting ICI. Leaving unanswered the question regarding the option of replacement of a treaty instrument, it implicitly classifies

[9] The contractual (consent) effect of a treaty recasting or replacement (conventional recasting) differentiates it from the recasting of legislation that has a repealing effect (legislative recasting). Used as a legislative technique, legislative recasting "enables amendments to, and codification of, acts to be carried out within the framework of a single legislative text," permitting "the adoption of a single legislative text which simultaneously makes the desired amendment, codifies that amendment with the unchanged provisions of the earlier act, and repeals that act." See the Inter-institutional Agreement of 28 November 2001 on a more structured use of the recasting technique for legal acts, OJ C 77, 28.3.2002, p. 1 (Preamble, paras. 4 and 5). This Agreement adopted by the European Parliament, the Council, and the Commission lays down "procedural rules enabling a more structured use to be made of the recasting technique pursuant to the Community's normal legislative process" (Art. 1).

[10] Raftopoulos, *The Inadequacy of the Contractual Analogy in the Law of Treaties*, op. cit., *passim*.

treaty replacement as an unchartered, "nonlegal" question, most myopically identifying legal logic with the private rather than public law logic.

The primary factor for the conventional reconstitution or recasting of the treaty or its protocols is its constitutive support by the hierarchical status order embodied in the particular treaty regime. Only if the core of the most powerful state parties of the treaty regime endorse the conventional reconstitution or recasting instead of amendment, is the transition possible and viable. During the Renegotiation process, the request for replacement instead of amendment should derive from the collective will of the stronger parties. At the same time, they anticipate that their "relational weight" for the ICI application of the replacing conventional instrument, combined with the early time effect of the latter, will generate a broader governance effect. As is clearly evidenced by international practice, this factor is conducive to the acceleration of the acceptance of the replacing treaty instrument by the rest of the contracting parties, thereby denoting the progressively obsolete character of the replaced instrument. Relatedly, the importance of the revision precipitation events and the pressing need for their effective management in the framework of the treaty regime should be showcased. The revision precipitation event, both in its positive version – applications of relevant scientific or technological developments,[11] relevant positive cooperative actions at the global level, overwhelming challenges by new strategic concepts changing the vision of managing issues and problems, like the sustainability concept, or change of political and military-strategic realities – and in its negative aspect (economic crisis, climate change, major accidents, malfunctions in governance caused by the lack or suppression of public participation, emerging attitudes or practices having a destabilizing effect on the treaty regime) may creatively mobilize the transformation of amendment into replacement during Renegotiation.[12]

Overall, the outcome of the Renegotiation process – to take the form of conventional reconstitution instead of the amendment of an instrumental version of the treaty regime – is the result of a negotiably shaped special decision, of a multifactorial basis, directly related to its more effective, efficient, cohesive, and legitimate empowered function. The horizontality of the international order and the contextuality of the treaty relations protecting and promoting ICI is consonant with an "operative" meaning of replacement of the treaty instrument and its conventional gradation until the replaced treaty instrument becomes obsolete.

[11] In relation to climate change, for instance, the recent development of more integrated methodology and new technologies capable of measuring ocean temperatures with a depth and precision that was previously lacking reveal that global warming is not only intensifying but it is also accelerating. See B. A. Steinman, M. E. Mann, and S. K. Miller, "Atlantic and Pacific Multidecadal Oscillations and Northern Hemisphere Temperatures." 347(6225) *Science* (27 February 2015), 988–991.

[12] Most characteristic in this case is, for instance, the renegotiation of several important arms limitation treaties after the end of the Cold War, like the Non-Proliferation Treaty (NPT), 1968, and the Conventional Forces in Europe (CFE) Treaty, 1990.

3.4 Alternative Options to Renegotiation?

The question concerning the basic alternative options to Renegotiation is of a rather limited value precisely because these options may only be vested with a "terminating" legal form associated with the law of treaties. Thus, when a change in the structure or function of a treaty instrument is no longer perceived by a state party as beneficial for it, then it may resort to "withdrawal from" or "denunciation of" the treaty regime as a whole. The individualizing legal effect of withdrawal or denunciation may be provided by the treaty itself – normally the "withdrawal clause" is part of the patternment of the treaty content – and applied according to their terms – if not, they may be invoked according to the relevant rules of the Vienna Convention on the Law of Treaties and the relevant international law decisions, practice, and academic constructions.[13] On the other hand, withdrawal or denunciation may hardly constitute alternatives to Renegotiation: they may normally be applied, if at all, as a result of Renegotiation but also at any time during the operation of the treaty regime and independently of Renegotiation.

The suggestion that the incorporation of a withdrawal clause into the treaty instrument precludes its opportunistic exercise because of its design referring to "the notice period" and "the withdrawal wait period," and, thus, makes withdrawal less likely, may, at first sight, have some merits, but it does not tell the whole story.[14] It is, in fact, the relational nature of the treaty as an ICI conventional regime that, through the operation of its particular institutional structure and the flexibility of its possible amendment, "internalizes" the application of the withdrawal clause and makes its exercise infrequent or, indeed, quite exceptional. After all, as was explained earlier, withdrawal may be exercised even when a treaty is silent on this matter and is directly related to the determination of the space of its implied operation. What finally seems to determine in practice the possibility or the probability of its exercise is directly related to the ad hoc regime institutional management of the matter and/or the related "weight" of the relational and contextual factors and their multifaceted aspects (public nature of the treaty, ICI legislative purpose, domestic, regime-internal and external context of reference, and the pragmatic circumstances surrounding the multilateral constitution of the treaty regime). Thus, whether expressly provided in a treaty regime or implied, withdrawal reflects the subjective power-right of the state party to repeal its individual participation in

13 See the "subjectivity" aspect of the patternment of the treaty content in Chapter 4.

14 B. Koremenos, *The Continent of International Law: Explaining Agreement Design*, Cambridge University Press, 2016, 140–157. In fact, Koremenos visualizes withdrawal through the distorting lenses of the inadequate game-theoretic framework, transposing its logic to the explanation of the exercise of withdrawal provision, ignoring its legal nature and, even more importantly, the legal nature of treaty as establishing an ICI regime. And looking at treaties as playing fields, she advances a rather disorienting international relations theory type of argument: "Even though withdrawing is lawful and not equivalent to defecting . . . strategically, in many cooperative settings, withdrawing has the same effect as defecting," thus, being preoccupied with the deterrence of an "early withdrawal" that may offer a strategic advantage to the withdrawing state. Ibid., 61.

any ICI treaty regime, but the complexity of the aforementioned treaty institutional practices and factors associated with its exercise make it exceptional and an opportunistic withdrawal a risky strategic possibility not affecting the continuity of the treaty ICI regime. The question of withdrawal is, in pragmatic terms, to be decided by a state party by navigating two opposing considerations: how harmful is the continuation of its participation in the dynamically evolving treaty regime versus how many "bridges" would burn due to its withdrawal from the treaty regime and the related political and functional cost, taking into account the relational nature of the treaty regime, its contextuality, and the associated interdependence of states in the horizontal international order.[15]

It should not be overlooked, however, that both denunciation and withdrawal, having a terminating legal effect of individual participation in a treaty, are likely to be employed as an intermediate strategy: they may be part of an individual strategy broadly aiming at triggering the process to an overall review of the treaty and accelerate the initiation of its Renegotiation for its substantial revision. And if this seems to be, in fact, rather unlikely to happen in multilateral treaty regimes, due to the flexibility of the initiation of the amendment procedure wrapped up in the relevant standard provision, withdrawal and denunciation may, nevertheless, find room for application in bilateral treaty regimes. The example of Bilateral Investment Agreements is instructive. Although they are generally subject to consensual Renegotiation (change "within" the conventional framework and not "of" the conventional framework), there have been instances of an overall rejection of the treaty regime – through the termination of Bilateral Investment Agreements and withdrawal from the International Center for Settlement of Investment Disputes. This alternative to Renegotiation strategy has been followed by certain Latin American countries, but now is avoided because of its serious political and legal implications and repercussions.[16]

3.5 *Renegotiating the Treaty Regime Declarative Components*

Although the Renegotiation phase fundamentally refers to the revisionary governance process amending or reconstituting the text of the treaty instrument, one

15 The famous expression "if you break it, you own it" is amply applicable in this case: it is a simple statement of the fact that if you decide to withdraw from/denounce a treaty regime, you may become the owner of unleashed uncontrollable powers, eroding relations with other states and possibly causing severe domestic shocks. This expression is a formulation of the Pottery Barn rule notoriously and most perceptively cited by US Secretary of State Colin Powell when warning President George W. Bush in 2002 about the consequences of an American invasion of Iraq: "You are going to be the proud owner of 25 million people," he told the president. "You will own all their hopes, aspirations, and problems. You'll own it all." B. Woodward, *Plan of Attack*, Wheeler Large Print Book Series, 2004, 150.

16 See UNCTAD, *Denunciation of the ICSID Convention and BITS: Impact on Investor-State Claims*, 2010, IIA Issues Note, No. 2 (December), available at: http://unctad.org/en/docs/webdiaeia20106_en.pdf.

should not overlook a marginal aspect of this phase, touching on the declarative components of a treaty regime, such as action plans. These declarative components are related to the constitution and/or the implementation of a treaty ICI regime, ingraining into it the necessary technical/scientific information and knowledge for its continuous, more effective, and more efficient operation. Because of their chronic quality and component function in a treaty regime, these declarative instruments may also be "refined" or "reassessed" by negotiated consensus, in conformity with the procedural steps applicable to the particular treaty regime. Such a reassessment of an existing treaty regime declarative component may result in its replacement by a new one. It goes without saying that the coordinating role of the Secretariat in this process is important.

The refinement or reassessment of a treaty regime declarative component may take three concrete, interconnected forms, in a similar fashion to the amendment of a treaty.

- It may update the existing regime declarative instrument, addressing specifically identified needs.
- It may elaborate the existing regime declarative instrument, addressing the inclusion of new or alternative up-to-date information and guidance provided to clarify existing guidance.
- It may provide new guidance on issues for which there is essentially no guidance in the existing regime declarative instrument.

In cases of a fundamental change of focus, due to contextual developments and identified shortcomings of the existing regime declarative instrument, a new regime declarative instrument may replace the old one after thorough review and renegotiation.

Environmental treaty regimes provide an excellent illustration of this aspect of Renegotiation, precisely because they encompass complementary components of scientific, technological, and social knowledge, interactively setting the tone for the direction and depth of their relational governance. The Mediterranean Action Plan (MAP), the scientific and technical component of the Barcelona Convention system (BCS) governing the marine environment and coastal region of the Mediterranean, is an instrumental example. Adopted in 1975,[17] MAP provided a model: it set up a comprehensive (multidisciplinary) and context-relevant (Mediterranean condition) Prenegotiation framework, promoting "the parallel development" of technical

[17] MAP was adopted by sixteen States bordering the Mediterranean and the European Community and it was the first-ever plan adopted as a Regional Seas Programme under UNEP's umbrella, serving as a model. The Regional Seas Programme, launched in 1974, was conceived as a global programme implemented through Regional Action Plans, shaped according to the needs of the region concerned and, thus "regionalizing" the interests of states with respect to the protection of the marine environment in an innovative manner. See Raftopoulos, *The Barcelona Convention and Protocols: The Mediterranean Action Plan Regime, supra* note 6, 1–5.

and legal governance aspects for the control of pollution in the Mediterranean,[18] on the basis of which the first phase of the BCS (1976–1995) was carried out. The fundamental revision of the BCS in 1995, shifting the focus from a sectorial approach to scaled pollution control to integrated management of marine environment and coastal zone contributing to the sustainable development of the Mediterranean Sea area, was inescapably coupled with the adoption of the second phase of MAP. The Action Plan for the Protection of the Marine Environment and the Sustainable Development of the Coastal Areas of the Mediterranean (MAP Phase II) was the outcome of a renegotiation, carried out within the institutional structure of the BCS regime, that thoroughly reassessed MAP I. After its detailed review negotiation and approval by the Joint Meeting of the Scientific and Technical Committee and the Socio-Economic Committee, the proposed Action Plan (MAP Phase II) was introduced and further negotiated at the 9th Meeting of the Contracting Parties (1995), where various elaborations and additional guidance were proposed and their negotiation led to the adoption of the revised MAP Phase II by the Meeting,[19] and its endorsement by the following Conference of Plenipotentiaries, included in its Final Act.[20] And for the first time, the Action Plan (MAP Phase II) was expressly raised as part of the consensual basis of the general obligations of the Contracting Parties (CPs) under Article 4(2) of the amended Barcelona Convention, prescribing the normative implications of the implementation of MAP in its relationship with the BCS.[21] In fact, the Action Plan (MAP Phase II), because of the fundamental change in its focus, replaced the Action Plan (MAP Phase I), "taking into account the achievements and shortcomings" of MAP Phase I, "as well as the results of recent developments," especially the

[18] On this "parallel development" approach, see ibid. From its inception, MAP contained three constituent elements, the environmental assessment component (a coordinated pollution and research programme in the Mediterranean), the environmental management component (integrated planning of the development and management of the resources of the Mediterranean Basin), and the legal and institutional component (the framework convention and related protocols for the protection of the Mediterranean environment – institutional and financial implications). Ibid., 5–80.

[19] MAP: Report of the 9th Ordinary Meeting of the Contracting Parties to the Convention for the Protection of the Mediterranean Sea Against Pollution and Its Related Protocols, Barcelona, 5–8 June 1995, UNEP(OCA)/MED IG.5/16, paras. 30, 31 and annex IX.

[20] See MAP: Final Act of the Conference of Plenipotentiaries on the Amendments to the Convention for the Protection of the Mediterranean Sea Against Pollution, to the Protocol for the Prevention of Pollution of the Mediterranean Sea by Dumping from Ships and Aircraft and on the Protocol Concerning Specially Protected Areas and Biological Diversity in the Mediterranean, UNEP(OCA)/MED IG.6/7, 1 July 1995, Appendix I, pp. 101–137.

[21] Art. 4(2) provides that the CPs "pledge themselves to take appropriate measures to implement the Mediterranean Action Plan" in pursuance of the protection of the Mediterranean marine environment and its natural resources "as an integral part of the development process" in a sustainable manner. It is also noteworthy that by decision IG.5/16 (Annex IX) of the 9th Meeting of the Contracting Parties, 1995, adopting MAP Phase II and the Barcelona Resolution on the Environment and Sustainable Development in the Mediterranean Basin IG.5/16 (Annex XI), the Ministers "commit themselves to the full implementation of the MAP Phase II, the Barcelona Convention and its Protocols."

UN Conference on Environment and Development (Rio, 1992) and the Conference "Med 21" on Sustainable Development in the Mediterranean (Tunis, 1994).[22]

Further important contextual developments, culminating in the UN Conference on Sustainable Development – Rio+20 (Rio, 2012), set the stage for a new reassessment of the Action Plan (MAP Phase II). Thus, the 18th Meeting of the Contracting Parties decided to launch the renegotiation process for the assessment of MAP Phase II, and, more specifically, to effectively address "the challenge of sustainable development and the irreversible nature of impacts on the environment and resources," with a view to propose "a Decision on the appropriate way forward including the possible adoption at the 19th meeting of the Contracting Parties of MAP phase III," and also "to give greater emphasis in MAP to concrete and operational activities" (Decision IG.21/16).[23] However, the time was not ripe for a new reassessment and policy considerations halted the renegotiation process. The lack of progress was further handled by the 19th Meeting of the Contracting Parties. It decided to implement Decision IG.21/16, emphasizing the need for MAP Phase II to be adjusted to reflect the key developments made in the MAP system with regard to thematic issues, and, for this purpose, to establish an open-ended Working Group of the MAP Focal Points to update the document for submission to the 20th Meeting of the Contracting Parties.[24] And there was a clear orientation of renegotiation towards a general updating, elaboration, and new guidance in the existing MAP Phase II instrument, precluding the need for a new MAP Phase III instrument. The outcome of renegotiation within the framework of the Open-ended Working Group on the Mediterranean Action Plan II Assessment was, rather predictably, conservative, providing an insight into the relevance and status of MAP II that may be beneficially used for its future strategic development. It paved the way for MAP II to be retained as originally formulated in 1995 and ensured that no update of the document will be carried out at the present time.[25] The recent 20th Meeting of the Contracting Parties consolidated this negotiably reached consensus: underlining the importance and relevance of the MAP II instrument, as well as its contribution to sustainable development, it decided to retain the original text of MAP Phase II.[26]

22 MAP: Action Plan for the Protection of the Marine Environment and the Sustainable Development of the Coastal Areas of the Mediterranean (MAP Phase II), Introduction, see *supra* note 20.

23 UNEP/MAP: Report of the 18th Ordinary Meeting of the Contracting Parties to the Convention for the Protection of the Mediterranean Sea Against Pollution and Its Related Protocols, Istanbul, Turkey, 3–6 December 2013, UNEP(DEPI)/MED IG.21/9, Decision IG.21/16, Annex II, 241.

24 UNEP/MAP: Report of the 19th Ordinary Meeting of the Contracting Parties to the Convention for the Protection of the Mediterranean Sea Against Pollution and Its Related Protocols, Athens, Greece, 9–12 February 2016, UNEP(DEPI)/MED IG.22/28, paras. 122–124, 20.

25 See UNEP/MAP: Meeting of the MAP Focal Points, Athens, Greece, 12–15 September 2017, UNEP(DEPI)/MED WG.443/19.

26 UNEP/MAP: Report of the 20th Ordinary Meeting of the Contracting Parties to the Convention for the Protection of the Mediterranean Sea Against Pollution and Its Related Protocols, Tirana, Albania, 15–18 December 2017, UNEP(DEPI)/MED IG.21/9, Decision IG.21/16, Annex II, 241.

4 THE OUTCOME OF RENEGOTIATION

When the series of the negotiating sessions of the Ad Hoc Working Group of Legal and Technical Experts is completed and the draft of the revised text (amendment or replacement) is finalized, the Secretariat introduces it to the Conference/Meeting of the Parties (or to the highest authoritative organ of the international organization) for its collective approval. This collective approval is accompanied by a special mandate to the Secretariat to convene and organize a Diplomatic Conference or a Conference of Plenipotentiaries, or a Review Conference, the highest political negotiating forum, for the official adoption of the revised draft text. Like in the Constitutive Negotiation process, the Secretariat undertakes the preparation of the draft of the Final Act that will be adopted by the Diplomatic Conference as well as of the Resolution to be annexed to the Final Act which, in the case of amendment, refers to the adoption of the specific amendments inviting the parties to accelerate the procedure of notification of their individual acceptances.

If amendment is the outcome of Renegotiation, the Diplomatic Conference convened by the Secretariat, officially adopts the amendment text normally by consensus, otherwise by the qualified majority defined in the treaty. The amendment text is annexed to the Final Act of the Conference, which is signed by the representatives of the Contracting Parties, the president of the Diplomatic Conference, and the head of the Secretariat. The Final Act provides the official testimony of the completion of the Renegotiation process and of the adoption of the amendments to the treaty attached as an annex and formulated in all official languages of the treaty. For the entry into force of the amendments, the standard rules on treaty amendment are strictly applied, having a contractual effect (in the case of the amendment of the substantive body of the treaty) or a relational effect (in the case of the amendment of technical annexes or of adding new technical annexes).

5 IN THE TWILIGHT ZONE BETWEEN RENEGOTIATION AND CONSTITUTIVE NEGOTIATION: RENEGOTIATING THE UNDER-DETERMINATE EDGES OF A TREATY REGIME

Interestingly, Renegotiation as an amendment process may, in some cases and because of the particular relational nature of the treaty regime, perform not a treaty-changing but a treaty-constitutive function when related to the development of a particular framework provision of a treaty requiring definitive specification. It may concern edges still to be determined. This account of renegotiation may proceed through layers of institutional negotiation operating within the framework of the particular treaty regime and generating its constitutive completion.

Thus, when Renegotiation refers to a treaty's under-determinate aspect requiring further specification, negotiation is initiated and carried out in accordance with the existing treaty regime. The fact that it unfolds between the contracting parties of a treaty regime, with the participation of the non-state entities vested with the status of observers, and that their focus is on negotiating for specifying and articulating a certain under-determinate thematic aspect of an already established treaty regime advancing its ICI implementation, indicates that Renegotiation may also have a constitutive function. Operating within its procedural limits and aiming at the constitutive completion of an operating treaty regime, Renegotiation builds ICI consensus through multiple layers of institutional negotiation and its process is prolonged, exhibiting particular structural characteristics. In brief, Renegotiation is performed through constituting the specific elements of an under-determined thematic aspect of the treaty, and, as a result, it undergoes subtle structural transformations and opens up new dimensions in negotiating techniques.

5.1 *Renegotiating the Undetermined Crime of Aggression of the Rome Statute of the ICC and the Way to the Kampala Revisionary Compromise*

The Kampala Review Conference on the crime of aggression amending the Convention establishing the Statute of the International Criminal Court, 1998, and its outcome, known as the Kampala Compromise, culminated a process providing a characteristic and stimulating paradigm of the constitutive function of Renegotiation as a treaty amendment process. Such a cross-cutting function of Renegotiation is basically related to the particular relational character of the treaty regime establishing the Statute of the ICC: it refers to the conventional establishment of an international court by State Parties governing certain operational and financial aspects of the court, while the law and competence, institutional structure, function, and powers of the court are specifically prescribed. It is therefore of special importance that the Statute of the ICC is set to enable it to administer Justice in a holistic and balanced manner, effectively protecting and promoting ICI in dynamic coherence with its context. And it is within this framework that its undetermined aspect concerning the crime of aggression was to be negotiably constituted as an amendment.

5.1.1 Referential Context, the Rome Compromise, and Institutional Layers of Renegotiation

Reflecting a creative negotiating process, Renegotiation has led from the so-called 1998 Rome Compromise, associated with the framework formulation of the crime of aggression in the ICC Statute, to the revisionary 2010 Kampala Compromise. In this long negotiating process, the definition and the elements of this crime were collectively fleshed out and consolidated by consensus while the related question of the Court jurisdiction was realistically and constructively set out. Thus, Renegotiation was geared to effectively build a bridge for the transition of the undetermined aspects of the crime of aggression in the ICC Statute into their constitutive legal formulation serving ICI as an amendment of the Statute process. And it was fashioned within a peculiar referential context. Despite the strong recognition of the crime of aggression as an international crime by important international instruments,[27] and by earlier renowned international instruments and tribunals judgments, namely the London Agreement establishing the Charter of the Nuremberg International Military Tribunals,[28] the Nuremberg Judgement,[29] and the Tokyo International Military Tribunal and judgment, the elements of this crime had remained undefined for decades to the effect that it had eventually slipped into the shadow of international law developments.[30] On the other hand, operating as an amendment to the established ICC Statute, Renegotiation reflected a performative aspect of this Statute and, as a result, it ought to secure the highest possible conceptual and functional coherence with it, avoiding deviations from it.

More specifically, the framework formulation of the crime of aggression originally provided in the ICC Statute was constructed as a dynamic and multifarious legal platform (the Rome Compromise) encompassing:

- The simple reference that the crime of aggression was within the jurisdiction of the Court (Art. 5(1)(d)).
- The *pactum de contrahendo* of a provision to define the crime and set out the conditions for the jurisdiction of the ICC with respect to this crime, in accordance with the prescribed rules of amendment of the Statute allowing such a process "after the expiry of seven years from the entry into force of this Statute," and in consistency with the relevant provisions of the UN Charter (Art. 5(2)).
- The complementing Resolution F of the Final Act of the UN Diplomatic Conference of Plenipotentiaries on the Establishment of an International Criminal Court establishing the Preparatory Commission for the ICC to

[27] See UNGA Resolution 95(1) "Affirmation of the Principles of International Law Recognized by the Charter of the Nürnberg Tribunal." UN Doc. A/RES/95 (1946), para.1 (11 December1946); ILC: "Draft Code of Crimes against the Peace and Security of Mankind with Commentaries," Report of the International Law Commission on the Work of Its Forty-Eighth Session (6 May–26 July 1996), GAOR A/51/10 (1996); YBILC, 1996, vol. II(2), Art. 16.

[28] See Art. 6(a) of the Charter of the Nuremberg International Military Tribunal prescribing "crimes against peace," 82 *UNTS* (1951), 280.

[29] Pronouncing the initiation of a war of aggression as a supreme international crime, in "Judicial Decisions, International Military Tribunal (Nuremberg), Judgment and Sentences," 41 *AJIL* (1947), 186.

[30] The fact that the UN General Assembly, in 1974, decided to adopt by consensus the definition of "the act of aggression" (UNGA Resolution 3314 [XXIX] Annex to UN Doc. A/RES/3314 [XXIX], 14 December 1974), providing that it should be construed within the scope of the Charter and in the context of the relevant provisions of the Charter, while entirely falling for its determination within the competence of the Security Council, was politically unable and legally inapt to revert this process.

> prepare proposals for a provision on aggression and mandating the UN Secretary General to convene the Commission "as early as possible" and to provide to it "such secretariat services as it may require."[31]

In pursuance of the Rome Compromise and pending the entry into force of the Rome Statute of the ICC, the Preparatory Commission for the ICC was set up and held ten negotiating sessions (1999–2002). At its third session, the Preparatory Commission created the Working Group on Aggression, which originally negotiated the specifying aspects of the crime of aggression as identified by the Rome Compromise (definition of the crime plus jurisdiction of the ICC in context), but was only able to produce a result that was modest in form (Discussion Paper 2002), though interesting in substance, usefully shaping the optional negotiating zone for these issues,[32] thus directing the constitutive function of their renegotiation.

The entry into force of the Rome ICC Statute in 2002 was coupled with the reinforcement and progressive enrichment in the constitutive function of the Renegotiation process. Thus, the Assembly of States Parties to the ICC Statute (ASP)[33] refuelled the renegotiation process for the continuation and completion of the work on the crime of aggression. Taking into account the Report of the Preparatory Commission for the ICC on the crime of aggression, containing Discussion Paper 2002 of the Working Group on Aggression, it proceeded to establish the Special Working Group on the Crime of Aggression (SWGCA) "for the purpose of elaborating proposals for a provision on aggression" in accordance with the Rome Compromise.[34] It also decided that the SWGCA "shall submit such proposals to the Assembly for its consideration at a Review Conference, with a view to arriving at an acceptable provision on the crime of aggression for inclusion in the Statute in accordance with the relevant provisions of the Statute."[35]

31 See United Nations Diplomatic Conference of Plenipotentiaries on the Establishment of an International Criminal Court, Official Records, Vol. I, Final Documents, Annex I, Resolution F, paras. 1, 7, 10, 72–73. According to para. 2 of this Resolution, the Preparatory Commission consisted of representatives of States that have signed the Final Act of the United Nations Diplomatic Conference and other States that have been invited to participate in the Conference. In accordance with the UNGA Resolution 56/85 (A/RES/56/85, 18 January 2002) the Secretary-General invited, as observers to the Preparatory Commission, representatives of organizations and other entities that have received a standing invitation from the General Assembly, representatives of interested regional intergovernmental organizations and other interested international bodies (such as the International Tribunal for the Former Yugoslavia and the International Tribunal for Rwanda), as well as NGOs (paras. 6 and 7).

32 See the Preparatory Commission for the International Criminal Court, Report, "Proposals for a Provision on the Crime of Aggression," PCNICC/2002/2/Add. 2, 3–6.

33 See Art. 112 of the Rome ICC Statute.

34 Resolution ICC-ASP/I/Res. 1 adopted by consensus at the 3rd Plenary Meeting on 9 September 2002, ICC-ASP/I/3, 328.

35 Ibid.

5.1.2 The Twinning Renegotiating Process

The SWGCA held its first meeting in September 2003 and completed its renegotiating rounds in February 2009. Its proposals for a provision on aggression were very properly characterized as "a watershed in the negotiations on the crime of aggression,"[36] and offered the creative platform for the Kampala Compromise. To reach a consensus on its proposals, the SWGCA fruitfully employed an integrating framework of negotiation – an interactive combination of formal and informal negotiating processes – which was instrumental in the construction of ICI. This complementarity framework orienting renegotiation was most insightfully decided by the SWGCA at an early stage of its work and effectively generated a significant increase in the time frame of its meetings, which were initially restricted to few formal meetings,[37] a clearly inadequate time allocation in view of the crucial, immensely complex political issues, legally and technically undefined, such as the crime of aggression. At the same time, the significant time expansion was associated with a twinning negotiating process (formal and inter-sessional negotiating sessions) in an interactive relationship, thus bringing to the fore more transparency and a more scholarly illuminated problem-oriented approach to the renegotiation constituting the crime of aggression.[38]

This twinning negotiating process, initiated and structured by the Chairman of the SWGCA and its team,[39] actually had its soul in the informal inter-sessional meetings the spirit of which infused the work of the SWGCA. They were designed as

36 S. Barriga, "Against the Odds: The Results of the Special Working Group on the Crime of Aggression," in R. Bellelli (ed.), *International Criminal Justice: Law and Practice from the Rome Statute to Its Review*, Ashgate Publishing, 2010, 621–643, 640.

37 The resolution of the Assembly of States Parties on the establishment of the SWGCA stated that the SWGCA will meet "during the regular sessions of the Assembly or at any other time that the Assembly deems appropriate and feasible." Resolution ICC-ASP/1/Res. 1, op. cit., para. 4.

38 In this process, one should not underestimate the impact of the authoritative volume prepared by the UN Secretariat entitled "Historical Review of the Developments Relating to Aggression" and presented to the Working Group on the Crime of Aggression at the ninth session of the Preparatory Commission, in 2002 (PCNICC/2002/WGCA/L1 and Add. 1). This volume usefully "provides an objective, analytical overview of the history and major developments relating to aggression before and after the adoption of the Charter of the United Nations," and "reflects developments relating to aggression as of mid-2001" (UN: *Historical Review of Developments Relating to Aggression*, New York, 2003, Preface, xviii) constituting a valuable resource for the ensuing negotiating process, as underlined in the Report of the Special Working Group on the Crime of Aggression, 2005 (ICC-ASP/4/SWGCA/1, 2005, para. 4).

39 The initiation of this twinning negotiating process emanating from the realization of its importance in the continuous negotiations and the consensus unfolding of the necessary knowledge was the work of the Chairman of the SWGCA, Ambassador Christian Wenaweser of Liechtenstein, supported by his inspired Liechtenstein negotiating team. Chairman Wenaweser "guided the negotiations in a skilled manner, displaying just the right combination of authority, expertise, patience and good humour," and, most effectively, he created the feeling that "despite the numerous obstacles that lay ahead, the SWGCA had a realistic chance of fulfilling its mission." C. Kress and L. von Holtzendorff, "The Kampala Compromise on the Crime of Aggression." 8 *Journal of International Criminal Justice* (2010), 1179, 1186.

open-ended and all-inclusive meetings, held in English only and focused exclusively on the crime of aggression, allowing representatives of non-state parties and experts from interested NGOs to actively participate in the negotiating process. All five inter-sessional meetings have taken place at the Woodrow Wilson School in Princeton University between 2004 and 2009 and were called "the Princeton Process." The Princeton Process signalled the potential importance that a complementary "academization" of the negotiating process may have in the context of certain relational treaty regimes.[40] The Princeton Process created a complementary, more academically (legally and technically) fuelled renegotiation, feeding the formal renegotiating formal sessions of the SWGCA, while opening the window of opportunity for an intensive contribution to it by the larger scholarly community.[41]

Interestingly, the Princeton Process was associated with an effective textual negotiation technique that immensely facilitated the thematic approach adopted by the Group, focusing on the legal and technical aspects of the crime of aggression that were not addressed before. Thus, each negotiating session of the Princeton Process was centred on a discussion paper prepared by the Chairman, which somehow transposed into the inter-sessional negotiating process the logic and practice of single negotiating text. The discussion papers effectively guided constitutive renegotiation in its informal terrain, contributing, step by step, to consensus-building on the crime of aggression and its elements of crime in consistency with the Rome Statute of the ICC. The question of "smooth incorporation" of the provision on the crime of aggression into the ICC Statute was a determinative factor properly injected by the discussion papers into inter-sessional renegotiation. Having a constant thematic focus (the elements of definition of the crime of aggression, the conditions for the exercise of jurisdiction and their consistency with the relevant provisions of the UN Charter and with the elements of the other crimes of the ICC Statute), the discussion papers, following a carefully balanced approach,[42] set the evolving stage (a constructing and explaining framework) for fruitful informal negotiation between the delegates. At the same time, the informal negotiating sessions were effectively facilitated by the introduction of non-papers by the Chairman, facilitating and deepening the understanding of the major outstanding issues and their interlinkages while testing the views of the participants through questionnaires. Correspondingly, the Reports of each informal negotiating session

40 The proposed term "academization" is, in my view, preferable to the often-used term "technical" because it is a process-term, indicating an ongoing activity enhancing the more academic vision of the issues involved, rather than a full-fledged state of their no-interest examination. At the same time, it implies an enhanced but realistic degree of dissociation from state-interests rather than a complete dissociation from them concealing their underlying guiding force.

41 See Kress and von Holtzendorff, "The Kampala Compromise on the Crime of Aggression," *supra* note 39, 1187.

42 See S. Barriga, "Introduction to the Negotiation History," in S. Barriga and C. Kress (eds.), *The Travaux Préparatoires of the Crime of Aggression*, Cambridge University Press, 2012, 17–18.

became important reference tools for the developing negotiating process. Reflecting the progress achieved in each such session and illuminating the "hardening" aspects in the defined zone of Renegotiation, they served to build trust among the participants and confidence for a successful outcome while consolidating the levels of the informally, legally, and technically achieved consensus.[43]

As a result of its successful twinning negotiating process and the special techniques developed in their interaction, the SWGCA was able to propose in February 2009 a consensus definition of the crime of aggression, thus achieving a major breakthrough in the constitutively-functioning renegotiation process. Its so-called "2009 Proposals," submitted to the Review Conference in Kampala, reflected this progress in a creative framework. It contained the draft amendments to the Rome Statute of the ICC on the Crime of Aggression: deletion of Art. 5.2 of the statute, a new article embodying a clean text on the definition of the crime of aggression (Art. 8bis), and a new article on the exercise of jurisdiction over the crime of aggression (15bis) with two alternatives regarding the jurisdiction of the ICC in the case of the absence of the determination of the crime of aggression by the Security Council.[44] It also contained the draft amendments to the elements of crimes complementing the definition of the crime of aggression in the additional Art. 8 (bis),[45]and consolidating its support. Finally, and in view of the particularly delicate nature of the negotiation process on these issues, it most usefully included draft understandings regarding the interpretation of the amendments on the crime of aggression, which comprised the referrals by the Security Council, jurisdiction *ratione temporis* of the Court, and the open-ended alternatives for the acceptance of the amendment on the crime of aggression and the related role of state consent.[46]

43 A standard paragraph was included at the end of the introduction of each Report of the SWGCA, providing, in an almost identical phrasing, that "[t]he present document does not necessarily represent the views of the Governments of the participants. It seeks to reflect conclusions and opinions regarding different issues on the crime of aggression. It is understood that these issues would have to be reassessed in light of further work on the crime of aggression. It is hoped that the material in the present document would facilitate the work of the Special Working Group on the Crime of Aggression." ICC-ASP/3/SWGCA/INF.1, para 4; ICC-ASP/4/32, para. 3; ICC-ASP/5/SWGCA/INF.1, para. 5; ICC-ASP/6/SWGCA/INF.1, para. 4; ICC-ASP/8/INF.2, para. 5. It is also interesting that, in this process, the SWGCA agreed to establish a "virtual working group" at its 2005 session, in order to "allow States to advance their discussion outside regular and inter-sessional meetings, it being understood that such a working group communicating by electronic means would be open to all interested States." ICC-ASP/4/32, para 91. Its main purpose was to "help prepare for future meetings of the SWGCA either in the framework of the Assembly of the Contracting Parties or in an inter-sessional format" (ICC-ASP/4/SWGCA/1, para. 6), and it was not meant as a decision-making body or as a substitute for meetings of the SWGCA. Ibid., para 11.

44 See ICC: Review Conference of the Rome Statute, The Conference Room Paper on the Crime of Aggression of 25 May 2010 (RC/WGCA/1), Annex I, 3.

45 Ibid., Annex II, 6.

46 Ibid., Annex III, 7.

5.2 THE KAMPALA REVISIONARY COMPROMISE

Within this successfully negotiated framework, the 2010 Review Conference in Kampala focused its efforts on bridging the remaining gaps. Relying on the achieved consensus on the definition of the crime of aggression and the solid support behind it,[47] the Review Conference focused on the still outstanding issue of the conditions for the ICC exercise of jurisdiction: whether some form of expressed consent by the aggressor state should be required and, hence, the crime of aggression should be subject to a more restrictive jurisdictional regime than the other three core crimes prescribed in the Statute,[48] and what the Security Council's role would be in the determination of an act of aggression in this context ("the question of questions"). A Conference Room Paper (CRP) prepared by the Chair served as the basis of the renegotiating process of the Review Conference in Kampala. Quite perceptively, the CRP on the crime of aggression provided a comprehensive framework of the package to be adopted by consensus as forwarded by the SWGCA in its 2009 Proposals:

- The draft enabling resolution on the crime of aggression, containing the "considering part" referring to the internal legal context and the "ordering part" by which the draft amendments and the draft understanding creating the package will be adopted.
- The draft amendments to the Rome Statute on the crime of aggression, containing the unbracketed draft Article 8bis on the definition of the crime of aggression and draft Article 15bis on the exercise of jurisdiction over the crime of aggression with two alternatives and six options (jurisdictional filters).[49]
- The unbracketed draft amendments to the Elements of Crimes.

47 In fact, the solid support for the achieved definition of the crime of aggression grew even stronger when challenged by criticisms developed at a later stage, where, despite "a certain level of understanding for the concerns advanced," the view consistently prevailed "that reopening the definition would inevitably lead to its total unravelling." However, state parties "were willing to address legitimate concerns outside the definition itself." C. Wenaweser, "Reaching the Kampala Compromise on Aggression: The Chair's Perspective." 23(4) *LJIL* (2010), 883–887, 883.

48 The crime of genocide, crimes against humanity, and war crimes. Rome Statute of the ICC, Art. 5.

49 The two broad alternatives were referring to the following jurisdictional filters: exclusive Security Council jurisdiction (alternative 1) and primary, but not exclusive, Security Council jurisdiction (alternative 2). Each of the two alternatives was accompanied by several options. For details, see Barriga, "Introduction to the Negotiation History," *supra* note 42, 33–36. During the negotiations within the SWGCA framework, the term "jurisdictional filter" replaced the term "conditions for exercise of jurisdiction" since it was agreed that each of the four existing mechanisms (Security Council, Pre-Trial Chamber, General Assembly, International Court of Justice) would constitute a condition for the exercise of jurisdiction and, hence, the question was what kind of filter should be applicable. See Informal Inter-Sessional Meeting on the Crime of Aggression 8–10 June 2009, Non-paper by the Chairman on the Conditions for the Exercise of Jurisdiction, paras. 14–19, available at: https://asp.icc-cpi.int/iccdocs/asp_docs/SWGCA/Non-paper-conditions-jurisdiction-28May2009-ENG.pdf.

- Draft understandings regarding the interpretation of the amendments on the crime of aggression as discussed at the last session of the SWGCA, open to further understandings.[50]

It is clear that coupling the consensus procedure with the package deal procedure as reflected in the CRP has had a catalytic impact on the development of the Kampala Compromise. Embracing the consolidated substantive definition of the crime of aggression and the elements of the crime, together with the clearly defined menu of alternatives and options and a few proposals regarding the jurisdictional aspect, as well as the open-ended understandings regarding their interpretation of the amendment, the CRP effectively framed the domain for the creative outcome of the Review Conference in Kampala. The Review Conference left intact the unbracketed draft amendments of Article 8bis on the definition of the crime of aggression and of the elements of crimes, considering them "locked" and not subject to reopening for negotiations. Instead, it was exclusively oriented towards the negotiation of the bracketed draft amendment of Article 15bis on the exercise of jurisdiction and to the finalization of the open-ended understandings of the amendments to the ICC Statute. After intense negotiations, which produced revised versions of the CRP, capturing creative and highly influential proposals reflected in non-papers submitted by the Chair and certain delegations,[51] and conducted in a uniquely constructive atmosphere at both levels,[52] the Working Group and the Plenary of the Review Conference, the Review Conference has finally achieved a successful compromise by consensus.

The Kampala Revisionary Compromise reflected an accommodation of interests based on a long and delicate process of a negotiated construction of ICI related to the determination of the crime of aggression and its jurisdictional filter management in the framework of the purposive operation of the ICC Statute and its institutional credibility. Resolution 6 of the Review Conference, embodying the final version of the CRP, contained a comprehensive package that included:

- The consolidated amendments of Article 8bis on the definition of the crime of aggression,[53] and to the elements of crimes,[54] inserted after Art. 8 of the Statute.

50 ICC: Review Conference of the Rome Statute, The Conference Room Paper on the Crime of Aggression, op. cit., *passim*.

51 See, for details, Barriga, "Introduction to the Negotiation History," *supra* note 42, 47ff.

52 As stressed by the Chair Christian Wenaweser, "the willingness of all sides to make massive concessions" reflected a unique spirit of negotiations that "would probably be very difficult to recreate in the future." Wenaweser, "Reaching the Kampala Compromise on Aggression," *supra* note 47, 887.

53 Resolution RC/Res. 6, "Amendments to the Rome Statute of the International Criminal Court on the Crime of Aggression," adopted at the 13th Plenary Meeting, on 11 June 2010, Annex I, 18. Available at: https://treaties.un.org/doc/source/docs/RC-Res.6-ENG.pdf.

54 Ibid., Annex II, 21.

- The compromise amendments of Article 15bis and Article 15ter on the exercise of jurisdiction over the crime of aggression inserted after Art. 15 of the Statute, which finally distinguished between the Security Council referral (Art. 15ter) and state referral, *proprio motu* investigation (Art. 15bis).

Being the hardest outstanding aspect of the ICC Statute Renegotiation process, this distinction incorporated the two-filter approach: the nonexclusive jurisdictional filter of the Security Council attributing to it a primary but not exclusive jurisdiction, and the additional jurisdictional filter of the Pre-Trial Division of the Court, which could authorize an investigation where no determination of the act of aggression has been made by the Security Council. However, this two-pillar jurisdictional regime where the Security Council has a primary but not exclusive jurisdiction is to be made operable on the basis of collectively specified, balancing, substantive, and procedural conditions. It was agreed that the vested referential power of the Security Council to the Court for a crime of aggression was undisputable, minimalistic,[55] and not subject to any state consent, while it can decide the deferral of ICC proceedings as provided in Art. 16 of the Statute. On the other hand, and in order to counterbalance the strong insistence on the monopoly of Security Council with respect to the ICC aggression proceedings, the referential power of states and the *proprio motu* investigation was extensively qualified: the Pre-Trial Division operates as an additional judicial filter to the Security Council, commencing the investigation in respect of a crime of aggression "where no such determination is made" by the Security Council and the latter has not decided to suspend the ICC proceedings according to Art. 16 of the Statute (Art. 15bis (8)); non-state parties are thoroughly exempted from the jurisdiction of the Court over the crime of aggression (Art.15bis (5)), whereas an opt-out regime applies to state parties if they have previously declared that they do not accept such jurisdiction "by lodging a declaration with the Registrar" (Art. 15bis (4)). Finally, the activation of the exercise of the jurisdiction of the Court over the crime of aggression under both new articles was conditioned, after intense negotiation until the last minute, upon the same activation formula: it is "subject to a decision to be taken after 1 January 2017 by the same majority of States Parties as is required for the adoption of an amendment to the Statute."[56]

- The frame of understandings regarding the amendments to the Rome Statute of the ICC on the crime of aggression.

[55] As Kress remarks, Article 15ter does not provide that the Security Council should "make a determination of an act of aggression," and, in effect, "(it) embraces the idea that the Council may wish to give the 'green light' to an investigation without making the strongest determination available under Article 39 of the UN Charter." Kress and von Holtzendorff, "The Kampala Compromise on the Crime of Aggression," *supra* note 39, 1211.

[56] Art. 15bis (3) and Art. 15ter (3), Resolution RC/Res. 6, op. cit., thus requiring a two-thirds majority of state parties in accordance with Art. 121(3) of the Statute on Amendments.

> These carefully formulated understandings set out an authoritative interpretative frame of the Statute that facilitated the consensus on its amendments. They provide clarifications regarding the exercise of the Court's jurisdiction on the basis of the referrals by the Security Council, the *ratione temporis* exercise of the jurisdiction of the Court, and the interpretation of the amendments as not creating "the right or obligation to exercise domestic jurisdiction with respect to an act of aggression committed by another State" (negation of the application of the ICC Statute complementarity principle).[57] The last two understandings concerning the criteria of establishing an act of aggression and the consideration of its three components (character, gravity, and scale) played an important role in achieving the widest possible balancing of interests and "in clearing the path to an overall agreement"[58] at the time of Renegotiation, while their institutional workability remains to be seen.

The Kampala revisionary compromise and its morphological pattern has taken the form of a *framework–specification provision continuum*, subject to the appropriate amendment procedure prescribed in the ICC Statute, also encompassing a space for interpretative understandings accommodating diverging interests. As such, on the one hand, it has a constitutive aspect and resembles Constitutive Negotiation,[59] and, on the other hand, it is properly adapted to the established treaty regime and functions within the bounds of its multilevel amendment procedure. In other words, negotiation, in this particular context, evolved in the twilight zone between the Constitutive Negotiation and Renegotiation processes. The negotiably achieved collective development of the underdetermined treaty substance is not a product of the "living experience" of the treaty regime. It is an intensely negotiated specification of its framework formulation carried out instrumentally, for the more comprehensive, contextually efficient, and institutionally effective implementation of the relational treaty regime serving ICI. Hence, the significance of inventing and employing a variety of complementary negotiating techniques guiding this hybrid Renegotiation process.

57 Ibid., Annex III, para. 5.

58 Kress and von Holtzendorff, "The Kampala Compromise on the Crime of Aggression," *supra* note 39, 1207.

59 Echoing this constitutive function, it was pertinently observed that the Kampala Compromise "allows the completion of the codification of the existing body of crimes under customary international law," and "it stands for a most significant legal development in the most sensitive area of international criminal justice and, by implication, in international security law in general." N. Blokker and C. Kress, "A Consensus Agreement on the Crime of Aggression: Impressions from Kampala." 23(4) *LJIL* (2010), 889, 894–895.

Bibliography

Allot, P. *Eunomia: New Order for a New World*. Oxford University Press, 1990.

Alvarez, J. E. *International Organizations as Law-Makers*. Oxford University Press, 2005.

"The New Treaty Makers." 25 *Boston College International and Comparative Law* (2002), 213–234.

Anderson, K. "The Ottawa Convention Banning Landmines, the Role of International Non-Governmental Organizations and the Idea of International Civil Society." 11 *EJIL* (2000), 91–120.

Andresen, S., Skodvin, T., Underal, A., and Wettestad, J. *Science and Politics in International Environmental Regimes: Between Integrity and Involvement*. Manchester University Press, 2000.

Antonakis, J. and House, R. J. "The Full-Range Leadership Theory: The Way Forward." In B. Avolio and F. Yammarino (eds.), *Transformational and Charismatic Leadership: The Road Ahead*. JAI, 2002, 3–34.

Aristotle. *Metaphysics*, vol. XVII (transl. by H. Tredennick). Loeb Classical Library, Harvard University Press, 1932.

Nicomachean Ethics, vol. XIX (transl. by H. Rackham). Loeb Classical Library, Harvard University Press, 1926 (reprinted 1999).

Physics, vol. IV (transl. by P. H. Wicksteed and F. M. Cornford). Loeb Classical Library, Harvard University Press, 1957.

Politics, vol. XXI (transl. by H. Rackham). Loeb Classical Library, Harvard University Press, 1932 (reprinted 1998).

Posterior Analytics, vol. II (transl. by H. Tredennick and E. S. Forster). Loeb Classical Library, Harvard University Press, 1960.

Aust, A. *Modern Treaty Law and Practice* (3rd edn). Cambridge University Press, 2013.

Barriga, S. "Against the Odds: The Results of the Special Working Group on the Crime of Aggression." In R. Bellelli (ed.), *International Criminal Justice: Law and Practice from the Rome Statute to Its Review*. Ashgate Publishing, 2010, 621–643.

"Introduction to the Negotiation History." In Stefan Barriga and Claus Kress (eds.), *The Travaux Préparatoires of the Crime of Aggression*. Cambridge University Press, 2011, 1–98.

Benedick, R. E. "Perspectives of a Negotiation Practitioner." In G. Sjosted (ed.), *International Environmental Negotiations*. SAGE Publications, 1993, 219–243.

Blokker, N. and Kress, C. "A Consensus Agreement on the Crime of Aggression: Impressions from Kampala." 23(4) *LJIL* (2010), 889–895.

Brown Weiss, E. "Strengthening National Compliance with International Environmental Agreements." 27(4) *Environmental Policy and Law* (1997), 297–303.
Cardiner, R. *Treaty Interpretation*. The Oxford International Law Library. Oxford University Press, 2008.
Cash, D. W., Clark, W. C., Alcock, F., Dickson, N. M., Eckley, N., Guston, D. H., Jager, J., and Mitchell, R. B. "Knowledge Systems for Sustainable Development." 100(14) *Proceedings of the National Academy of Sciences* (2003), 8086–8091.
Charney, J. I. "Technology and International Negotiations." 76 *AJIL* (1982), 78–118.
Chossudovsky, E. M. *The Helsinki Final Act Viewed in the United Nations Perspective: Towards Strengthening the Continuity and Coherence of the Follow-Up to the Conference on Security and Cooperation in Europe*, UNITAR 1980, Research Report No. 24.
Churchill, R. R. and Ufstein, G. "Autonomous Institutional Arrangements in Multilateral Environmental Agreements: A Little-Noticed Phenomenon in International Law." 94 *AJIL* (2000), 623–659.
Collingwood, V. "Non-Governmental Organisations, Power and Legitimacy in International Society." 32 *Review of International Studies* (2006), 439–454.
Commission on Global Governance. *Our Global Neighborhood*. Oxford University Press, 1995.
Cook, S. D. N. and Brown, J. S. "Bridging Epistemologies: The Generative Dance between Organizational Knowledge and Organizational Knowing." 10(4) *Organization Science* (1999), 381–400. Edited version (2005). Available at: www.sagepub.com/upm-data/9926_039585Ch03.pdf.
Cooney, R. and Lang, A. "Taking Uncertainty Seriously: Adaptive Governance, Alien Invasive Species and the WTO." 18 *EJIL* (2007), 523–551.
Costa, A. et al. "Your Morals Depend on Language." *Plos One*, 23 April 2014. Available at: www.plosone.org/article/info%3Adoi%2F10.1371%2Fjournal.pone.0094842.
Crawford, J. "Responsibility for Breaches of Communitarian Norms: An Appraisal of Article 48 of the ILC Articles on Responsibility of States for Internationally Wrongful Acts." In U. Fastenrath, R. Geiger, D.-E. Khan, A. Paulus, S. von Schorlemer, and C. Vedder (eds.), *From Bilateralism to Community Interest: Essays in Honour of Judge Bruno Simma*. Oxford University Press, 2011, 224. Doi: 10.1093/acprof:oso/9780199588817.003.0017
Cross, J. "Negotiation as Adaptive Learning." 1 *International Negotiation* (1996), 153–178.
David, A. E. *The Strategy of Treaty Termination: Lawful Breaches and Retaliations*. Yale University Press, 1975.
De Bono, E. *Lateral Thinking: Creativity Step by Step*. Harper & Row, 1970.
Serious Creativity: Using the Power of Lateral Thinking to Create New Ideas. HarperBusiness, 1992.
De Burca, G. "The European Union in the Negotiation of the UN Disability Convention." 35 (2) *European Law Review* (2010), 174–196.
Dobelli, R. *The Art of Thinking Clearly* (transl. by N. Griffin). Harper, 2013.
Dowdle, M. W. (ed.). *Public Accountability: Design, Dilemmas and Experiences*. Cambridge University Press, 2006.
Drury, J. L. et al. "Sympathetic Decisions: Incorporating Impacts on Others into Emergency Response Decision Spaces." In T. Comes, F. Fiedrich, S. Fortier, J. Geldermann, and T. Müller (eds.), *Proceedings of the 10th International ISCRAM Conference*. Baden-Baden, Germany, May 2013, 199–209. Available at: www.iscramlive.org/ISCRAM2013/files/132.pdf.

Dworkin, R. M. "Is Law a System of Rules?" In R. M. Dworkin (ed.), *The Philosophy of Law*. Oxford Readings in Philosophy. Oxford University Press, 1977, 38–65.

Edmonds, M. "Government Contracting and Renegotiation: A Comparative Analysis." 50(1) Public Administration (1972), 45–64. Published online in April 2007. http://onlinelibrary.wiley.com/doi/10.1111/j.1467-9299.1972.tb00080.x/pdf

Fellmeth, A. X. and Horwitz, M. *Guide to Latin in International Law*. Oxford University Press, 2009.

Fisher, R. and Ury, W., with Patton, B. (ed.). *Getting to YES: Negotiating Agreement without Giving In*. Penguin Books. 1991.

Frei, D. *Evolving a Conceptual Framework of Inter-Systems Relations: Elements for a Common Theoretical Approach to Cooperative Transactions in East–West Relationships*. UNITAR 1980, Research Report No. 25.

Fuller, L. L. "The Forms and Limits of Adjudication." 92 *Harvard Law Review* (1978–1979), 353–409.

Funtowicz, S. O. and Ravetz, J. R. "Global Risk, Uncertainty, and Ignorance." In J. X. Kasperson and R. E. Kasperson (eds.), *Global Environmental Risk*. United Nations University Press, Earthscan, 2001, 73–94.

Galinksy, A. D. "When to Make the First Offer in Negotiations." Available at: http://hbswk.hbs.edu/archive/4302.html.

Gigerenzer, G. and Gaissmaier, W. "Heuristic Decision Making." 62 *Annual Review of Psychology* (2011), 451–482.

Goldman, A. and Rojot, J. *Negotiation: Theory and Practice*. Kluwer Law International, 2002.

Haas, P. *Saving the Mediterranean: The Politics of International Environmental Cooperation*, Columbia University Press, 1990.

"Science Policy for Multilateral Environmental Governance." In N. Kanie and P. M. Haas (eds.), *Emerging Forces in Environmental Governance*, United Nations University Press, 2004, 115–136.

Hall, D. L., Hellar, B., and McNeese, M. "Rethinking the Data Overload Problem: Closing the Gap between Situation Assessment and Decision Making." In *Proceedings of the 2007 National Symposium on Sensor and Data Fusion (NSSDF) Military Symposia (MSS)*, Mc Lean, VA, 2007.

Hall, N., Displacement, Development, and Climate Change: International Organizations Moving beyond Their Mandates, Global Institutions Series, Rutledge, 2016.

Kahn-Freund, O. *Labour and the Law*. Stevens & Sons, 1977.

Kelley, J. G. *Scorecard Diplomacy*. Cambridge University Press, 2017.

Keohane, R. "The Concept of Accountability in World Politics and the Use of Force." 24 *Michigan Journal of International Law* (2003), 1121–1141.

Keysar, B., Hayakawa, S. L., and An, S. G. "The Foreign-Language Effect: Thinking in a Foreign Tongue Reduces Decision Biases." 23 *Psychological Science* (2012), 661–668.

Kirton, M. J. *Adaption-Innovation: In the Context of Diversity and Change*. Routledge, 2003 (Repr. 2011).

Klabbers, J. "The EJIL Foreword: The Transformation of International Organizations Law." 26 *EJIL* (2015), 9–82.

Koh, T. "A Constitution for the Oceans." Remarks. Available at: www.un.org/depts/los/convention_agreements/texts/koh_english.pdf.

Koh, T. B. and Jayakumar, S. "The Negotiating Process of the Third United Nations Conference on the Law of the Sea." In M. H. Nordquist (ed.), *United Nations Convention on the Law of the Sea 1982: A Commentary*, vol. 1. Martinus Nijhoff, 1985, 29–134.

Koremenos, B. *The Continent of International Law: Explaining Agreement Design*. Cambridge University Press, 2016.

Koskenniemi, M. "Constitutionalism as a Mindset: Reflections on Kantian Themes about International Law and Globalisation." 8 *Theoretical Inquiries in Law* (2007), 9–36.

"The Fate of Public International Law." 70 *MLR* (2007), 1–30.

Kratochwil, F. *The Status of Law in World Society: Meditations on the Role of the Rule of Law*. Cambridge Studies in International Relations. Cambridge University Press, 2014.

Kress, C. and von Holtzendorff, L. "The Kampala Compromise on the Crime of Aggression." 8 *Journal of International Criminal Justice* (2010), 1179–1217.

Kuhn, T. S. "Dubbing and Redubbing: The Vulnerability of Rigid Designation." In C. Savage (ed.), *Scientific Theory*. University of Minnesota Press, 1990, 298–318.

The Essential Tension: Selected Studies in Scientific Tradition and Change. University of Chicago Press, 1977.

"Objectivity, Value Judgment and Theory Choice." In *The Essential Tension: Selected Studies in Scientific Tradition and Change*. University of Chicago Press, 1977, 320–339.

Levinson, S. C. *Pragmatics*. Cambridge University Press, 1983.

Lichtenberg, G. C. *"Waste Books" (Sudelbücher)* (translation, with an introduction by R. J. Hollingdale). NYBR Classics, 2000.

Llewellyn, K. N. "What Price Contract? An Essay in Perspective." 40 *Yale Law Journal* (1931), 704–751.

MacNeil, I. R. *The New Social Contract: An Inquiry into Modern Contractual Relations*. Yale University Press, 1980.

Majone, G. "Science and Tran-Science in Standard Setting." 9 *Science Technology and Human Values Journal* (1984), 15–22.

Martineau, A.-C. "The Rhetoric of Fragmentation: Fear and Faith in International Law." 22 *LJIL* (2009), 1–19.

Matthews, J. T. "Power Shift." 76(1) *Foreign Affairs* (1997), 56–66. Also available at: www.foreignaffairs.com/articles/52644/jessica-t-mathews/power-shift.

Maslow, A. H. *The Farther Reaches of Human Nature*, Viking Press, 1971.

Motivation and Personality. Harper, 1954.

McConnell, M. L. "The Relationship between Science and Politics in Environmental Negotiations." In E. Raftopoulos and M. L. McConnell (eds.), *Contributions to International Environmental Negotiation in the Mediterranean Context*. MEPIELAN Studies in International Environmental Law and Negotiation-2, Nomiki Bibliothiki SA – Bruylant, 2014 (Repr. first edn, 2004) Part II, 81–92.

McDougal, M. and Reisman, W. M. "The Prescribing Function in World Constitutive Process: How International Law Is Made" (1980). Faculty Scholarship Series. Paper 2661. Available at: http://digitalcommons.law.yale.edu/fss_papers/2661.

McGann, J. and Johnstone, M. "The Power Shift and the NGO Credibility Crisis." 11 *Brown Journal of World Affairs* (2005), 159–171.

Merrills, J. G. *International Dispute Settlement* (3rd edn). Cambridge University Press, 1998.

Meyer, M. "The Rise of the Knowledge Broker." 32(1) *Science Communication* (2010)SAGE Publications, 118–127. Available at: http://scx.sagepub.com/content/32/1/118.

Michels, R. *Political Parties*. Free Press, 1962.

Minsky, M. "A Framework for Representing Knowledge." In P. H. Winston (ed.), *The Psychology of Computer Vision*. McGraw-Hill, 1975, 211–281. Also available at: http://web.media.mit.edu/~minsky/papers/Frames/frames.html.

Monk, R. *Ludwig Wittgenstein: The Duty of Genius*. Vintage, 1991.

Narlikar, A. (ed.), *Deadlocks in Multilateral Negotiations: Causes and Solutions*, Introduction. Cambridge University Press, 2010.

O'Neill, K. *The Environment and International Relations* (2nd edn). Cambridge University Press, 2017.

Oldham, G. and McLean, R. "Approaches to Knowledge-Brokering." 1997. Available at: www.iisd.org/pdf/2001/networks_knowledge_brokering.pdf.

Oppenheim, L. (ed.), *The Collected Papers of John Westlake on Public International Law*. Cambridge University Press, 1914 (paperback edn, 2014).

Osborn, A. F. *Applied Imagination: Principles and Procedures of Creative Thinking*. Scribner, 1953.

Parry, C. *The Sources and Evidences of International Law*. Manchester University Press-Oceana Publications Inc., 1965.

"Of Treaties." In A. Parry (ed.), *Collected Papers of Clive Parry*, vol. II. Wildy, Simmonds and Hill Publishing, 2012, 289–307.

Patton, B. "On Teaching Negotiation." In M. Wheeler (ed.), *Teaching Negotiation: Ideas and Innovations*. PON Books, 2000, 7–61.

Peters, A. "Universalist Assumptions and Implications of Comparative Law: Should They Be Deconstructed?" In *Proceedings of the 93rd Annual Meeting of the American Society of International Law*, 1999, 366–369.

Peters, B. G. and Pierre, J. *Comparative Governance: Rediscovering the Functional Dimension of Governing*. Cambridge University Press, 2016.

Polanyi, M. *Personal Knowledge: Towards a Post-Critical Philosophy*. University of Chicago Press, 1958.

Pollux. "The Interpretation of the Charter." 23 *BYBIL* (1946), 54–82.

Program on Negotiation Harvard Law School. "About the Harvard Negotiation Project." 19 April, 2009. Available at: www.pon.harvard.edu/research_projects/harvard-negotiation-project/hnp/.

Pound, R. *An Introduction to the Philosophy of Law*. Yale University Press, 1954.

Raftopoulos, E. *Barcelona Convention and Protocols: The Mediterranean Action Plan Regime*. Simmonds & Hill Publishing Ltd., 1993.

Conventional Environmental Governance and the Mediterranean or PLUS ULTRA (In Greek). Nomiki Bibliothiki SA, 2014 (Repr. first edn, 2006).

"Conventional Environmental Governance in the Mediterranean and Its Evolving Institutional and Fiduciary Aspects in a Pragmatic Perspective." 30 *Ocean Yearbook* (2016), 129–173.

Course, Theory and Language of International Law: "Objectivity" or International Common Interest?" (In Greek). Nomiki Bibliothiki SA, 2014 (Repr. first edn, 1997).

The Inadequacy of the Contractual Analogy in the Law of Treaties. Publications of the Hellenic Institute of International and Foreign Law. Athens, 1990.

"International Environmental Negotiation as a Governance Technique." In E. Raftopoulos and M. L. McConnell (eds.), *Contributions to International Environmental Negotiation in the Mediterranean Context*. MEPIELAN Studies in International Environmental Law and Negotiation-2. Nomiki Bibliothiki SA – Bruylant, 2014 (Repr. first edn, 2004) Part I, 3–64.

"Theorizing about Conventional Environmental Sea-Regimes as International Trusts: The Case of the Barcelona Convention System." In R. Wolfrum, M. Seršić, and T. M. Šošić (eds.), *Contemporary Developments in International Law: Essays in Honour of Budislav Vukas*. Brill-Nijhoff, 2015, Part 2, Law of the Sea, 263–290.

Raiffa, H. *The Art and Science of* Negotiation. Harvard University Press, 1982.

Rajamani, L. "The Cancun Climate Agreements: Reading the Text, Subtext and Tea Leaves." 60 *ICLQ* (2011), 499–519.

Renton Commission. *The Preparation of Legislation*. Report of the Renton Commission, London, Cmnd. 6053, 1973.

Riles, A. "Models and Documents: Artifacts of International Legal Knowledge." 48 *ICLQ* (1999), 805–825.

Roucounas, E. "Facteurs Privès et Droit International Public." 299 *Recueil des Cours de l' Académie de Droit International de la Haye* (2002), 1–419.

Rovelli, C. *Reality Is Not What It Seems: The Journey to Quantum Gravity* (transl. by S. Carnell and E. Serge). Allen Lane-Penguin Random House UK, 2016.

Rowold, J. "Instrumental Leadership: Extending the Transformational-Transactional Leadership Paradigm. Zeitschrift für Personalforschung." 28(3) *German Journal of Research in Human Resource Management* (2014), 367–390.

Sand, P. "Sovereignty Bounded: Public Trusteeship for Common Pool Resources?" 4(1) *Global Environmental Politics* (2004), 47–71.

Schwarz, M. and Sonin, K. "A Theory of Brinkmanship, Conflicts, and Commitments." 24(1) *Journal of Law, Economics & Organization* (2008), 163–183.

Scott, B. *The Skills of Negotiating*. Wildwood House, 1986.

Sebenius, J. K. "International Negotiation Analysis." In V. A. Kremenyuk (ed.), *International Negotiation: Analysis, Approaches, Issues* (2nd edn). Jossey-Bass – A Wiley Company, 2002, 229–255.

"Negotiation Arithmetic: Adding and Subtracting Issues and Parties." 37 *International Organization* (1983), 292–298.

Sjostedt, G. "Negotiation on Trade and the Environment: Variation in the Multilateral Approach." In V. A. Kremenyuk (ed.), *International Negotiation: Analysis, Approaches, Issues* (2nd edn). Jossey-Bass – A Wiley Company, 2002, 362–374.

Smith, T. H. "Metaphors for Navigating Negotiations." 21(3) *Negotiation Journal* (2005), 343–364.

Sohn, L. B. "United National Decision-Making: Confrontation or Consensus?" 1 *Harvard International Law Journal* (1974), 438–445.

Spector, B. I. *Negotiation as Learning: Pedagogy and Theory*. A paper in Honor of Bill Zartman. Presented at the Annual Conference of the International Studies Association, March 2, 2007, Chicago.

Starkey, B., Boyer, M. A., and Wilkenfeld, J. *International Negotiation in a Complex World*. Rowman & Littlefield, 2015.

Steinman, B. A., Mann, M. E., and Miller, S. K. "Atlantic and Pacific Multidecadal Oscillations and Northern Hemisphere Temperatures." 347(6225) *Science* (2015).

Susskind, L. E. *Environmental Diplomacy: Negotiating More Effective Global Agreements*. Oxford University Press, 1994.

Trebilcock, A. "Labour Resources and Human Resources Management." In *ILO Encyclopaedia of Occupational Health and Safety* (4th edn), Part III, Chapter 21. Available at: www.ilocis.org/documents/chpt21e.htm.

Tribe, L. H. "The Curvature of Constitutional Space: What Lawyers Can Learn from Modern Physics." 103 *Harvard Law Review* (1989), 1–39.

Triepel, H. *Völkerrecht und Landesrecht, Leipzig, 1899/Droit International et Droit Interne* (transl. by René Brunet). Bibliothèque Française de Droit des Gens de la Fondation Carnegie, 1920.

Twining, W. and Miers, D. *How to Do Things with Rules* (5th edn). Cambridge University Press, 2010.

UNESCO. The Future of Scientific Advice to the United Nations: A Summary Report to the Secretary-General of the United Nations from the Scientific Advisory Board, September 2016, 1–32.
Viñuales, J. "The Paris Climate Agreement: Less Is More." 59 *GYIL* (2017), 11–45.
Waldron, J. "Legislators' Intentions and Unintentional Legislation." In E. Marmor (ed.), *Law and Interpretation: Essays in Legal Philosophy*. Clarendon Press, 1997, 329–357.
Walton, R. E. and McKersie, R. B. A *Behavioral Theory of Labor Negotiations: An Analysis of a Social Interaction System*. McGraw-Hill, 1965.
Webber, G. C. N. *The Negotiable Constitution: On the Limitation of Rights*. Cambridge University Press, 2009.
Wenaweser, C. "Reaching the Kampala Compromise on Aggression: The Chair's Perspective." 23(4) *LJIL* (2010), 883–887.
Wendt, A. *Quantum Mind and Social Science: Unifying Physical and Social Ontology*. Cambridge University Press, 2015.
Whorf, B. L. "Language, Mind and Reality." In J. B. Carroll (ed.), *Language, Thought and Reality: Selected Writings of Benjamin Lee Whorf*. MIT Press, 1956.
Widdows, K. "The Unilateral Denunciation of Treaties Containing No Denunciation Clause." 53 *BYBIL* (1982), 83–114.
Wittgenstein, L. *Philosophical Investigations* (transl. by G. E. M. Anscombe). Basil Blackwell, 1976.
Woodward, B. *Plan of Attack*. Wheeler Large Print Book Series, 2004.
Young, O. *Protecting the Environment in a Stateless Society*. Cornell University Press, 1994.
Zartman, I. W. and Berman, M. R. *The Practical Negotiator*. Yale University Press, 1982.

Index

Aarhus Convention on Access to Information, Public Participation in Decision-Making and Access to Justice in Environmental Matters, 117, 163–164, 171, 175, 183, 190–191
"Academization," 244
Ad Hoc Multilateral Conferences
overview, 105
agendas, 110–113
Declarations, patternment of, 113–118
Diplomatic Conferences, 106–108
Final Communiqués, 118–119
functions of, 106–108
initiators, role of, 110–113
management techniques, 108–109
personalities, 111–113
place, 110–111
plan, 110–111
Preparatory Conferences, 106–108
purpose, 110–111
single negotiating texts, 109–110
structure of, 106–108
Supporting Reports, 109
Ad Hoc Working Groups of Legal and Technical Experts
in constitutive phase of negotiation, 58, 122–123, 218
in multilateral governance, 190–191
in prescriptive transformative model of negotiation, 36
in renegotiation phase, 58–59, 224, 227, 239
Ad referendum
agreements, 125, 136
views, 70
Agendas
Ad Hoc Multilateral Conferences, 110–113
Rules of Procedure, 139
Aggression, crime of
codification of, 249
Conference Room Paper (CRP), 246–249
defined, 246
Kampala Review Conference, 246–249
Princeton Process, 244–245
renegotiation phase and, 240–249
Rome Compromise, 240–242
Rome Statute of ICC and, 240–242, 244–245, 246–249
Special Working Group on the Crime of Aggression (SWGCA), 242–247
twinning renegotiation, 243–245
Agreement on Trade Related Aspects of Intellectual Property Rights (TRIPS Agreement), 166–167
Allott, P., 60, 66, 72
Alvarez, J.E., 34
Amendments
multilateral governance and, 197–202
renegotiation phase, amendment versus replacement, 231–233
Rules of Procedure, 148
Analogies
in domestic law, 20–21
in law of treaties, 45–46, 157, 189
private law contract, 45–46, 156–157, 189, 232
Analysis stage, 23
Anchoring effect, 16
Anderson, K., 64–65
Aristotle, 60, 62, 68
Arms Trade Treaty, 160
Asia Pacific Economic Council (APEC), 62–63
Athens Convention relating to the Carriage of Passengers and their Luggage by Sea, 205–206
Aust, A., 146–147, 163

Bamako Convention on the Ban of the Import into Africa and the Control of Transboundary Movement and Management of Hazardous Wastes Within Africa, 167–168, 187
Bank for International Settlements, 62–63
Barcelona Convention for the Protection of the Marine Environment and Coastal Region of the Mediterranean
- morphological patternment and, 156
- multilateral governance and, 183, 185, 191
- normative patternment and, 167–168, 169–170
- referential patternment and, 151, 152
- renegotiation phase and, 228, 236–238
- Rules of Procedure, 137

Barcelona Convention Protocol on Integrated Coastal Zone Management in the Mediterranean, 179
Barcelona Convention Protocol on Specially Protected Areas and Biodiversity, 167
Barnier, M., 54
Barriga, S., 246
Basel Convention on the Control of Transboundary Movements of Hazardous Wastes and Their Disposal, 117, 124, 137, 152, 162, 167–168, 195
Battle of Balaklava (1854), 17
Berman, M.R., 76
Best Alternative to a Negotiated Declaration (BATNDE), 24–26
Best Available Solution to a Negotiated Agreement (BATNA), 24–26
Bilateral investment agreements, 235
Brackets system, 216–217
Brainstorming sessions, 211–213
Brexit, 53–54
"Brinkmanship," 131–132
Brown Weiss, E., 188
Bucharest Convention on the Protection of the Black Sea Against Pollution, 199, 204
Bush, George W., 235

Cairo Guidelines and Principles for the Environmentally Sound Management of Hazardous Wastes, 117
Cancun Agreements, 130
Charney, J.J., 104
Charter for European Security (1999), 62–63
Charter of Paris for a New Europe (1990), 62–63
Chemical Weapons Convention. *See* Convention on Chemical Weapons
Chess metaphor, 52–53
Chossudovsky, E.M., 27
Cicero, 60
Climate change, 233
Collective agreements, 43–45
Collective bargaining process, 43–45
Collective institutional entities, 62–64
Committee against Torture, 186–187
Committee of Enforced Disappearances, 193
Committee on the Protection of the Rights of All Migrant Workers and Members of Their Families, 193
Committee on the Rights of the Child, 193
Compatibility test, 205–206
Complementarity
- overview, 20–21
- creative negotiation and, 45–48
- between negotiation and treaty, 1–2, 4–5

Comprehensive Test Ban Treaty, 187, 192–193
Conference on Environmental and Development, 237–238
Conference on the Law of the Sea, 163–164
Conference Room Papers (CRPs), 218, 246–249
Conferences of Plenipotentiaries, 219–221
Conferences of the Contracting Parties (COPs), 183–185, 191, 198–200
Consensus procedure
- overview, 26
- consensus relational level, 128–131
  - individual objection, 129, 130, 131
  - package deal procedure, 129, 131–133, 247
- "constructing-negotiating" aspect, 127–128
- defined, 127
- organizational management level, 132–136
  - overview, 132–133
  - conference-scaling practices, 134–136
  - fragmentation of issues and, 133–134
  - inner-communication system, 135
  - lateral expansion of issues and, 133–134
  - miniaturization of conferences, 134–136
  - sub-fora, 134–136
- "resulting-normative" aspect, 127–128
- strategic management level, 131–132
  - "hold-out position" strategy, 132
- UNCLOS and, 127
- Vienna Convention on the Law of Treaties and, 126–127, 131

Constitutive phase of negotiation
- overview, 7–8, 120–121
- Ad Hoc Working Groups of Legal and Technical Experts in, 58, 122–123, 218
- Conferences of Plenipotentiaries, 219–221
- consensus procedure (*See* Consensus procedure)
- creative negotiation and, 57–58
- Diplomatic Conferences, 219–221

Final Acts and, 125–126, 219–221
Intergovernmental Negotiating Committees, 122–123
multilateral governance and (*See* Multilateral governance)
negotiation-generating decision, 122
methodological elements, 122
procedural elements, 122
referential elements, 122
outcome of, 219–221
political initiative, 121
Rules of Procedure (*See* Rules of Procedure)
Secretariat, role of, 58, 123–126
Special Techniques and Practices
overview, 210
brackets system, 216–217
brainstorming sessions, 211–213
inter-sessional workshops, 213–215
non-negotiation texts, 218–219
"non-papers," 218–219
opening statements, 210–211
recording of names, 217–218
side-events, 215–216
textual pattern, negotiation of, 149
morphological patternment (*See* Morphological patternment)
normative patternment (*See* Normative patternment)
referential patternment (*See* Referential patternment)
Contextual nature of creative negotiation, 59–69
overview, 42
collective institutional entities and, 62–64
"jigsaw configuration," 68
NGOs and, 64–66
ordering-induced context, 66–68
reference configuration conditions, 55–56, 100, 150, 227
sovereign states and, 61–62
subjectively-induced context, 60–61
teleological causation and, 68
Contextual order, 227–228
Contract view of treaties, 45–47
Controllability level of multilateral governance
overview, 187–188
accountability and, 188
compliance and, 189–193
dispute settlement and, 193–197
"umbrella procedural system," 193–197
Convention Against Corruption, 117, 174, 184, 207
Convention Against Torture and Other Cruel, Inhuman or Degrading Treatment or Punishment, 162, 168–169, 177, 186–187, 193
Convention Against Transnational Organized Crime, 156
Conventional Forces in Europe Treaty, 233
Conventional recasting, 231–233
Convention on Biological Diversity, 162, 195, 204
Convention on Chemical Weapons
multilateral governance and, 174, 175, 185–186, 192, 196, 200–201, 208
normative patternment and, 163–164, 168–169
Convention on Combating Bribery of Foreign Public Officials in International Business Transactions (OECD), 117
Convention on the Law of the Non-Navigational Uses of International Watercourses, 195–196
Convention on the Law of the Sea (UNCLOS)
consensus procedure and, 127
multilateral governance and, 204–205
normative patternment and, 162–164, 166
referential patternment and, 151, 152, 154
Convention on the Privileges and Immunities of the United Nations, 1946, 74
Convention on the Prohibition of the Development, Production, Stockpiling and Use of Chemical Weapons and on their Destruction, 162
Convention on the Protection and Promotion of Diversity of Cultural Expressions, 153
Convention on the Protection of the Underwater Cultural Heritage, 162
Convention on the Rights of Persons with Disabilities, 64, 65, 123
Convention on the Rights of the Child, 193
Conventions. *See specific Convention*
Conventions on Nuclear Accidents (IAEA), 195
Convention to Combat Desertification, 158, 204
Costa, A., 49
"Craving for generality," 14
Crawford, J., 61
Creative attribution of meaning, 163–164
Creative negotiation
overview, 6–7, 41
contextual nature of, 59–69
overview, 42
collective institutional entities and, 62–64
"jigsaw configuration," 68
NGOs and, 64–66
ordering-induced context, 66–68
reference configuration conditions, 55–56, 100, 150, 227
sovereign states and, 61–62
subjectively-induced context, 60–61
teleological causation and, 68

Creative negotiation (cont.)
defined, 45
international relations (IR) theory and, 47
phased-structure of, 54–59
overview, 42
constitutive phase (*See* Constitutive phase of negotiation)
dual referentiality and, 54–55
multilateral governance process in, 55–56
prenegotiation phase (*See* Prenegotiation phase)
renegotiation phase (*See* Renegotiation phase)
positivist international law and, 45–47
relational nature of, 43–48
overview, 41
collective bargaining process and, 43–45
complementarity and, 45–48
subjectivity of
overview, 42–43, 69
accountability of negotiating team, 79–81
decision configuration of negotiating team, 74–79
organization of negotiating team, 74–79
process advisory role of negotiating team, 81–82
setting up of negotiating team, 69–74
textual nature of, 48–54
overview, 42
"hard law" versus "soft law," 48
negotiating metaphors and, 52–54
working language and, 48–52
Crimean War, 17

Deadlock, 144
De Burca, G., 65
Declaration against Corruption and Bribery in International Commercial Transactions, 117
Declarations
"considering part," 113–114, 116–117
elaboration, 236
Memoranda of Understanding (MOU), 117–118
new guidance, 236
"ordering part," 114–117
patternment of, 113–118
renegotiation phase and, 235–238
updates, 236
Definitions, 161–164
Denunciation clauses, 206–210, 234
Destabilizing tactics, 17–18
Diagnostic level of prenegotiation phase. *See* Prenegotiation phase
Dialectical approach, 19–20
Diplomatic Conference of Plenipotentiaries on the Establishment of an International Criminal Court, 241–242
Diplomatic Conferences, 219–221, 239
Disclaimer clauses, 166–167, 168–169
Discussion papers, 76, 244–245
Discussion stage, 23
Distributive negotiation model
overview, 2–3, 6, 13–14
anchoring effect, 16
attitude of negotiators, 16
destabilizing tactics, 17–18
multi-tiered framework in, 16–17
opening of negotiation process, effect of, 16
power of parties in, 16
strategic misrepresentations, 17–18
"zero-sum" situations and, 15–18
Divorce metaphor, 53–54
Dobelli, R., 37
Domestic order, 77–78
Drafting, legislative, 137, 162
Due institutional diligence, 224–227
Dworkin, R., 173

Earth League, 95–96
Environmental treaties, renegotiation phase, 236–238
Equitable assessment, 90
Equitable geographical distribution, 141, 142–143, 183
Equitable geographical representation, 141, 214
Equitable solution, 195–196
European Bank for Reconstruction and Development, 62–63
European Union, 62–63
"Expertise" concept, 225

FCCC. *See* Framework Convention on Climate Change (FCCC)
Final Acts
constitutive phase of negotiation and, 125–126, 219–221
prenegotiation phase and, 118–119
renegotiation phase and, 239, 241–242
Final Communiqués, 118–119
Fisher, R., 33
Foreign Corrupt Practices Act of 1977 (US), 116
Fragmentation
consensus procedure and, 133–134
of international law, 101
of issues, 31–32, 133–134

Framework Convention for the Protection of the Marine Environment of the Caspian Sea, 178, 199, 204
Framework Convention on Climate Change (FCCC), 97, 130, 162, 181, 184–185, 204
Frei, D., 26–27

Game theory, 3, 26–28
Group of Experts on Scientific Aspects of Marine Pollution (GESAMP), 163–164

Haas, P.M., 35
Hambro, E. (Pollux), 146–147
Harvard Negotiation Project, 22
Harvard Principled Negotiation Model
  overview, 2–3, 6
  analysis stage, 23
  as anthropocentric model, 23–24
  BATNA and, 24–26
  BATNDE and, 25–26
  consensus and, 26
  discussion stage, 23
  methodological axes, 22–23
  planning stage, 23
  programmatic stages, 23
  Vienna Convention on the Law of Treaties and, 24
Helsinki Convention on the Protection of the Marine Environment of the Baltic Sea Area, 199, 207
Helsinki Convention on the Transboundary Effects of Industrial Accidents, 207
Helsinki Final Act (1973), 14–15, 26–27, 30, 62–63
"Hierarchy of needs" theory, 111–113
High-level segment, 217
Horizontal coherence, 164
Horizontal management, 194, 197
Horizontal normativity, 9, 153

ICC. *See* International Criminal Court (ICC)
ICI relations. *See* International common interest (ICI) relations
ICZM Protocol, 170
Implementative Annexes, 197–198
Indicators of thematic management. *See* Normative patternment
Industrial relations, 43
  collective agreements, 43–45
  collective bargaining process, 43–45
Information Sharing Center, 186
Initiators, 88–90, 110–113
Institutional dualism, 226
Institutionality level of multilateral governance, 182–187
Integrative negotiation model
  overview, 2–3, 6, 13–14
  collective identification and determination of issues, 19
  dialectical approach, 19–20
  "non-zero-sum" situations and, 18–22
  "packaging" of issues, 19
  relational norms, 20–22
Intergovernmental Negotiating Committees, 58, 122–123
Intergovernmental Panel on Climate Change (IPCC), 51, 97, 184–185
International Atomic Energy Agency (IAEA) Conventions on Nuclear Accidents, 195
International Bank for Reconstruction and Development, 62–63
International Center for Settlement of Investment Disputes, 235
International Civil Aviation Organization (ICAO) Convention on the Making of Plastic Explosives, 204–205, 207
International common interest (ICI) relations
  overview, 1–2
  collective identification and determination of issues, 19
  consensus procedure and (*See* Consensus procedure)
  constitutive phase of negotiation (*See* Constitutive phase of negotiation)
  creative negotiation and, 6–7 (*See also* Creative negotiation)
  dialectical approach, 19–20
  multilateral governance (*See* Multilateral governance)
  "packaging" of issues, 19
  prenegotiation phase (*See* Prenegotiation phase)
  refocusing of international law, 4–5
  relational norms, 20–22
  renegotiation phase (*See* Renegotiation phase)
International Convention for Suppression of Acts of Nuclear Terrorism, 166–167
International Convention for the Protection of All Persons from Enforced Disappearance, 193
International Convention on Oil Pollution Preparedness, Response and Cooperation, 174
International Convention on the Protection of the Rights of All Migrant Workers and Members of Their Families, 193
International Court of Justice (ICJ), 126–127, 190

International Court of Justice (ICJ) (cont.)
  evolutionary approach to duty to negotiate, 190
  obligation-duty to negotiate, 190
  relational approach to treaties, 126–127
International Criminal Court (ICC)
  Diplomatic Conference of Plenipotentiaries on the Establishment of an International Criminal Court, 241–242
  Preparatory Commission, 241–242
  Rome Statute, 240–242, 244–245, 246–249
International Labour Organization (ILO) Convention 169, 151
International Law Commission (ILC), 131, 146–147
International law order, 68
International Maritime Organization (IMO), 182, 201–202, 205–206
International Monetary Fund, 62–63
International ordering
  contextual negotiation and, 42, 59–60, 68, 116
  horizontal normativity of, 9
  in international society, 62
  negotiating team and, 71
  NGOs and, 64
  polycentricity in, 101, 120
  relational negotiation and, 41
International relations (IR) theory
  challenges to, 1–2
  creative negotiation and, 47
  narration of negotiation in, 2–4
International Seabed Authority, 127
International Union for Conservation of Nature (IUCN), 184
Inter-sessional workshops, 213–215

"Joint learning," 21–22
Joint Vienna Institute (JVI), 62–63
Juncker, Jean-Claude, 53–54
Jurisdictional filters, 246

Kahn-Freund, O., 44
Kampala Review Conference, 240, 246–249. *See also* Aggression, crime of
Kampala Revisionary Compromise, 240, 246–249. *See also* Aggression, crime of
Kelley, J.G., 65
Keysar, B., 49
Klabbers, J., 63
Knowledge
  management of, 90–97
  in negotiation, 8, 35–36, 49–50, 70, 72–74, 81–82
  practical knowledge, 215
  tacit knowledge, 94–95
  usable knowledge, 92, 224–225
Knowledge brokers, 224–225
Knowledge gaps, 96, 135
Knowledge in negotiation
  relational ICI engineering, 92, 93, 94–95
  tacit knowledge, 94–95
  usable knowledge, 92
Koh, T., 134, 136
Koremenos, B., 234
Kratochwil, F., 72
Kress, C., 248
Kuhn, T.S., 93, 94
Kuwait Regional Convention for Cooperation on the Protection of the Marine Environment from Pollution, 199–200
Kyoto Protocol, 97

Labour relations, 43
Land-Based Sources Protocol, 170
Languages, 145–148
Lateral expansion of issues, 133–134
Law of the Sea. *See* Convention on the Law of the Sea (UNCLOS)
Law of the Sea Conference, 104
Law of treaties
  analogies in, 45–46, 157, 189
Legislative view of treaties
  drafting, 137, 162
  international conferences, 81
  legislative intent, 187–188
  "legislativeness" of text, 71
  negotiating team and, 71–72, 81–82
  in negotiation, 71–72, 81–82
  purpose of, 44–45, 164–170, 172–173, 174, 202
  quasi-legislative role of negotiation team, 81
  realm of, 44–45, 229
  recasting technique, 232
  use of treaty terms, 161–164
Lichtenberg, Georg Christoph, 52
Lima Convention for the Protection of the Marine Environment and Coastal Area of the South-East Pacific, 124
Local knowledge, 225
London Agreement Establishing the Charter of the Nuremberg International Military Tribunals, 241
Lugano Convention on Civil Liability for Damage Resulting from Activities Dangerous to the Environment, 150–151

MacNeil, I.R., 67
MARPOL 73/78 Convention, 201–202

Maslow, A.H., 112
McKersie, R.B., 43
"Med 21" Conference on Sustainable Development in the Mediterranean, 237–238
Mediterranean Action Plan (MAP), 228, 236–238
Meetings
- place and time, 138
- public and private sessions, 138

Meetings of the Contracting Parties (MOPs), 183–185, 191, 198–200, 236–238
Memoranda of Understanding (MOU), 117–118
Miers, D., 173
Miniaturization of conferences, 134–136
Minimata Convention on Mercury, 152–153, 219
Ministerial segment, 217
Morphological patternment
- overview, 155
- Barcelona Convention and, 156
- framework agreement – performative protocols *in processu* approach, 156–158
- integrative agreement – executing annexes *in processu* approach, 158–159
- renegotiation phase and, 229–231

Multilateral Conference on the Environment on the Causes and Prevention of Damage to Forests and Waters by Air Pollution in Europe, 105
Multilateral governance
- Ad Hoc Working Groups of Legal and Technical Experts in, 190–191
- amendments and, 197–202
- Barcelona Convention and, 183, 185, 191
- Conferences of the Contracting Parties (COPs) and, 183–185, 191, 198–200
- controllability level
  - overview, 187–188
  - accountability and, 188
  - compliance and, 189–193
  - dispute settlement and, 193–197
  - "umbrella procedural system," 193–197
- Convention on Chemical Weapons and, 174, 175, 185–186, 192, 196, 200–201, 208
- institutionality level, 182–187
- Meetings of the Contracting Parties (MOPs) and, 183–185, 191, 198–200
- prenegotiation phase and (*See also* Ad Hoc Multilateral Conferences)
  - overview, 86
  - agendas, 110–113
  - Declarations, patternment of, 113–118 (*See also* Declarations)
  - defined, 56–57
  - functions of Ad Hoc Multilateral Conferences, 106–108
  - initiators, role of, 110–113
  - institutional organization and management, 105
  - management techniques, 108–109
  - single negotiating texts, 109–110
  - structure of Ad Hoc Multilateral Conferences, 106–108
  - Supporting Reports, 109
- Secretariat, role of, 183–184
- subjectivity level, 202–210
  - denunciation clauses, 206–210
  - "plurality-in-treaty-relation," 202
  - reservations, 204–205
  - subjectification of participation, 202–204
  - withdrawal clauses, 206–210
- thematization level
  - overview, 172–173
  - assistance in developing countries, 179–180
  - financial governance, 180–181
  - general duties and obligations, 173–174
  - implementative measures, 176–178
  - information, scientific, and educational development, 178–179
  - institutional responsiveness, 176
  - internal capacity building, 179–180
  - procedural and substantive duties, 174–176
  - public participation, 178
  - relationship with other conventional regimes, 180
  - technology transfer, 179–180
- transformability level, 197–202
- UNCLOS and, 204–205
- Vienna Convention on the Law of Treaties and, 205–206, 209–210

Nagoya Protocol on Access to Genetic Resources and the Fair and Equitable Sharing of Benefits Arising from their Utilization to the Convention on Biological Diversity, 151
Narlikar, A., 144
Negotiating team
- accountability of, 79–81
- author of texts, role of, 70–72
- decision configuration of, 74–79
- ground guidelines, 74–76
- head, role of, 70
- international ordering and, 71
- inter-team negotiation, 76–77
- intra-team negotiation, 76
- legislative view of treaties and, 71–72, 81–82
- organization of, 74–79

Negotiating team (cont.)
process advisory role of, 81–82
quasi-legislative role of, 81
reports, 79–81
scientific-technical expert, role of, 72–74
setting up of, 69–74
special weight of representation, 77–78
"Neutralization" of information, 36
Non-governmental organizations (NGOs), 64–66
Non-negotiation texts, 218–219
"Non-papers," 218–219
Non-Proliferation Treaty, 190, 233
"Non-zero-sum" situations, 18–22, 28–30, 37–38
Nordic Council, 62–63
Normative patternment
overview, 159
Barcelona Convention and, 167–168, 169–170
controllability
overview, 187–188
accountability and, 188
compliance and, 189–193
dispute settlement and, 193–197
"umbrella procedural system," 193–197
Convention on Chemical Weapons and, 163–164, 168–169
disclaimer clauses, 166–167, 168–169
general duties and obligations, 170–172
general power-rights, 171, 186
geographical scope of application, 169–170
institutionality, 182–187
legislative definitions, 153–154, 161–164
creative attribution of meaning, 163–164
transference of meaning, 163–164
material scope of application, 165–169
Preamble, 160–161
scaled specification of scope of application, 167–168
statement of purpose, 164–165
subjectivity, 202–210
denunciation clauses, 206–210
"plurality-in-treaty-relation," 202
reservations, 204–205
subjectification of participation, 202–204
withdrawal clauses, 206–210
system of multilateral ICI governance (*See* Multilateral governance)
thematization
overview, 172–173
assistance in developing countries, 179–180
financial governance, 180–181
general duties and obligations, 173–174
implementative measures, 176–178
information, scientific, and educational development, 178–179
institutional responsiveness, 176
internal capacity building, 179–180
procedural and substantive duties, 174–176
public participation, 178
relationship with other conventional regimes, 180
technology transfer, 179–180
transformability, 197–202
UNCLOS and, 162–164, 166
use of terms, 161–164
Vienna Convention on the Law of Treaties and, 160
Noumea Convention for the Protection of the Natural Resources and Environment of the South Pacific Region, 124, 164, 169
Nuremberg International Military Tribunals, 241
Nuremberg Judgment, 241

Observers, 138
Opening statements, 210–211
Order
contextual order, 227–228
domestic order, 77–78
international law order, 68
polycentric order, 101
in processu, 150
referential order, 227, 229
relational order, 150–151
status order, 128, 229
Organization for Economic Cooperation and Development (OECD), 62–63, 117
Organization for the Prohibition of Chemical Weapons, 175, 185–186, 192, 196
Osborn, A.F., 211
Ottawa Convention Banning Landmines, 65, 123, 208

Pactum de contrahendo, 189–190, 241
Palestine, 61
"Parallel development" approach, 237
Paris Agreement on Climate Change, 50, 97, 165, 192, 219
Parry, C., 5, 156–157
Patternment
of Declarations, 113–118
morphological patternment (*See* Morphological patternment)
normative patternment (*See* Normative patternment)

referential patternment (*See* Referential patternment)
treaty-patternment effect, 46–47
Patton, B., 33
Phase-structure of international negotiation
overview, 42
constitutive phase (*See* Constitutive phase of negotiation)
dual referentiality and, 54–55
multilateral governance process in, 55–56
prenegotiation phase (*See* Prenegotiation phase)
renegotiation phase, SeRPrenegotiation phase
Piecemeal procedure, 28–30
Planning stage, 23
Point of information, 143–144
Point of order, 143–144
Point of personal privilege, 143–144
Polanyi, M., 94
Pollux (Edvard Hambro), 146–147
Polycentricity, 54
Polycentric order, 101
Positional negotiation model. *See* Distributive negotiation model
Positivist international law
challenges to, 1–2
creative negotiation and, 45–47
problems with, 5
Powell, Colin, 235
Practical knowledge, 215
Preamble, 160–161
Prenegotiation phase
BATNDE and, 25–26
creative negotiation and, 56–57
diagnostic level
overview, 86, 87
"added value," 102
alternative solutions, 103–105
cognitive management, 90
consistency of context, 101–102
contextual approach, 93–95
contextuality, 100–102
defined, 56
determination of issues, 90–105
framing entities, 98
heuristic, 102
horizontal operation, 86
identification of context, 100–101
initiator, role of, 88–90
instrumental leadership role, 88–90
interpretative framings, 98–99
knowledge, management of, 90–97
level of negotiation focus, 87–88
Memoranda of Understanding (MOU), 117–118
ordering effect, 85–86
performative framings, 99–100
primae impressionis problem, 85–86, 105
procedural approach to relevant knowledge, 95–97
relational ICI engineering, 92–93, 95
subjective diagnostic approach, 97–100
subjective framings, 98–100
thematic diagnostic approach, 90–97
multilateral governance level (*See also* Ad Hoc Multilateral Conferences)
overview, 86
agendas, 110–113
Declarations, patternment of, 113–118 (*See also* Declarations)
defined, 56–57
Final Communiqués, 118–119
functions of Ad Hoc Multilateral Conferences, 106–108
initiators, role of, 110–113
institutional organization and management, 105
management techniques, 108–109
single negotiating texts, 109–110
structure of Ad Hoc Multilateral Conferences, 106–108
supporting reports, 109
outcome of, 118–119
structured nature of, 86
as transformative governance, 7, 85–87
Prescriptive transformative model of negotiation
overview, 14–15, 26–28
addition of issues, 31
Ad Hoc Working Groups of Legal and Technical Experts in, 36
fragmentation of issues, 31–32
game theory and, 3, 26–28
gradation in, 28–30
information and, 34–37
number of issues, 30–32
piecemeal procedure, 28–30
positivity and, 39
"prisoner's dilemma" and, 26
responsiveness and, 39
situational characteristics and, 32–38
size of payoffs, 28–30
strategic choice and, 38–40
structural characteristics and, 28–32
subtraction of issues, 31–32
temporality and, 39–40
thematic multiplicity, 30–32

Prescriptive transformative model (cont.)
time horizon and, 37–38
time pressure and, 32–34
"zero-sum" situations versus "non-zero-sum" situations, 28–30, 37–38
Primae impressionis problem. *See* Prenegotiation phase
Princeton Process, 244–245. *See also* Aggression, crime of
Principled negotiation model. *See* Harvard Principled Negotiation Model; Integrative negotiation model
"Prisoner's dilemma," 26
Procedural motions, 143–144
"Public trust," 35

Quantum theory, 91–92, 93, 95
Quasi-legislative role of negotiating team, 81

Raftopoulos, E., 178
Ramsar Convention on Wetlands of International Importance especially as Waterfowl Habitat, 184
Realist School of New Haven, 149
Recasting technique, 232
Recording of names, 217–218
Referential order, 227, 229
Referential patternment
overview, 150
"added value" and, 154–155
Barcelona Convention and, 151, 152
consistency with context, 152–154
functional consistency, 152–153
quasi-legislative consistency, 153
constructive heuristic field, 154–155
identifiability of context, 150–151
UNCLOS and, 151, 152, 154
Regional Cooperation Agreement on Combating Piracy and Armed Robbery Against Ships in Asia, 186
Regional Seas Programme, 236
Relational ICI engineering, 92–93, 95. *See also* Prenegotiation phase
Relational nature of creative negotiation, 43–48
overview, 41
collective bargaining process and, 43–45
complementarity and, 45–48
Relational norms, 20–22
Relational order, 150–151
Renegotiation phase
Ad Hoc Working Groups of Legal and Technical Experts in, 58–59, 224, 227, 239
alternatives to, 234–235
amendment versus replacement, 231–233
Barcelona Convention and, 228, 236–238
contextuality of, 227–229
conventional recasting, 231–233
creative negotiation and, 58–59
Declarations and, 235–238
denunciation clauses and, 234–235
derivative context, 228–229
Diplomatic Conferences and, 239
due institutional diligence, 224–227
environmental treaties, 236–238
Final Acts and, 239, 241–242
formal consolidated text, 230–231
initiation of, 223–224
institutional dualism, 226
knowledge brokers, 224–225
Mediterranean Action Plan (MAP), 228, 236–238
Meetings of the Contracting Parties (MOPs) and, 236–238
morphological patternment and, 229–231
outcome of, 239
participatory trust of parties and, 222–223
political significance of, 222
referential order, 227, 229
renegotiation zone, 227
Reports on Proposed Amendments, 224–226
as revisionary governance, 8–9, 222–223
Secretariat, role of, 58–59, 224–227, 239
under-determinate aspects
overview, 239–240
aggression, crime of, 240–249
institutional layers, 240–242
referential context, 240–242
Rome Statute of ICC and, 240–242
twinning renegotiation, 243–245
Vienna Convention on the Law of Treaties and, 231–233, 234
withdrawal clauses and, 234–235
Reports on Proposed Amendments, 224–226
Representation, 140
Reservations, 204–205
Rio+20 Conference on Sustainable Development, 237–238
Rio Declaration on Environment and Development, 86
Rome Compromise, 240–242. *See also* Aggression, crime of
Rome Statute of ICC, 240–242, 244–245, 246–249
Rotterdam Convention on the Prior Informed Consent Procedure for Certain Hazardous Chemicals and Pesticides in International Trade, 178, 184
Rovelli, C., 92

Rowold, J., 88–89
Rules of Procedure
overview, 127–128, 136–137
agendas, 139
amendments, 148
Barcelona Convention and, 137
Bureau of Negotiating Meeting or Conference, 140–142
conduct of business, 143–144
decision-making, 144–145
definitions, 137
languages, 145–148
meetings
place and time, 138
public and private sessions, 138
observers, 138
organization, 142–143
point of information, 143–144
point of order, 143–144
point of personal privilege, 143–144
procedural motions, 143–144
purpose, 137
representation, 140
Vienna Convention on the Law of Treaties and, 146–147
Russel, W., 17

Scepticism, 51
Sebenius, J., 21–22
Secretariat
constitutive phase of negotiation, role in, 58, 123–126
inter-sessional workshops and, 213–215
multilateral governance, role in, 183–184
renegotiation phase, role in, 58–59, 224–227, 239
Side-events, 215–216
SPA and Biodiversity Protocol, 170
Special Techniques and Practices
overview, 210
brackets system, 216–217
brainstorming sessions, 211–213
inter-sessional workshops, 213–215
non-negotiation texts, 218–219
"non-papers," 218–219
opening statements, 210–211
recording of names, 217–218
side-events, 215–216
Special Working Group on the Crime of Aggression (SWGCA), 242–247
Status order, 128, 229
Stockholm Conference on Human Development, 163–164
Stockholm Convention on Persistent Organic Pollutants, 158
Strategic misrepresentations, 17–18
Sub-fora, 134–136
Subjectivity
of creative negotiation
overview, 42–43, 69
accountability of negotiating team, 79–81
decision configuration of negotiating team, 74–79
organization of negotiating team, 74–79
process advisory role of negotiating team, 81–82
setting up of negotiating team, 69–74
multilateral governance and, 202–210
denunciation clauses, 206–210
"plurality-in-treaty-relation," 202
reservations, 204–205
subjectification of participation, 202–204
withdrawal clauses, 206–210

Tacit knowledge, 94–95
Teleological causation, 68
Textual nature of creative negotiation, 48–54
overview, 42
"hard law" versus "soft law," 48
negotiating metaphors and, 52–54
working language and, 48–52
Thematization level of multilateral governance
overview, 172–173
assistance in developing countries, 179–180
financial governance, 180–181
general duties and obligations, 173–174
implementative measures, 176–178
information, scientific, and educational development, 178–179
institutional responsiveness, 176
internal capacity building, 179–180
procedural and substantive duties, 174–176
public participation, 178
relationship with other conventional regimes, 180
technology transfer, 179–180
Theorization of negotiation
overview, 6
distributive negotiation model (*See* Distributive negotiation model)
Harvard Principled Negotiation Model (*See* Harvard Principled Negotiation Model)
integrative negotiation model (*See* Integrative negotiation model)
prescriptive transformative model of negotiation (*See* Prescriptive transformative model of negotiation)

"Theory of hierarchy of needs," 111–113
"Thin red line," 17
Tokyo International Military Tribunal, 241
Torture Convention. *See* Convention Against Torture and Other Cruel, Inhuman or Degrading Treatment or Punishment
Transactional leadership, 88–89
Transference of meaning, 163–164
Transformability level of multilateral governance, 197–202
Transformational leadership, 88–89
Transformative model of negotiation. *See* Prescriptive transformative model of negotiation
Treaties. *See specific Treaty*
Treaty on the Non-Proliferation of Nuclear Weapons, 190, 233
Treaty-patternment effect, 46–47
Tribe, L.H., 93, 95
"Tunnel vision," 35
Twining, W., 173
Twinning renegotiation, 243–245

UNCLOS. *See* Convention on the Law of the Sea (UNCLOS)
Under-determinate aspects in renegotiation phase
  overview, 239–240
  aggression, crime of, 240–249
  institutional layers, 240–242
  referential context, 240–242
  Rome Statute of ICC and, 240–242
  twinning renegotiation, 243–245
United Nations. *See also specific Entity or Agreement*
  Charter, 146–147, 166, 208
  Commission on Crime Prevention and Criminal Justice, 117
  Economic and Social Council, 117
  Economic Commission for Europe (ECE), 105, 117, 190
  Environmental Programme (UNEP), 117, 124, 137, 184–185, 226, 236
  High-Level Political Forum on Sustainable Development, 96
  Institute for Training and Research (UNITAR), 3, 15, 26–27
  Permanent Commission of the South Pacific, 124
  Scientific Advisory Board, 89, 96
  South Pacific Commission, 124
  UNCTAD, 117
  UNESCO, 153, 162
United States-European Union Agreement on Extradition between the United States of America and the European Union, 174
Unum e pluribus, 71, 82, 216–217
Unum in processu, 69
Ury, W., 33
Usable knowledge, 92, 224–225
Use of terms, 161–164

Verhofstadt, Guy, 53–54
Vertical management, 194
Vienna Convention on the Law of Treaties
  consensus procedure and, 126–127, 131
  contract view of treaties and, 45–46
  Harvard Principled Negotiation Model and, 24
  multilateral governance and, 205–206, 209–210
  normative patternment and, 160
  renegotiation phase and, 231–233, 234
  Rules of Procedure and, 146–147
von Gierke, O., 149

Waldron, J., 82
Walton, R.E., 43
Webber, G.C.N., 94
Wenaweser, C., 243, 247
Westlake, John, 60
Whorf, B.L., 49
Withdrawal clauses, 206–210, 234
Wittgenstein, L., 14, 69
Working Group of the MAP Focal Points, 238
Working Group on the Mediterranean Action Plan II Assessment, 238
Working language, 48–52, 106, 145–148
World Trade Organization (WTO), 62–63, 127

Yale Law School Realist School, 149

Zartman, W.I., 76
"Zero-sum" situations, 15–18, 28–30, 37–38